Follett Social Studies

People, Time, and Change

Program Directors
Phillip Bacon
M. Evelyn Swartz

Authors
Charles B. Myers
Gordon Wilk

Allyn and Bacon, Inc., Newton, Massachusetts

*Rockleigh, NJ Atlanta Warrensburg, MO Dallas Rancho Cordova, CA
London Sydney Toronto*

Teacher Consultants

Joan Sánchez Augerot
Seattle Public Schools
Seattle, Washington

Silvio Guglielmo Benvenuti
Detroit Public Schools
Detroit, Michigan

Margaret L. Boyd
Fairfax County Schools
Vienna, Virginia

Gary L. Caldwell
Omaha Public Schools
Omaha, Nebraska

Elizabeth G. Charette
West Tampa Middle School
Tampa, Florida

Carolyn E. Comey
Washington School #6
Phoenix, Arizona

Patricia DeBardeleben
Treadwell Elementary School
Memphis, Tennessee

Jeanette Hadley
Public School 154, Manhattan
New York, New York

ISBN 0-205-09526-7

Printed in the United States of America

3 4 5 6 7 8 9   93 92 91 90 89 88

Lynne K. Hollomon
Portland Public Schools
Portland, Oregon

Dolores K. Horwitz
William Hibbard School
Chicago, Illinois

Sister St. Rita Marotta, I.H.M.
St. Dorothy School
Drexel Hill, Pennsylvania

Edith Naiser
Spring Branch Schools
Houston, Texas

Helen Rogers
Gary School Corporation
Gary, Indiana

Edith B. Rudder
Wake County Schools
Raleigh, North Carolina

Martha Doerr Toppin
Oak Grove Intermediate School
Concord, California

Ronald J. Walker
William H. Ohrenberger School
Boston, Massachusetts

3

Table of Contents

4

Table of Contents

Map List

Map List

The Atlas

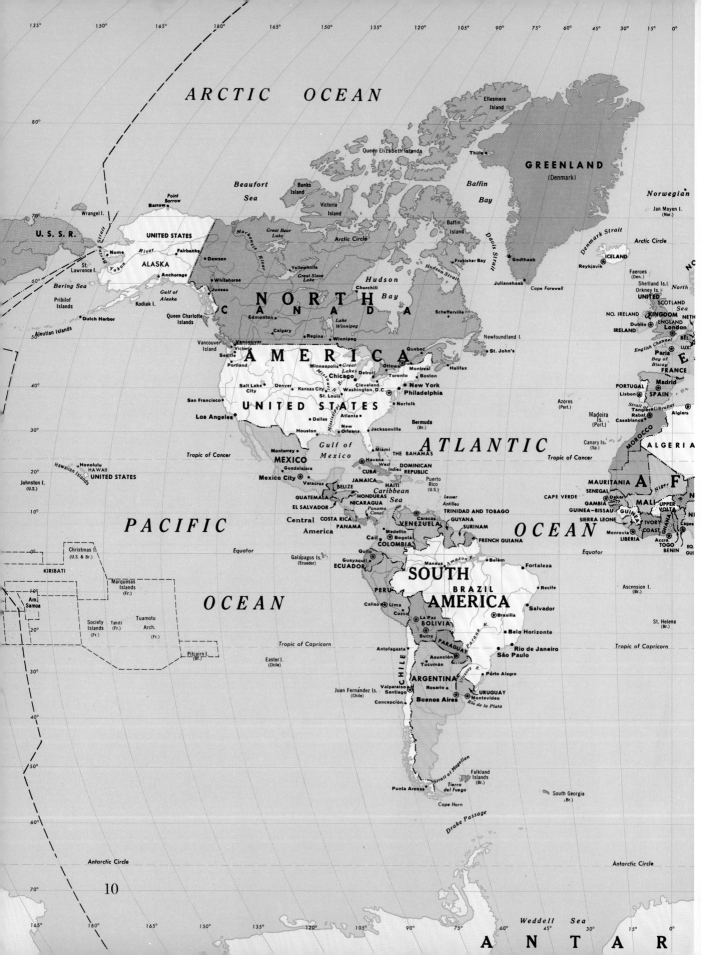

The World
Political Map

⊛ National Capitals
★ Other Capitals • Other Cities

SCALE 1:105,000,000 or One Inch—About 1660 Miles

Miles
0 500 1000 2000 3000 4000 5000

Kilometers
0 2500 5000 7500

Projection Modified Van Der Grinten

11

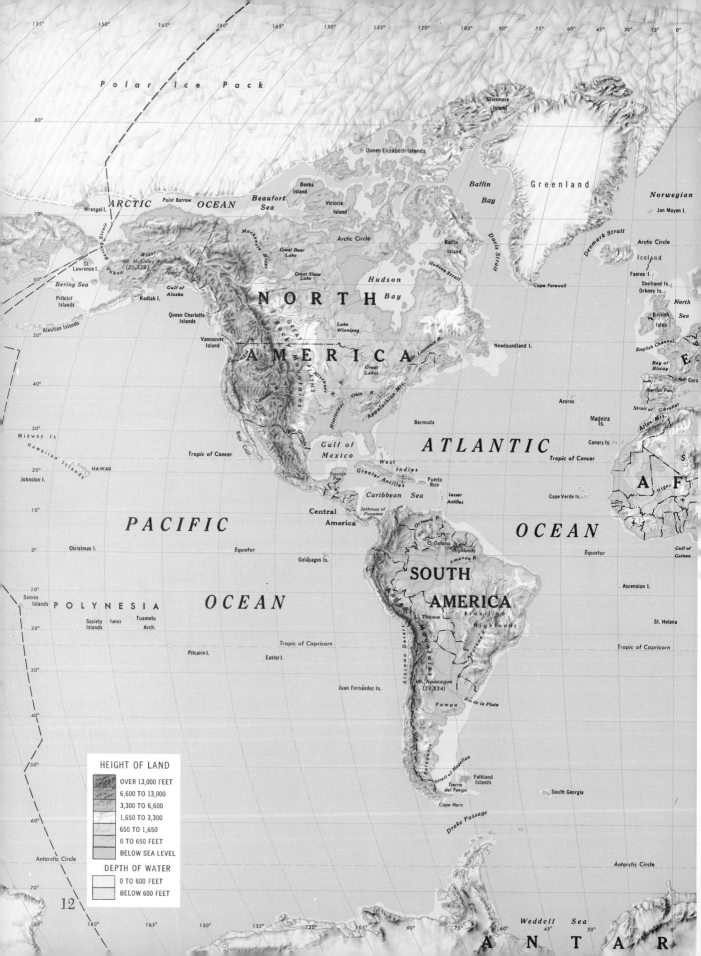

Polar Ice Pack

ARCTIC OCEAN

Wrangel I.
Point Barrow
Beaufort Sea
Banks Island
Victoria Island
Queen Elizabeth Islands
Ellesmere Island
Baffin Bay
Greenland
Norwegian
Jan Mayen I.

Bering Strait
St. Lawrence I.
Mt. McKinley (20,320)
Yukon River
Mackenzie River
Great Bear Lake
Arctic Circle
Baffin Island
Davis Strait
Denmark Strait
Arctic Circle
Iceland
Faeroe I.
Shetland Is.
Orkney Is.

Bering Sea
Pribilof Islands
Gulf of Alaska
Kodiak I.
Great Slave Lake
Hudson Strait
Cape Farewell
North Sea
British Isles

Aleutian Islands
Queen Charlotte Islands
Vancouver Island
NORTH
Hudson Bay
Lake Winnipeg
St. Lawrence R.
Newfoundland I.
English Channel
Bay of Biscay
Iberian Pen.
Cors.

Columbia R.
Rocky Mountains
GREAT PLAINS
AMERICA
Great Lakes
Missouri R.
Ohio R.
Appalachian Mts.
Azores
Madeira Is.
Strait of Gibraltar
Atlas Mts.

Midway Is.
Hawaiian Islands
HAWAII
Johnston I.
Colorado R.
Baja Calif.
Rio Grande
Tropic of Cancer
Gulf of Mexico
Bermuda
ATLANTIC
Tropic of Cancer
Canary Is.
A F
S

Christmas I.
Yucatán Pen.
West Indies
Greater Antilles
Puerto Rico
Lesser Antilles
Caribbean Sea
Cape Verde Is.
Niger R.

PACIFIC
Central America
Isthmus of Panama
OCEAN
Galápagos Is.
Orinoco R.
Guiana Highlands
Amazon R.
SOUTH
AMERICA
Equator
Gulf of Guinea

Equator
Samoa Islands
POLYNESIA
OCEAN
Andes
L. Titicaca
Brazilian Highlands
Ascension I.
St. Helena

Society Islands
Tahiti
Tuamotu Arch.
Atacama Desert
Tropic of Capricorn
São Francisco R.
Tropic of Capricorn

Pitcairn I.
Easter I.
Mt. Aconcagua (22,834)
Rio de la Plata

Juan Fernández Is.
Pampa
Patagonia
Falkland Islands

HEIGHT OF LAND
OVER 13,000 FEET
6,600 TO 13,000
3,300 TO 6,600
1,650 TO 3,300
650 TO 1,650
0 TO 650 FEET
BELOW SEA LEVEL

DEPTH OF WATER
0 TO 600 FEET
BELOW 600 FEET

Strait of Magellan
Tierra del Fuego
Cape Horn
Drake Passage
South Georgia

Antarctic Circle
Antarctic Circle
Weddell Sea
ANTAR

12

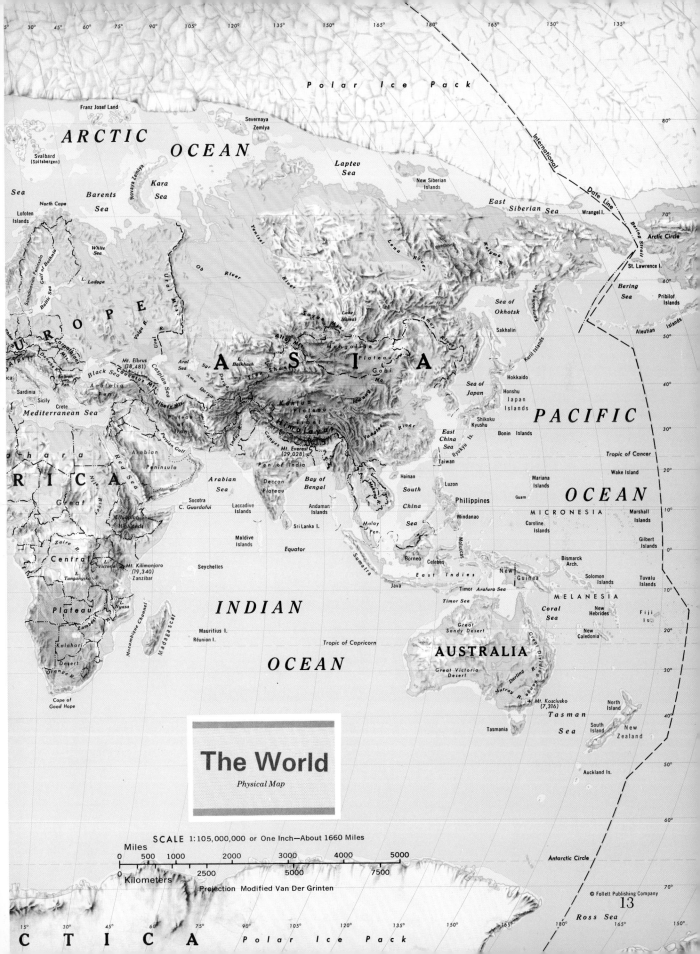

The World

Physical Map

SCALE 1:105,000,000 or One Inch—About 1660 Miles

Miles
0 500 1000 2000 3000 4000 5000

Kilometers
0 2500 5000 7500

Projection Modified Van Der Grinten

© Follett Publishing Company

13

World Landforms

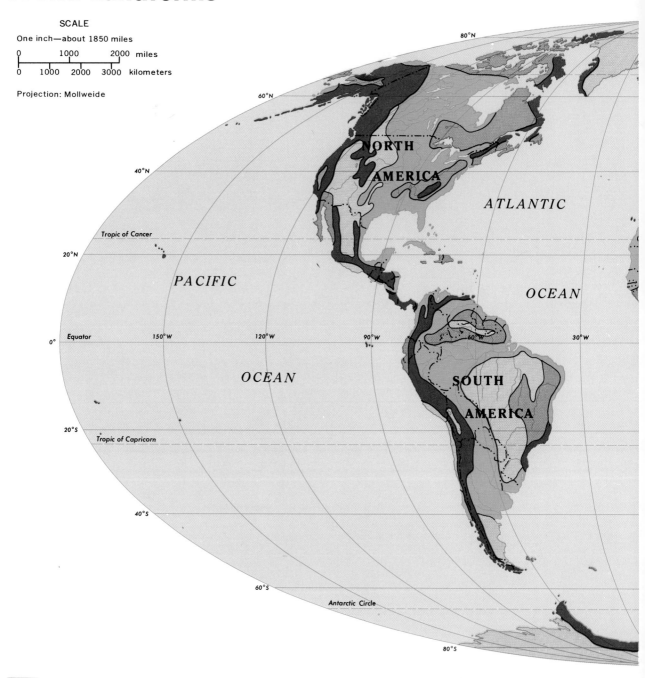

SCALE

One inch—about 1850 miles

0   1000   2000 miles

0   1000   2000   3000 kilometers

Projection: Mollweide

80°N

60°N

40°N

Tropic of Cancer

20°N

NORTH
AMERICA

ATLANTIC

PACIFIC

OCEAN

Equator   150°W   120°W   90°W   60°W   30°W   0°

OCEAN

SOUTH
AMERICA

20°S

Tropic of Capricorn

40°S

60°S

Antarctic Circle

80°S

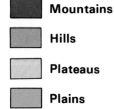

■ Mountains

■ Hills

□ Plateaus

■ Plains

14

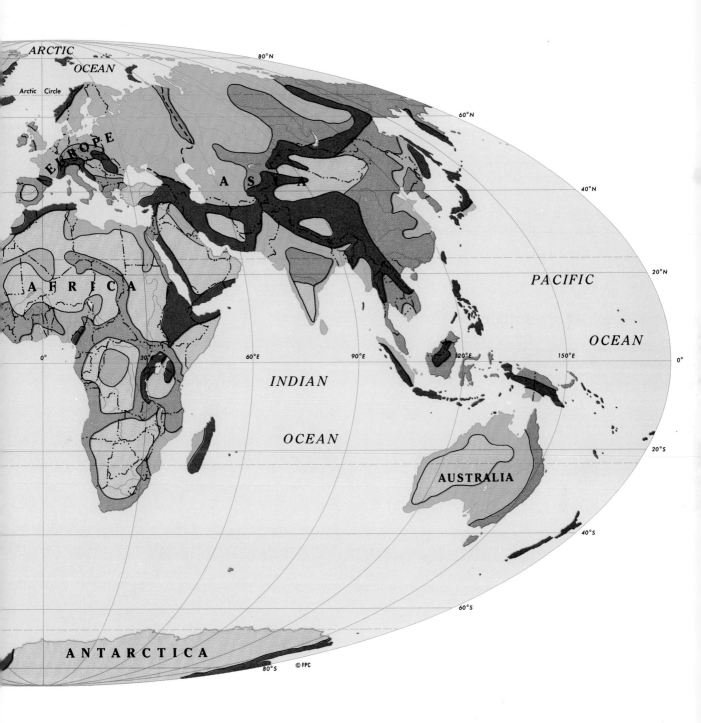

ARCTIC

OCEAN

Arctic Circle

80°N

60°N

40°N

EUROPE

ASIA

PACIFIC

20°N

OCEAN

AFRICA

0°

30°

60°E

90°E

120°E

150°E

0°

INDIAN

OCEAN

20°S

AUSTRALIA

40°S

60°S

ANTARCTICA

80°S © FPC

World Climates

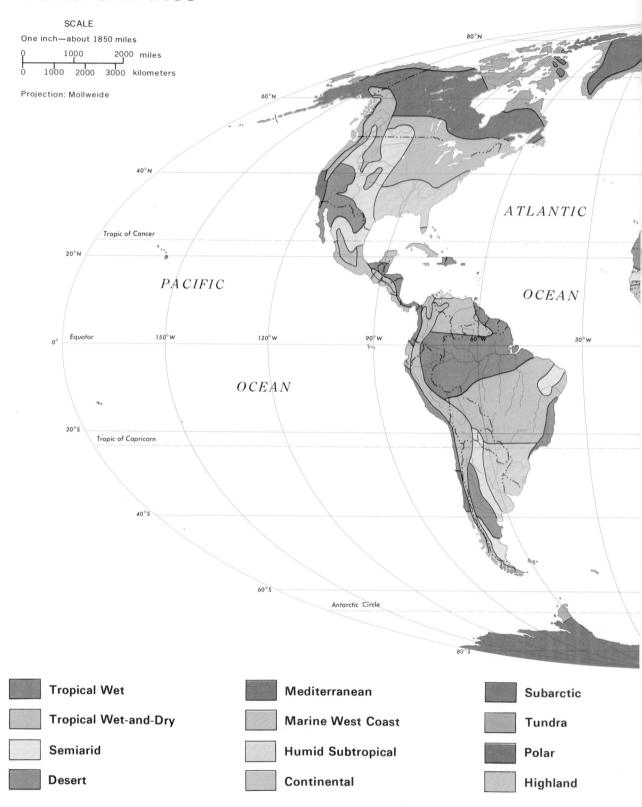

SCALE

One inch—about 1850 miles

0   1000   2000 miles

0   1000   2000   3000 kilometers

Projection: Mollweide

80°N

60°N

40°N

Tropic of Cancer

20°N

PACIFIC

Equator   150°W   120°W   90°W   60°W   30°W
0°

OCEAN

20°S

Tropic of Capricorn

40°S

60°S

Antarctic Circle

80°S

ATLANTIC

OCEAN

Legend:

Tropical Wet	Mediterranean	Subarctic
Tropical Wet-and-Dry	Marine West Coast	Tundra
Semiarid	Humid Subtropical	Polar
Desert	Continental	Highland

16

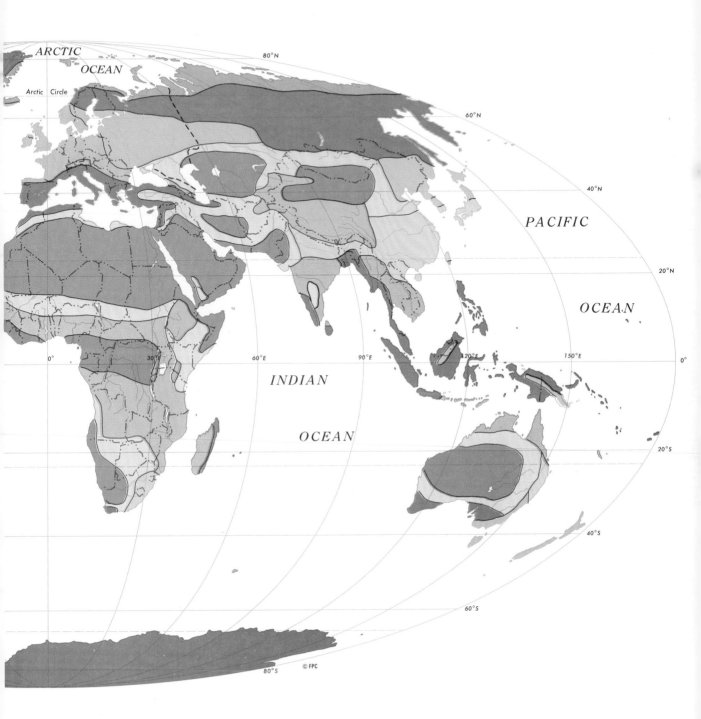

ARCTIC
OCEAN

Arctic Circle

80°N

60°N

40°N

PACIFIC

20°N

OCEAN

INDIAN

OCEAN

0°

30°E

60°E

90°E

120°E

150°E

0°

20°S

40°S

60°S

80°S

© FPC

17

Natural Vegetation

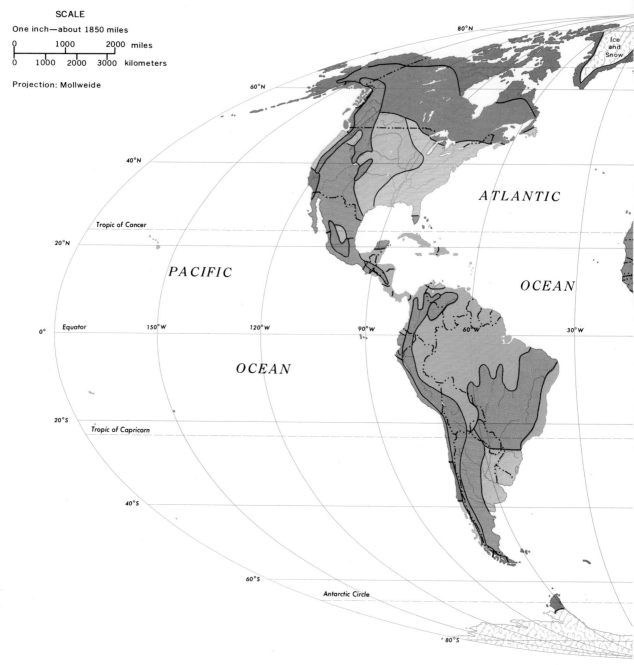

SCALE

One inch—about 1850 miles

0   1000   2000   miles

0   1000   2000   3000   kilometers

Projection: Mollweide

80°N

60°N

40°N

Tropic of Cancer

20°N

PACIFIC

ATLANTIC

OCEAN

Equator

0°

150°W

120°W

90°W

60°W

30°W

OCEAN

20°S

Tropic of Capricorn

40°S

60°S

Antarctic Circle

80°S

Ice and Snow

FOREST

Tropical Broadleaf

Scrub

Mixed

Needleleaf

GRASSLAND

Savanna

Steppe

DESERT

TUNDRA

HIGHLAND

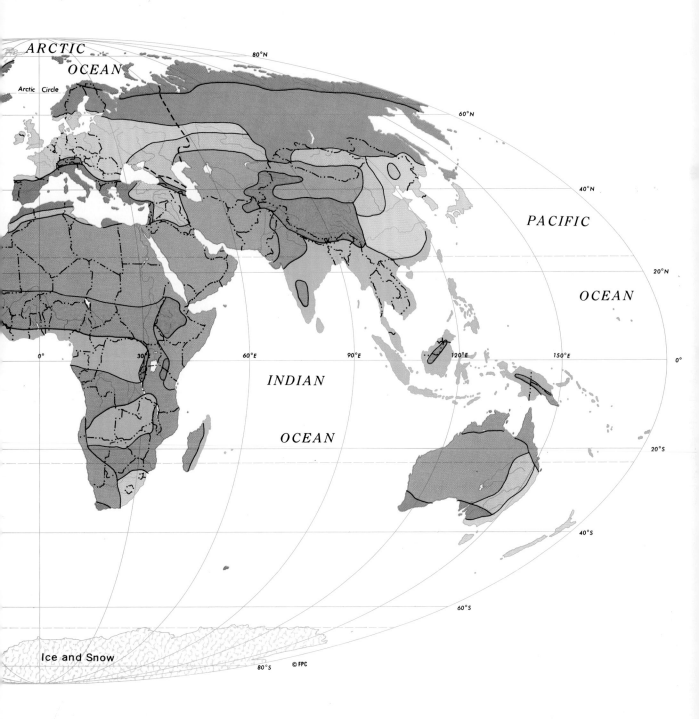

ARCTIC
OCEAN

Arctic Circle

80°N

60°N

40°N

PACIFIC

20°N

OCEAN

0°   30°E   60°E   90°E   120°E   150°E   0°

INDIAN

OCEAN

20°S

40°S

60°S

Ice and Snow

80°S   © FPC

World Land Use

SCALE
One inch — about 2000 miles

0   1000   2000   miles

0   1000 2000 3000   kilometers

Projection: Goode's Homolosine

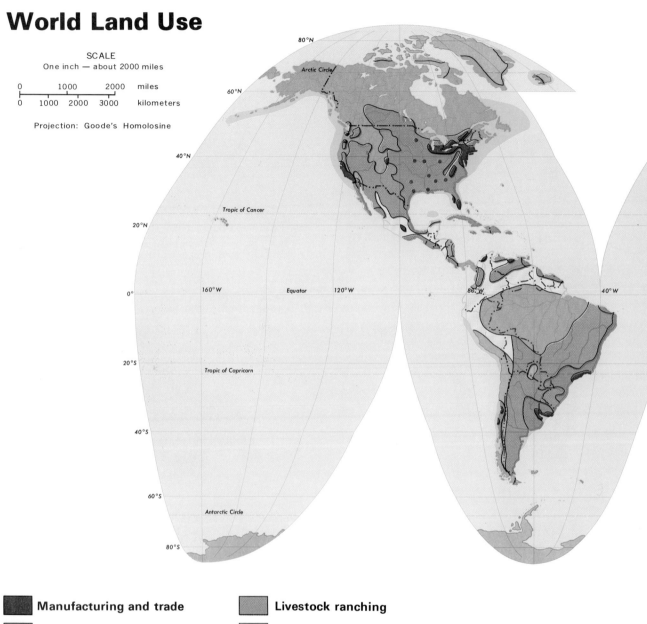

- ■ **Manufacturing and trade**
- **Commercial farming**
- **Subsistence farming**
- **Lumbering, gathering, hunting, and fishing**
- **Livestock ranching**
- **Nomadic herding**
- **Commercial fishing**
- **Unproductive land (except mining)**

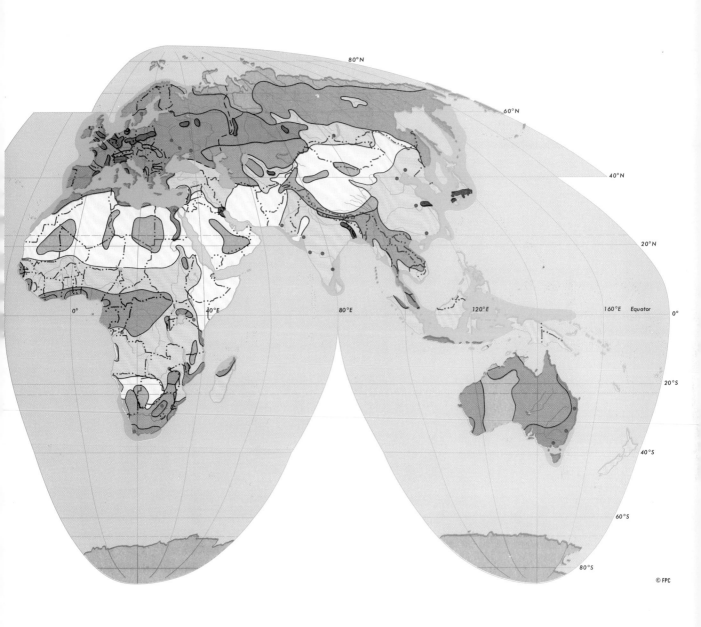

80°N

60°N

40°N

20°N

Equator

0°

40°E

80°E

120°E

160°E

0°

20°S

40°S

60°S

80°S

© FPC

21

World Population

SCALE
One inch — about 2000 miles

| 0 | 1000 | | 2000 | miles |
| 0 | 1000 | 2000 | 3000 | kilometers |

Projection: Goode's Homolosine

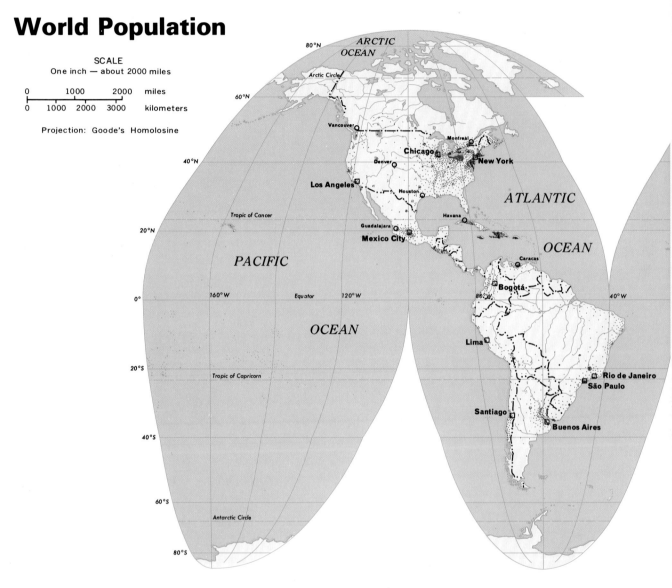

1 dot equals 100,000 people

□ **Selected cities with more than 3 million people**

o **Selected cities with fewer than 3 million people**

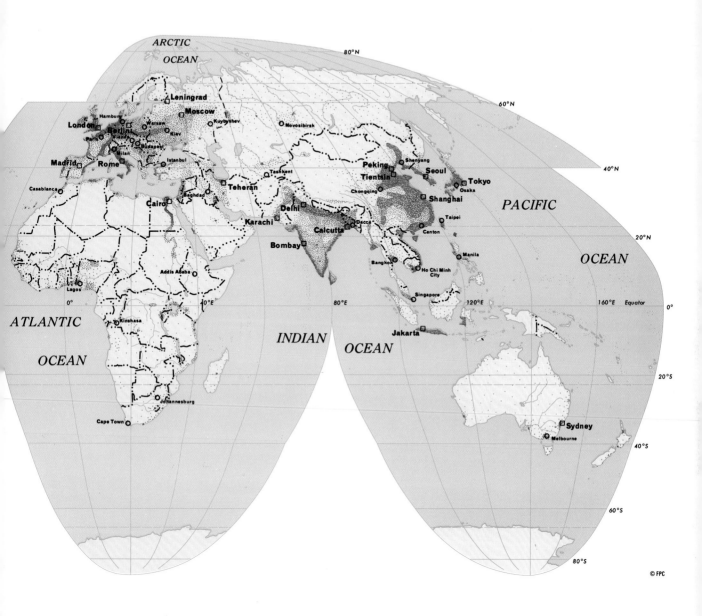

ARCTIC

OCEAN

80°N

60°N

40°N

Leningrad

Moscow

Hamburg

London

Berlin

Warsaw

Paris

Vienna

Milan

Kiev

Kuybyshev

Novosibirsk

Budapest

Madrid

Rome

Istanbul

Tashkent

Peking

Shenyang

Seoul

PACIFIC

Tientsin

Tokyo

Osaka

Casablanca

Baghdad

Teheran

Chongqing

Shanghai

Cairo

Karachi

Delhi

Dacca

Canton

Taipei

20°N

OCEAN

Calcutta

Bombay

Manila

Addis Ababa

Bangkok

Ho Chi Minh

City

Lagos

0°

10°E

80°E

Singapore

120°E

160°E

Equator

0°

ATLANTIC

Kinshasa

INDIAN

OCEAN

Jakarta

OCEAN

20°S

Johannesburg

Sydney

Cape Town

Melbourne

40°S

60°S

80°S

© FPC

23

World Connections

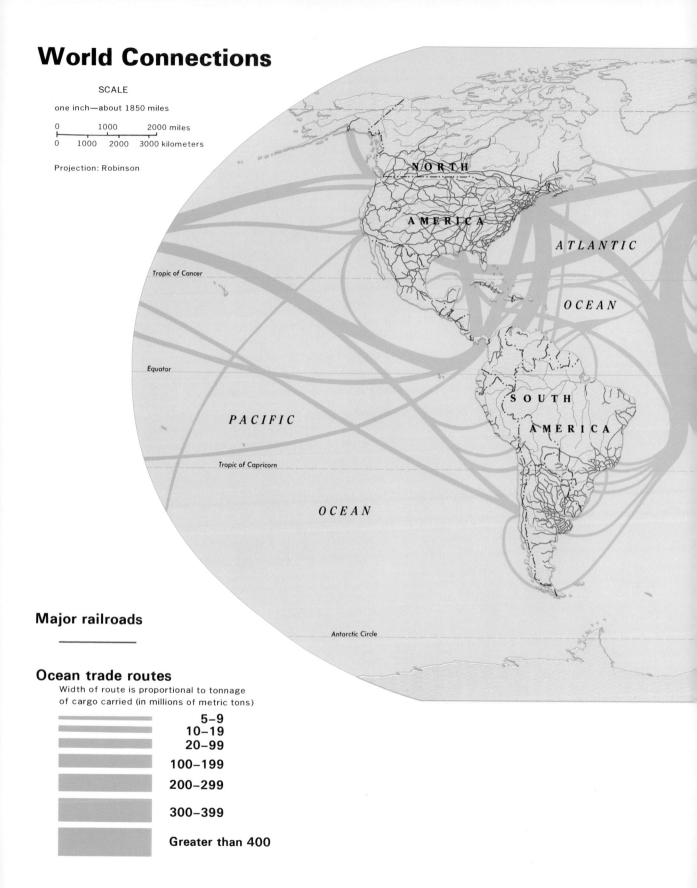

SCALE

one inch—about 1850 miles

0   1000   2000 miles

0   1000   2000   3000 kilometers

Projection: Robinson

NORTH AMERICA

ATLANTIC OCEAN

Tropic of Cancer

Equator

PACIFIC

SOUTH AMERICA

Tropic of Capricorn

OCEAN

Antarctic Circle

Major railroads

Ocean trade routes

Width of route is proportional to tonnage
of cargo carried (in millions of metric tons)

5–9
10–19
20–99
100–199
200–299
300–399
Greater than 400

ARCTIC OCEAN

Arctic Circle

EUROPE

ASIA

AFRICA

INDIAN OCEAN

PACIFIC OCEAN

AUSTRALIA

ANTARCTICA

© FPC

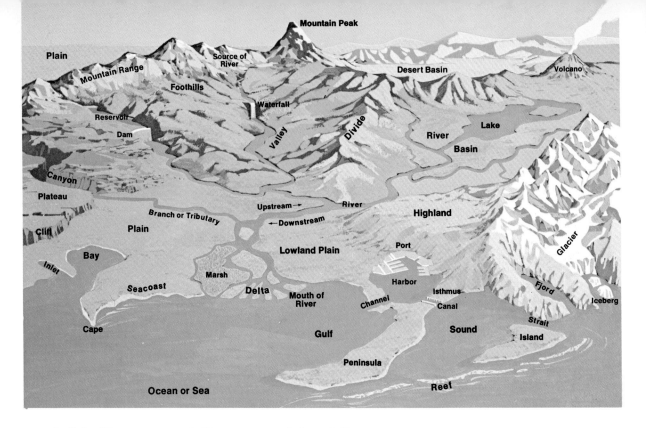

Labels on the illustration: Mountain Peak, Plain, Mountain Range, Source of River, Foothills, Desert Basin, Volcano, Reservoir, Dam, Waterfall, Valley, Divide, River, Lake, Basin, Canyon, Plateau, Cliff, Branch or Tributary, Upstream, River, Highland, Plain, Downstream, Inlet, Bay, Marsh, Lowland Plain, Port, Glacier, Seacoast, Delta, Mouth of River, Channel, Harbor, Isthmus, Canal, Fjord, Iceberg, Cape, Gulf, Sound, Strait, Island, Peninsula, Reef, Ocean or Sea

A Dictionary of Geographical Terms

altitude The height above sea level.

basin An area of land largely enclosed by higher land.

bay Part of a body of water that reaches into the land.

bed The bottom of a body of water, as riverbed or ocean bed.

branch A river or stream that flows into a larger river or stream.

canal A channel dug for irrigation or transportation.

canyon A deep, narrow valley with steep sides.

cape A point of land stretching out into a body of water.

channel A narrow body of water connecting two larger bodies of water; the deepest part of a waterway.

cliff A high, steep wall of rock.

coast Land along a sea or ocean.

continent One of the seven largest bodies of land on the earth.

current The flow of a stream of water.

dam A wall built across a river to stop or slow down the flow of water.

delta Land built up by deposits at a river's mouth.

desert A dry, barren area of land where few plants can grow.

dike A wall of earth or stone built by people to hold back flooding.

divide A highest point of land separating river basins.

downstream The direction of a river's flow—toward its mouth.

drainage basin An area of land drained by a river and its tributaries.

elevation The height above sea level.

equator The imaginary line around the earth that is halfway between the North and South poles.

fjord A narrow inlet of the sea between steep banks or cliffs.

foothills Hills at the base of mountains.

glacier A large body of slowly moving ice.

gulf Part of a sea or ocean that reaches into the land.

harbor A sheltered place where ships may anchor safely.

highland An area of hills, mountains, or plateaus.

hill A rounded part of the earth's surface with sloping sides.

iceberg A large floating mass of ice that has broken off from a glacier.

inland Away from the coast.

inlet A small part of a body of water that reaches into a coast.

island Land that is entirely surrounded by water.

isthmus A narrow strip of land that connects two larger land areas.

lake An inland body of water.

latitude The distance in degrees north or south of the equator.

longitude The distance in degrees east or west of the prime meridian.

lowland An area of low and usually level land.

map key An explanation of the meaning of the symbols on a map.

map scale The measuring device found on maps that compares distances on the map with distances on the earth's surface.

marsh An area of low, wet land where tall grasses grow.

mountain High, rocky land, usually with steep sides and a pointed or rounded top, higher than a hill.

mountain peak The pointed top of a mountain.

mountain range A long chain of mountains.

mouth (of a river) The place where a river flows into a larger body of water.

North Pole The point on the earth that is farthest north.

oasis A place in a desert where water is found in a spring or a well, making the growing of crops possible.

ocean One of the four largest bodies of water on the earth.

ocean current A flow of water that moves in a definite direction in the ocean.

pampa A grass-covered plain in South America.

peninsula A body of land nearly surrounded by water.

plain An area of broad, level land.

plateau An area of high, flat land.

port A harbor, town, or city where ships can load and unload their cargoes.

prairie A large plains region with tall grasses.

prime meridian The imaginary line on the earth's surface running through Greenwich, England, from the North Pole to the South Pole. The line is used as the starting point from which degrees of longitude are measured.

rain forest A tropical woodland, with heavy rainfall throughout the year, marked by tall broad-shaped, evergreen trees that form a continuous canopy.

rapids A part of a river, generally shallow, where the current moves swiftly over rocks.

reef A ridge of rock or sand at or near the surface of water.

reservoir A lake where water is stored for future use.

river A large stream of water flowing through the land.

river valley Low land through which a river flows.

savanna A level, tropical grassland with scattered trees.

sea A large body of water, usually salt water, partly or completely enclosed by land.

shore Land next to a lake.

sound A wide channel connecting two bodies of water or an inlet between the mainland and islands.

source (of a river) The place where a river begins.

South Pole The point on the earth that is farthest south.

steppe A vast area of short grass that is often dry and level.

strait A narrow stretch of water that connects two larger bodies of water.

swamp An area of land that is always soaked with water.

tide The regular rising and falling of the water of the ocean and waters connected with the ocean.

timber line A line in mountain regions above which trees do not grow.

tributary A river or stream that flows into a larger river or stream.

tropics The warm region lying on both sides of the equator.

tundra A cold, treeless plain in polar regions.

upstream The direction toward a river's source, opposite to its flow.

valley Low land between hills or mountains.

volcano A mountain formed of rock or ash thrown up from inside the earth.

waterfall Water falling over a steep drop in the land.

Map Symbols

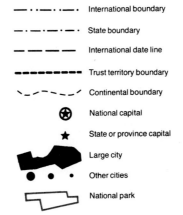

Physical Features

- River or stream
- Lake
- Ice pack
- Mountains
- Mountain peak
- Swamp or marsh
- Grassland
- Woodland
- Desert

Cultural Features

- International boundary
- State boundary
- International date line
- Trust territory boundary
- Continental boundary
- National capital
- State or province capital
- Large city
- Other cities
- National park

- Reserve or reservation
- Canal
- Dam
- Railroad
- Pipeline
- Bridge
- Airport
- Main road
- Secondary road
- Other road

The Atlas Tells a Story

As you read, think about these words.

grid   longitude   meridian   projection
latitude parallel   prime meridian   International Date Line

Our Round Earth

Planet Earth is a sphere. It is round like a globe, which is a model of the earth. Yet standing on the earth's surface, you cannot really see the earth's roundness. Even from the tallest building or from an airplane, you have no real way of proving that the earth's surface really does curve off in all directions.

Even so, we do have proof that the earth is a sphere. Photographs taken from far in space show the earth's shape.

Page 9 of your Atlas shows you positive proof of the round shape of Planet Earth. Look at it carefully. Beneath the swirling clouds, you can find the outline of parts of North America. You can also clearly see the roundness of the earth.

In what ways does space travel help us understand our own planet better? Here astronaut Edwin Aldrin walks on the moon's surface.

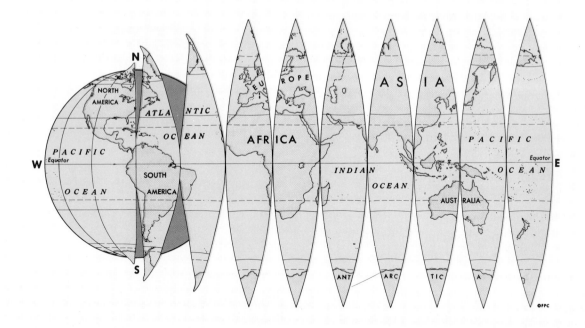

Globes and Maps

Globes are accurate in ways that maps can never be. The reason is simple. The earth is round, and globes are round. So a globe is an accurate scale model of the earth. A map, on the other hand, is flat. Just as an orange skin tears when it is peeled, so does a globe's surface tear when it is flattened to make a map.

Distortion on maps. When the features of the round earth are put on a flat map, things change. The actual shapes of land and water become distorted. Look, for example, at the world physical map on pages 12–13. Find the Antarctic continent. Compare it with the Antarctic continent on a globe. What differences can you see?

The diagram on this page will help you see exactly what has happened. Distortion is greatest in the polar regions. Here the tearing of the globe's surface is greatest. Distortion is least in areas near the equator. Here there is much less tearing and twisting.

A World Grid

We live in a world of lines. Look at the maps in your Atlas. Look at your classroom globe. All of them have crisscrossing lines. These lines form a **grid**.

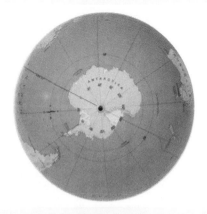

Why does this globe show the most accurate shape of Antarctica?

29

The global grid helps us locate places on the earth's surface.

Familiar grids. You have used many grids. Seats in your classroom or school auditorium may have a grid pattern.

Look at the classroom grid on this page. Find the seat in row C across and row 3 down. The seat is at an intersection, or meeting point, of two lines—C and 3. What directions would you give someone who wanted to find the seat directly behind that one? in front of it? to the right? to the left? You are using a grid to find locations.

Lines on the globe. Places can be found on the earth's surface by using a global grid. It works in exactly the same way that the rows of chairs work in the classroom drawing. A global grid is simply two sets of lines used on a globe. One set runs east and west. These are lines of **latitude**. The other set runs north and south. These are lines of **longitude**. The unit used for measuring latitude and longitude is the degree. The symbol for *degree* is °.

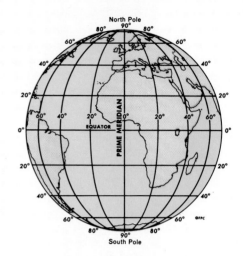

The lines running east and west on the global grid are called **parallels**. These are lines of latitude. Parallels, like railroad tracks, are always the same distance from one another.

The equator. The equator is the key parallel, or line of latitude. It is halfway between the poles. Its latitude is 0°. All places are north or south of 0°. The North Pole is at 90° north. The South Pole is at 90° south.

Look at the world political map on pages 10–11. Find the equator. Now find

Teacher's [ ] Desk

	1	2	3	4	5	6
Row A	▢	▢	▢	▢	▢	▢
Row B	▢	▢	▢	▢	▢	▢
Row C	▢	▢	▢	▢	▢	▢
Row D	▢	▢	▢	▢	▢	▢
Row E	▢	▢	▢	▢	▢	▢

Times around the world are based on the official time at the Greenwich Observatory, on the prime meridian.

the first parallel north of the equator. It is 10° north. What is the first parallel south of the equator? On the world map in the Atlas, the parallel lines of latitude are at 10° intervals. On some globes and other maps, they may be at 10°, 15°, 20°, or even 30° intervals.

Lines of longitude. A second set of lines runs from pole to pole on your map. They are called **meridians**, or lines of longitude. We use these lines to measure places east and west. Just as the equator is the starting point for measuring distances north and south, the **prime meridian** is the beginning point for measuring distances east and west. The longitude of the prime meridian is 0°. It runs through Greenwich (gren'ich), England.

The prime meridian. Look again at the world map on pages 10–11. Find the prime meridian. It is marked 0°. Every place on earth can be measured east or west from this line. For example, find the line that runs through the city of Denver in the United States. What is Denver's longitude? It is west of the prime meridian, so you must say 105° west to give Denver's correct longitude. At what latitude is Denver? You can see that Denver is located at about 40° north and 105° west. Check your understanding of this idea by finding the latitude and longitude of these three places: New Orleans in the United States, Belo Horizonte in Brazil, and Leningrad in the Soviet Union.

31

Mercator's Map

Gerhardus Mercator (ger·här'dəs mər·kāt'ər), a European map maker, was born in 1512. He lived during a time of worldwide exploration. He wanted to draw a map that would help explorers. Explorers needed a map in which directions would always be right, no matter where they were traveling.

You can see Mercator's map below. You can also see how the map seems to be "thrown forward" from a globe. Mercator imagined a globe with a light inside. He imagined that the light could shine through the globe. The light would make a pattern appear on a sheet of paper, which was wrapped around the globe. With this pattern in mind, Mercator drew his map of the world.

On Mercator's map, lines of latitude and longitude are stretched. They are also straight. These straight lines allowed sea captains to plot a straight course between any two places. Following a straight-line course might make their trip longer. But the explorers could be sure of arriving at their exact destination. Ship and airplane captains still use Mercator's map today.

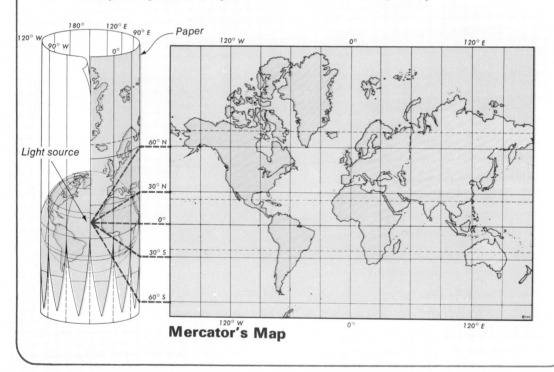

Mercator's Map

Map Projections

As you know, maps are not as accurate as globes. It is impossible to put a curved surface on a flat piece of paper without some tearing and twisting. The map maker, above everything else, must save the global grid. This is essential because, no matter what else happens, location must be true on all maps. If the locations on the maps in your Atlas were changed, the maps would be useless.

Saving the grid. A map is a **projection,** or a take-off, on the globe. In other words, it is making something flat look as much as possible like something round. The word *project* (prə·jekt′) means "to throw forward." A map projection is a grid—the lines of latitude and longitude—picked off the globe and thrown forward onto a flat piece of paper.

Your Atlas contains four different examples of projections. The names of each of the projections the map maker used are found in the map key. In each of these projections, the global grid has been placed on flat paper differently.

To see the differences between map projections and the globe, think about these points. On a globe—

1. latitude lines are parallel;
2. longitude lines come together at the poles;
3. lines of longitude are exactly the same length everywhere; and
4. lines of latitude become shorter in length as you move from the equator (the longest line of latitude) toward the poles.

Look at the grid on the world political map, pages 10–11. Check the list above. How many points from the list are true in this projection? Do the same thing for the world climate map. Find two other maps in your Atlas that use still different projections. Notice how the grid differs in each of these maps.

The fact that the grids on these maps are different does not mean that the maps are wrong. In fact, there is simply no way to keep the globe's grid accurate on a flat map. Each map has been drawn to fit the purpose for which the map was meant to be used.

Time and Longitude

Time and longitude are related to each other. The earth makes one complete turn on its axis every 24 hours. If you divide 24 (the number of hours in a day) into 360 (the number of degrees in a complete circle), the answer is 15. This means that the earth turns through 15° of longitude every hour.

International Date Line. Look again at the world political map in your Atlas. Find the prime meridian (0° longitude). Now locate the 180° meridian. You can see that the 180° line has a dashed black line that follows it for part of its path from the North Pole to the South Pole. You can also see that it varies from the 180° line in several places, especially in the Bering Sea area between Alaska and the USSR. This line is called the **International Date Line**.

Days begin at the International Date Line. Days also end there. This is the way a new day begins: As the earth turns toward the east, a new day begins at midnight at the International Date Line (180°). One hour later it will be 1 A.M. along the 180° line. At the same time, it will be midnight at 165° east. The new day will be just beginning here. Look at your map. One hour later the new day will start at 150° east. Name the next place where the new day will start.

When it is midnight at 180°, it will be noon at 0°. Why? The prime meridian is exactly half a world, or 180°, away from the International Date Line.

Look again at the location of the International Date Line. Why is it a conve-

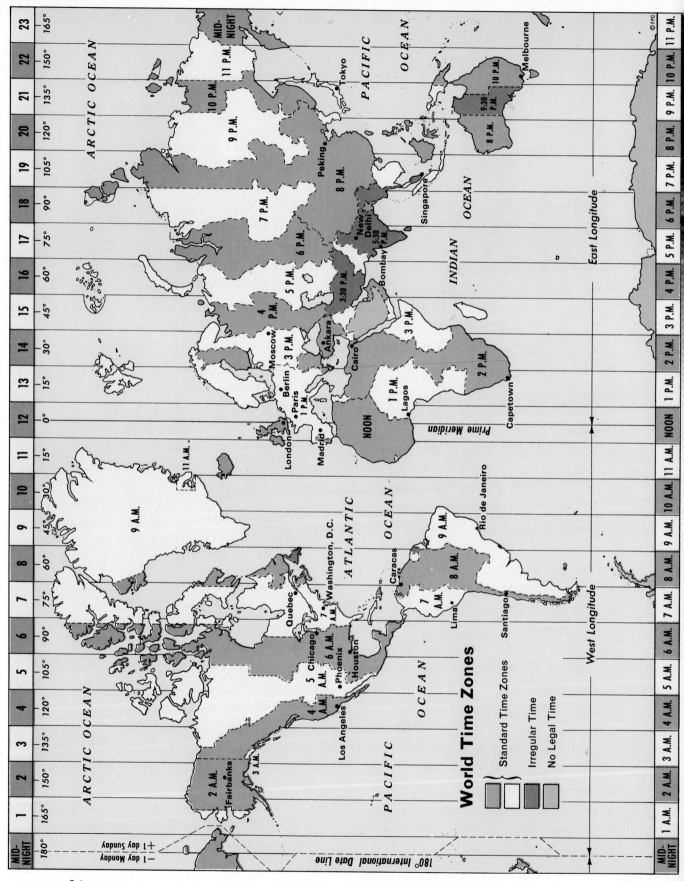

World Time Zones

Standard Time Zones

Irregular Time

No Legal Time

34

What is the London time in this photograph? the New York time?

nient place for days to begin and end? What would be the problem if days began and ended at 90° west?

World time zones. The map to the left shows the world's time zones. Like most world maps, it centers on the prime meridian. The chart shows noon along this line. If you look to the east 15°, it is 1 P.M. It was noon there one hour ago. If you look to the west 15°, it is 11 A.M. Noon will not arrive for another hour.

You can see that time zones do not follow longitude lines precisely. People have juggled time zones so that the boundaries usually pass through sparsely settled areas. It would not be very convenient for a city to be in two time zones. For example, 105° west runs right through Denver, Colorado. If time zone lines followed longitude lines precisely, it might be 5 P.M. in the eastern part of Denver and 4 P.M. in the western part. Such a system surely would not be very convenient.

Use your world political map with the time zone map. Imagine that you wanted to call someone in London at noon London time. At what time in your hometown would you have to call?

Become familiar with all the maps in your Atlas. You will use them often as you study the units in this book. Skill in reading maps will be helpful to you all your life.

Checking Up
1. What is the global grid?
2. Define *parallel*. Define *meridian*.
3. At what degree of longitude is the prime meridian? What is the purpose of the prime meridian?
4. What is a map projection?
5. Name four points that are true of the grid on a globe.
6. How are time and longitude related?
7. How are the prime meridian and the International Date Line related?
8. If it is noon along the prime meridian, what time would it be along the International Date Line?

Part One
The Beginnings

Throughout time people have learned to live in their environment. They have also learned to change the environment and to develop new ways of living. People have lived as gatherers, hunters, herders, farmers, and workers in cities. They have lived in small hunting groups, farm villages, city states, and vast empires.

From earliest times people have invented, discovered, and developed new techniques that changed their ways of living. Achievements in art, scientific advances, and systems of government are some of the records left to show us what the past was like.

Today we study the records and the people who left them. Learning about them helps us understand our world today and plan for tomorrow. People have always asked questions about their world. The ways in which they have answered these many questions are a part of the story of people on earth. They are *our* story.

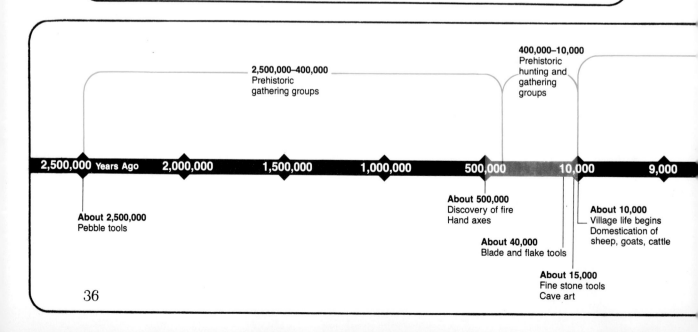

2,500,000–400,000
Prehistoric gathering groups

400,000–10,000
Prehistoric hunting and gathering groups

2,500,000 Years Ago   **2,000,000**   **1,500,000**   **1,000,000**   **500,000**   **10,000**   **9,000**

About 2,500,000
Pebble tools

About 500,000
Discovery of fire
Hand axes

About 40,000
Blade and flake tools

About 15,000
Fine stone tools
Cave art

About 10,000
Village life begins
Domestication of
sheep, goats, cattle

36

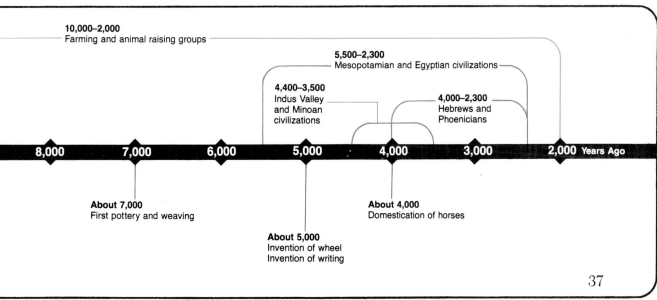

10,000–2,000
Farming and animal raising groups

5,500–2,300
Mesopotamian and Egyptian civilizations

4,400–3,500
Indus Valley
and Minoan
civilizations

4,000–2,300
Hebrews and
Phoenicians

| 8,000 | 7,000 | 6,000 | 5,000 | | 4,000 | 3,000 | 2,000 | Years Ago |

About 7,000
First pottery and weaving

About 4,000
Domestication of horses

About 5,000
Invention of wheel
Invention of writing

37

Unit 1

An Ice Age World of People

About 15,000 years ago, an artist painted this bison on the wall of a cave.

39

Before History

As You Read

1. Think about these words.
   prehistory   glacier   anthropologist
   history   archaeologist   geologist
2. Look for answers to these key questions.
   a. What effects did the Ice Age have on the earth?
   b. What divides history from prehistory?
   c. What do we call the scientists who study prehistory, and what are their methods?
3. Use this reading skill.
   Each chapter in this book begins with a list of important social studies words. You will also find these words in **bold** type the first time they are used. The Glossary at the back of your book tells you the pronunciations and definitions of these words. As you finish each chapter, be sure you can pronounce each word and understand its meaning.

How can we learn about people who lived during the Ice Age? The earliest people left no written records for us to read. In fact, writing was not invented until about 5,000 years ago. We call this earliest period of time—all the years before the development of writing—**prehistory**. The period of time that comes after the development of writing is known as **history**.

Turn to the time line on pages 36–37. Look at both prehistoric and historic periods of time. We know more about historic time than we do about prehistoric time. You can see, though, that we do know some things about prehistoric time. However, all that we know has been learned from the remains in the earth. We know less about these thousands and thousands of years of prehistoric time because there are no written records.

Understanding Time

When you study the story of people, you deal with thousands and even millions of years. Understanding these periods of time is not easy. Your own history goes back only about twelve years. The history of the United States as a nation covers a little over two hundred years, from 1776 to the present. Even the whole of history, the 5,000 years or so since writing was developed, is not too difficult to understand.

Prehistory, on the other hand, deals with such long periods of time that it is

This glacier fills a mountain valley on New Zealand's South Island.

difficult to imagine them. Farming began around 10,000 years ago. Some scientists believe that people have been using fire for about 500,000 years. Some scientists even believe that people lived on earth at least 2.5 million years ago. The time of the huge dinosaurs goes back 200 million years. The earth itself may be 2.5 billion years old. Look at the time line on page 36. How far back does it go? It is almost impossible to show all these events on a time line.

The Ice Age

Our story, the story of people on earth, begins during the Ice Age. During this time large areas of the continents of North America, Europe, and Asia were covered with sheets of ice called **glaciers**. The average temperature of the earth was lower than it is today. The snow never completely melted. As the snow piled higher and higher, the pressure caused glaciers to form. Some scientists believe that there may have been several

periods of warming and cooling during the Ice Age.

Glaciers developed when the temperature was lower. They retreated or melted when the temperature was warmer. The Ice Age lasted until about 11,000 years ago. There are many unanswered questions about the Ice Age. What caused the periods of warming and cooling? How long did they last? Where were the people? How did they survive?

Although they are not complete, there are some answers to these questions. We know some things about the Ice Age. For example, we know that glaciers move from higher ground to lower ground. We know that they have changed the landscape of many parts of the world.

During the Ice Age huge quantities of water on earth were frozen in glaciers. As a result, oceans were about 300 feet lower than they are today. Some land that is beneath the ocean today was above water during the Ice Age. Some of this land formed land links, or bridges,

41

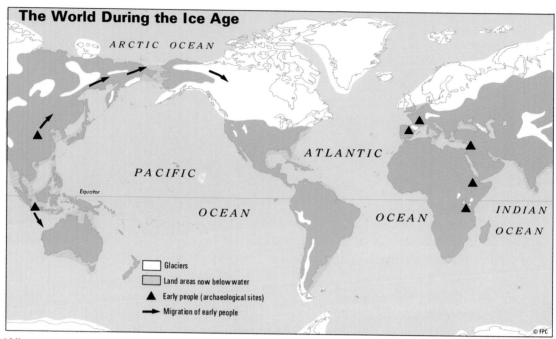

The World During the Ice Age

ARCTIC OCEAN

ATLANTIC

PACIFIC

Equator

OCEAN

OCEAN

INDIAN
OCEAN

Glaciers
Land areas now below water
▲ Early people (archaeological sites)
→ Migration of early people

© FPC

Why were people able to migrate easily from Asia to North America?

between continents. Look at the map above. What continents and islands were connected during the Ice Age? These land bridges made it possible for people and animals to move for thousands of years to lands that were later separated by water.

Learning About the Past

We also know that questions about where the people lived and how they survived have some answers. Scientists are sure that people lived on earth during the last part of the Ice Age. The remains of these people and their tools have been found buried beneath the surface of the earth.

All that we know about the dates, the inventions, and the locations of early people has come from the earth itself.

The earth is a storehouse of information. Many scientists have worked to discover information about early people.

Archaeologists. Scientists who study very old remains in order to learn about the past are **archaeologists** (är′kē·äl′ə·jəsts). The remains include the bones of long-dead animals and people, as well as remains of things people made in the past. Most wooden objects, clothing, and houses are completely gone. Yet some things remain, often buried in the earth. Archaeologists dig up these things and study them. Archaeologists have learned much about early people.

Anthropologists. Scientists who study people and their culture, or way of living, are **anthropologists** (an′thrə·päl′ə·jəsts). Some anthropologists study people living today to find out about people in the past. There are still a few small groups of people in some parts of the world who live as the people did thousands of years ago. Anthropologists study these groups. By learning about their ways of living, we can often make some intelligent guesses about how similar groups lived long ago. This information also helps archaeologists.

Other anthropologists study the remains of early people and animals to learn more about them. They study the size of the bones of early people to learn about the size of the people. We know, for example, that during most of prehistory people were much smaller than people are today. With the help of still other sciences, anthropologists can date or discover the age of a set of bones fairly accurately. We can learn, therefore, just about the date that the bones belonged to a living person.

Careers

Archaeologists

Archaeologists work all over the world at sites where human remains are found. They choose sites from both prehistoric and historic ages. Archaeologists have made important discoveries in such places as caves and dry riverbeds. More often they have to dig far beneath the surface of the ground.

As they dig, archaeologists keep records of the things they find at each level. Each level was once at the surface of the ground. Over long periods of time, wind, running water, lava flows, and glaciers buried the surface with soil and dust. The farther down a level is, the older any remains are. By studying the bone and tool remains from each level, archaeologists try to understand the people who at one time lived on that piece of land.

Archaeologists carefully choose the sites for digging. They search for a site that is likely to have been used by early people. A hill near a lake or river is a good place. Here early humans could easily have gotten water and hunted the animals that also came to drink.

Archaeologists must have many years of university education. They take courses in anthropology, dating methods, and fossil remains. They also learn about the period and region in which they expect to do their work.

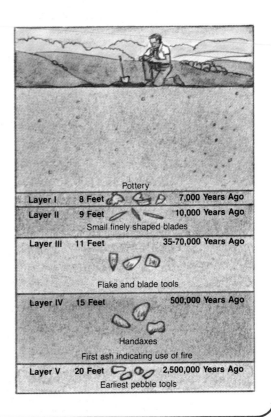

		Pottery	
Layer I	8 Feet		7,000 Years Ago
Layer II	9 Feet		10,000 Years Ago
		Small finely shaped blades	
Layer III	11 Feet		35-70,000 Years Ago
		Flake and blade tools	
Layer IV	15 Feet		500,000 Years Ago
		Handaxes	
		First ash indicating use of fire	
Layer V	20 Feet		2,500,000 Years Ago
		Earliest pebble tools	

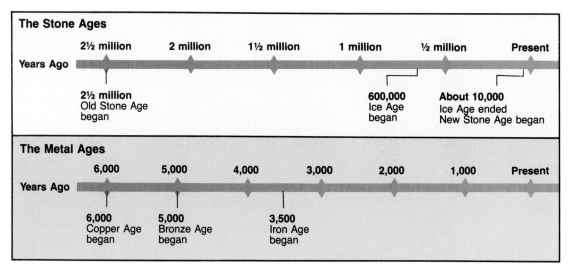

The Stone Ages

Years Ago	2½ million	2 million	1½ million	1 million	½ million	Present

2½ million
Old Stone Age
began

600,000
Ice Age
began

About 10,000
Ice Age ended
New Stone Age began

The Metal Ages

Years Ago	6,000	5,000	4,000	3,000	2,000	1,000	Present

6,000
Copper Age
began

5,000
Bronze Age
began

3,500
Iron Age
began

Geologists. Scientists who study the earth itself are **geologists** (jē·äl′ə·jəsts). They also help us learn about the past. Rocks and rock formations can give us some ideas about what the earth was like in past ages and how it has changed over long periods of time. It was geologists who first learned about the Ice Age. By studying rocks and soil, they have been able to figure out the movements of Ice Age glaciers. Geology can also help an archaeologist know when certain levels now under the ground were at the surface. This knowledge also helps to date things that are unearthed.

The ages of prehistory. Scientists have divided the long prehistoric period into several ages. These ages have been named for the kinds of tools early people made and used. The first tools were made of stone, so the first prehistoric age is called the Stone Age. Look at the time line above. Notice that the long Stone Age is divided into two shorter periods, the Old Stone Age and the New Stone Age.

The ages occurring after people learned to use metals are named after the metals used. These are the Copper Age, the Bronze Age, and the Iron Age. Look at the time line again. When was metal first used for tools?

Checking Up
1. How do glaciers move?
2. What are the two ways in which anthropologists help us understand early people?
3. How do scientists divide the prehistory of people?
4. What answers would you give to the key questions at the beginning of this chapter?
5. *Imagine finding the remains of human bones and stone tools at the bottom of a ravine. How could an archaeologist, an anthropologist, and a geologist help you understand what you had found?*

44

Maps Tell a Story of Glaciers

As you read, think about these words.
moraine   loess   fjord

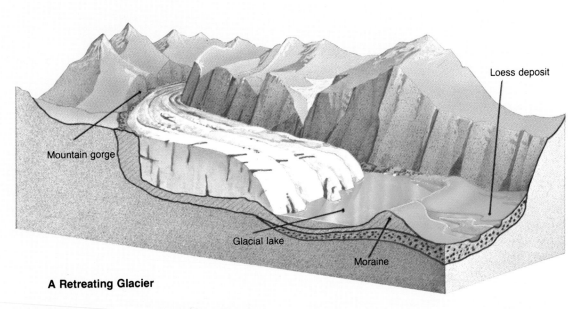

Loess deposit

Mountain gorge

Glacial lake

Moraine

A Retreating Glacier

The growth and movement of glaciers created many different kinds of landforms. As glaciers spread, they picked up sand, gravel, and rocks. Later, the melting glacier left a ridge of rocks and soil known as a **moraine** (mə·rān′). Find the moraine formation on the map.

Glaciers were powerful enough to crush hard rock into fine particles, which were then carried along by the moving ice. Later, the melting glacier left this fine soil on the earth. Known as **loess** (les), this soil is especially good for farming. Loess, carried from what is now Canada, covers much of the state of Kansas. Find the area covered by loess on the map.

Glaciers even cut deep gorges in river valleys. In some places, as the glaciers melted and sea level rose, the gorges filled with seawater. These gorges are known as **fjords** (fē·ôrdz′). The weight of some glaciers was great enough to make great depressions, or low areas, in some regions. Then melting glaciers flooded some of these low-lying areas. Lakes formed. The Great Lakes are glacial lakes that were at one time formed in this way. Find the mountain gorge and glacial lake on the map.

Checking Up

1. How did the forward motion of glaciers change the land?
2. How did the melting of the glaciers change the land?
3. Explain each word listed at the top of this page.

45

People Are Special

As You Read

1. Think about these words.
   migrate   nomad   division of labor
2. Look for answers to these key questions.
   a. What are the special characteristics of human beings that have helped them survive?
   b. Why were tools, language, and fire important to early people?
   c. What are gathering and hunting groups?
3. Use this reading skill.
   At the beginning of each chapter in this book, there are key questions. As you read, keep these questions in mind. They give you clues about what the chapter is about.

It is hard for people today to imagine how people survived during early times. The climate was harsh, and the animals were fierce. People did survive, however, because of their special characteristics.

Special Characteristics

Four characteristics make human beings special. One of these characteristics is the ability to walk upright. Hands are then free to hold things or to perform tasks.

Hands themselves are also a special characteristic. Hold your book up in front of you. Notice how you grip it. Your fingers grip from one direction. Your thumb grips from another. The inside of your thumb can touch the inside of your fingers. Our thumbs make it possible for us to use tools such as screwdrivers and pencils.

The way humans see is another important characteristic. Our eyes are set in the front of our heads. This characteristic enables us to see depth and distance. Think how important measuring distance might have been for early people. Without this kind of vision, a hunter could not be sure how far away an animal was. That could mean a lot of trouble if the animal were attacking.

Walking upright, gripping with our thumbs, and having a frontal eye set are three important characteristics. Yet an even more important characteristic is the large and complex human brain. Our ability to think makes it possible for us to change the environment as well as to adapt, or adjust, to it.

Tools. Early people used their brains in many ways. One way was to invent tools. Tools helped them survive.

How did people hold a hand ax? What do you think they used it for?

Which of these tools do you think was good for chopping? for scraping?

The earliest tools that have been found are pebble tools. This kind of tool was a small chipped stone that had a sharp point. Pebble tools were used for chopping, cutting, and digging.

As time passed, people made better tools. People chipped away the sides of the stone more carefully to make a sharp, pointed hand ax. They gripped the axes in their hands and used their arms as handles. Look at the photograph of the hand ax shown above.

At some time people must have noticed that the flakes of rock that were chipped off to make a hand ax were often very sharp. They had a cutting edge even sharper than the hand ax. People began to use these flakes as tools. Flake tools were used for cutting, scraping, and chopping.

Throughout prehistoric time people invented different tools for different purposes. Improved tools made it possible for people to have more control over their environment.

Language. Language is certainly one of the most important developments of early people. It, too, was possible because of the complex human brain. Language made it possible for one generation to teach the next generation what had been learned. For example, parents could use language to teach their children toolmaking and the customs of their group. The use of language made it much easier for people to live and work together.

Fire. Learning to use fire was a big step forward for early people. Fire could frighten off dangerous animals. It could be used to stampede a herd of animals into a ravine, where they could be killed more easily. Archaeologists have also found wooden spears with tips hardened by fire.

People began to cook their food over fire. Cooking softens food and makes it easier to digest. It also kills bacteria that can cause illness. People learned to smoke meat to keep it from spoiling.

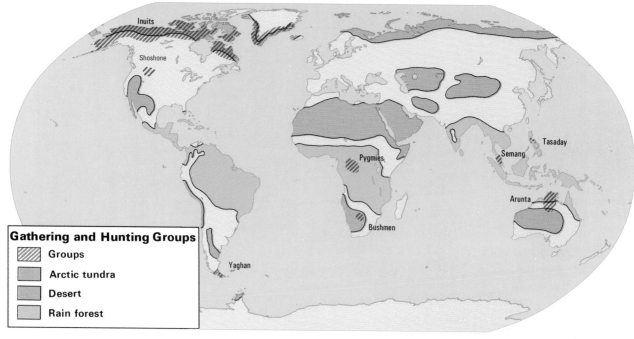

Gathering and Hunting Groups
- [//] Groups
- Arctic tundra
- Desert
- Rain forest

Gatherers and hunters once lived in many parts of the world. Today only a few groups remain. They live in remote areas.

Fire provided a new source of light. The number of working hours in a day increased. Possibly people gathered around the evening fire, telling tales and making tools.

Fire, along with improved tools, helped people to survive during the Ice Age. Although the earliest people probably lived close to the equator, where the climate was warm, some **migrated**, or moved, to colder parts of Europe, Asia, and North America. Even during the Ice Age, people who had fire were able to live in the northern lands.

Gatherers and Hunters

The most important task for early people was finding food. The earliest people lived by gathering and hunting. Food gatherers lived on the food they found.

This mother and child belong to a present-day gathering group in the Philippines.

Gatherers. The food that gatherers ate included fruits, nuts, seeds, and edible leaves. Perhaps they also caught small animals, but they were not hunters.

Gatherers were wanderers. They moved from place to place in search of food. When they used up the food in one place, they moved to a new location. Gatherers lived in caves or camped in the open. If they built shelters, the shelters were very simple ones.

Gatherers could never be very far away from a good supply of food. They probably did not live in places that had long, cold winters.

Hunting people may have tamed the dog as early as 30,000 years ago.

Gathering people taught their children skills. What do you think this man is teaching the children sitting around him?

Coming-of-Age Ceremonies

Becoming an adult is an important event for any person. Most of us become adults gradually. Many years of education help prepare students for later careers. Throughout their teen years, young people take on more and more responsibilities.

In present-day hunting and gathering groups, however, special ceremonies mark the time when a young person becomes an adult. In these groups, the roles of men and women are strictly separated. During the coming-of-age ceremonies, girls receive lessons that prepare them for marriage. Boys become members of the hunting group.

The ceremonies include instruction in both adult life and the special customs of their people. Often there is also a test of physical hardship for the young boys. By enduring pain, the boys prove their courage.

Although coming-of-age ceremonies vary from people to people, they are found in almost every remaining hunting and gathering group.

Suppose you were an anthropologist studying the coming-of-age ceremonies among present-day hunting and gathering groups. What guesses might you make about ways of life among earlier hunters and gatherers?

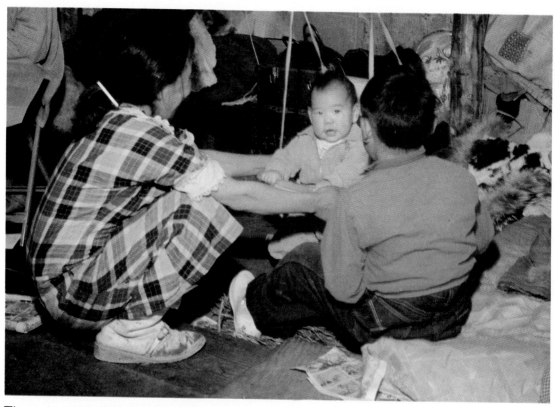

There is more time for leisure in hunting groups than in gathering groups. What do you think this family may be doing?

Hunters. Hunters probably had a better supply of food than gatherers. Hunters could kill enough small animals, or one large-enough animal, to provide food for many people for many days. Not everyone in a hunting group hunted. Some gathered food. Thus members of hunting groups had a wider variety of food than did people who were only gatherers.

Hunters, like gatherers, moved from place to place. They usually moved when the animals they hunted migrated. Many of the large game animals, such as bison and deer, migrated north and south every year. As winter approached, the animals moved south. When the weather got warmer, they moved north. The animals followed their food supply. The hunters followed theirs.

Archaeologists have found evidence that shows some early hunting groups may have returned to the same area every summer, year after year. Because they followed their food supplies, early hunters and gatherers can be considered the first **nomads**.

Families and groups. Throughout time the basic human group has been the family. Gatherers probably lived in groups of related families. These groups probably had no more than twenty people. Larger groups would have used up the available food supplies too fast.

Scientists believe that most members of gathering groups worked to provide food. Men, women, and even young children gathered the plants, leaves, and roots used for food.

Hunting groups were probably larger than gathering groups. Some hunting groups may have had as many as sixty people. Hunting could provide more food than gathering.

From the evidence we have, it seems that in hunting groups only the men were the hunters. Women and children were probably not included in the hunts.

Women stayed at the campsite to care for the children and to gather food. Caring for children was easier and much safer at the campsite. It is possible that the first **division of labor**, or assigning of certain jobs to certain people, took place in early hunting groups.

Hunting large game animals was dangerous. Therefore, even boys were usually not included in the hunt until they had developed adequate strength and skills with weapons.

Checking Up
1. What is the most important of the special characteristics of people?
2. Name three kinds of stone tools and their different uses.
3. What advantages did hunting groups have over gathering groups?
4. What answers would you give to the key questions at the beginning of this chapter?
5. *Why might there have been a division of labor between the men and the women in hunting groups but not in gathering groups?*

People at the End of the Old Stone Age

If you could look at a person who lived about 35,000 years ago, you would find a human being very much like people today. There are few differences between yourself and a person of your age from that time.

New Tools

Over many thousands of years, people improved their tools. Tools became more **specialized**. People developed special tools for special purposes. They made tools for scraping, boring, cutting, and chopping.

In Europe and Asia, people began to make greater use of bone, reindeer antler, and wood. Stone tools were chipped into shape and sharpened. New kinds of tools appeared. Archaeologists have found fishhooks, harpoons, and parts of bows and arrows. People in Europe and Asia also made blade tools that are similar to modern knife blades. Many tools were decorated with carved designs.

Art, Magic, and Religion

Improvements in tools were remarkable achievements. Even more remarkable was the artistic work of early people. Their sculptures and paintings probably had a magical purpose.

A blade tool has sharp edges. It is good for scraping and cutting.

People made these clay animals toward the end of the Ice Age.

Notice the fine craftwork on this ivory carving of a woman's head.

Art. When the cave paintings of late Ice Age people were first found, many experts did not believe the paintings could be prehistoric. They did not think that people who lived so long ago could have done such fine work. Since then, many more examples of such work have been discovered. These include carvings and drawings scratched on bone and antler. Similarities between the cave paintings and these carvings indicated they were from the same time period. Since bone and antler once belonged to living animals, they could be dated by the carbon 14 method. The results showed that these works were done between 10,000 and 15,000 years ago, as the Ice Age was finally ending. Northern Spain and southern France are especially rich in these discoveries.

Most of the art shows animals that hunting people depended on for food. Some pictures show animals that are now **extinct**, or no longer in existence, such as the woolly rhinoceros and the mammoth, a hairy elephant. Drawings of people are rarer, and they are never as detailed as those of animals.

The cave paintings are deep inside caves, far from the cave openings where people lived. Paintings cover the walls and ceilings. It must have been difficult doing this work by fire or torchlight. Why did people do it?

Many experts think the art had a connection with a kind of magic. A number of the painted animals are shown with arrows or spears in their sides. The painters may have hoped that a picture of a successful hunt would give the group's hunters a kind of magical power or special luck in their hunting. If this idea is true, some early art may have had a connection with early religious practices.

This cave painting shows horses and oxen thousands of years before either animal was tamed.

Early religion. Since there are no written records, we cannot be certain of the religious beliefs early people held, or even if they had a religion. Anthropologists, however, have studied many different groups of hunting people who live today and have learned a great deal about their religious beliefs. People late in the Old Stone Age may have held similar beliefs.

We know that early people buried their dead with great care. They often included many burial gifts with the bodies. People were buried wearing ornaments made of carved bone or strings of animal teeth or seashells. Weapons and evidence of food have also been found in graves.

This ceremonial dancer wears animal horns and skins.

54

Why do you think this shaman might be dancing?

Many present-day hunting people follow similar practices in burying their dead. There are special burial ceremonies. Gifts of weapons and food included in the burial show a belief in a life after death. These items are for the spirit, or soul, of the dead person as it travels to another land.

People in hunting groups may believe that all things, both living and nonliving, have a spirit. They also may believe that a person, called a shaman, can talk to and even influence these spirits. A shaman is supposed to have the power to bring about a good hunt. In prehistoric times, the shaman was probably the cave painter.

Checking Up

1. What new materials did people late in the Old Stone Age use to make tools? What were some of the specialized tools that they made?

2. How do we know that the cave paintings were done between 10,000 and 15,000 years ago?
3. What is a shaman? What did Old Stone Age people believe a shaman could do?
4. What answers would you give to the key questions at the beginning of this chapter?
5. *What do the cave paintings and burial places of Old Stone Age people tell us about their beliefs?*

Unit 1 Summary

- Some scientists believe that people may have lived on the earth for more than 2½ million years.
- Prehistory includes all time on earth until the invention of writing.
- The work of many different kinds of scientists helps us learn about what happened in prehistory.
- We can know something about the way of life of prehistoric people by the things they left behind.
- The earliest people made very simple tools and lived by gathering food and hunting. Later, hunting people gradually improved and made a wider variety of tools.
- Toward the end of the Ice Age, about 11,000 years ago, people began to produce artistic work, both paintings and tools. People late in the Old Stone Age may have lived lives very similar to those of present-day hunting and gathering groups.

Unit 1 Review Workshop

What Have You Learned?

1. How did toolmaking improve during the time of the Stone Age?
2. Why do archaeologists keep records of the things they find at each level of a site?
3. Explain what walking upright, gripping with thumbs, and having a frontal eye set enable people to do. What other human characteristic is the most important?
4. How were hunting groups different from gathering groups?
5. In what way might early artistic works have been connected with ideas of magic?

Use Your Reading Skills

Determine which word best fits each sentence. Choose from the following words.

prehistory	division of labor
glaciers	specialized
archaeologist	extinct
anthropologist	shaman
geologist	migrate

1. A _____ studies the earth itself.
2. The level of the sea rose after the _____ melted.
3. The period in the past before the invention of writing is known as _____.
4. An _____ digs up and studies ancient remains.
5. The tools of people late in the Old Stone Age were more _____ than the tools of the people of earlier times.
6. In hunting groups, the _____ left hunting to the men and gathering to the women and children.
7. Several Ice Age animals are now _____.
8. Deer and bison _____ with the seasons.
9. An _____ studies how people lived long ago.
10. The person in a hunting group who is supposed to be able to influence spirits is called a _____.

Use Your Map Skills

Look at the map on page 42. Determine whether the following countries were covered by glacial sheets during the Ice Age. If you do not know where each country is located, use the Atlas map on pages 10–11.

Mexico	Sweden	Spain
Canada	England	Japan

Use Your Thinking Skills

1. Anthropologists and historians have tried to understand the meaning of the cave paintings. They believe there was some connection between the paintings and magic. Do you agree with this idea? Explain why. How is the purpose of our art different?
2. Look at the drawing of Stone Age hunters. What does it tell you about how they hunted together? What was

their hunting plan? What are the two important early human discoveries they are using to drive on the animals? What type of tool is the spear point?

Use Your Research Skills

Find out about a hunting and gathering people who still exist or who did so until recently. Choose one from the following list and use your school or local library to help you. Tell where the group lives, how large it is, what kinds of food the people eat, and what their daily lives are like.

Inuits (Eskimos) of the Arctic Circle
Shoshone Indians
Yaghan or Yamana of Tierra del Fuego
Arunta (Australian Aborigines)
Kung Bushmen of the Kalahari Desert
Pygmies of the Ituri rain forest

Semang of Malaya
Tasaday of the Philippines

Learn by Doing

Use clay to make models or draw pictures of prehistoric tools such as pebble, flake, and blade tools. Use the pictures in this and other books to help you. Label each tool. Tell what kind of tool it is, when it was used, and what purpose it was used for.

Read to Learn More

Find the topics listed below in the card catalog of your library. Read all or part of a book listed under one of the topics. Share what you learn with your classmates.

ARCHAEOLOGY   FOSSIL

ANTHROPOLOGY   STONE AGE

RADIO CARBON DATING

Unit 2

The Rise of Civilization in the Middle East

Statues of winged lions, such as this one, guarded the palaces of the Assyrians, who lived in northern Mesopotamia.

The Agricultural Revolution

As You Read

1. Think about these words.
   agriculture   revolution   domesticate   adapt   population
2. Look for answers to these key questions.
   a. What changes in climate took place at the end of the Ice Age?
   b. How did farming probably begin?
   c. How do domesticated plants and animals differ from wild ones?
3. Use this reading skill.
   Each chapter has headings. The larger headings tell you the main topics. Important ideas about these topics are found in the smaller headings. You can make an outline by using these headings. Make an outline of this chapter.

When the Ice Age was ending, hunting and gathering groups lived in many parts of the world. These small groups of people hunted different animals or gathered different plants, depending on where they lived. Their basic pattern of life, though, was the same. Within the thousand years following the end of the Ice Age, patterns of life began to change dramatically. People in some areas started producing food by farming.

The New Stone Age

The Ice Age came to an end when a warming trend occurred. This warming trend continued for several thousand years. The glaciers that covered the northern parts of Europe, Asia, and North America began to melt. Look at the time line on page 44. When did the Ice Age end? About 9,000 years ago, cli-

mates throughout the world were about the same as they are today.

As the climate changed, plant and animal life changed. Warmer weather and more rainfall gradually turned many northern areas in Europe, Asia, and North America into forests. Areas with less rain became grasslands. Find these forests and grasslands on the map on pages 18–19. The plants and animals that began to live in these areas were much like the wild plants and animals found there today.

The period following the Ice Age is called the New Stone Age. People used the finely shaped and highly polished stone tools described in Unit 1. They also invented new tools for producing food. Look at the time line on page 44. When did the New Stone Age begin? It lasted until the beginning of the Copper Age.

60

totally different kind of life for humans. Such a change is called a **revolution**.

How Farming Began

People have always used plants for food. It took people thousands of years, however, to become farmers. They also continued hunting and gathering long after they began planting crops.

We do not know how agriculture was discovered. After thousands of years of gathering plants, however, people must have seen that plants grow from seeds. They tried planting seeds to grow crops.

People began to **domesticate** many plants and animals. Domestication is the process of **adapting**, or changing, a plant or an animal so it can be produced more easily by people. Domestication occurs over many years of plant and animal life. Right up to our own time, people have continued the process of domestication. Many scientists believe that some of the first people to domesticate plants and animals lived in the part of the world today called the Middle East.

The Middle East

Look at the map on this page. It shows the area where the continents of Europe, Asia, and Africa meet. This area is known as the Middle East. Developments in farming in the Middle East eventually spread across much of Europe, Asia, and Africa.

The Fertile Crescent. Find the large valley of the Tigris and Euphrates rivers at the center of the map. Locate the highland area farther to the north and

Because they knew much about plants, women may have discovered farming.

The development of **agriculture**, or farming practices, took place over thousands of years. It happened at different times in different places. Nevertheless, the development of agriculture led to a

Ancient Middle East

⌂ Early farming villages

Miles
0 100 200 300 400 500 600

0   200   400   600   800
Kilometers

Black Sea

Caspian Sea

Mediterranean Sea

Euphrates River

Tigris River

Nile River

Red Sea

Persian Gulf

© FEC

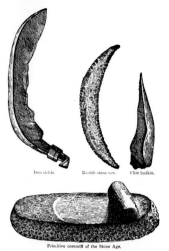

These New Stone Age tools were used to cut grain and grind it into flour.

nearer the eastern Mediterranean. Trace the highland region along the eastern coast of the Mediterranean Sea. Together the river valley and highland area near the Mediterranean coast form a curved, or crescent-shaped, area. Because of its rich soil, the area is called the Fertile Crescent. Agriculture seems to have had its beginning in the highlands of the Fertile Crescent.

This highland area of the Middle East provided a rich source of plants and animals. Wild wheat and barley were already used as food by early people. In fact, these grains grow wild in parts of the Middle East today. Animals suitable for domestication, especially goats and sheep, roamed the same grasslands and were among the animals hunted by the people there.

Farming people used tools that were different from those of earlier hunters and gatherers. In the New Stone Age, gatherers developed sickles to cut wild grains such as wheat and barley. When people began to plant and grow their own grains, they improved these sickles.

They also made stone tools for grinding grain into flour.

As people became farmers, they were able to produce a greater food supply. With more food, the **population**, or the number of people in the area, could continue to grow. More and more land could be farmed to produce food for this increasing population.

The Development of Agriculture

About the same time people began growing crops, they also started raising animals. The stalks of plants they raised furnished food for their animals. Agriculture could, therefore, provide food for both people and animals.

Plants. Farmers learned as they planted and harvested. The seeds of wild grain were attached to the stalk by a brittle stem. When the grain was ripe, the seeds broke off easily and fell to the ground. Wild grain, therefore, presented a problem to farmers. As a farmer harvested the stalks, most of the seeds fell off. The seeds, or grain, were what the farmer wanted, but collecting them was difficult.

Some plants, however, had a less brittle stem. The seeds did not fall off as easily. Such plants did not do well in natural conditions because their seeds did not fall to the ground at the right time. They were, however, valuable to the farmer, who could harvest the plants without losing the grain.

The early farmers learned to plant only the seeds from the plants with less brittle stems. The seeds of the new plants, then, did not fall off when the plants were harvested. Farmers also chose seeds from the plants that had more and larger seeds. Year after year, farmers carefully selected the seeds that would produce the best crops.

In time, the domesticated wheat and barley were quite different from the wild plants. They were so different, in fact, that the domesticated plants would have had difficulty growing wild. They needed the care of the farmers. Scientists today can tell whether seeds found at an archaeological site came from wild or domesticated plants.

Animals. The first animals to be domesticated in the Middle East were dogs, goats, and sheep. Scientists estimate that domestication occurred about 11,000 years ago. Some scientists believe that dogs may have been kept even earlier. They may have been trained to help hunters.

The goats and sheep that roamed wild in the Middle East would have provided

As in early times, this Middle Eastern girl of today tends the village herd.

a good source of meat for hunting people. Hunters probably followed the herds of animals as they roamed their grazing lands. At some point these hunters may have decided to round up some of the younger animals and keep them. This assured the people of a steady supply of food. They no longer had to hunt.

Goats and sheep were the easiest animals to domesticate. Farmers bred animals so that they got the kind they wanted. For example, domesticated sheep and goats had shorter horns than wild ones. Domestic sheep were bred to have longer woolly hair after farmers began to use wool for cloth. After thousands of years, the domesticated animals changed so much that they looked quite different from their wild relatives. Like the plants, they had become more dependent on the farmers.

Checking Up
1. Where is the Middle East? the Fertile Crescent?
2. What different kinds of tools did early farmers use?
3. What were the first plants and animals to be domesticated in the Middle East?
4. What answers would you give to the key questions at the beginning of this chapter?
5. *Once people began farming, it became impossible for them to return to being only hunters and gatherers. Why do you think this was so?*

63

A New Way of Life

As You Read

1. Think about these words.
   permanent   surplus   property
2. Look for answers to these key questions.
   a. In what three ways did the agricultural revolution change the way of human life?
   b. What inventions followed the beginnings of agriculture in the Middle East?
3. Use these reading skills.
   Learn to summarize the main ideas in the chapter. Skim the chapter. Remember to read the headings. Write a three-sentence summary of the main ideas.

The change from food gathering to food producing was only part of the agricultural revolution. What made it a true revolution were all the other changes that resulted from the development of agriculture.

Instead of using animal skins, people began to weave cloth for clothing.

Settling Down

Agriculture forced people to settle, or stay in one place. People had to be near their fields all year long. Farmers began to build lasting, or **permanent**, houses. Early farmers built their houses close together to have protection from any enemies. People lived in communities of 100 or more. In time, some villages grew into towns of several thousands.

New Tools and New Jobs

As time passed, there were more different kinds of jobs to perform in farming communities than there were in hunting and gathering groups. People began to specialize, or to do only certain jobs. Some worked in the fields. Others took care of the farm animals. Women spent much of their day grinding grain into flour and preparing meals.

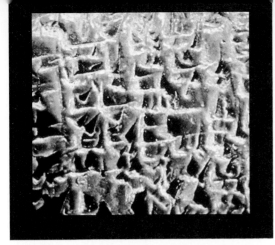

The Mesopotamians used baked clay for jars, writing tablets, and toys.

People in Mesopotamia still build their houses with sun-dried brick.

New inventions. As people found new ways of making things, specialization increased. Pottery was probably discovered when someone noticed that fire hardened clay. Soon people were making clay pots and dishes and baking them in ovens to harden them. Making pottery took skill, and some people began to specialize in it.

The invention of the plow made farming even more efficient. Just one person with an ox-drawn plow could loosen more earth than several people working with hoes. It took fewer farmers to provide enough food for a village. Some farmers, then, were able to change jobs

The earliest plows appeared about 6,000 years ago, several thousand years after the beginning of farming.

and specialize in some other kind of work. Specialization led to more trading among people of the community.

A Surplus

Improved farming methods enabled some farmers to grow a **surplus** of crops. This meant that they raised more food than they could use. This surplus became wealth—something that could be traded for other things the family needed or wanted. Trade increased. People even began to think differently. Ownership became important. There were few ideas of **property**, or things owned, among hunting and gathering people. Gatherers had few possessions, and almost everything belonged to the group as a whole. In the farming villages, ownership was

Signature seals were carved stone cylinders that left an imprint on clay.

limited to land, animals, the house, tools, and the few other belongings of the family. They were passed down from parents to children within the family.

After a time, some people owned more land or goods than others. Some people became rich and important while others did not.

Writing. People needed ways to prove they were the owners of things. How could a farmer, for example, prove that a jar of grain belonged to him?

All that remains of this ancient village in Mesopotamia is a mound.

The development of writing helped solve this problem. Look at the time line on pages 36–37. When was writing developed? At first people used stamps called seals to mark the things they owned. Later, as writing developed, it was used to record business dealings. Still later, writing allowed people to record events, laws, and literature.

The development of writing marks the end of the prehistoric period. As the use of writing spread, more and more evidence of what early life was really like was left for future archaeologists and historians to find.

Checking Up
1. What are some examples of specialization in early farming villages?
2. How did people show they owned something?
3. Why did people develop a system of writing?
4. What answers would you give to the key questions at the beginning of this chapter?
5. *If you had lived thousands of years ago, would you rather have been a food gatherer or a food producer? Why? What are some advantages and disadvantages of each way of life?*

Maps Tell a Story of Agriculture

The agricultural revolution has continued for centuries. Different methods of agriculture and different crops have been developed in various places and at various times. From these places, plants and animals have been taken to new places. The map on this page shows where plant and animal domestication probably began. The map on page 68 shows the areas where some of these crops are grown today.

Farmers may have first grown grains in both the Middle East and in northern China. Find these areas on the map on this page. Now look at the map on page 68. How has the growing of grain spread?

Growing root crops such as yams seems to have begun in western Africa.

Other root crops were grown in the tropical regions of Central and South America and the South Pacific. Look for the areas where people first grew root crops on the map on this page.

People in Southeast Asia learned to grow another grain. They grew rice. From Southeast Asia, growing rice spread to China and India. Find the area where people first grew rice. In what present-day areas is rice grown?

In the Western Hemisphere, some entirely different plants were domesticated. In Central America and Mexico maize, or corn, was a grain grown as the major source of food. In the Andes, white potatoes were the most important crop. Locate the areas where corn and potatoes were first grown. Find where

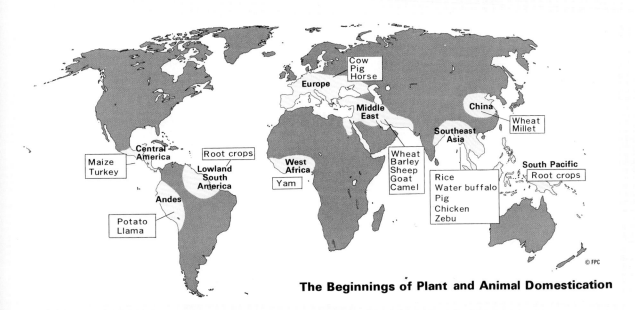

The Beginnings of Plant and Animal Domestication

Early people in different parts of the world learned to grow wheat, yams, rice, corn, and potatoes.

67

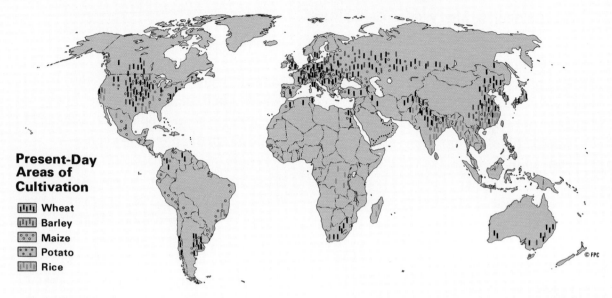

**Present-Day
Areas of
Cultivation**

|▥| Wheat
|▥| Barley
|⚬⚬| Maize
|⦙⦙| Potato
|▥| Rice

All over the world, people now grow wheat, barley, rice, corn, and potatoes.

the growing of corn and potatoes has spread. European explorers introduced these crops into many parts of the Eastern Hemisphere. Many other plants from Central America and Mexico, such as tomatoes, beans, and squash, were also taken to Europe, Asia, and Africa. There they became important sources of food.

In the same way that crops spread around the world, various animals have also been introduced to new areas. For example, cattle, sheep, and horses were brought to the Americas and Australia by the Europeans.

Harvesting the crop had to be done fast, before birds ate it or rain ruined it.

Checking Up
1. Name seven areas where different crops were first developed.
2. What plants first grown in the Western Hemisphere have been introduced into the Eastern Hemisphere?
3. Name the animals domesticated in each of these places: the Middle East, Europe, Southeast Asia, Central and South America.

From Village to City

As You Read

1. Think about these words.
   irrigation   astronomy   civilization   urban   rural   empire
2. Look for answers to these key questions.
   a. Why was Mesopotamia a good location for agriculture?
   b. Who were the Sumerians? What were their achievements?
   c. How did cities develop?

The many changes brought about by the agricultural revolution occurred over a long period of time. It seems that many came about after agriculture had spread from the highlands to other areas of the Middle East.

The Spread of Agriculture

As early as 8,000 years ago, there were many farmers in the Middle East. Agriculture had also begun to spread. Sometimes farmers from one area moved elsewhere, taking their agricultural way of life with them. Agricultural knowledge probably also spread as people from different areas traded with one another.

Mesopotamia. Sometime around 7,000 years ago, farmers began to move into the valley of the Tigris and Euphrates rivers. This area is called Mesopotamia, which means "between the rivers." Here people began to farm.

Mesopotamia was a dry land. There was little rainfall. Each spring, however, as the snow in the northern mountains melted and the rains came, the rivers overflowed their banks. Since the land in Mesopotamia was very flat, the flooding covered a wide area.

The rivers carried rich soil from the highlands and deposited it along the flooded banks. Every year this flooding renewed the soil of Mesopotamia, making it good farming. The area, however, had one problem. In some years floods might wash everything away.

Before people could farm successfully in Mesopotamia, they had to learn to control the flooding. They built up the river banks to form levees, or earthen walls to hold back the floodwaters. They also built canals and ditches to carry the river water to their fields. This method of directing water, which is called **irrigation**, allowed people to keep their fields watered during the long dry season.

Such large-scale projects could not be done by single farm families. Entire villages had to work together. The work was probably supervised by the village elders, a small group of older people who were the village leaders.

69

Citizenship

The Code of Hammurabi

Whenever people live in a group, there are likely to be problems among them. Laws are rules to govern the behavior of people.

The Sumerians were the first people to have written laws. However, the best-known set of early laws was drawn up by the Babylonians after the decline of the Sumerians. These laws are known as the Code of Hammurabi (həm·ə·räb′ē). Hammurabi was king of Babylonia, a country north of Sumer. His laws were carved on a large stone slab that was found by archaeologists in 1901.

Many of Hammurabi's laws follow the principle of "an eye for an eye." If a person put out someone's eye, the eye of that person would be put out as punishment. The laws were divided according to different groups of people. There were separate laws for the wealthy; for people without any special rank, or the common people; and for the slaves. For example, a wealthy person who broke another wealthy person's arm would have his own arm broken. If he broke a common person's arm, he would only have to pay a fine. The fine for breaking a slave's arm was even less. Sometimes, however, punishments were more severe for wealthy people because they were supposed to know better. The ideas in the Code of Hammurabi are very different from our own principle of equality before the law.

The Code of Hammurabi gave women many rights. They could own property, buy and sell things, and lend and borrow money. Wives, however, were placed under the control of their husbands. Husbands were even allowed to punish wives if, for example, the wives were poor housekeepers.

This pillar containing Hammurabi's law shows the king receiving it from a god.

We probably do not agree with much of the Code of Hammurabi today. The code did show the king's concern for his subjects. The idea of written laws was also an important step in bringing about a system of justice known to all.

Changes in Religion

Religious beliefs changed as farming became more important. Success at farming was always uncertain. The farmers looked on the growth of their plants as a miracle. Farmers prayed to gods of nature—the sun, the sky, the earth, water, and storms. They believed good harvests depended on these gods.

In the farming villages, a special group of people, the priests, took charge of religious ceremonies. Each village had a temple for these ceremonies. The priests prayed and made sacrifices to the gods. Being a priest was a full-time job. Priests did not work in the fields.

As villages grew larger, the priests grew more important and more powerful. Temples became larger and more grand. The temple was usually the most impressive building in a town. Priests studied the movements of the moon, the planets, and the stars. They believed there was a god of the moon, a god of the planet Jupiter, and a goddess of the planet Venus.

Using their knowledge of the heavenly bodies, or **astronomy**, they began to make calendars. Their calendar was based on the twelve movements of the moon around the earth in a little less than a year. Their calendar was unlike ours, which is based on the movement of the earth around the sun. A calendar based on the moon, however, is still used by people in much of the present-day Middle East.

The Rise of Cities

Between 5,000 and 5,500 years ago, many changes took place in the Middle East. It was during this time that the calendar, the plow, the potter's wheel, and the weaver's loom were all developed. For the first time people probably used wheels on carts pulled by donkeys. They also began to use metals—copper, tin, gold, and silver. Soon they also learned to make bronze and iron. The sail came into use on boats built of reeds or planks. People developed writing. Some villages even grew into cities.

Picture Writing about 3100 B.C.	Sign about 2500 B.C.	Sign about 1800 B.C.	Sign about 700 B.C.	
				All of the symbols in the top row meant "fish." Notice how the symbols changed as the years passed. The symbols became simpler so that they could be written more quickly with a stylus.
				The sign for "star" changed over the centuries. The meaning also changed to include "heaven" and "god."

Sumerian writing originally stood for pictures of things. Later it represented the syllables of words.

Nomads Choose a Different Way of Life

About 4,500 years ago, large areas of central Asia, the Arabian Peninsula, and Saharan Africa were grasslands. These steppes, or dry short-grass regions, were not as suitable for agriculture as were the highland areas of the Middle East. The thick grasses that covered the steppes were difficult to break up with a plow. Several thousand years after the development of farming and village life in the Middle East, people living in the grasslands developed a different way of life.

Saharan nomads traded salt for the gold of the kingdoms south of the desert.

Nomads live in movable tents because they have to migrate with their herds.

They began to raise large herds of cows and sheep and wandered with them in search of fresh grass. People who lived in this way were nomads. Once the nomads began riding horses and camels, it became even easier for them to move with their herds. The horse was originally domesticated by nomadic people of the eastern European steppe. Camels were domesticated by nomads who lived in central Asia and Arabia.

The life of nomads was very different from the life of settled farmers. Nomads were constantly on the move. Their homes were tents that they carried with them. Nomads and farmers often fought over land. Animals were the nomads' only real property. Nomads believed that land should be used only as pasture for their herds.

The gods of the nomads did not have anything to do with the earth or even with the animals the nomads tended. Instead, their gods were of the sky above—the one thing that stayed with them wherever they wandered.

Nomads have been important throughout history. Nomads have often served as a link between distant areas of civilization. They have helped in the exchange of goods and ideas. For example, nomads guided merchants and their camels bringing silk from China, across central Asia, to the Middle East.

Many of the people you will later read about were once nomads. The history of the Middle East is especially the story of nomadic invasions. Nomads have also played important roles in the history of North Africa, India, China, central Asia, and eastern Europe.

The Sumerians thought of a temple as the home of a god. They may have tried to build their temples in the shape of mountains.

The Sumerians. At this time, a group of people living in the southern part of Mesopotamia grew in importance. They were known as the Sumerians. Their land was called Sumer. The Sumerians made many contributions to **civilization,** or the overall development of human thought and way of living. Throughout the river valley, people adopted the Sumerian way of life. They learned the Sumerian language and studied Sumerian ideas.

Many of the new developments, including writing, first began in Sumer. Sumerian writing is called cuneiform (kyōo·nē′ə·fôrm′), a word which means "wedge-shaped." The characters were pressed into soft clay tablets with a tool that left wedge-shaped marks. At first these marks were picture symbols. Over time they became symbols that stood for whole words or syllables.

The Sumerians built many of the world's first cities. Earlier agricultural villages sometimes grew into large towns. The city, however, was different in one way. It became the center of power. Cities were where the rulers lived. Kings controlled their territory from cities.

Sumerian cities also became important religious centers. The Sumerians built large temples called ziggurats (zig′ə·rats′). These temples were more than places of worship. The city's grain was often stored there. Written records of all sorts were also kept in the temple. Business records, records of court cases, and wills are among the records that have been found in Sumerian ziggurats. Much of what we have learned about the Sumerians comes from these clay tablets.

The city. As population increased, a number of cities grew up in Sumer. The largest may have had as many as 25,000

The works of Sumerian craftworkers tell us much about how the Sumerians lived, dressed, and enjoyed themselves.

people. In some places people built walls around the city to protect themselves from attacks by outsiders. Not all the people, however, lived within the walls of the city. Most farmers lived in small villages outside the walls.

In addition to the ziggurat and the king's palace, each city had a marketplace where farmers, merchants, and craft workers traded their goods. Most of the houses in the city were the same kind of dried-mud homes the farmers built. Some of the wealthier people, however, had larger stone or brick houses. These were usually two stories high, with many rooms built around a central courtyard.

The specialization that began with agriculture increased in the cities. Potters, weavers, metalworkers, and other craft workers had their homes and places of business there. The city dwellers depended on the outlying farms for their food. Both people in the **urban** areas, or cities, and people in the **rural** areas, or farms, were ruled by the same leaders.

At first the priests ruled the Sumerian cities. In time warfare among the cities

increased the power of army leaders. Some of these army leaders eventually became kings.

The armies of the cities often fought wars over boundaries and water rights.

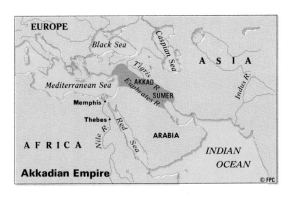

Akkadian Empire

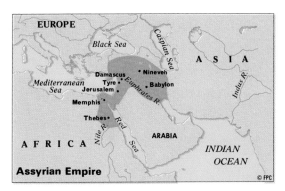

Assyrian Empire

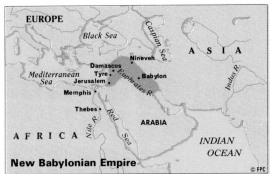

New Babylonian Empire

Ancient Mesopotamia was the center of many highly organized empires.

The armies also had to defend the cities and farms against raiding nomads. Nomads, or people who were always moving with their herds, often traded with the cities. They exchanged their milk, cheese, wool, or animal hides for farm products and things made in the city. Often, however, they attacked a city, taking what they wanted.

Kings and empires. Some kings were not content to rule a single city. Many kings had their armies attack other cities in order to extend their power. In time, the king of the Akkadians (ə·kād′ē·ənz), a neighboring people who lived farther north in the valley, overcame the Sumerians. Around 4,300 years ago the Akkadian king, Sargon, defeated each of the Sumerian cities. He extended his control over all Mesopotamia, and conquered the land northwest of the valley up to the Mediterranean. He became the ruler of an **empire**, an area of several cities and different groups of people, all under the control of a single power.

The Akkadian Empire lasted less than 200 years. Many other empires rose and fell in Mesopotamia. Yet the pattern of civilization that the Sumerians created—their religion, their system of writing, and their urban life—continued for 3,000 years.

Checking Up

1. How did agriculture spread into new areas?
2. What were five new inventions made between 5,000 and 5,500 years ago?
3. Why did kings take control of the Sumerian cities?
4. What answers would you give to the key questions at the beginning of this chapter?
5. *Why did religion change as farming became more important?*

The Hebrews and the Phoenicians

As You Read

1. Think about these words.
   monotheism   navigation
2. Look for answers to these key questions.
   a. What were the religious beliefs of the Hebrews?
   b. What is the significance of the Ten Commandments?
   c. Why were the Phoenicians important?

The Hebrews and the Phoenicians (fi·nish′ənz) were two groups of people who lived in the western part of the Fertile Crescent. Look at the map on page 79. Find Phoenicia. The Hebrews lived to the south. The Phoenicians and Hebrews borrowed many ideas from neighboring Mesopotamia and Egypt. Although they never built powerful empires, the Hebrews and the Phoenicians did make special contributions to civilization.

Hebrews

The first people to believe in the idea of one God were the Hebrews, or Jewish people. This belief, called **monotheism**, set them apart from all the other people in the ancient Middle East. All the other people believed in many gods who represented natural forces such as the earth or the sky. The Hebrews believed their God was the creator of everything. The Hebrews also believed their one God took a special interest in them as His people. God expected them to follow His rules of behavior. They believed this God sent them prophets, or messengers, to warn them to mend their ways and to lead them back to the correct path.

The Hebrews' special book, the Bible, tells how Abraham, the father of the Hebrews, originally lived in lower Mesopotamia. He and his family, however, left this area and traveled westward, where they lived as nomads. A shortage of food forced the Hebrews to move to Egypt. Having been made slaves by the Egyptian kings, they finally managed to escape from Egypt. Their leader, Moses, led the Hebrews out of Egypt. This event is known in the Bible as the Exodus, or "going out."

After leaving Egypt, the Hebrews passed through a wilderness. It was here that the Bible says Moses received the Ten Commandments, or rules of behavior, from God. Much of Hebrew law is based on the Ten Commandments. It became the most important duty of the Hebrews to follow this sacred law.

The Hebrew kingdom reached its peak during the reigns of King David and his son, Solomon. David made Jerusalem the capital city, and there Solomon built a magnificent temple. Find Jerusalem on the second map on page 75.

After Solomon's death the Hebrew kingdom declined. Over the following centuries, or hundreds of years, the Hebrews fell to conquerors from Mesopotamia and were carried off as captives. Later they were allowed to return to their land. A new Hebrew state again arose. It too was soon conquered.

The history of the Hebrews became one of repeated revolts against foreign rulers. After an unsuccessful uprising against the Romans, the last of these conquerors, the Jewish population was scattered throughout the Mediterranean world. In this later period of Jewish defeat and foreign rule, many Jews began to look to God for a Messiah, or Savior. They believed the Messiah would save them and reestablish the Jewish state.

The Hebrews' monotheism has become part of the religious beliefs of many of the world's people. The idea that a just and merciful God judges our deeds is important not only to Jews but also to Christians and Muslims.

Phoenicians

In the ancient Mediterranean world, the Phoenicians were especially important to trade and **navigation**, or the art of guiding ships at sea. In the course of their voyages, the Phoenicians came into contact with the Egyptian and Mesopotamian systems of writing. From these various systems of writing, they devel-

Jerusalem, located in the modern nation of Israel, is a sacred city for Jews, Christians, and Muslims.

oped a phonetic alphabet. A phonetic alphabet is one in which the symbols or letters stand for individual sounds, rather than for words or syllables. Our own phonetic alphabet is based on the alphabets of other Mediterranean people who got the idea from the Phoenicians.

The Ten Commandments explain how people should worship God and live properly.

It may have been the lack of good farming land that caused the Phoenicians to turn to the sea. The mountains behind the coastal plain were covered with cedar, cypress, and oak trees. The Phoenicians used the wood of these trees to build their ships.

The Phoenicians also developed the art of navigation. On their first voyages, they carefully followed the Mediterranean coastline. In time, however, they learned to tell direction by using the stars and began to sail the open sea.

Their ships reached the western Mediterranean, and they established colonies in many places. Look at the map on page 79 to find the areas they colonized. On one three-year voyage, their sailors rounded the entire coast of Africa. This accomplishment was not repeated for 2,000 years.

Phoenicia grew wealthy from the trade that was carried on between the cities and colonies. Craft workers in the Phoenician cities skillfully produced glassware, pottery, and jewelry. These wares were traded for agricultural goods and metal ores from the lands of the Phoenician colonies.

The Phoenicians, like the Hebrews, were conquered again and again by more

The Phoenicians used oars and sails, but the compass was unknown to them.

powerful neighbors. Phoenician ships were used by many of these conquerors in their own navies. Although Phoenicia never became an important Mediterranean power, one of its colonies did.

Carthage, on the coast of North Africa, was for several centuries the main rival of another Mediterranean power—the city of Rome. Their rivalry, however, is a story for a later unit.

Checking Up
1. What is the Bible? Who were Abraham, Moses, and David?
2. What happened to the Hebrews after the decline of their kingdom?

Phoenician alphabet	𐤀	𐤁	𐤂	𐤃	𐤄	𐤅	𐤆	𐤇	𐤈	𐤉	𐤊	𐤋	𐤌	𐤍	𐤎	𐤏	𐤐	𐤑	𐤒	𐤓	𐤔	𐤕
Greek alphabet	A	B	Γ	Δ	E	Y	I	B	⊗	५	K	L	M	N	Ξ	O	Γ	M	Q	P	Σ	T
Roman alphabet	A	B	C,G	D	E	F,V		H		I		L	M	N	X	O	P		Q	R	S	T

The Phoenicians had twenty-two letters that stood for consonants. The Greeks invented letters for the five vowel sounds. Try to follow how the Romans took their letters from the other two alphabets.

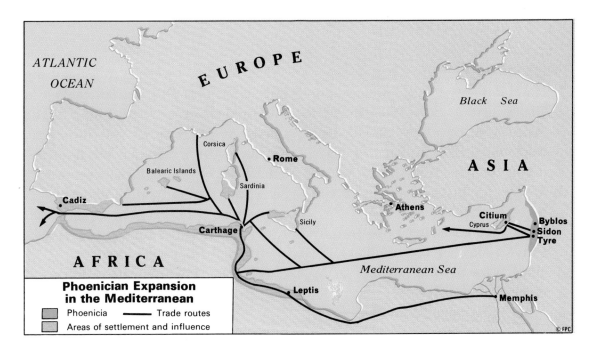

Phoenician Expansion
in the Mediterranean

◻ Phoenicia ——— Trade routes
◻ Areas of settlement and influence

3. What is a phonetic alphabet? How did we get our phonetic alphabet?
4. What answers would you give to the key questions at the beginning of this chapter?
5. *How was the monotheism of the Hebrews different from the religious beliefs of their neighbors?*

Unit 2 Summary

- At the end of the Ice Age, people began to turn from food gathering and hunting to food producing.
- People learned to domesticate plants and animals and began to settle in permanent villages. Specialization increased after the discovery of new ways of making things.
- Food producers could feed an increasing population.
- Farming began in the highlands of the Middle East and then spread to the fertile valley of the Tigris and Euphrates rivers, where farmers learned to use irrigation.
- The production of a surplus led to more trade and an idea of property.
- The Sumerians developed the earliest civilization. Among their contributions are a calendar, a system of writing, and the world's first cities.
- Priests ruled the Mesopotamian cities, but in time powerful kings took control of the cities. Some kings established great empires.
- Nomads had a way of life quite different from that of settled farmers.
- The Hebrews were the first to believe in one God.
- The Phoenicians developed the phonetic alphabet and were important to trade.

Unit 2 Review Workshop

What Have You Learned?

1. How did plant and animal life change at the end of the Ice Age?
2. When was the New Stone Age? Name three changes that took place during the New Stone Age.
3. Where did the agricultural revolution probably begin?
4. What were the main crops grown by early farmers in the Middle East? What were the first animals to be domesticated there?
5. What is a surplus? Why was a surplus important?
6. Why was irrigation needed in the Tigris and Euphrates valley?
7. Who were the Sumerians?
8. How did cities differ from villages?
9. How did the nomads contribute to civilization?
10. Why were the Hebrews and Phoenicians important?

Use Your Reading Skills

Match the words with the correct definitions.

1. environment	a. something left over
2. surplus	b. everything around us
3. property	c. the art of guiding ships
4. levee	d. the things a person owns
5. navigation	e. an earthen floodwall

The weather turned warmer and the glaciers melted. This is an example of a cause-and-effect relationship. The change in the weather was the cause. The melting of the glaciers was its effect.

Each set of two statements below contains both a cause and an effect. Label each either C for cause or E for effect.

1. a. Domesticated animals became different from wild ones.
   b. People bred animals to bring out certain qualities.
2. a. Farmers began to trade.
   b. Farmers had a surplus.
3. a. Trade and business increased.
   b. A way of recording accounts was developed.
4. a. Priests studied astronomy.
   b. Priests made calendars.
5. a. cities fought wars.
   b. army leaders took power.
6. a. The Phoenicians came into contact with different writing systems.
   b. The Phoenicians developed the phonetic alphabet.

Use Your Thinking Skills

Write three paragraphs comparing the different ways of life of rural people, urban people, and nomadic people in the ancient Middle East. Use one of the following questions as the main topic for each paragraph. What type of work would each group have done? Where would they have lived? How could they depend on one another?

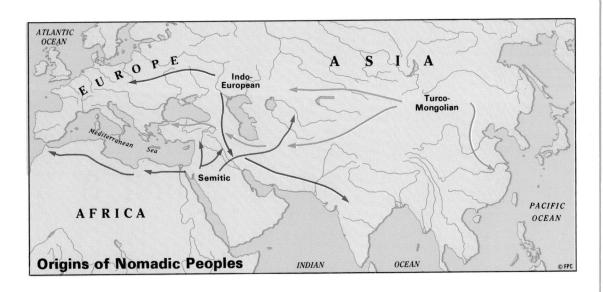

Origins of Nomadic Peoples

Use Your Map Skills

On the basis of language, historians have been able to group many of the nomadic peoples. The three most important language families that can be traced back to nomadic origins are the Semitic (sə·mit′ik), the Indo-European, and the Turco-Mongolian. Find the original areas of these three language groups on the map above.

Over the course of history, these three groups have spread to many regions of the Old World. Name three areas to which each of these groups spread. Choose from the regions below.

Europe   Middle East   North Africa
India   Central Asia   China

Use Your Time Skills

Look at the time line at the beginning of Part I. List the six human achievements below in the order they occurred.

writing
pottery and weaving
domestication of horses
invention of the wheel
village life
domestication of sheep and goats.

Learn by Doing

Prepare a report for the class on one of the special topics listed below.

Sumerian writing
Mesopotamian number system
The kingdom of Ebla
Assyrian methods of conquest
Babylon under Nebuchadnezzar
Phoenician trade
Cedars of Lebanon

Read to Learn More

Find the topics listed below in the card catalog of your library. Read all or part of a book listed under one of the topics. Share what you learn with your classmates.

IRRIGATION   CALENDAR
SUMERIANS   ALPHABET

Unit 3

Early Civilization in Egypt, India, and Crete

This gold mask covered the face of the mummy of the boy king Tutankhamen.

Maps and Graphs Tell a Story of Egypt

As you read, think about these words.

delta   source   cataract

Across North Africa stretch thousands of miles of deserts. In the northeastern corner of these lands lies Egypt. Egypt of today probably looks very much like Egypt of ancient history. Even then, the only break in the barren deserts was the green valley of the Nile River.

The Land and the River

Find Egypt on the map below. What seas border Egypt on the north and on the east? Although these seas provided ancient Egypt with trade routes with other civilizations, the most important waterway was the Nile River.

The Nile. The Nile is the longest river in the world. It flows north through Egypt to the Mediterranean. Just before it reaches the sea, it branches into many smaller rivers. These rivers flow through the land and empty into the Mediterranean. This triangular area of land is called a **delta** because it is shaped like the Greek letter called *delta* △. Find the Nile and its delta.

Two smaller rivers in the highlands of central Africa are the **source**, or beginning, of the Nile. Find these rivers on the map. What are their names? Trace them to their sources. Where do the rivers meet to form the Nile? From Khartoum the Nile flows to Aswan.

Now look at the map on the next page. Along this section of the river are sev-

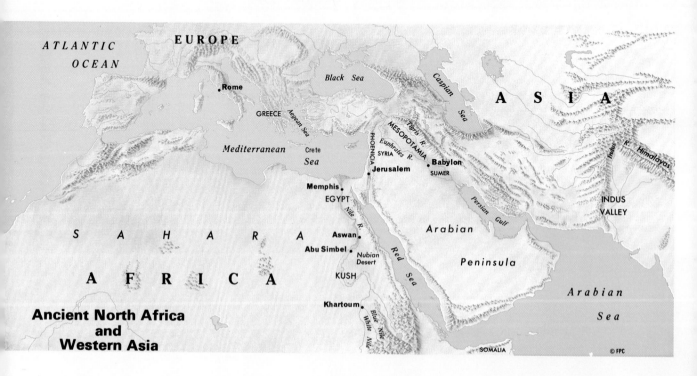

Ancient North Africa
and
Western Asia

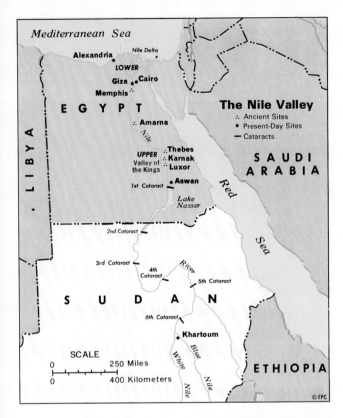

Mediterranean Sea

The Nile Valley
- ∴ Ancient Sites
- • Present-Day Sites
- — Cataracts

rainfall. The red wavy line at the top shows average monthly temperature, which is measured in degrees Fahrenheit and Celsius along the left side of the graph. The blue bars show average monthly rainfall, measured in inches and centimeters along the right side. The letters across the bottom stand for the months of the year.

These climatographs show information for which two cities? Locate them on the map. Which city is closer to the equator? Which city has warmer temperatures? About how many degrees does the temperature in each city vary from the warmest to the coolest months? Which city has the least rainfall? The precipitation map on the next page also shows the pattern of rainfall in this area.

eral **cataracts**, or high waterfalls. Locate these cataracts on the map. From Aswan the Nile flows through a valley surrounded by limestone cliffs. In ancient times this area was known as Upper Egypt. The Nile continues 600 miles (960 km) from Aswan to the ancient city of Memphis, near present-day Cairo. Here the Nile branches and flows through the marshy delta. The Nile Delta was known as Lower Egypt.

The Climate

Look at the climate map in the Atlas on pages 16–17. What kind of climate does Egypt have? The two climatographs will help you understand what a desert climate is like. Each graph shows two kinds of information: temperature and

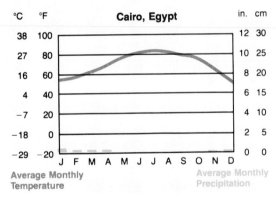

Cairo, Egypt

Average Monthly Temperature

Average Monthly Precipitation

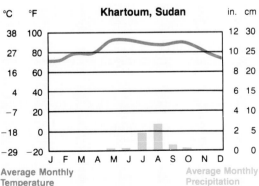

Khartoum, Sudan

Average Monthly Temperature

Average Monthly Precipitation

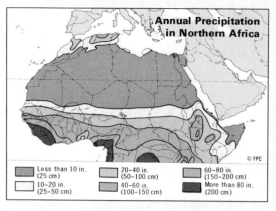

Annual Precipitation in Northern Africa

Less than 10 in. (25 cm)
10–20 in. (25–50 cm)
20–40 in. (50–100 cm)
40–60 in. (100–150 cm)
60–80 in. (150–200 cm)
More than 80 in. (200 cm)

© FPC

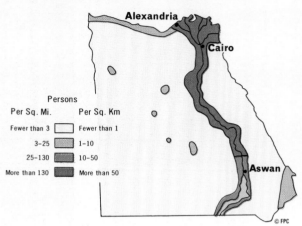

Population Density of Egypt

Alexandria
Cairo
Aswan

Persons	
Per Sq. Mi.	Per Sq. Km
Fewer than 3	Fewer than 1
3–25	1–10
25–130	10–50
More than 130	More than 50

© FPC

In some desert areas, absolutely nothing grows. In others, some plants and shrubs can survive. Look at the land use map on pages 20–21 of the Atlas. Away from the Nile what is the main activity? Now look along the Nile. How is the land used there?

Farming and Irrigation

In ancient times, as today, life along the Nile was possible because of the annual flooding of the river. Rainfall and melting snow in the highlands at the sources of the Nile caused the river to swell and overflow its banks. The floodwaters spread across the lowlands of the narrow valley. From earliest times farmers counted on the flood for water. They learned to irrigate their land and so were able to lengthen the growing season.

The Aswan High Dam. As time passed, people wanted to control the floodwaters even more. They began building dams across the river. The greatest of these is the Aswan High Dam, which was completed in 1971. The water held behind the dam flooded the valley of Abu Simbel and created an enormous new lake, Lake Nasser.

The dam releases water from Lake Nasser for use over the whole year. Farmers can irrigate more land than ever before. They can also grow crops all year round. Egypt's agricultural production has greatly increased.

The People

Look at the population map above. Where do the people of Egypt live? Why? Where do you think they lived in ancient times? Why? As you can see from looking at information about climate and land use, Egypt and its people still depend on the Nile. It was, and still is, the lifeline of that country.

Checking Up

1. In which direction does the Nile River flow?
2. What makes farming possible in this desert area?
3. From what you have learned, how would you describe this desert region?

86

Egypt, Gift of the Nile

As You Read

1. Think about these words.
   floodplain   pharaoh   dynasty
2. Look for answers to these key questions.
   a. What was agriculture like in the Nile Valley?
   b. How was Egypt protected from invaders?
   c. How is the history of Egypt divided?
3. Use this reading skill.
   Every paragraph you read has a main idea. This idea may be stated directly in one of the sentences in the paragraph. Sometimes, however, it is not. You should attempt to find the main idea in every paragraph of the lesson. Practice finding the main idea in the first three paragraphs of this chapter.

About the time civilization was developing in Mesopotamia, other civilizations were developing in other river valleys. One of these civilizations was in Egypt. The story of Egypt is one of pyramids and temples, of farmers and pharaohs. Most of all, though, the story of Egypt is the story of the Nile.

The River and the Land

Between 5,000 and 7,000 years ago, nomads from western Asia and other parts of northern Africa settled in the Nile Valley. They began farming along the **floodplain**, the level land beside the river. These early farmers lived in farm villages scattered along the Nile.

The early farmers prospered. As time went on, more and more farms and villages lined the length of the Nile. Some people specialized in such things as trade or craftwork. Powerful rulers and armies arose. Builders constructed large temples, palaces, and fine homes for the wealthy. A number of cities grew up beyond the farms and villages.

The Nile, however, never lost its importance throughout the entire history of Egyptian civilization. In Egypt the Nile was more than just a river. It was the source of life.

The yearly flood. The priests at the temple near the city of Memphis studied the eastern sky in the hours before dawn. They looked for Sirius, the Dog Star. They knew that when Sirius reappeared the Nile would soon flood the valley. With the flood would come new soil.

The Egyptian farmers prepared for the rising of the river. Eagerly they prayed for the return of the flood. Then it came. The reddish-brown water spilled over the riverbanks and covered the land. Priests and farmers rejoiced. They made sacrifices to the god of the river. The yearly flood had come again, as it had for thousands of years.

Farming. Most farmers planted their first seed in October when the floodwaters were gone. The land was still wet and muddy. Some farmers used wooden plows hitched to oxen or other farm animals to turn the soil. Others used only a stick to make small holes for their seeds. Then they led a herd of sheep, goats, or cattle across the field. The animals trampled the mud and covered the seeds.

The farmers knew the only source of water for their crops was the yearly flood. They learned to collect some of the floodwater so they could irrigate their land. By carefully using their water, farmers were able to harvest three crops a year.

Usually the harvests were good. The Egyptians grew many of the same crops that the Mesopotamians did. There were wheat for bread, barley for a kind of beer they drank, and flax, a plant from which linen is made, for the clothes they wore. Grapes, dates, and other foods were part of the harvest. The farmers also raised cattle and caught fish and water birds in the Nile.

Sometimes the harvests were not good. The Egyptians planned for these times. They stored grain from good harvests for food in those years when there was little water.

An Isolated Land

Without the Nile, farming in Egypt would not have been possible. Without farming, it is doubtful that the great Egyptian civilization would have developed. However, it was not farming alone that helped Egyptian civilization flourish. Egypt's location helped, too.

These farmers are cutting wheat with sickles, stacking it with long forks, and threshing it with bent sticks.

Look again at the map on page 84. The Nile cataracts protected Egypt from invasion from the south. The rocky deserts east and west of the Nile also were protection. Only along the Mediterranean Sea was Egypt open to invaders. In 2,000 years, Egypt was invaded only three times! The Egyptians did not have to prepare for war all the time. They had time to develop their civilization.

Then and Now

Irrigation Along the Nile

Ancient Egyptian farmers invented the shadoof (shə·dōof′) to help them lift floodwaters to irrigate their land. Look at this picture of the shadoof. Notice the bucket on one end of the beam and the weight, usually a rock or clump of dried mud, on the other. The weight helped farmers raise and lower the bucket.

Egyptian farmers today still use the shadoof. They must still irrigate their land. They need not wait, however, for the yearly floods to bring their water supply. The system of modern dams along the Nile provides a steady source of water the year around. Agricultural production has doubled. Since the floodwaters are now controlled, however, they do not renew the soil along the floodplain. Now the farmers must provide fertilizer to enrich the soil.

This Egyptian painting shows a gardener using a shadoof to draw water.

Crown of Upper Egypt

Crown of Lower Egypt

Pharaoh's Double Crown

The cobra and the vulture were the symbols on the pharaoh's crown.

The Pharaohs

The strong government of Egypt also helped civilization develop. Early Egypt was made up of Lower Egypt, or the delta of the Nile, and Upper Egypt, the area to the south. Find these places on the map on page 85.

The first pharaoh. About 5,100 years ago Menes (mē′nēz), a king of Upper Egypt, conquered Lower Egypt. With this conquest Upper and Lower Egypt were united into one kingdom. Many of the fine achievements that came with Egyptian civilization took place after Menes united the country. Menes was the first Egyptian **pharaoh**, or king. He started the first **dynasty**, a line of kings belonging to the same family. Menes made Memphis his capital city. Find Memphis on the map on page 85. Now find the same location on the Atlas map on pages 10–11. What modern city was built near Memphis?

After Menes there were hundreds of other pharaohs. Some are remembered, but most are not. Yet their power is not forgotten. They ruled over a rich land. They led strong armies and protected the people from nomad warriors. They conquered other lands. They led Egypt for almost 3,000 years of civilization.

The Three Kingdoms

Historians divide the long history of ancient Egypt into three periods. They are the Old Kingdom, the Middle Kingdom, and the New Kingdom. Although they are called kingdoms, it is best to think of them as periods of time.

The Old Kingdom. During the Old Kingdom, the Egyptians developed their art, writing, architecture, and burial practices. They learned to make tools out of copper. They developed a calendar. They began to irrigate.

Egypt could produce most of the goods it needed. There were, however, luxury goods that the Egyptians sought in nearby lands. During the Old Kingdom, the Egyptians traveled to Phoenicia to get fine wood, the cedars of Lebanon, for shipbuilding. They traveled up the Nile into the land of Kush to the south. There they got gold, ivory, and hardwood. From other places they got copper and spices.

The Middle Kingdom. Toward the end of the Old Kingdom, the pharaohs became weak. Officials began to increase their power. No strong ruler governed the entire country. The Old Kingdom period came to an end.

The Nile was a busy trade route. The Nile current carried boats down the river. Mediterranean winds powered sailboats up the river.

Finally, however, a powerful pharaoh again united Egypt. Thebes became the new capital city. Find Thebes on the map on page 85.

The Middle Kingdom ended when the Hyksos (hik′sos′), nomads from western Asia, invaded Egypt. The Hyksos used horses and chariots to conquer the Egyptians. Some historians believe that the Hebrews you read about in Unit 2 came to Egypt during the time of the rule of the Hyksos.

The New Kingdom. The Egyptians learned to fight with horses and chariots. A pharaoh led armies that drove the Hyksos from the country. During the New Kingdom period that followed, the pharaoh extended the boundaries of Egypt to the banks of the Euphrates River and up the Nile to the Fourth Cataract. Egypt became an empire.

The trade begun in the Old Kingdom continued throughout Egyptian history. One pharaoh, Queen Hatshepsut (hat′shep·sət), was especially eager to increase trade. She ruled early in the New Kingdom.

Queen Hatshepsut sent five cargo ships down the Red Sea to the land of Punt. Historians think Punt was along the present-day coast of Somalia. Find the Red Sea and Somalia on the Atlas map on pages 10–11. The cargo ships brought back myrrh trees to be planted in the queen's capital. The Egyptians used the resin of myrrh for incense and perfume.

Checking Up

1. How did the Egyptians prepare for years of poor harvests?
2. Why was Menes considered to be an important pharaoh?
3. What goods did the Egyptians get through trade? From what countries did they get them?
4. What answers would you give to the key questions at the beginning of this chapter?
5. *Why do you think a strong pharaoh was important to the development of Egyptian civilization?*

Pyramids and Pharaohs, Temples and Priests

As You Read

1. Think about these words.
   myth   mummy   sphinx
   pyramid   obelisk
2. Look for answers to these key questions.
   a. Why and how were the pyramids built?
   b. Why was the tomb of Tutankhamen important?
   c. What were the duties of Egyptian priests?
3. Use this reading skill.
   Taking notes means listing important ideas in your own words. As you read this chapter, practice taking notes on what you read under these headings: Religious Beliefs, Pyramids—The Tombs of the Pharaohs, The Valley of the Kings, Priests and Temples, and Obelisks and Sphinxes. Use short phrases rather than long sentences to list the important ideas. Taking notes will help you remember what is in the chapter and will make it easier for you to review its contents.

Religion was important to the ancient Egyptians. Like other early people, they believed in gods of nature. They worshiped gods of the sun, the plants, and the Nile. Their gods were often shown as animals, humans, or humans with animal heads or bodies.

Religious Beliefs

Before Egypt was united, each village had its own gods. After Menes united the country, the villages kept their own gods, but all worshiped the most important god, Ra (rä), the god of the sun. Everyone, even the pharaoh, believed the pharaoh to be the son of Ra. They also thought Ra was the father of Queen Hatshepsut, who was one of the few women pharaohs.

The Egyptians had many **myths**, or stories, about their gods. One myth told about the beginning of Egypt: In the beginning, there was only an ocean. The ocean waters dropped, and a mound of earth appeared. That mound was Egypt. A hawk landed on the mound. On his head the hawk, who was really Ra, wore a sun disk circled by a cobra. The cobra became the symbol for the pharaohs.

An important part of the religion of Egypt was the belief in life after death, the afterlife. People believed that they

From left to right stand Osiris, ruler of the land of the dead; Horus, god of plants; Isis, the moon goddess; and Ra, the sun god.

entered a new life after they died. The pharaoh would rule the land of the dead, just as he had ruled the land of the living.

People believed so strongly in the afterlife that they spent much time planning for it. They believed that the afterlife would be like life on earth. Maybe it would be even better.

We can tell from the paintings and writings left in the tombs of the Egyptians that they enjoyed life. They had games, dances, music, and festivals. Those who could afford them had beautiful furniture, fine clothing, and jewelry. They wanted all these things in the afterlife also.

Pyramids—The Tombs of the Pharaohs

Treasures for the afterlife were buried with the pharaohs. Because of these great riches, the pharaohs feared grave robbers. So they built great tombs called **pyramids.**

Building a pyramid. Twenty years before his death, King Khufu (kōō′fōō) of the Old Kingdom ordered his pyramid to be built. He wanted to be sure that his tomb would be ready when he died. He wanted a burial place safe from robbers.

A small group of workers charged with laying the ground plan for Khufu's pyramid gathered in the desert beyond the farms, villages, and cities. It was night. The master builder and his helpers sighted the North Star. Using the star as a direction finder, they staked out the square base of the pyramid. The sides were lined up with the directions north, south, east, and west.

In the weeks that followed, the work of building the base of the pyramid began. Most of the workers were farmers. When the Nile flooded, the fields were too wet for farming, so the farmers worked for the pharaoh. By serving the pharaoh, they thought they could join him in the afterlife. Only the pharaoh and those who served him could make the wonderful journey.

The workers quarried, or cut, rocks from the cliffs farther up the Nile. It was hard work. Their only tools were made of stone, bronze, or copper. However, the Egyptians learned to cut giant rocks.

Some weighed 2½ tons each! Day after day, year after year, the workers quarried rock for the tomb that would be Egypt's largest pyramid.

The workers floated the huge rocks on barges down the Nile to the building place in the desert. More workers pulled the rocks up ramps to the pyramid.

Khufu's pyramid, like others, was built in steps. There was an entrance on the north side. Deep inside were many rooms and passageways to confuse any grave robbers.

Finally, the workers placed the last rock on the pyramid. Then they covered the whole thing with shiny limestone. Now the pyramid was smooth from top to bottom. It was ready for the burial of Khufu.

The photograph on page 96 shows this Great Pyramid. When it was finished, it covered 13 acres (5.2 ha) and was 481 feet (116 m) high! That is about the height of a forty-story building. It took more than 100,000 workers twenty years to complete the tomb.

Other pharaohs built pyramids in the desert. All were robbed. Later pharaohs decided to build tombs in the stone cliffs in the river valley. These tombs would be safer. The valley had only one entrance. It was easy to guard. So many pharaohs were buried in the valley that it became known as the Valley of the Kings.

The Valley of the Kings

Tutankhamen (tōōt′änk·ä′mən), the boy king, was dead. In the valley the priests prepared his tomb, already carved from one of the cliffs.

The burial. Special workers prepared the king's body for burial. The workers embalmed the body to preserve it for the afterlife. First, workers removed all the organs except the heart. They placed the organs in a special jar. Then they washed the body with spices, rubbed it with oils, and coated it with resin. Finally, they wrapped the body in long strips of fine linen. The work took seventy days. Now the **mummy**, or the preserved body, was ready for burial.

Workers had to cut the huge stone blocks in quarries, and load them onto barges.

Priests treated a body with spices, oils, and resin, and then wrapped it in linen.

Priests and high-ranking citizens carried the body to the tomb. Everything needed for the afterlife was there. There were pieces of furniture, food, chariots, weapons, and statues of servants.

Priests said prayers to protect the young king from evil. Someone may have placed a small basket of fruit on the coffin. The priests and members of the family left. Seals were placed on the doors of the tomb. Workers shoveled rock and dirt to hide the entrance. The king's journey to the afterlife began.

The search. King Tutankhamen was buried over 3,000 years ago. During those thousands of years, the way of life of the ancient Egyptians was forgotten. Modern archaeologists thought we could learn much about ancient Egypt if they could find just one tomb that had not been robbed. One of these people was Howard Carter, a British archaeologist.

By the year 1924, Carter had done much searching for the tomb of Tutankhamen. So far, he had found nothing. His sponsor, the person who paid for the search, wanted him to stop. Carter asked for and got one last chance.

Carter's search continued. Finally, one morning in November, Carter's workers uncovered sixteen steps that led down into a cliff. Could these steps lead to the tomb? The workers continued to dig. At last they found a door with two seals. One was the pharaoh's seal. It was broken. Had grave robbers been there? Were the mummy and treasure gone?

They then transported the blocks down the Nile to where the pyramid was being built.

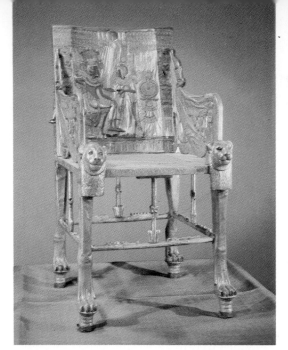

Treasures from Tutankhamen's tomb included the pharaoh's throne, and a statue of the jackal god guarding the tomb.

Carter noticed a small hole in the door. He enlarged it with a steel rod. Holding a candle to the opening, he squinted to see inside. He saw wonderful things. Gold was everywhere. There were gold couches, gold statues, a gold throne, and other objects fit for a king!

Tutankhamen was only eighteen when he died. He was not an important pharaoh. Yet his name lives on because of the treasures in his tomb. These have helped people today learn about life in ancient Egypt.

Priests and Temples

The early Egyptians were master builders. Not only did they build great pyramids, but they also built great temples. Their temples were not places for worship. They were private homes of the gods. The Egyptians made the temples beautiful places for the gods to live.

The temple at Karnak was the largest building the ancient Egyptians built. This great temple was built by one pharaoh and added to by many other pharaohs. The columns and walls of the temple had carvings and paintings that told of the greatness of the pharaoh and the gods.

The Great Sphinx has the face of the pharaoh Khafre and the body of a lion. It seems to be guarding Egypt's largest pyramids.

The priests of the temples had many duties. For a few, the special duty was caring for the god in the temple. Only priests could enter the place where the statue of the god was kept. On special festival days, however, they carried the statue out of the temple so the people could see it.

Some priests were astronomers, or people who study the stars. Others knew about medicine and helped cure sick people. Others were teachers who taught boys how to write. A few priests even became advisers to the pharaohs.

Obelisks and Sphinxes

The tombs and temples built by the ancient Egyptians have lasted thousands of years. Other structures stand beside them in the desert along the Nile.

Tall, tapering pillars called **obelisks** (äb′ə·lisks′) are beside the temples. The carvings on them tell stories about the pharaohs.

Leading to the entrance of the temple at Karnak is a double row of stone-carved **sphinxes** (sfink′səz). A sphinx was a creature in a number of ancient myths. A sphinx always had the body of a lion. The head of a sphinx might be that of a man, a ram, or a hawk. Ancient Egyptians made many statues of sphinxes.

The Great Sphinx, built for the pharaoh Khafre (käf′rə), stands beside his pyramid. The head of the Great Sphinx is an enormous portrait of Khafre. Standing 66 feet (20 m) high, the Great Sphinx seems to be guarding the pyramids of Egypt.

Egyptian temples have a sense of timelessness about them.

Checking Up
1. How did the Egyptians explain the beginning of their land?
2. How were the bodies of the pharaohs prepared for burial?
3. What were Egyptian temples?
4. Why did later pharaohs have tombs built in cliffs rather than pyramids?
5. What answers would you give to the key questions at the beginning of this chapter?
6. *Why do you think some pharaohs would have wanted priests as their advisers?*

97

Life Along the Nile

As You Read

1. Think about these words.
   scribe   hieroglyphics   papyrus
2. Look for answers to these key questions.
   a. What were the duties of the farmers, scribes, and nobles?
   b. How do ancient Egyptian artists help us understand Egyptian life?
   c. How did the Egyptians enjoy themselves?

The paintings in the tombs and temples and the writings left by the Egyptians tell us about ancient life along the Nile. They show us the way people dressed and what they did for entertainment. They also tell us about the kinds of work people did.

Workers in Ancient Egypt

Almost everyone in Egypt had a job to do. Most of the people were farmers. Some were artists and craftworkers. A few were government workers, scribes, or wealthy nobles. Slaves, captured during wars, also worked in Egypt.

Farmers. All Egyptians depended on the farmers. Rich harvests provided food for every Egyptian and for trade with other people. During the growing season, the men worked daily in the fields. Remember that they also worked on the pyramids and other buildings during the flood season. Sometimes they even served in the pharaoh's army. The women cooked, made the clothing, and cared for the children. Often children helped their parents working in the fields and at home.

Scribes. Very few people in ancient Egypt could read or write. They depended on **scribes** to write letters and to keep records. Sometimes scribes became important government workers and advisers to the pharaoh.

Scribes were usually from wealthy families, but sons of poor families might become scribes too. Boys attended school for as long as twelve years to learn to be scribes. It took this long to learn to make the hundreds of small pictures and signs that made up the **hieroglyphics** (hī′rə·glif′iks), the Egyptian system of writing. After they learned to write, they were allowed to write on **papyrus**, or paper made from reeds.

Craftworkers. Some craftworkers were carpenters, shipbuilders, or bricklayers. Others were bakers, butchers, brewers, or fishers. Still others made beautiful jewelry and clothing. The things they made were prized by people in Egypt and other countries.

Modern Readers of Egyptian Hieroglyphics

For hundreds of years after the decline of Egyptian civilization, no one knew how to read Egyptian hieroglyphics. People had forgotten what the symbols meant. People of modern times, therefore, knew little about life in ancient Egypt. In 1799 a French soldier stationed in Egypt made an important discovery, though at the time he probably did not know how important it was. The soldier found a black stone covered with three sets of writing. One set was written in ancient Greek, one was in picture hieroglyphics, and the third was written in a cursive form of hieroglyphics. Known as the Rosetta Stone because it was found near the Rosetta Branch of the Nile, the black stone held the key to hieroglyphics.

Many people who study languages wondered if each set of writing told the same story but in a different language. If so, they thought the Greek words, which scholars did understand, might unlock the mystery of hieroglyphics. Jean Francois Champollion (zhän fran·swä shän·pôl·yōn), another Frenchman, was one of these people.

Champollion noticed that the same hieroglyphics appeared five times inside certain oval forms. He also noticed that the Greek writing mentioned a certain king's name five times. Champollion

The hieroglyphics for the name of Tutankhamen appear above.

guessed that the ovals contained the king's name.

Champollion carefully began matching Greek letters with Egyptian hieroglyphics. He was right. The Greek writing was the key to the hieroglyphics on the Rosetta Stone.

After the hieroglyphics on the Rosetta Stone were understood, more scholars worked on other hieroglyphics. The work was hard and took many years. Although we still do not know exactly how the Egyptians pronounced their words, scholars can read the hieroglyphics and learn about Egyptian life.

Artists. Artists were important in Egypt. Their paintings and sculpture were a part of Egyptian religious life. The Egyptians believed that paintings and statues in the tombs came to life and cared for the dead in the afterlife. The tomb paintings have given us a clear idea of life in ancient Egypt. Art did not change much during Egypt's history. Statues almost always had the same pose. Look at the statue on page 101. The figure is shown staring ahead. There are few Egyptian statues showing figures looking sideways.

The homes of wealthy Egyptians had gardens and pools where the families could enjoy picnics.

The painting of the boy using a shadoof on page 89 shows the pose for most Egyptian paintings. Notice that the head is shown from the side but that there is a front view of the eye. There is a front view of the shoulders but a side view of the legs. Try this pose. You will find that it is impossible.

Nobles. The nobles were the wealthy people in Egypt. They owned much land. The nobles helped the pharaoh rule Egypt. They often looked after things in the different provinces Egypt was divided into. They kept up the irrigation systems and collected taxes from the farmers.

The nobles had servants and slaves to work for them. Their homes were filled with fine furniture and vases made by the craftworkers. They dressed in linen, just as the poorer people did, but their clothing was much finer. Both men and women used makeup and wore wigs and jewelry.

Daily Life

The homes of the ancient Egyptians were made of mud brick. The poorer people lived in small houses. The wealthier lived in larger and grander houses. The grandest home of all was the pharaoh's palace. Few houses stood on the floodplain of the Nile. This land was reserved for farming. Egyptians built their homes on the drier land beyond the fields of the floodplain.

Although the farmers worked hard, they enjoyed the days of festivals. Then they danced, played games, and listened to music. Sometimes there were even magicians. Wealthy people liked these things too. Wealthy people often invited their friends to great feasts. The guests enjoyed talking, eating many different foods, and watching dancers and acrobats perform. Egyptian children played many games. They had toy dolls, animals, and houses.

The Decline of Egypt

About 3,200 years ago, ancient Egyptian civilization began to decline. Some territories conquered in earlier wars broke away from Egyptian rule. After another 500 years, a series of invasions began. The first invaders to conquer Egypt came from Mesopotamia and Persia. Then came armies from Greece and Rome, two later civilizations that developed across the Mediterranean Sea. The once-great civilization built by the Egyptians gave way to its conquerors.

Did You Know?

- The early Egyptians had a fairly accurate calendar. Their year had 365 days divided into twelve months. Each month had 30 days. The 5 days that remained were used for festivals.
- Egyptian doctors were skilled surgeons and healers. They could set bones and perform brain operations. They probably learned about the human body from the preparation of mummies.
- The Egyptians were the first people to survey, or measure, land. They learned to survey land because the flooding of the Nile often removed landmarks.
- The Egyptians had drinking straws made from reeds along the Nile River.
- The Egyptians were the first people to make glass.
- The Egyptians drew maps on papyrus. Their maps showed the way to the tombs, temples, and cities in Egypt.

Imhotep was the earliest known physician in Egypt.

This statue is of Tutankhamen hunting on the Nile for sport.

Checking Up

1. Why did the wealth of Egypt depend on farming?
2. What were hieroglyphics? Why are modern scholars interested in them?
3. Why were paintings and statues placed in the tombs of pharaohs?
4. What answers would you give to the key questions at the beginning of this chapter?
5. *What job would have most interested you if you had been an ancient Egyptian? Give reasons for your answer.*

101

The Indus Valley and Crete

As You Read

1. Think about these words.
   granary   caste   outcaste
2. Look for answers to these key questions.
   a. How do we know about the people in the Indus Valley and on Crete?
   b. What two major religions developed in India?

The first civilization in India also began in a river valley. Find India on the Atlas map on pages 10–11. Notice that India juts out into the Indian Ocean. In the northern part are the Himalayas, the highest mountains in the world. Two rivers flow from these mountains, the Ganges (gan′jēz) and the Indus. Find these rivers on the map on pages 12–13.

The Indus Civilization

Mystery surrounds the rise of the Indus Valley civilization. No one knows for sure where the people came from. The people had a system of writing, but no one knows yet how to read it. All that we know has come from their cities' ruins.

The Indus Valley people made seals showing pictures of animals and writing samples.

Planned cities. Archaeologists first found the ruins of one city. Then they found the ruins of another. They were surprised to discover that the two cities were built in the same way. Both cities were planned cities.

Each city had a large section that was surrounded by a strong brick wall. This

This photograph of one of the Indus Valley cities was taken from the air.

102

section of the city was a fort. People probably went there for safety when enemies attacked their city. In the fort section were a temple, a **granary**, or a place to store grain, and other buildings. There was also a heated pool. It is possible that the pool was used for bathing, a part of the religion of the people.

Living in the Indus Valley. As in Egypt, farming was very important in the Indus Valley. The crops grown included wheat and barley. There were goats, sheep, and a special kind of humped cattle. The people in this valley were probably the first to raise chickens and to grow cotton.

The Indus people also traded with other countries. Using horses, camels, and elephants, they took trade goods overland. They traveled by sea to Mesopotamia. Mesopotamian clay tablets record the rare woods, copper, and ivory sold by traders from the Indus Valley.

The decline of the Indus Valley civilization. No one is really sure just what happened to the ancient civilization in the Indus Valley. It is likely that the end came when Aryans (ãr′ē·ənz), nomads from the northwest, invaded. They came through mountain passes in the Hindu Kush and used chariots and axes to conquer the people.

The Aryans

After the conquest of the early people in the Indus Valley, the Aryans settled down in villages in the Indus and Ganges valleys. They learned to farm. Some became traders and craftworkers.

Language. The Aryans brought their language and religion with them. They spoke an Indo-European language. The present-day languages of northern India all come from this parent language.

Hinduism. The religion of Hinduism developed out of the beliefs of the Aryans and the local people they had conquered. Hinduism became the main religion in India.

An important part of the Hindu religion was the **caste** (kast) system. The Aryans divided people into four castes, or groups, according to the kind of work they did. The people in the highest caste were priests and teachers called Brahmans. Next were the warriors. The third caste included the craftworkers, traders, and farmers. Landless workers made up the fourth and lowest cast. Each caste had strict rules of conduct. People who did not obey these rules became **outcastes**. They were no longer members of any caste.

Hindus believed that if a person led a good life, the soul of that person would return in a higher being. For this reason, Hindus accepted the duties of their caste.

Buddhism. People in the lower castes were poorer than those in the higher castes. Yet according to Hindu belief, they would have to wait until the next life for things to get better.

One Hindu, Gautama (gaut′ə·mə), wondered why this should be so. Although Gautama was a wealthy prince, he was unhappy because of the suffering and poverty he saw. He left his wife and

Young people on Crete may have been taught to jump over bulls. Bull leaping probably gave rise to the myth of the minotaur.

young son to find out how to end suffering for himself and for the other people of India.

Gautama searched far and wide for the answer to his question. He found it while he sat deep in thought under a fig tree. His answer was that to escape suffering, people had to give up all wants. People could help rid themselves of want through correct conduct.

Gautama preached his ideas to other people. Soon he had many followers. His followers called him Buddha, the Enlightened One. His teachings became the main part of the religion of Buddhism.

Buddha's followers traveled throughout India, China, Korea, Japan, and the countries of Southeast Asia. Many people in those places accepted Buddhism as their religion. In India, however, most people remained Hindus.

Ancient Crete

Look at the time line on pages 36–37. Notice that other civilizations were developing during the same time that the Egyptian and Indus Valley civilizations developed. One of these other civilizations was on the island of Crete. It is called the Minoan civilization. Find Crete on the Atlas map on pages 10–11.

Mountains and valleys cover the island. The rich soil and mild climate make it a good place to live.

Knossos. Early in this century, a British archaeologist became interested in Crete. He knew the ancient myths that said there was once a huge palace where a king named Minos lived. The myth also said that Minos kept a minotaur, a monster with the head of a bull and the body of a man.

The archaeologist knew that myths are sometimes based partly on fact. The archaeologist decided to explore Knossos, the location of King Minos's palace in the myth.

The Minoans. At Knossos the archaeologist found a huge palace with two hundred rooms. There were storerooms, workrooms, bedrooms, and bathrooms. The bathrooms even had drainage pipes. The whole palace covered six acres! The ruins and the civilization were named Minoan after the king in the myth.

Beautiful paintings decorated the walls of the palace. Many of them were of young people jumping over bulls. You can see an example in the photograph above. Statues of bulls and snakes were found in the palace. Perhaps the Minoans worshiped bulls and snakes.

Minoan writing. Also in the palace at Knossos were tablets filled with writing. No one has yet been able to read this writing. Perhaps someday someone will be able to do this, just as Champollion figured out the Egyptian hieroglyphics. Then we may know more about the early people on Crete.

Crete and the sea. Look again at the Atlas map on pages 10–11. What sea surrounds Crete? See how close Crete is to Egypt, Syria, and Greece. Crete had a good location for trading by sea. The Minoans traded food grown on the island, such as grapes, olives, wheat, and barley. They also traded objects made by their craftworkers. Beautiful pottery vases and jars were made by these Minoan workers.

The decline of the civilization. About 3,600 years ago, groups of nomads settled around the Aegean (i·jē′ən) Sea. Some of them conquered Crete and learned the Minoan way of living. Later, groups of these same nomads again invaded Crete. Either because of these conquests or because of volcanic eruptions that might have occurred, the civilization on Crete disappeared.

Checking Up
1. Why are the ancient cities in the Indus Valley called planned cities?
2. What did the Aryans contribute to Indian civilization?
3. How did a British archaeologist discover the Minoan civilization?
4. What answers would you give to the key questions at the beginning of this chapter?
5. *How were the civilizations in ancient Crete and the Indus Valley alike? How were they different?*

Unit 3 Summary
● Egypt was called the Gift of the Nile because the yearly flood brought new soil for the land. The Egyptians learned to collect the floodwater for irrigation. Today the Egyptians use dams to control the floodwaters.
● Pharaohs ruled Egypt for almost 3,000 years.
● Egyptian civilization developed during the Old Kingdom. Egypt became an empire during the New Kingdom.
● The Egyptians invented a calendar, used hieroglyphics, and knew about medicine.
● The Egyptians built pyramids and cliff tombs for the pharaohs' mummies and the things they would need in the afterlife.
● Many Egyptians were farmers. Some were craftworkers. Others, such as scribes, nobles, and priests, helped the pharaoh rule.
● Early civilizations also arose in the Indus Valley and on Crete.
● The religions of Hinduism and Buddhism developed in India. Hinduism has remained the religion of India. Buddhism has spread throughout much of Asia.

Unit 3 Review Workshop

What Have You Learned?

1. What contributions did the Egyptians make to civilization?
2. Why was the location of Egypt important for the development of Egyptian civilization?
3. Who was Menes? Hatshepsut?
4. What groups were the Egyptians divided into?
5. Who was Champollion?
6. What were the religious beliefs of the Egyptians?
7. What were the purposes of Egyptian pyramids, cliff tombs, and temples?
8. What were the achievements of the Indus Valley people?
9. What are the beliefs of Hinduism? of Buddhism?
10. Who was King Minos? Where was his palace?

Use Your Reading Skills

A. As you read, it is important for you to make connections. Some of the topics you read about in Unit 2 appeared again in this unit. Some of the ideas that were discussed in one chapter of this unit came up again in another. Choose the word in parentheses that correctly completes each of the statements that follow.

1. The Hyksos who conquered Egypt, the Aryans who invaded India, and the people who overran Crete were all (urban, nomadic) groups.

2. The ancient Egyptians, the Indus Valley people, and the Minoans all had writing systems. Only the writing of the (Egyptians, Indus Valley people) can be read.

3. All three ancient civilizations described in this unit built cities. The planning of the cities of the (Egyptians, Indus Valley people) was the most advanced.

4. The civilizations of the Indus Valley people and of the Minoans probably declined because of (disease, invasions).

5. Ancient people invented myths. The (Egyptians, Minoans) told of the beginning of their country as the appearance of a mound above the ocean waters.

B. Match each of these words with its correct definition.

1. pyramid	a. one of the four divisions of Hindus
2. hieroglyphics	b. a story about gods
3. dynasty	c. tomb for a pharaoh
4. myth	d. a line of kings from the same family
5. caste	e. Egyptian writing

C. The people of all three civilizations we have studied in this unit, thought of the bull as sacred. Which of the

bulls shown on this page is Egyptian? Which is Minoan? Which is from the Indus Valley people? Explain how you can identify each.

Use Your Math Skills

The ancient Egyptian pyramid builders knew they could always make a perfect square corner by using a knotted cord. You can do this too. Take a piece of string. Mark it off into twelve even parts. Knot it once after the first three parts and again after the next four parts. Now use the three sections to lay out a triangle. These lengths will always give you a triangle with one square corner.

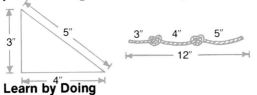

Learn by Doing

By now you have learned much about ancient Egypt. Egypt is still an important country. It has more people than any other Middle Eastern country. In a group of several of your classmates read about one of the topics below and list five facts you find on a sheet of paper.

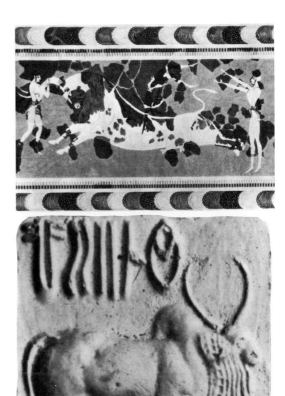

Yours and the other groups in the class can arrange these sheets on a bulletin-board display about present-day Egypt.

government   schools
agriculture   trade
population   religion

Read to Learn More

Find the topics listed below in the card catalog of your library. Read all or part of a book listed under one of the topics. Share what you learn with your classmates.

HIEROGLYPHICS   MYTHOLOGY
SPHINX   BRAHMA

Part Two
Early Civilizations Flourish

The oldest civilizations of the world developed in the river valleys of western Asia and northern Africa. About 2,500 years ago, however, the influence of these people was declining. Across the Mediterranean Sea the civilizations of Greece and Rome were rising.

Civilization did not continue to develop only around the Mediterranean. It also developed up the Nile from Egypt in the land of Kush, spreading to central Africa. The Chinese were also developing their own civilization. Only hundreds of years later did they discover there was civilization to the west. During this same time period, Mayan civilization was developing in Central America.

In Part Two we shall start to use a different system of dating. Until now dates in this book have been given in terms of how many years ago something happened. Historical events, however, are often dated according to the birth of Christ. Those happening before Christ are dated B.C. Those taking place since Christ are dated A.D. The time line below uses this system of dating.

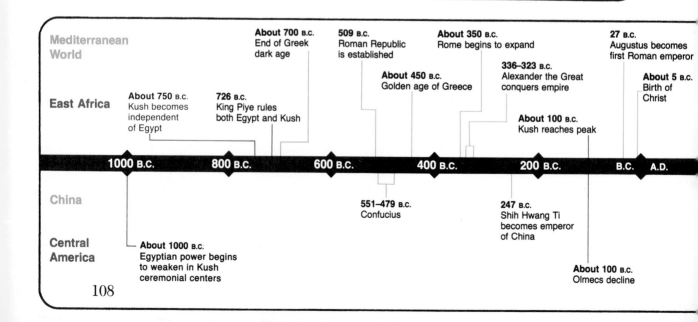

Mediterranean World

About 700 B.C.
End of Greek dark age

509 B.C.
Roman Republic is established

About 350 B.C.
Rome begins to expand

27 B.C.
Augustus becomes first Roman emperor

About 450 B.C.
Golden age of Greece

336–323 B.C.
Alexander the Great conquers empire

About 5 B.C.
Birth of Christ

East Africa

About 750 B.C.
Kush becomes independent of Egypt

726 B.C.
King Piye rules both Egypt and Kush

About 100 B.C.
Kush reaches peak

1000 B.C.   800 B.C.   600 B.C.   400 B.C.   200 B.C.   B.C.   A.D.

China

551–479 B.C.
Confucius

247 B.C.
Shih Hwang Ti becomes emperor of China

Central America

About 1000 B.C.
Egyptian power begins to weaken in Kush ceremonial centers

About 100 B.C.
Olmecs decline

108

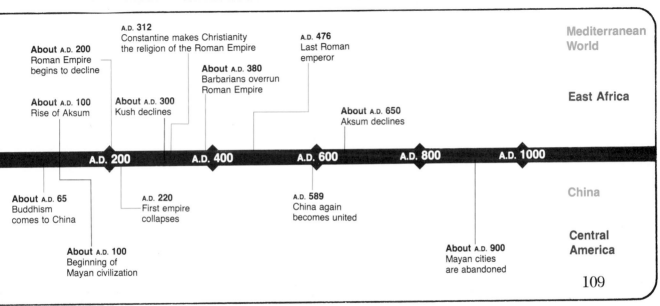

A.D. **312**
Constantine makes Christianity
the religion of the Roman Empire

A.D. **476**
Last Roman
emperor

Mediterranean World

About A.D. **200**
Roman Empire
begins to decline

About A.D. **380**
Barbarians overrun
Roman Empire

About A.D. **100**
Rise of Aksum

About A.D. **300**
Kush declines

About A.D. **650**
Aksum declines

East Africa

A.D. **200**   A.D. **400**   A.D. **600**   A.D. **800**   A.D. **1000**

About A.D. **65**
Buddhism
comes to China

A.D. **220**
First empire
collapses

A.D. **589**
China again
becomes united

China

About A.D. **100**
Beginning of
Mayan civilization

About A.D. **900**
Mayan cities
are abandoned

**Central
America**

109

Unit 4

The Ancient Greeks

The temple of Athena stood on a hill overlooking Athens. Athena was the goddess of the city.

Maps and Diagrams Tell a Story of Greece

As you read, think about these words.
physical map   elevation   erode

The country of Greece lies northwest of Egypt on the northern coast of the Mediterranean Sea. Find Greece on the Atlas map on pages 10–11. You can see that Greece is not far from Egypt. Both border the Mediterranean, but they have different climates and landscapes.

Climate

Egypt has a desert climate, but Greece and other areas along the Mediterranean share a very different climate. Look at the climate map on pages 16–17 in the Atlas. What is this climate region called? Only four other areas in the world have this same kind of climate. Where are they? At approximately what latitude is each area located? Which of all five areas is the largest? Which is the smallest?

Dry summers, wet winters. Most places on the earth either have precipitation all year round or, like Egypt, have almost none at all. The mediterranean climate has a different precipitation pattern. In areas with a mediterranean climate, the summers are dry and the winters are rainy. Look at the climatographs on this page. During which months does each place receive precipitation? These months are the winter season. Because Santiago is south of the equator, the seasons there are just the opposite of those north of the equator. About how much total precipitation does each place receive? Which place receives

the most? Although the annual amount of precipitation is much greater than in desert areas, the amount is not great compared with that of many other climate regions. Even though these are the rainy months, the weather is generally sunny.

Now look at the temperatures for each place. During which months is it the warmest? Compare these months with the climatographs for Cairo and Khartoum on page 85. How are they alike? The mediterranean climate during these summer months is very much like the climate of the Sahara. Look again at the

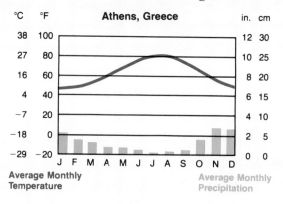

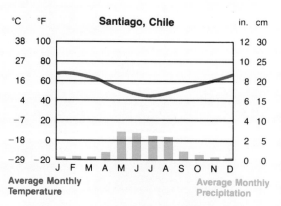

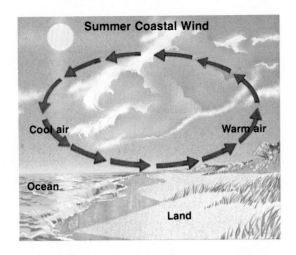

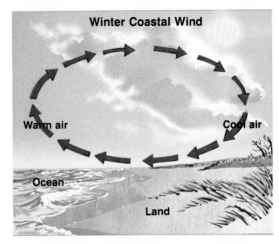

temperatures for the winter months. What is the coolest month in each place? What is the average temperature then? In the mediterranean regions all around the world, these mild, sunny winters make them popular resort areas.

The influence of large bodies of water. All mediterranean climate regions are located on large bodies of water. Look again at the climate map on pages 16–17. On which body of water is each of these regions? These nearby bodies of water help make the climate mild. Look at the diagrams above. Oceans and seas warm up slowly in the summer and cool off slowly in the winter. This gradual warming and cooling keeps mediterranean regions from having extremely warm or cool temperatures.

The Landscape

Not only are mediterranean regions located on large bodies of water, but they also have mountains. To locate the mountains in these areas, turn to the **physical map** on pages 12–13. This map uses shades of black and colors to tell you about the landscapes of the earth. Find the map key in the lower left corner. The diagrams on the next page show you how to read the map key for physical maps. Notice how the shading becomes darker as the land becomes more mountainous. Different colors show **elevation,** or height of the land above sea level. Sea level is the place where the ocean meets the land. Which color shows land near sea level? Which color shows the land with the greatest elevation?

Find Greece on the physical map on pages 12–13. Using the map key, how would you describe the landscape? Use the climate map on pages 16–17 to help you locate the other mediterranean climate regions around the Mediterranean Sea. How do the landscapes of these regions compare with the landscape of Greece? with the landscape of Egypt?

The mountains and the climate. Mountains help create mediterranean climate regions. The Alps in Europe and the Sierra Nevada in California help

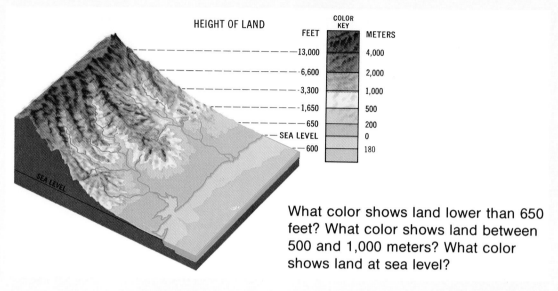

HEIGHT OF LAND

FEET	COLOR KEY	METERS
13,000		4,000
6,600		2,000
3,300		1,000
1,650		500
650		200
SEA LEVEL		0
600		180

What color shows land lower than 650 feet? What color shows land between 500 and 1,000 meters? What color shows land at sea level?

keep winters mild. They block cold bursts of polar air. Thus, frosts are quite rare in these mediterranean regions.

Mountains in some mediterranean regions also help make water available during the dry summers. Look again at the physical map on pages 12–13. Which mediterranean regions have mountains

over 13,000 feet (3,962 m)? These mountains have elevations high enough that snow builds up during the winter months. This snow is actually stored water. In the spring, as temperatures become warmer, the snow begins to melt. This water can then be used to irrigate the land. Look at the physical map of Greece on this page. The Pindus Mountains often have enough snow to provide the water needed for farming during the dry months.

People and the Land

The next two maps help tell the story of both ancient and present-day Greece. Compare the population map with the physical map of Greece. Today, as in ancient times, the people of Greece cluster along the low coastal areas and in the river valleys. Now look at the map showing land use. What is the main activity in the areas where the people live? How would you explain this pattern? The soil in these areas also makes them good

Adriatic Sea

Black Sea

Sea of Marmara

•Thessaloníki

+Mt. Olympus

Pindus Mts.

Aegean Sea

Ionian Sea

•Athens

Greece
Physical Map

SCALE
0   100   200 Miles
0   100   200 Kilometers

Crete

© FPC

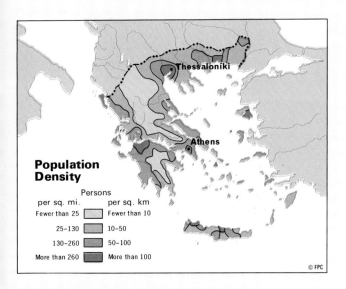

Population Density

Persons

per sq. mi.		per sq. km
Fewer than 25		Fewer than 10
25–130		10–50
130–260		50–100
More than 260		More than 100

Thessaloníki

Athens

© FPC

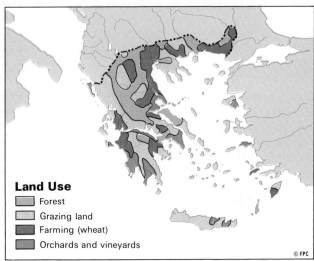

Land Use

- Forest
- Grazing land
- Farming (wheat)
- Orchards and vineyards

© FPC

farming locations. As in Egypt, this soil is highly productive when water is available. The crops grown today include grains, tobacco, olives, grapes, citrus fruits, and figs. Greece also produces enough olive oil for trade with other countries, just as it did in ancient times.

Look again at the land-use map. What is the main activity in the more rugged areas? In some of these places, olive trees and vineyards produce good crops, but in most places the soil is thin and the land is steep and rocky. The vegetation, typical of other mediterranean areas, is stunted in growth. The plants often have thick bark and waxy leaves, which help protect them during the dry summers. Across this landscape goats and sheep pick their way, grazing on the patches of vegetation.

Interestingly, the vegetation of ancient Greece may have been quite different. Like the mediterranean region of California today, the true natural vegetation of Greece was probably woodland—

open forests and grasslands. However, over the course of thousands of years, people cut enough trees to deforest the land. They used the wood for homes, for ships, and for fuel. Little did they know that as they cut more and more trees, the rains **eroded** more and more of the land. Much soil was washed away. Now much of this rich soil lies in the river valleys. It cannot be replaced, and new forests cannot be planted. The pattern of erosion continues. Sheep and goats graze today on the sparse vegetation as they have for hundreds and hundreds of years.

Checking Up

1. What are the two important characteristics of the mediterranean climate region?

2. What do the locations of these regions have in common?

3. Where do most of the people in Greece live? Why?

115

The Early Aegean World

As You Read

1. Think about these words.
   odyssey   legend   peninsula
2. Look for answers to these key questions.
   a. How did the Achaeans' way of life change after they entered Greece?
   b. What were the achievements of the Achaeans?
   c. How did the Mycenaeans remember their past?
3. Use this reading skill.
   When you finish a chapter, it is useful to draw a conclusion about what you have read. For example, this chapter will examine two groups of nomads who settled in ancient Greece. The level of civilization of the first group was much higher than that of the second group. What might you conclude about the effect the second group had on the development of Greek civilization?

About 1600 B.C. groups of nomads began to make their way southward into Greece. They had lived on the steppes of eastern Europe, north of the Black Sea. Look at the map of Greece on page 123. Find the Black Sea. Find the land north of this body of water. There the nomads had raised sheep, goats, and cattle and had learned to use the horse for riding and for pulling carts.

The Achaeans

For the next several hundred years, groups of nomads pressed farther and farther into Greece. They brought with them their herds of animals, their horses, their gods, and their customs. They also brought their Indo-European language that was an early form of Greek. They were the first Greeks, and were called the Achaeans (ə·kē′ənz).

We know very little about events that occurred during the hundreds of years when these invasions took place. Writing had not yet come to Greece, so there are no written records.

The land. Moving into Greece, the Achaeans found a land of tree-covered hills and snowcapped mountains. These highlands divided Greece into many small valleys, especially the eastern coast along the Aegean Sea. Look at the Dictionary of Geographical Terms on pages 26–27. Find some of the landforms you have just read about. How many landforms can you name?

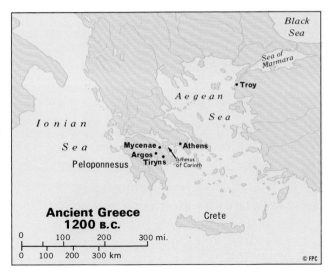

Ancient Greece
1200 B.C.

What advantages could the hills and the sea offer the Achaeans?

The sea itself was something new to the Achaeans, who were used to the endless grasslands of the northern steppes. Their language, in fact, did not have a word for *sea*. Eventually, however, the Achaeans became skilled sailors who used their ships to trade with other parts of the Aegean world.

The small valleys provided lowlands for farming, and nearby hills were good grazing land. The climate was warmer and less harsh than that of the northern steppes. The Achaeans found that they did not need to wander from place to place in search of good grazing land.

The settlements. As nomads the Achaeans had lived in small groups. Each group was ruled by a leader who was the group's mightiest warrior. As the groups moved into Greece, each leader seized a valley or a plain for himself and his people. In time, each of these areas became a small kingdom of its own.

In the centuries that followed their invasions, the Achaeans built and settled in cities. Each city had a great palace for its king at the center. The palaces were surrounded by thick walls. In times of trouble, the people gathered behind the palace walls to fight off attackers.

The cities were usually built on high ground some distance from the sea. The high ground provided a further advantage in case of attack by outsiders. Most cities were also close enough to the sea for the Achaeans to build ports and sailing ships. They fished, and they used their swift ships to trade with other parts of the Aegean world.

As trade grew, the Achaeans learned to use writing. Examples of this early Greek writing show that it was used mainly for record keeping by trading people.

The Mycenaeans. The civilization of the Achaeans lasted from 1600 to 1100 B.C. By 1450 B.C. the Achaeans controlled the Aegean islands and the surrounding land.

Among the greatest of Achaean cities of this time were Mycenae (mī·sē′nē), Tiryns (tir′ənz), Argos (är′gäs), and Athens. Mycenae may have been the strongest and most powerful of all. For this reason, the Achaean civilization is often referred to as Mycenaean (mī′sə·nē′ən). Find the cities of Mycenae and Athens on the map above.

Most of the Mycenaeans remained simple farmers, fishers, and craftworkers. The ruling group controlled trade and continued the warrior way of life.

117

The Lion Gate was the entrance to Mycenae. Why were walls necessary?

They had weapons and shields made of bronze, and their palaces were filled with wall paintings, beautiful pottery, and objects made of gold and precious stones. The Mycenaeans are probably best known for their part in a war that would be remembered for thousands of years to come.

The Trojan War

About 1200 B.C. a war broke out between the Trojans, the people in Troy, and the Mycenaeans. Troy was destroyed during this war. Find Troy on the map of ancient Greece. The Trojan War has been remembered because it was described in a long poem written hundreds of years later.

Homer. Homer is remembered as the first and greatest poet of ancient Greece. No one is certain just where and when he lived. According to tradition he was blind, but we do not have proof. About all we know is that he was the author of two great poems. The *Iliad* tells about the Trojan War. The *Odyssey* concerns the adventures of Odysseus (ō·di′sē·əs),

a Greek warrior on his way home from the war. Today we use the word **odyssey** to describe any long, wandering trip.

Writing was not used to tell stories during the time of the Mycenaeans, nor for hundreds of years to come. Stories were memorized and passed on from person to person over the years. These stories were told in verse, and they were the chief form of entertainment among the ancient Greeks. They were also a way of keeping alive the events and the traditions of the past.

As the story of the Trojan War was passed down by word of mouth, it probably grew and changed as each storyteller added something to it. According to tradition the Trojan War took place around 1200 B.C. It was probably not until 800 B.C. that Homer put together the story as we know it today in the *Iliad*, a poem of over 15,000 lines.

The Greeks remembered the Trojan War through **legends**, stories that may or may not be true. One of the legends

Homer told of Odysseus's long journey home from the Trojan War.

According to legend, how did the Mycenaeans surprise the Trojans?

explains how the Trojan War was won. According to this legend, the Mycenaeans built a giant wooden horse. Some of their soldiers hid inside the horse, which was hollow. The Trojans brought the horse into their city. At night the Mycenaean soldiers came out of the horse. They helped defeat the Trojans.

Homer's account of the war presents other legends too. We are, however, fairly certain that the Trojan War did take place. If it took place in 1200 B.C., it was probably one of the last great victories of the Mycenaeans.

The Dorian Invasions

About 1100 B.C. Greece was once again invaded by nomads from the north. The new invaders, called Dorians, quickly conquered most of Greece. They destroyed the Mycenaean cities, killed the rulers, and took over the farmlands. Athens was the only major city to escape capture.

The Dorians were interested mainly in taking over useful farmland. They swept southward into a land called the Peloponnesus (pel′ə·pə·nē′səs), a **peninsula** between the Aegean and Ionian seas. A peninsula is a body of land almost surrounded by water. Look at the map on page 117. Find the Peloponnesus and the seas around it. The Dorians settled here in the inland valleys and plains.

The Dorians destroyed much of Mycenaean culture. Writing was lost. Dorian buildings and art were simple compared to the fine palaces and art of the Mycenaeans. For hundreds of years—between 1100 and 700 B.C.—life in Greece centered around small, simple farming villages. This period is often called the "Greek dark age."

Because writing had vanished, we know very little about events during the Greek dark age. Changes were occurring, however, during this time that led to the achievements of the Golden Age of Greece.

Checking Up
1. How did the climate in Greece influence agriculture?
2. Who was Homer?
3. What was the Greek dark age?
4. What answers would you give to the key questions at the beginning of this chapter?
5. *What was the main difference between the Achaean and the Dorian invasions?*

The Development of Democracy

As You Read

1. Think about these words.
   city-state   aristocracy   democracy   tyrant
2. Look for answers to these key questions.
   a. Why did the kings in Greece gradually lose their power?
   b. What was democracy like in Athens?
   c. Why did the Greeks set up colonies?
3. Use this reading skill.
   As you read this chapter, you will learn that not all Greek city-states were alike. To understand how they were different, read for details about the two city-states mentioned in the chapter. Ask yourself what made Athens and Sparta different. What form of government did Athens develop? What form did Sparta develop? What else was very different about the two city-states?

After the Dorian invasion, Greece remained divided into many small kingdoms. By the end of the dark age, the kings had lost their power in much of Greece. Changes were taking place. The city-state was becoming important.

The City-State

A **city-state** was a self-governing unit, like a country in the world today. It included a city and the villages and farmlands surrounding it. At the heart of the city-state was a single city.

From kings to aristocrats. During the Dorian period, each farming village was ruled by a king. The power of the kings was not great enough, however, to allow them to remain as rulers for long. If fighting had to be done, it was done by the king and his family. As the unrest continued, more soldiers were needed.

Those who could afford to buy weapons and armor could fight. Only the wealthy, however, could afford to buy such equipment. More and more, the rich farmers began to demand their share of power. Kings were replaced by an **aristocracy** (ãr′ə·stäk′rə·sē), a form of government by the wealthy.

The aristocrats passed on their wealth, land, and power from fathers to sons. They thought of themselves as "the best." Their form of government, the aristocracy, was "the rule of the best."

Democracy. By the 500s B.C. many of the city-states like Athens had grown larger. Trade was increasing, and the traders and craftworkers became wealthy. With their new wealth, these people could buy weapons and fight for their city just as the older aristocracy did. Athens now began to build a navy. Even the poor could serve in the navy.

Many more people now began to demand some of the same rights that the aristocracy enjoyed. They set up a form of government in which more people took part. They called this new form of government **democracy**, or "the rule of the people."

Athens and Sparta

Problems in Athens. Many people in Athens now began to demand their share of power. The small farmers were also becoming unhappy. Many were losing their land to the large landholders. It was not easy to grow grain in a dry year. The harvest was poor. After a poor harvest, the small farmer had to borrow money from the large landholder until the next harvest.

The reforms of Solon. In the early 500s B.C., Solon (sō′lən) was elected to lead Athens. He saw that something had to be done to help the small farmers. He canceled their debts. He also forced them to switch from raising grain to planting more olive groves. Olives were better suited to the soil and the dry mediterranean climate.

Solon's most important reform was extending the right of citizenship. He made it possible for the city merchants and craftworkers to become citizens of Athens. They could serve in the Assembly, the group that made the laws.

The Athenians met on Pnyx Hill, shown at the right, to govern the city.

Tyrants. At this time conflict developed between the aristocrats and the other groups of craftworkers, traders, and farmers. Some people used this unrest as a means to gain power. The Greeks called such men **tyrants** (tī′rəntz). Today we think of a tyrant as a cruel or evil person. To the Greeks, a tyrant could be a good leader or a bad one. The word simply meant someone who seized and held power illegally.

Athenian democracy. By the early 400s B.C., democracy had reached its peak in Athens. Citizenship had been extended to free men in Attica, the farmlands and villages around Athens. Any citizen could attend and vote in the Assembly. All citizens had the right to speak there or to introduce laws. At times as many as 6,000 people would gather in Athens to discuss and vote on important issues.

121

A limited democracy. By today's standards, Athens was a very limited democracy. Only free men could enjoy all the rights of citizenship. A person born outside of Attica could not become a citizen. Women had almost no rights. Neither did the many slaves.

Sparta. Like Athens, Sparta had gone through political changes. Earlier, Sparta had been ruled by two kings who were the leaders of two powerful families. Later, the kings lost much of their power to the aristocracy, though they kept their position as war chiefs.

Warriors were the most important group in Sparta.

Citizenship

Democracy

The Greek word *democracy* means "government by the people." Democracy was taken very seriously by the Greeks. They fought among themselves and with foreign powers to keep the right to govern themselves.

In Athens the Assembly met on a hillside in the city about every nine days. Any citizen could propose a new law and speak for or against it. All citizens were allowed to vote. Voting was by voice. The crowd shouted out a yes or a no. Judges listened to the shouts and decided the result.

Greek democracy was called a direct democracy. All citizens took a direct part in the decisions. The Greek city-states were small enough for this kind of democracy to work. Direct democracy can still be found in America today. In some small towns, for example, the citizens gather in a meeting and vote on local matters.

Most nations today, however, are much too large for a direct democracy

In our form of democracy we elect representatives to two assemblies that make up the United States Congress.

to work. Many nations are representative democracies. The people elect representatives to speak for them and to pass laws. The idea of democracy is the richest part of our heritage from ancient Greece.

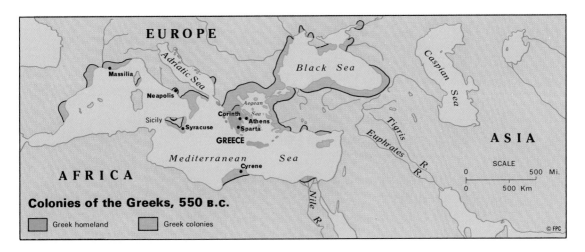

EUROPE

Adriatic Sea

Massilia

Neapolis

Black Sea

Caspian Sea

Aegean Sea

Sicily

Corinth

Athens

Syracuse

Sparta

GREECE

ASIA

Tigris R.

Euphrates R.

Mediterranean Sea

SCALE

0   500 Mi.

0   500 Km

AFRICA

Cyrene

Nile R.

Colonies of the Greeks, 550 B.C.

Greek homeland   Greek colonies

© FPC

As Sparta grew stronger, it began to take over neighboring villages. If a village resisted, it was conquered and its people were forced to become Helots. Helots were a class of people who had to work to feed and supply the Spartans. They had no rights.

About 650 B.C. the Helots of one of these conquered villages revolted. After that, Sparta became much more military in its outlook. Only by keeping strong and ready to fight did the Spartans feel safe from further revolts. In Sparta citizenship was limited to its soldiers.

Greece Expands

Even though the years during and after the Greek dark age were not peaceful ones, population continued to grow. Cities were becoming crowded. There was not enough land for those who wanted to farm. The Greeks began to spread out into less-crowded areas called colonies.

Once a new colony was established, it became a new city-state in its own right. Its people made their own laws and con-

trolled their own trade. Some colonies then set up new colonies of their own.

By 500 B.C. Greek settlements and Greek ideas extended far beyond the Aegean. Greek city-states circled the Black Sea. They extended as far west as the Mediterranean coasts of present-day France and Spain. Most of Sicily and the southern part of Italy were under Greek control. There were Greek colonies even in Africa. Find Greece on the map on this page. Find its colonies.

Checking Up

1. How did Solon help Athens become more democratic?
2. Who were the Helots?
3. Where did the Greeks establish their many colonies?
4. What answers would you give to the key questions at the beginning of this chapter?
5. *Why is the idea of democracy the richest part of our heritage from ancient Greece?*

123

The Greeks at War

As You Read

1. Think about these words.
   marathon   tribute   isthmus
2. Look for answers to these key questions.
   a. What brought about the Persian Wars?
   b. Why did other Greek city-states dislike the leadership of Athens?
   c. What was the result of the Peloponnesian War?

While the Greeks were moving toward democracy, lands to the east continued to be ruled by powerful kings. One of these lands was Persia, present-day Iran. The Persians had been nomads who settled in the highlands east of Mesopotamia. Their kings ruled like the kings who had ruled Mesopotamian empires.

In the later 500s B.C., Persian kings began to conquer other areas and bring them under Persian control. Persia built a great empire. Included in this empire were some of the Greek city-states in western Anatolia (an′ə·tō′lē·ə) and along the coast north of the Aegean Sea. Look at the map of the Persian Empire on the next page. Find Greece, Anatolia, and the Aegean Sea. Name some other parts of the world that were part of the Persian Empire.

These Greek city-states were forced to pay taxes to Persia. They also had to accept as their leaders tyrants who were favored by Persia. This did not please the freedom-loving Greeks.

The Persian Wars

In 499 B.C. some of the Greek city-states tried to free themselves from Persian rule. They asked other Greeks for help. Athens sent them a little aid. Even so, the Greeks were unable to drive out the Persians.

Darius (də·rī′əs), the Persian king, decided to punish Athens for interfering with Persian rule. In 490 B.C. he landed Persian soldiers on the Greek mainland near Marathon (măr′ə·thän). The Greeks managed to defeat the Persian invaders. According to legend a long-distance runner raced all the way from Marathon to Athens to tell the Athenians the good news. This was the origin of the race of 26 miles, 385 yards (42 km, 16. m) called the **marathon**.

Darius died soon after the defeat at Marathon, but his son, Xerxes (zərk′sēz), prepared for an even greater invasion. In 481 B.C. he brought 600 ships and 180,000 soldiers to the coast of Anatolia. The next spring they crossed the Helles-

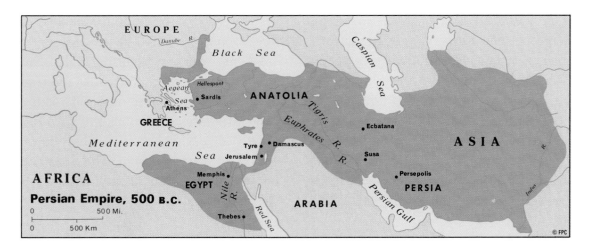

Persian Empire, 500 B.C.

0   500 Mi.

0   500 Km

pont, a narrow body of water between Anatolia and Greece. Find the Hellespont on the map above.

The Greeks stopped fighting among themselves and worked together. Thirty different city-states voted to fight the Persians. Sparta, which had the best army, led the fighting forces. Athens provided the navy.

The Persian Wars lasted until 479 B.C. There were battles both on land and at sea. The Persians captured Athens and destroyed much of the city. Many thousands were killed on both sides, but the Greeks finally drove the invaders from the Greek mainland.

The Leadership of Athens

Once the Persians had left the mainland, the Spartans went home. The Athenians, however, wanted to drive the Persians out of the Aegean area entirely. Under the leadership of Athens, a number of Greek city-states formed a league. Each contributed ships, troops, or money to support a strong navy. Because the treasury for this league was kept on the island of Delos, it was called the Delian League.

Together the league members continued to push the Persians back into Asia. Finally, in 449 B.C., the Persians agreed to stay out of the Aegean. Athens, which had been the leader of the Delian League, was unwilling to give up its leadership even though it had accomplished its goal. It forced the other members to continue paying a yearly **tribute**, or a tax for protection, to Athens. Much of this money was used to rebuild parts of Athens that had been destroyed by the Persians earlier in the century.

Pericles. Pericles (per'ə·klēz) came to power in Athens in 461 B.C. A popular leader, he controlled Athens for the next thirty years. Pericles made Athens into a fortress. He strengthened the walls around the city. He built the "long walls" that protected the five-mile stretch between Athens and its port at Piraeus (pī·rē'əs). If attacked, Athens could still protect its way to the sea. Look at the map on page 127. See how the walls created a passage to Piraeus.

Pericles had a law passed so people could be paid for serving in the government. The law allowed more poor people to hold public offices. Pericles also spent large amounts of money on temples and other public buildings. To meet the expenses of all these projects, Pericles continued to collect tribute from other areas. These actions did not make Athens very popular with the city-states that were forced to pay tribute for an alliance they no longer wanted or needed.

Athens, which took pride in its own democratic tradition, was now interfering with the freedom of other city-states. Some city-states were unhappy with this growth of Athenian power. They began to look to Sparta for help. The Spartans, too, were becoming uneasy with Athenian expansion.

People Who Made a Difference

Socrates, Plato, and Aristotle

Some people say that warriors and leaders are the most important people in history. Greece, however, will always be remembered for three of the world's greatest philosophers, or thinkers seeking truth.

Socrates (säk′rə·tēz′), who lived in Athens, was concerned with how we know the things we know. He asked questions such as, What is truth? and What is justice? He stressed that people must question their ideas. He did this with his students. He asked a question, and for every answer he followed it with another question. He led his students to see that many of their ideas were false. His goal was to strip away all false ideas. Only then could a person find the true answers.

Plato was one of Socrates' students. Much of what we know about Socrates comes from the writings of Plato, since Socrates left no writings of his own. Plato started a school called the Academy. Here he taught that everything in our world was only an imperfect copy of something in an ideal world. In his work *The Republic*, he tried to show what a perfect city-state would be like.

Plato shared his ideas with students.

Plato's most famous student was Aristotle (ăr′ə·stät′əl). Aristotle differed from his teacher. Instead of looking for an ideal world, Aristotle studied things as they were in the real world. He based his own work about the city-state on a study of how politics, or government, worked in 158 different city-states in Greece. Aristotle wrote about many different sciences. His work was always based on careful study of how things really worked. Modern scientists use methods similar to those used by Aristotle.

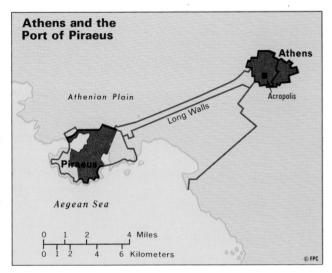

Athens and the Port of Piraeus

Athens

Athenian Plain

Acropolis

Long Walls

Piraeus

Aegean Sea

0 1 2 4 Miles
0 1 2 4 6 Kilometers

© FPC

How did the "long walls" give the Athenians access to the sea?

The Peloponnesian War

Sparta controlled or had friendly relations with most of the Peloponnesus, the area south of the Isthmus of Corinth. An **isthmus** is a narrow strip of land that connects two larger bodies of land. The Isthmus of Corinth connects the Peloponnesus to the rest of Greece. Athens was extending its control over more and more of the area north of the isthmus.

Finally, fearful of Athens's growing power, Sparta declared war. Other city-states of Greece became involved in the war as allies of either Athens or Sparta.

The war lasted about twenty years. There were victories and defeats on both sides. In 405 B.C. the Spartans surprised the Athenian fleet and destroyed it. They then attacked Athens itself. In 404 B.C. Athens surrendered to Sparta.

The Peloponnesian War brought political chaos to all of Greece. Both Athens and Sparta were weakened by it.

Pericles strengthened Athens' power and led the city in its "Golden Age."

Years of unrest followed, with various city-states fighting one another. No single power in Greece remained strong enough to end this unrest. In spite of the troubled times, Greek civilization continued to flourish.

Checking Up

1. Who was Darius? Xerxes?
2. What were the achievements of Pericles as leader of Athens?
3. What answers would you give to the key questions at the beginning of this chapter?
4. *What was the Delian League?*

127

The Golden Age

Even though there was much unrest in Greece because of war, the middle 400s B.C. has been called the Golden Age of Greece. Much of what we remember best and admire most about Greece is a part of that period. It was the time when many Greek artists, writers, and thinkers were producing their finest work. Athens reached its height in this Golden Age.

Life in the Golden Age

If you lived in Athens in the 400s B.C., your day would start early. People were up with the sun, and by early morning the streets were filled. The bustling agora (ag′ə·rə), or marketplace, was a gathering area. In this broad, open space at the center of the city, the farmers set up stalls to sell their products, and trad-ers from outside the city displayed their wares. Around the agora were schools, law courts, and craft shops where pottery and other objects were made and sold. Nearby was the hill where the Assembly met. Spreading out from the agora were the homes of the city dwellers. Towering above the city was a hill called the Acropolis (ə·kräp′ə·ləs). The Acropolis held the Parthenon (pär′thə·nän′), the temple of the goddess Athena. Athena was Athens's special protector.

Whenever they were not working, the Greeks liked to gather and discuss the important events of the day. The agora, the barbershop, and the **gymnasium** were favorite gathering places for the men. The gymnasium was an open field where the men could take part in sports.

The sports included racing, boxing, and wrestling.

Women. Ancient Greece was a man's world. Most women led a sheltered life. They could not vote, hold office, or buy and sell property. Their main purpose in life was to serve as wives and mothers. When a woman married, she became the property of her husband. Anything she owned became his. If the husband died before his wife did, she was given back to the care of her father or a brother.

Caring for children, spinning and weaving, and taking care of the household duties were a woman's main concerns. Some women seldom left the house.

Life in Sparta was different. Spartan women had much more freedom. Since the Spartan men were always busy with their military duties, the women often took charge of the farm or business as well as of the household. They were free to move about and were not sheltered as the Athenian women were. Spartan girls and women took part in sports and games and often exercised as much as the boys and men did.

Children and education. Children stayed under the care of their mothers until the age of six. After that, Greek boys and girls began to lead separate lives. The girls stayed at home to learn to spin, weave, and take care of the home.

In Athens nearly all boys learned to read and write. Fees for schools were low, so even the poor were able to send their boys to school. Elementary schooling lasted from age six to age fourteen.

The main subjects were reading, writing, and some arithmetic. Public speaking was also stressed, since the boys might have to speak in the Assembly when they became citizens. Children from wealthy families also attended a special school to learn music and art. A third kind of school taught sports and other forms of exercise.

At the age of fourteen, the children of poor families often began to work. Wealthy Greek children continued their education for another four years by studying with one of the great teachers. Athens was famous for its teachers.

Reading and writing were far less important in Sparta. There the goal was to become a good soldier. At the age of seven, a boy left home to join a troop led by older youths. The boys learned to obey orders and to survive with little food or clothing. They continued training until they were twenty. Then they became part of the army and lived with their fellow soldiers for the next ten years. Even married soldiers lived away from their wives until they were thirty years old.

Religion. Religion was an important part of Greek life. Like many other early peoples, the Greeks worshiped many gods and goddesses. When the northern nomads invaded Greece about 1600 B.C., they brought the belief in their gods with them. The sky gods of these wandering herders became the chief gods. Zeus (zōōs), the father of the gods and the god of weather, became the most important of all.

The ancient Greeks came to the temple at Delphi (del'fī) to hear the oracle, a woman prophet, tell the future.

The earth gods of the farming people, however, were not forgotten. Over the years the sky gods and the earth gods were brought together into a family of Olympians, gods and goddesses who were said to dwell at the top of Mount Olympus, Greece's highest mountain.

Games and festivals. Festivals were held frequently throughout the year. Many were religious festivals only. Others were devoted to athletic games or presentations of plays, but even these included religious ceremonies.

Athletic games were held often. The most important of these events was the Olympic celebration held at Olympia every four years. These games began in 776 B.C. Athletes gathered from all over Greece to take part in the various events. There were races, jumping and throwing events, riding competitions, and boxing and wrestling matches. These games are

the origin of the Olympic Games today. The Greeks were so fond of these games that they even stopped fighting in the middle of a war to attend them. An athlete who won a prize at the games was treated like a hero at home.

The Greek Heritage

The idea of democracy is part of our Greek heritage, as are the Olympic Games. The Greeks made other contributions to our heritage.

Drama. The Greeks held special festivals for **drama.** Plays were performed in huge outdoor theaters. Nearly every important city had a theater. Drama festivals lasted for several days, and nearly everyone came to see the plays.

Many of the old Greek plays are still performed today. Some modern writers have written new plays and stories based on these older plays.

Discus-throwing was an Olympic sport. Notice how real the body looks.

Athenians still enjoy plays in this ancient circular theater.

Art and architecture. Much Greek art has been lost. The great statue of Athena that was housed in the Parthenon, for example, is gone. Nevertheless, much remains that we can still admire.

Vases and other pottery were used by the Greeks in their everyday lives. Still, they were beautifully made and decorated with fine painting.

Greek sculpture shows their admiration for the human body. The Greeks thought of their gods as having perfect human form. Their statues were meant to show that perfection. The earlier Greek statues are similar to those of the Egyptians. The figures are stiff and unrealistic. However, by the Golden Age, statues had become more lifelike and realistic. Figures were often shown as though they were in motion.

The best Greek architecture was devoted to the temples of the gods. Since all religious ceremonies were held outside the temples, the exterior of a temple was very important. Look at the picture of the Parthenon on page 111. Huge stone columns, or pillars, held up the temple roof. The top part of the temple was decorated with sculptures and paintings. In ancient times, these temples were painted in bright colors, though none of the paint remains today.

Checking Up

1. What was the agora? the Acropolis?
2. What subjects did Greek children study?
3. What answers would you give to the key questions at the beginning of this chapter?
4. *How was life in Athens different from life in Sparta?*

Alexander's World

As You Read

1. Think about these words.
   cavalry   barbarian
2. Look for answers to these key questions.
   a. What were the achievements of Alexander?
   b. What happened to Alexander's empire after his death?
   c. What was the result of Alexander's conquests?

North of Greece another power, Macedonia (mas'ə·dō'nya), was growing stronger. Find Macedonia on the map on the next page. The Macedonians were Greek in language and customs. Macedonia, however, had never developed into separate city-states. It had been ruled by kings. One of these kings finally invaded Greece. Weakened by wars the Greeks could not drive out the invaders.

The Rise of Macedonia

Philip of Macedonia became king in 359 B.C. His kingdom was large but weak. Philip began to strengthen it. He improved its army and conquered other areas around Macedonia.

Macedonian fighting methods were similar to those of the Greeks, though Philip made greater use of massing shielded foot soldiers to break through enemy lines. He backed these troops with horse-mounted warriors, or **cavalry**. Philip also used spies to learn his enemies' weaknesses. He even bribed enemy officials to get them on his side.

In 338 B.C. Philip's forces defeated those of Athens and Thebes, another important Greek city-state. He then called for a meeting of all Greek city-states at Corinth. Only the stubborn Spartans refused to send representatives to the meeting. The other city-states knew that Philip had the power to defeat them. They agreed to join a league under Philip's rule.

Philip wanted to lead a united Greece against Persia. He did not get a chance to lead this invasion. He was killed in 336 B.C., leaving his kingdom to his twenty-year-old son, Alexander.

Alexander the Great

Although he ruled for only thirteen years, Alexander succeeded far beyond what his father had planned. First he strengthened his claim as king of Macedonia. While Alexander was in Macedonia, however, Athens and Thebes tried to break away. He swiftly put down the revolts. Alexander punished Thebes by destroying the city.

Alexander spared Athens. His own teacher, Aristotle, had studied in Athens under Plato. Alexander admired Athens and thought highly of its accomplishments. He treasured Greek literature and art. It was said that he always slept on a copy of the *Iliad*.

Persia and the East. In 334 B.C. Alexander led his Greek army into Persia. He defeated all who stood in his way. He fought along with his troops and earned their respect and admiration.

In 331 B.C. the Greeks met the main Persian army in Mesopotamia and defeated it. In the following year, the Persian king was killed by his own soldiers. Alexander declared himself king of Persia. He then continued to move eastward with his army. He was determined to conquer the entire world.

In 327 B.C. the Greeks crossed into India. Soon after that, however, the exhausted Greek soldiers wanted to return to their homes and families. Most of them had been fighting on foreign soil for over six years. Reluctantly, Alexander agreed to turn back. On the long trip

Alexander conquered the largest empire the world had yet known.

back to Greece, Alexander became ill and died. He was not yet thirty-three years old.

The spread of Greek ideas. Alexander brought the many non-Greek people of his empire into contact with Greek ideas. He opened the east to Greek trade. He also adopted ideas and customs from the people he had conquered.

The Greeks did not care much for foreigners. They called them **barbarians.** The Greek word *barbarian* simply meant anyone who did not speak Greek. Alexander had a much more open mind. He

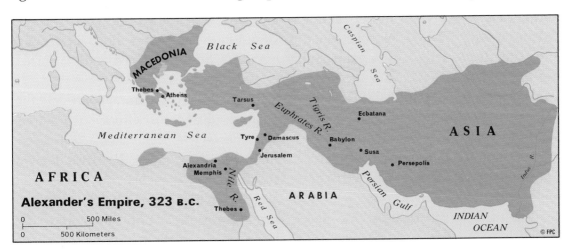

Alexander's Empire, 323 B.C.

Alexandria's towering lighthouse was famous in the ancient world.

found much to admire in the Persian Empire. He married a Persian princess. Persians also served in his army.

Wherever his conquests took him, Alexander established new cities. They followed the Greek model, with an agora, a gymnasium, and temples. Greek became the language of the empire, and Greek ideas spread from Egypt to the border of India.

Alexander named many of his new cities after himself. The most famous was Alexandria, which he built in Egypt.

The Hellenistic World

Greek civilization after the time of Alexander is called Hellenistic. This word means "Greek-speaking" or "acting like a Greek." The Hellenistic world spread far beyond the Greek mainland and the Aegean islands. After the death of Alexander, the center of the Hellenistic world shifted from Greece to Alexandria in Egypt.

The empire collapses. Without Alexander the great empire he had built could not survive. His leading generals divided it among themselves. One took Macedonia; another took Egypt. Still others took control of different parts of the eastern lands.

In Greece the city-states became independent again. Except for Athens and Sparta, none of them was strong enough to defend itself. The military and governing power of Greece declined.

Alexandria. Greek civilization continued to thrive, especially in Alexandria. Ptolemy (täl′ə·mē) had been one of Alexander's leading generals. He took control of Egypt after Alexander's death. The Ptolemies ruled for nearly 300 years.

Alexandria became the capital of the Egyptian kingdom. The Ptolemies brought many Greeks to Egypt to help them rule the country. Alexandria had a great museum and a library that was the largest in the ancient world. Scholars and scientists were welcomed and supported by the Ptolemies.

Advances in science. Some of the greatest advances in Greek science took place during the Hellenistic age. Hero of Alexandria invented the first known steam engine, though it was never used except as a toy. Herophilus (hi·rä′fə·ləs) made many discoveries about how the human body works.

134

One of the most remarkable of the Hellenistic scientists was Eratosthenes (er′ə·täs′thə·nēz), who computed the circumference of, or distance around, the earth. His figure was very close to today's measurement.

Greeks had long been interested in mathematics. The discoveries of Euclid (yoo′klid) of Alexandria and Archimedes (är′kə·mēd′ēz) of Syracuse established mathematical and scientific ideas that are still used today.

A lasting heritage. In the 200s B.C., a new power arose. Rome conquered Greece and before long built a new empire even larger than Alexander's.

Greek civilization, however, did not disappear. It continued to influence the Roman world, and it continues to influence the world today. People still read and enjoy Greek stories and poems. Greek plays are performed all over the world. We still admire Greek buildings and art. Greek ideas still play a part in modern thought. The glory of Greece has not been forgotten.

Checking Up
1. What special military skills helped Philip conquer Greece?
2. How did Alexandria become a center of Hellenistic civilization?
3. Name three important Hellenistic scientists and list their achievements.
4. What answers would you give to the key questions at the beginning of this chapter?

5. *Although Alexander treasured Greek civilization, he also admired much in the Persian Empire. How did he contribute to bringing the Greeks and Persians together?*

Unit 4 Summary
- The first Greeks were the Achaeans. Their invasion of Greece took place around 1600 B.C.
- In 1100 B.C. the Dorians came to Greece and destroyed the Mycenaean civilization.
- City-states developed at the end of the dark age. They were ruled by kings and later by the aristocrats.
- In Athens the rule of the aristocrats was replaced by democracy.
- The Persians tried to invade Greece in the 400s B.C. The Greek city-states joined together to defeat them.
- Sparta and Athens fought each other in the Peloponnesian War. This war weakened Greece so Philip conquered it easily.
- Philip's son, Alexander, united Greece and went on to conquer the Persian Empire.
- Alexander's conquests spread Greek civilization throughout western Asia. In Egypt he founded the city of Alexandria, which became a great center of learning.
- The Greeks made contributions to philosophy, science, drama, art, architecture, and the ideas of democracy and the Olympic Games.

Unit 4 Review Workshop

1. Why did the Achaeans stop being nomads?
2. What early poet wrote about the Mycenaeans? What poems did he write?
3. Why was the Dorian period called the dark age?
4. How were Sparta and Athens alike? How were they different?
5. What great things did Solon accomplish for Athens?
6. Where were Greece's colonies?
7. Why did the Greeks and Persians fight a war?
8. What organization did the Greeks form to fight against the Persians?
9. How did Pericles help make Athens a strong city?
10. What was the reason Athens and Sparta fought a war?
11. Why were the 400s B.C. called the Golden Age of Greece?
12. What questions were Greek philosophers interested in?
13. Why was Philip of Macedonia such a success in his wars with the Greek city-states?
14. What were the greatest accomplishments of Alexander the Great?

Use Your Reading Skills

A. Put the following events in time order. Put the earliest first and the latest last.

Trojan War   Hellenistic Age

Persian Wars   Achaean invasion
Dark age   Dorian invasion
Alexander's   Peloponnesian
  conquests   War

B. Many of our English words come from Greek words. For example, *diameter* is a combination of two Greek words. These words are *dia*, meaning "across," and *metron*, meaning "measure." The study of the origin and changes of meanings of words is called etymology. This word, too, comes from Greek. It is formed from the words *etymos* ("true") and *logos* ("speech"). Look at the English words and their Greek origins below. Using the information given, answer the questions that follow.

geography [from *geo* ("earth") and *graphein* ("to write or describe")]
astronomy [from *astron* ("star") and *nomos* ("set of laws")]
drama [from *dran* ("to do or act")]
alphabet [from *alph* and *beta*, the names of the first two letters of the Greek alphabet]
barbarian [from *barbaros* ("foreign")]

1. What word comes from the Greek word meaning "foreign"?
2. What Greek words make up our word *alphabet*?
3. What is the meaning of the two Greek words that make up the word *geography*?

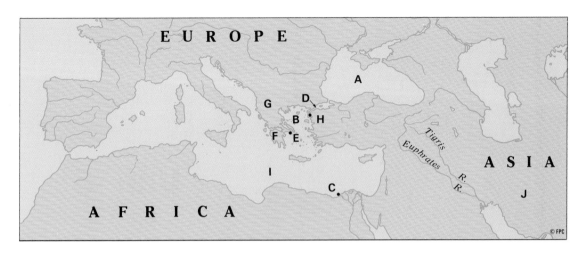

4. What is the Greek meaning of the word *astronomy*?

5. What word do we get from the Greek word meaning "to do or to act"?

Use Your Thinking Skills

Write these headings across the top of your paper.

Government	Philosophy
Literature	Science

Write each of the names below under the heading that describes the contribution made by the person. You may want to put some names under more than one heading.

Homer	Solon
Eratosthenes	Socrates
Pericles	Archimedes
Aristotle	Plato

Use Your Map Skills

The following are names of places that are important in Unit 4. Look at the map above. Match each name with the letter showing its location.

Macedonia	Black Sea
Troy	Persia
Hellespont	Peloponnesus
Alexandria	Mediterranean Sea
Athens	Aegean Sea

Learn by Doing

The Greeks had many gods to explain things they did not understand. Choose five of the gods in the list below. Do some research in your school library. Use an encyclopedia to find out what area of life each god was thought to govern. Write a sentence about each.

Hephaestus	Zeus	Apollo
Demeter	Ares	Hermes
Poseidon	Pan	Athena

Read to Learn More

Find the topics listed below in the card catalog of your library. Read all or part of a book listed under one of the topics. Share what you learn with your classmates.

OLYMPICS	ARCHITECTURE (GREEK)
DRAMA (GREEK)	TROJAN WAR

Unit 5

The World of the Romans

The ruins of Rome give us an idea of how large and beautiful the city of Rome was in ancient times.

Rome Begins

As You Read

1. Think about these words.
   capitol   forum
2. Look for answers to these key questions.
   a. How was the geography of Italy favorable to establishing a Mediterranean empire?
   b. How did the Romans explain the founding of their city?
   c. Where was the city of Rome built?
3. Use this reading skill.
   We can call attention to important information in many ways. We can use italicized words, bold type, parentheses, underlining, and colored or shaded boxes around words or whole sentences. As you read this chapter, notice which ways of calling attention are used.

As the Greeks were coming out of their dark age, a few small farming villages were being started along the Tiber River in what is today Italy. In time, these villages were to become Rome, the greatest city of the ancient world.

The Land

Look at the map on page 141. Notice that Italy, like Greece, is a peninsula. What large sea separates this peninsula from northern Africa? *Mediterranean* comes from two words meaning "between land." Why is *Mediterranean* a good name for this body of water?

The Romans called the Mediterranean Sea *mare nostrum*. In Latin, the language of the Romans, this meant "our sea." It was along the shores of this sea that the Romans established their empire.

The climate of southern Italy, where Rome is located, is also mediterranean. Like Greece, Rome has dry summers and mild, rainy winters. Trace the mountains located in Italy. The Apennines divide Italy into an eastern and a western part. The eastern part has good grazing land for sheep and cattle. Some early settlers raised livestock. The western plains are rich in fertile volcanic soil. On these plains, early settlers farmed.

The Legend of Romulus and Remus

The early Romans, like other people, had many legends about their past. One legend was that the city of Rome was founded by twin brothers, Romulus (räm'yə·ləs) and Remus (rē'məs). According to legend, the brothers were set adrift on the Tiber River in a basket.

140

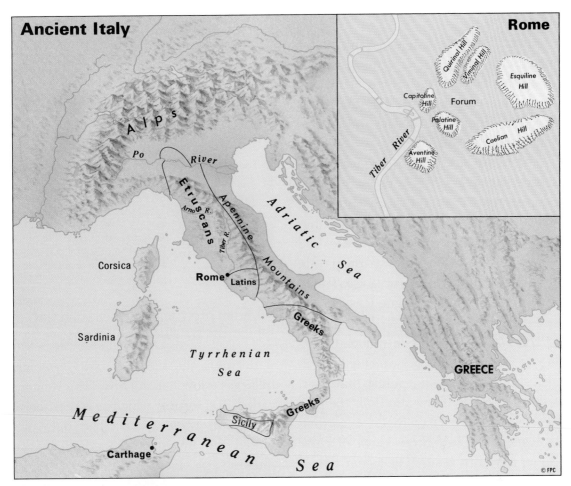

Ancient Italy

Alps

Po   River

Etruscans

Arno R.

Apennine Mountains

Tiber R.

Corsica

Rome • Latins

Adriatic Sea

Sardinia

Tyrrhenian Sea

Greeks

Mediterranean   Sea

Sicily   Greeks

Carthage •

GREECE

© FPC

Rome

Quirinal Hill

Viminal Hill

Capitoline Hill

Forum

Esquiline Hill

Palatine Hill

Caelian Hill

Tiber River

Aventine Hill

Rome began as several farming villages. Farmers built the early city.

When the basket finally got stuck in the mud along the shore, a she-wolf found the boys and nursed them. Later a shepherd found Romulus and Remus and raised them.

The boys grew up. They decided to build a city but could not agree over where it should be located. The brothers argued and argued until finally Romulus killed Remus. Romulus built his city and gave it his name, Rome. He ruled Rome for thirty-seven years. The legend says that as he ascended to heaven he shouted, "My Rome shall be capital of the world."

141

Early Rome

About 3,000 years ago, groups of nomads settled and began farming villages along the Tiber River. Some of the villages were on the seven hills that overlook the Tiber. One village was near a small island in the Tiber River.

The Etruscans. Early Rome was really several farming villages, not a city. Its people grew crops and raised cattle and sheep. Its early kings were warrior kings like those in early Greece. Rome had more advanced neighbors to the north. Known as the Etruscans (i·trəs′kənz), they probably helped Rome grow to the size of a city.

The early Etruscans introduced writing to Rome. They were excellent builders who built temples, public buildings, and many roads. They also built the first bridge across the Tiber River. According to legend, the last three kings of early Rome were Etruscans. The legend seems to be supported by archaeological finds.

The hills of Rome. For a long time, the Palatine Hill was the most important part of the city. Rome's richest citizens built their homes here. Much later, a Roman emperor built his home on this hill and named it Palatium. We get our word *palace* from Palatium.

On the Capitoline Hill, the Romans built a temple and a fortress. The temple was for the most important Roman god, Jupiter. Our word **capitol**, which is the name of the building where a legislature meets, comes from the word for the Capitoline Hill. Find these two hills on the map on page 141.

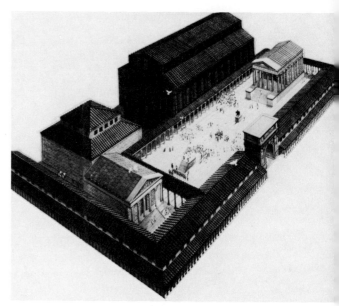

An artist drew this reconstruction of the Forum by studying its ruins.

Between the Palatine and Capitoline hills was a low marshy area. The Romans called it a **forum**, which was a place to meet and trade goods. The hills protected the Forum and made it a safe meeting place. As Rome grew, the marshes were drained. The Forum became the chief marketplace in Rome.

Checking Up

1. Into what agricultural areas did the Apennines divide ancient Italy?
2. Who were the Etruscans?
3. What did the Etruscans contribute to early Rome?
4. What answers would you give to the key questions at the beginning of this chapter?
5. *Why do you think the location of Rome was a good one for a city?*

142

The Roman Republic

As You Read

1. Think about these words.

   republic   social class   senator

   representative   consul   veto

2. Look for answers to these key questions.

   a. What is a republic? How was the Roman Republic organized?

   b. What was the "course of honor"?

   c. How was the conflict between the patricians and the plebeians settled?

The city of Rome grew large and important under the Etruscan kings. The Romans, however, did not want to be ruled by kings. Look at the time line below. When did the Etruscan kings rule? Finally, in the early 6th century B.C., the people of Rome overthrew the kings and established a form of government that lasted over 400 years.

Establishing a Republic

The new government the Romans formed was called a **republic**. In this form of government, the citizens elect officials and **representatives**, people who look after the government.

The Roman Republic was different from Greek democracy. In the democratic Greek city-state, all citizens voted in one assembly on laws. In the Roman Republic, groups of citizens belonging to different assemblies voted on laws. They elected officials to carry out these laws.

How the republic worked. The chart on the next page shows how the Roman government worked. Roman citizens

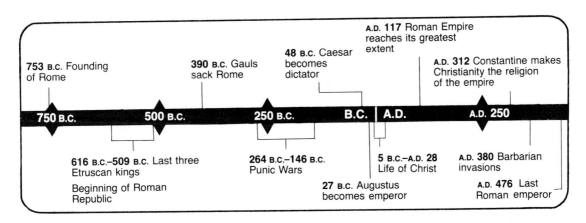

753 B.C. Founding of Rome

390 B.C. Gauls sack Rome

48 B.C. Caesar becomes dictator

A.D. 117 Roman Empire reaches its greatest extent

A.D. 312 Constantine makes Christianity the religion of the empire

750 B.C.   500 B.C.   250 B.C.   B.C. | A.D.   A.D. 250

616 B.C.–509 B.C. Last three Etruscan kings

Beginning of Roman Republic

264 B.C.–146 B.C. Punic Wars

27 B.C. Augustus becomes emperor

5 B.C.–A.D. 28 Life of Christ

A.D. 380 Barbarian invasions

A.D. 476 Last Roman emperor

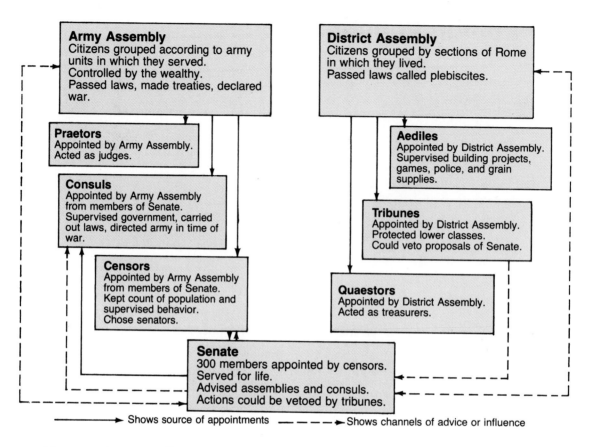

Army Assembly Citizens grouped according to army units in which they served. Controlled by the wealthy. Passed laws, made treaties, declared war.	**District Assembly** Citizens grouped by sections of Rome in which they lived. Passed laws called plebiscites.

Praetors
Appointed by Army Assembly.
Acted as judges.

Aediles
Appointed by District Assembly.
Supervised building projects, games, police, and grain supplies.

Consuls
Appointed by Army Assembly from members of Senate.
Supervised government, carried out laws, directed army in time of war.

Tribunes
Appointed by District Assembly.
Protected lower classes.
Could veto proposals of Senate.

Censors
Appointed by Army Assembly from members of Senate.
Kept count of population and supervised behavior.
Chose senators.

Quaestors
Appointed by District Assembly.
Acted as treasurers.

Senate
300 members appointed by censors.
Served for life.
Advised assemblies and consuls.
Actions could be vetoed by tribunes.

———————➤ Shows source of appointments   – – – – ➤ Shows channels of advice or influence

could serve in one of two assemblies. These were the Army Assembly and the District Assembly. Members of the assemblies elected a number of important officials. These officials took care of taxes, roads, public buildings, and city government.

The Army Assembly was the first assembly in the republic. Only the wealthiest Romans served in the Army Assembly. This assembly controlled the army. Its members could declare war and make laws.

Later the District Assembly was organized. All the citizens of the city were divided into groups according to where they lived. Each division, or ward, of the city had one vote in the District Assem-

bly. This assembly elected some of the Roman officials. It also appointed people called tribunes to protect the lower **social classes**, or groups of people with the same rank.

The most important leaders in the republic were **consuls**. The Army Assembly elected two members of the Senate, an advisory body, to serve as consuls. The consuls held office for one year.

The two consuls had the power that once belonged to the kings. The consuls were heads of the army when Rome was at war. They supervised the government. By having two people share the power of running the government, the Romans hoped to avoid having any one person act as king.

The Romans demanded fairness and firmness from their public officials.

The Senate. Another group of people, known as **senators**, advised the consuls. Senators also advised members of the assemblies about what laws should be passed for Rome. In all, there were 300 members of the Senate. The senators served for life.

The Roman Republic was a system of checks and balances so no one group of people had too much power. The tribunes held **veto** power over the recommendations of the Senate and the consuls. The Latin word *veto* means "I forbid." The censors, officials who collected taxes and counted the people to find out where they lived, held some power over the Senate. They named a new senator when a senator died. Even the assemblies held some power over the Senate because they had the right to approve or reject its laws.

The "course of honor." As the republic developed, it became the tradition for wealthy Romans from important families to seek careers in the government. A career in the government followed a pattern. The first position was of low rank. Then the person would run for a higher office, and then a still higher one. At least two years had to pass before a person could go from one office to another. The Romans called this process the *cursus honorum*, or "course of honor."

Only the wealthiest citizens could hold high offices. A Roman had to be wealthy enough to be able to devote time and money to getting elected and serving the republic. Those who held high offices were usually admitted to the Senate.

Priests and Gods

You have read about the different government workers whom the assemblies appointed to help govern the people. Other officials who were needed by the government were the priests. Priests took care of the temples built for the many gods the Romans worshiped. There were temples throughout the country.

When gods granted wishes, grateful citizens would bring gifts to honor them. Priests also helped the people with sacrifices. Pigs and sheep were often killed to honor a god. The Romans believed that the gods helped them both in war and in daily life. Houses usually had a place set aside for a statue of a favorite god.

Many of the gods were borrowed from the Greeks. The names of the gods, though, were changed to Roman names. As the Romans conquered other people, they also borrowed their gods. For example, after the Romans conquered the Egyptians, the Egyptian goddess Isis became popular in Rome.

When Rome became an empire, the Romans worshiped their emperors as gods of the state. The emperors became symbols of the unity of the empire. The Romans let people believe in whatever gods they wanted as long as they agreed to honor the state god as well.

Patricians and Plebeians

All the citizens of Rome could be divided into two groups based on money and the length of time their families had lived in Rome. Patricians (pə·trish′ənz) were people who could trace their families back to the beginnings of Rome. Anyone not born into one of these families could never hope to be a patrician.

The other people were called plebeians (pli·bē′ənz). Plebeians were the workers in Rome. For example, they were farmers, merchants, or carpenters. They did not hold offices in the government. However, they were not content to be powerless.

As Rome grew, many plebeians became very wealthy through trade and business. These upper-class plebeians led the poor of the city and the small farmers in a struggle for more rights. The weapon the plebeians used was the threat to leave the city.

Finally they did leave. The plebeians walked out of Rome and met in an assembly of their own. They elected tribunes to protect their rights. With the plebeians gone, work in the city and on the farms stopped. The Senate had no choice but to agree to the demands of the plebeians. The tribunes, elected by the plebeians, were made a part of the government. They were given the power to veto the actions of the Senate and of other officials. A tribune could not be dismissed for anything he did or said.

More changes benefited mainly the wealthier plebeians, who gained entry to offices that earlier had been open only to patricians. Although the common people gained rights and representation, the wealthy continued to hold most of the power in the government.

Checking Up

1. What were the duties of a Roman consul? of a tribune? of a censor?
2. Who were the members of the Army Assembly? of the District Assembly? of the Senate?
3. What were the religious beliefs of the Romans?
4. What answers would you give to the key questions at the beginning of this chapter?
5. *Why did a Roman citizen in high office need to be wealthy?*

The Growth of the Roman Empire

As You Read

1. Think about these words.
   legion   province   gladiator   emperor
   ally   estate   dictator

2. Look for answers to these key questions.
   a. How did Rome conquer an empire?
   b. What problems resulted from the growth of Rome?
   c. What were the achievements of Julius Caesar? of Augustus?

3. Use this reading skill.
   Seeing relationships helps you make sense out of what you read. Something happens that makes something else take place. The something that happens is the *cause*. The something that is made to take place is the *effect*. As you read, find the causes and effects of Roman expansion.

During the years of the Roman Republic, Rome expanded its territory. Its power and influence stretched far beyond the banks of the Tiber River.

Roman Conquests

Rome first conquered surrounding villages and land areas. These conquests were possible because the people in these places were not united. They were not as well organized as the Romans. Rome conquered one place and then another. With each conquest, Rome became more experienced and confident.

Rome also had a well-trained army. The Roman army was divided into **legions**, or groups of about 4,000 men. Each legion was further divided into smaller fighting groups.

Roman soldiers were away from home for long periods of time, often for several years. The soldiers were needed not only to fight for the land but also to stay and keep the peace once a land was conquered. Soldiers were given land in areas they conquered to encourage them to remain with the army.

Rome usually treated the people of conquered lands fairly. Therefore, the Romans had little trouble holding on to their captured territory. Some newly conquered people were even granted Roman citizenship. Other conquered people were allowed to govern themselves as long as they agreed to become **allies**. An ally is a country that agrees to join with another country for purposes of protection and trade.

147

Threats to Rome

Twice Rome's power was seriously threatened. Early in the history of the republic, the Gauls swept down from the north and invaded Rome. The Romans considered the Gauls barbarians, or less civilized people. The Gauls were not interested in staying in Rome. They were raiders fighting for whatever they could take from the people they defeated. Rome was able to get them to leave by paying great sums of money.

Punic Wars. Another, more serious threat occurred later. Rome fought three wars with Carthage called the Punic (pū′nik) Wars. Locate Carthage on the map on page 150. As you may recall, Carthage had been a Phoenician colony. The Carthaginians were traders. They controlled much of northern Africa.

Hannibal came close to defeating Rome. He used elephants to cross the rugged Alps.

The navy of Carthage controlled the shipping lanes of the western Mediterranean. They could cut off Rome's supply of grain from overseas. In the First Punic War, Rome had to build its own navy to defeat Carthage. Soon the Romans became as skilled at fighting at sea as they were on land.

The Second Punic War was fought over gold and silver in Spain. During this war the Carthaginians had a great advantage in that their leader, Hannibal, was one of the greatest military men of all times.

Hannibal decided to fight the Romans on their own ground. He led an army from Spain across the Alps and into northern Italy. Hannibal won battle after battle, always surprising the Romans with an unexpected move. He reached the walls of the city of Rome before being forced to withdraw.

In the last Punic War, the city of Carthage was destroyed. Roman soldiers tore down buildings. Men, women, and children who were not killed in the battles were sold into slavery. The site of the city was plowed up, and Roman soldiers spread salt over the land so that crops could not grow. Rome now controlled most of the lands of the western Mediterranean.

Rome and the eastern Mediterranean. During the Second Punic War, the king of Macedonia had sided with Carthage. Find Macedonia on the map on page 150. The Macedonian king hoped to end the growing power of Rome in the Adriatic Sea, the sea that separates Italy from

The Romans built this wall in northern Britain to hold back invaders.

the peninsula that Macedonia was located on. The Romans declared war on Macedonia. They defeated it and even took over Greece. The Romans also began to extend their control into western Asia. By about the year 100 B.C. Rome controlled nearly all the lands circling the Mediterranean.

Growth Brings Problems

Problems resulted from Rome's rapid expansion. The more territory Rome won, the more decisions had to be made on how to govern it. The assemblies could not easily settle such problems. The senators were better trained and took over the leadership of the government. The Senate became more and more powerful.

Conquered territories outside Italy were called **provinces**. A province was governed by officials sent from Rome. Many Roman officials did their jobs well, but some were corrupt and dishonest.

Some stole land or forced people to pay bribes for favors. Others took tax money.

Land. Land was considered the most respectable form of wealth. Each senator wanted to own great amounts of land. The senators made sure that lands gained through conquest were divided among themselves. With these lands, they formed large holdings of land called **estates**. Slaves worked these large estates. Slaves were usually captives who worked hard and were often treated poorly. A number of slaves revolted during this time. Such unrest only added to Rome's problems.

As senators took more and more land, many citizens were left landless. Small farmers were especially hurt. Hannibal's invasion of Italy ruined large areas of farmland. The smaller farmers could not compete with the large landowners who used slaves on their estates. The smaller farmers were forced to sell their lands, usually to the rich senators. These farmers went to Rome for help. Soon the city was filled with hungry people without work. To keep these people from rebelling, the Senate gave them free grain from the government warehouses.

The jobless people were kept amused and quiet with entertainment. Crowds watched **gladiators**, professional armed fighters who were usually slaves, fight to the death. Animals were sent to Rome from faraway lands. Lions, elephants, hippos, and bears fought with the gladiators and with each other. Wild animals were also trained to perform tricks for the approving crowds. Chariot races

149

thrilled the audiences. Sometimes the Colosseum, a big arena, was even flooded with water for naval battles.

The End of the Republic

Julius Caesar was a successful Roman military commander who conquered Gaul, or present-day France, and invaded Britain. Find these territories on the map on this page. When Caesar's rivals attempted to take his command away, Caesar marched on Rome. His rivals fled. Caesar became **dictator** for life. As dictator, he had all the power to make laws, and his word had to be obeyed. Find the time Caesar ruled on the time line on page 143.

Caesar defeated his rivals in wars fought in Spain, Syria, and North Africa. He then set about to correct the problems of Rome. Julius Caesar made improvements in the Roman government. The number of senators was increased so people from the provinces could be appointed. Caesar extended full Roman citizenship to many people in the conquered lands. New Roman colonies provided much needed land for citizens. Caesar even reworked the Roman calendar, which had been so inaccurate that many seasonal festivals were being celebrated at the wrong time of year.

Augustus. After Caesar was killed by enemies in the Senate, Augustus came to

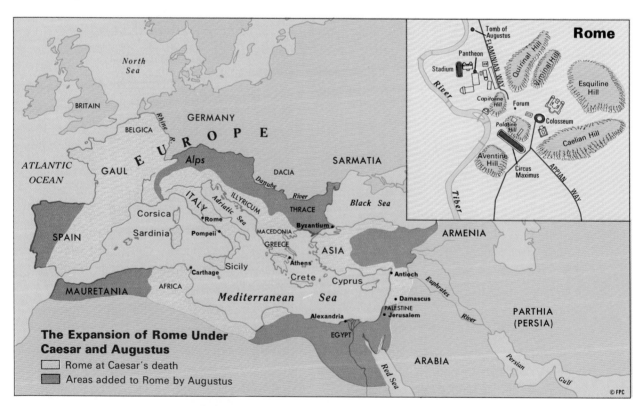

The Expansion of Rome Under Caesar and Augustus
☐ Rome at Caesar's death
☐ Areas added to Rome by Augustus

© FPC

The conquests of Julius Caesar brought the Roman Empire to the banks of the Rhine. Augustus extended its border to the Danube.

Julius Caesar was an army leader, a statesman, a reformer, and a writer.

toms, and ideas throughout the empire. Above all, Augustus brought peace to Rome. For this reason the Romans honored and supported him. Later they would speak of the time he ruled as a golden age.

Pax Romana. The peaceful times that Augustus brought to the Roman Empire marked the beginning of the Pax Romana, or Roman peace, which lasted 200 years. Roman territory reached its greatest size shortly after A.D. 100. No power was strong enough to threaten Rome. Rome did not have to use all of its money for wars and armies. Instead, money could be spent on public buildings and works of art.

power. He was Caesar's eighteen-year-old nephew and adopted son. Augustus fought for the right to take Julius Caesar's place as ruler. He defeated his rivals and took charge of Rome and all its territories. As supreme ruler of the Roman Empire, or **emperor**, Augustus proved to be an able and effective leader. He created an efficient government at home and in the provinces. He also appointed people to government office on the basis of their ability rather than their wealth. Even some freed slaves were able to rise to power under Augustus.

Augustus kept armies stationed throughout the provinces. He continued to establish Roman colonies in distant areas. Look at the map on page 150. Compare the size of the Roman Empire during the time of Caesar with its size during the time of Augustus. This colonization helped to spread Roman laws, cus-

The name Augustus meant the emperor was not just a man, but a god.

151

The Early Christians

Christianity had its start shortly after the time of Augustus. Locate Palestine on the map on page 150. Here a Jewish teacher began to attract followers. His name was Jesus.

Early Christians showed Jesus as a good shepherd guarding his flock.

The Jews, or Hebrews, who lived in Palestine wanted a king who would free them from Roman rule. Their holy books told them that such a Messiah would appear one day. Jesus' followers saw him as the Messiah, or Christ, one sent by God who would lead them to freedom.

Jesus was put to death by the Romans. His followers continued, however, to preach his message of brotherly love and heavenly salvation. The Christian religion began to attract more and more followers, especially among the poor.

The Romans could not understand a religion that taught that there was only one God. They insisted that everyone worship the Roman emperors. This the Christians, like the Jews, refused to do.

The Romans had many Christians put to death for refusing to worship the emperor. Some emperors thought the Christians threatened the state. Nevertheless, Christianity continued to spread from the poor to the ruling classes. Constantine, one of the last great Roman emperors, accepted the religion and made it the empire's official religion.

Christianity eventually united the empire in one belief as the Roman government had united it under one law.

The End of the Empire

About 200 years after Augustus died, the empire began to break apart. The emperors during this time were army generals who had seized power. They ruled without regard for the lives or property of citizens. Barbarians from the north attacked frequently. Rome had to spend more and more money to support its army. Taxes were raised to provide more funds. It became difficult for many people to pay their taxes. It seemed that the problems of the empire were too many for any one person to handle. The empire was divided into an eastern and a western part.

Finally, in A.D. 476 the last Roman emperor was forced from the throne by a barbarian who took his place. The power of Rome ended.

Checking Up

1. How were Roman soldiers encouraged to remain with the army?
2. What were the Punic Wars?
3. What were the teachings of Jesus?
4. What answers would you give to the key questions at the beginning of this chapter?
5. *How did the Roman Empire decline?*

Life in Roman Times

The family was the most important group in ancient Rome. It was much larger than an average family is today.

The Family

The wealthy household included the father and mother, the children, the uncles and aunts, and the slaves.

Men. The father was the head of the household. Even more powerful, though, was the head of the family. That person was the oldest man in the family. Think about your own family. Do you have a living grandfather or great-grandfather? In Roman times he would have been the head of both your family and the families of your uncles and cousins. He would make all the important decisions for all the other men, the women, and the children in the family. When he died, the next oldest male member of the family would become the head.

Women. When a woman married, she became a part of her husband's family. Any property she brought into the marriage became the property of her husband. Any decisions concerning her would be made by the head of her new family.

Roman women were not confined to the home as Greek women were. They freely attended festivals and other public gatherings. Men and women ate their meals together. Women, as well as men, were entertained at special dinners.

Women spun wool and made cloth. They brought up the children and looked after their earliest education. They supervised the household duties and made sure the household ran smoothly.

153

Toward the end of the republic, women gained the freedom to inherit property. Women, however, were still not able to vote, to hold office, or to have the other privileges of citizenship.

Children. Children were expected to follow in their parents' footsteps. Girls were trained to become good wives and mothers. Boys were taught to become good citizens. Every family hoped its boys would grow up to serve Rome.

Children played games with dice, hoops, seesaws, and balls. Dolls, doll-houses, and building bricks were also popular toys. Roman children kept pets just as children do today. They played with dogs and birds, but cats were not common pets.

Most boys received only enough education to do simple arithmetic and some reading and writing. However, they learned farming or a trade from their fathers. Their lifelong occupations were decided for them.

Upper-class boys received more schooling. Besides reading, writing, and arithmetic, they learned Greek and studied Homer and other great poets. It was also important to learn how to speak in front of large crowds.

Childhood did not last very long. Girls were married in their early teens. By the age of fourteen, boys were considered citizens. They began to learn the jobs they would have as adults.

Slaves. Slavery was an accepted part of Roman society. When Rome began to expand its territory, captives in war were taken as slaves. Slaves were also crimi-

A Roman artist painted this couple in a lifelike manner.

nals, people captured and sold by pirates, and children sold by their parents. All but the poorest families owned at least one slave. The rich owned many.

Slaves could be bought and sold. Slaves were not citizens and had no legal rights. They had to obey all orders of their masters. Many Romans treated slaves who worked in their houses well. Some slaves were given their freedom as a reward for good service.

City Life in Rome

Rome was the most glorious city in the empire. By the time of Augustus, its population had grown to nearly a million people. Its busy streets and forum were filled with Romans and visitors from the distant provinces.

The Romans divided their cities into regular blocks. They even provided stepping stones across streets.

The streets were crowded and noisy. Butchers, bakers, barbers, and craftworkers did much of their work in the streets. All night long chariots, wagons, and carts could be heard. During the day they were forbidden in the streets, because they would have created traffic jams.

Homes. Working people and the poor generally lived in large, overcrowded apartment buildings. The dark, gloomy apartments had no running water. People bathed in public baths. Water for cooking was hauled up from fountains in the streets.

Homes of the rich were large, comfortable, and beautiful. Statues and wall paintings decorated the courtyards.

Then and Now

Pompeii

Today as visitors walk the streets of Pompeii in the hot sun, they meet only lizards scuttling among the scattered ruins. Tourists visiting this city before August 24, A.D. 79 would have viewed a different scene.

The people of Pompeii thought that nearby Mount Vesuvius was a dead volcano. The volcanic soil made the area around Pompeii especially good for farming. Many people worked in the orchards and vineyards on the slopes of the mountain. Merchants in the city were busy selling clothes, hardware, and other items. The town flourished.

Mount Vesuvius was not dead, however. It began erupting again. A cloud of ash and gas moved over the city and buried it.

The catastrophe struck the town in the midst of its normal routine. People died instantly from the poisonous gas. The ash preserved things just as they were when people dropped them to run for their lives.

Archaeologists have now uncovered Pompeii. From these excavations we have learned more about how people in the Roman Empire lived, how they decorated their homes, what they used for cooking, and even what they wrote when scribbling on the walls.

Now visitors can tour the cramped quarters of ordinary townspeople or stroll through the block-long houses of the wealthy. They can see the shops that line the narrow streets.

A walk through the remains of the forum reveals temples, shops, markets, and government buildings. A sundial gives the time of day in both past and present-day Pompeii.

The eruption of Mount Vesuvius covered the city of Pompeii with a cloud of ash.

A tourist visiting Pompeii today would find these ruins.

The rich lived better. The houses of the wealthy included many rooms built around a central courtyard called the **atrium**. There were few windows on the outside walls. This helped keep out burglars and the noises from the street. The atrium let in plenty of air and light.

Important rooms had wall paintings and sometimes **mosaics**. A mosaic is a pattern or picture made with small pieces of stone or tile. Look for the pieces of tile in the picture of a Roman mosaic on this page.

Food. The poor lived mostly on bread or wheat porridge, olives, and grapes. They had a wide choice of vegetables but seldom had meat of any kind.

The rich dined well. They reclined on couches as they ate. Slaves did the cooking and serving. Sometimes dancers, singers, or poets performed while the Romans and their guests ate.

Entertainment. You have already read of the many kinds of entertainment Rome provided for its citizens. The emperor or a rich citizen usually planned and paid for the circuses, plays, races, and gladiator contests. They hoped that by providing fun they would be popular with the people or impress their friends.

Romans also spent a great deal of time at the baths. These were huge, beautiful places where people could bathe in both hot and cold water. The bathing area was surrounded by gardens, exercise rooms, meeting halls, and beauty shops. Romans could even buy snacks from the merchants who walked around the baths and sold food and drinks. Admission to

Gladiators and wild animals attracted Roman crowds to the arenas.

the baths was so cheap that almost anyone could afford to enter.

For a visitor from the provinces, the city was an exciting place to be. The rich temples and other public buildings, the busy forum and crowded streets, and the many and varied activities of a million Romans provided a never-ending show.

Checking Up
1. In what ways were Roman women freer than Greek women?
2. What kind of schooling did Roman boys receive?
3. Who were the slaves?
4. What answers would you give to the key questions at the beginning of this chapter?
5. *Why would Rome be an exciting place to a visitor from the provinces?*

Our Roman Heritage

As You Read

1. Think about these words.
   civil law   aqueduct   Romance language
2. Look for answers to these key questions.
   a. How did Roman law and government influence our own law and republic?
   b. What were the accomplishments of the Romans in architecture?
   c. What are the Romance languages? Where are they spoken?

The power of the Roman Empire declined and eventually vanished. However, the power of Roman ideas and accomplishments continued long after the empire was gone. Laws on how people should treat others are based on Roman laws. Some buildings today are built to look like those that stood in Rome. Languages spoken in many countries are based on the language that Romans spoke. Many of our English words come from Latin words.

Government and Law

The branch of law that deals with the affairs of private citizens is **civil law**. Roman law strongly influenced European civil law. Civil law includes legal decisions on the ownership of property. It covers agreements between people. It deals with rules for lending, borrowing, and collecting money.

Roman political ideas continued to influence people long after the empire fell. The ideas of the ancient Romans were known to the men who worked to create a new republic in the late 1700s for the United States of America. The Constitution of the United States contains ideas that were born in the Roman Republic.

Architecture

The Romans were skillful builders. They borrowed ideas from both the Greeks and the Etruscans, but they improved them and gradually developed a style of building that was Roman.

Many of the public buildings of our nation's capital show Roman influence.

What two features of Roman architecture can you identify in these ruins of a Roman city in North Africa?

The Romans perfected the arch, a curved structure used as a support over an open space, and the vault, a kind of stretched-out arch. Look at the picture on the next page. Find the arches. Using the arch, the Romans were able to build large bridges across water and to widen the space between the posts supporting their buildings.

Compare the photograph above with the one on page 130. Notice how the Romans borrowed the beautiful columns of the Greeks. They learned of arches from the Etruscans. The combination of arches and columns became Roman architecture.

The Romans invented and used concrete as a building material. Before concrete was invented, stone slabs or blocks were used for building. The large, heavy blocks were cut by hand and were hard to lift into place. Concrete could be used alone to make walls and columns, or it could be used to cement bricks together. It provided the Romans with a cheap material for construction. Building was much faster using concrete.

Thousands of miles of road crisscrossed the empire. Many remained the only roads in Europe for centuries after the fall of Rome. Many roads were so strong that today's heavy buses and trucks travel roads that were built for Roman carts. In France and Spain, small Roman bridges are still in use.

The Romans were also excellent town planners. The layout of a town was in a checkerboard pattern. Streets intersected at square corners. For variety, Romans lined some streets with columns

Notice the checkerboard street pattern in this Roman town.

Many Roman aqueducts still carry water today. This aqueduct is located in southern France.

and arches. Public buildings, forums, and temples were located at the end of many avenues.

To provide a constant supply of fresh water to their settlements, the Romans built miles and miles of graceful **aqueducts**. Parts of aqueducts look like bridges, but they are really troughs or open pipes that carry water. Aqueducts began in the hills near a source of fresh water. They sloped down gently as they carried the fresh water supply to the city.

Language and Literature

Latin, the language of the Romans, was used throughout the empire. After the fall of Rome, the different provinces went separate ways. Travel between them decreased. The people in each area continued to use the Latin language, but it changed slowly over hundreds of years. Eventually, the changes became so great that people from one area could no longer understand those from another area. They were speaking different languages even though their languages began as Latin.

Modern Italian, French, Spanish, Portuguese, and Rumanian are all languages that came from Latin. They are called **Romance languages**, not because they are romantic but because they came from the language of the Romans.

Latin itself lived on in the language of the Roman Catholic church. It was used

160

in religious ceremonies and for all writings. Since Christianity had spread all over Europe, Latin remained a language that was understood by people of many countries.

Latin literature is another important gift from the Romans. Much Latin writing was lost during the hectic times that followed the fall of Rome. Once again, it was the church that preserved much of what we have today. Latin writings, even though they had nothing to do with religion, were saved and copied by church members.

Much of what we know about early Roman history comes from Roman writers such as Livy and Tacitus. Livy wrote a history of the republic. Tacitus wrote about the times of the early emperors. Julius Caesar's accounts of his military encounters are still read today.

Signs of Rome's gifts are found everywhere. Roman influence is in our language, buildings, and law. The world still remembers the greatness of the Roman Empire.

Checking Up

1. What architectural forms did the Romans borrow from the Greeks and Etruscans?
2. What was the plan of Roman towns?
3. Name three Roman writers and the subjects they wrote about.
4. What answers would you give to the key questions at the beginning of this chapter?

5. *Compare the achievements of the Greeks and Romans. In what areas did they both make contributions? In what areas were the contributions of each different?*

Unit 5 Summary

- Rome was founded on seven hills near the Tiber River in Italy.
- The Etruscans helped Rome grow from a village to a city.
- The Romans had an organized form of government called a republic. Citizens elected officials to carry out the laws and run the government.
- Patricians were originally the only ones who had the rights of citizens. Later, plebeians also gained rights and representation.
- The family was the most important social group in Rome. Fathers were the heads of families.
- Rome extended its power and territory throughout the Mediterranean world.
- The republic ended when Julius Caesar became dictator.
- Augustus was the first emperor. He brought peace and prosperity to the Roman Empire.
- The Roman Empire lasted until A.D. 476 when barbarian invasions led to the fall of Rome.
- Some of Rome's contributions to civilization are in the areas of law, government, architecture, language, and literature.

Maps Tell a Story of Roman Roads

In the shadow of the temple near the center of the Forum stood an immense golden pillar. It was called the golden milestone, and from this point all Roman roads began.

The Romans built roads for many reasons. Armies had to be sent quickly to areas where they were needed. Government and army leaders had to send messages from Rome to the outlying provinces. Trades routes were needed to supply Romans with goods from all corners of the empire. Citizens needed roads to tour foreign lands or just to travel to the sea for vacations.

Slaves and captives most often built the roads. When they were not available, the Roman soldiers did. It was hard work. The road had to be dug by hand, and stone had to be cut for the gravel and pavement.

Roman roads were carefully built. For each road the land was surveyed, or looked at, to find the shortest, straightest route. Then it was marked out with stakes. Look at the diagram on the next page. Notice the different materials used for Roman roads. Ditches and sloping sides kept water off the surface. A deeper ditch was dug and filled with

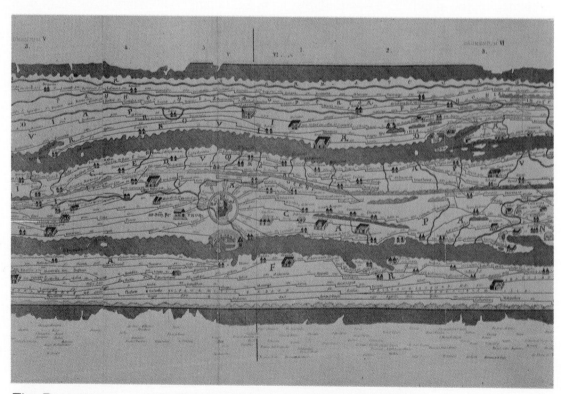

The Roman map maker who drew this map showed the Italian peninsula as it would appear if it were turned sideways.

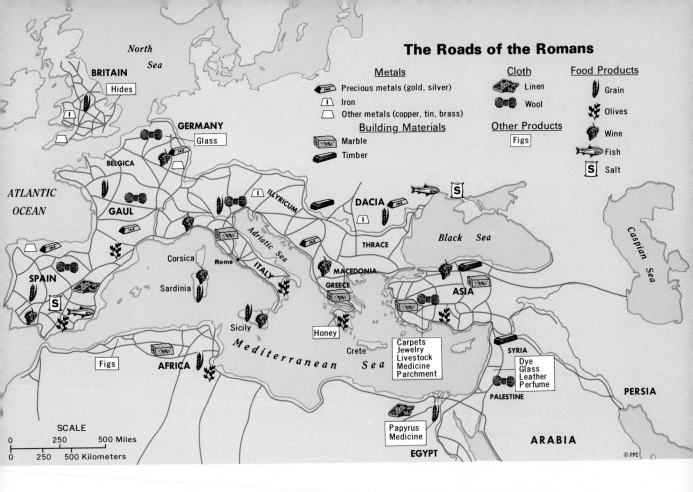

The Roads of the Romans

Metals
- Precious metals (gold, silver)
- Iron
- Other metals (copper, tin, brass)

Building Materials
- Marble
- Timber

Cloth
- Linen
- Wool

Other Products
- Figs

Food Products
- Grain
- Olives
- Wine
- Fish
- Salt

SCALE
0   250   500 Miles
0   250   500 Kilometers

sand, stones, and pebbles. A curb was laid to hold the final layer of paving stones in place.

Look at the map on page 162. It is the only copy that remains of an early Roman map. Notice the symbols that show

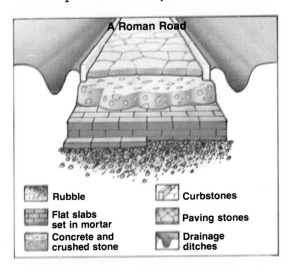

A Roman Road

- Rubble
- Flat slabs set in mortar
- Concrete and crushed stone
- Curbstones
- Paving stones
- Drainage ditches

rivers and hills. What symbols show sites such as temples and government buildings? What symbol do you think stands for the city of Rome?

Buildings with cisterns were colored with blue interiors. Cisterns are pools where water is collected. Travelers could be certain to find water wherever one of these buildings stood.

The remaining map shows the roads that connected the different parts of the empire. This map provides information not only on roads but also on the products that were traded along the highways. Compute the farthest distance a trader journeyed to bring his goods to Rome. What products did Rome import from Spain, Sicily and Sardinia, Egypt, Asia Minor, and Greece?

163

Unit 5 Review Workshop

What Have You Learned?

1. What does *mediterranean* mean? What did the Romans call this sea?
2. What did the Etruscans contribute to Rome?
3. What was the difference between the Roman Republic and Greek democracy?
4. Why was there a conflict between the patricians and the plebeians?
5. How was Rome able to extend its power over the Mediterranean world?
6. What were some of the problems the growth of Rome created for the Roman Republic?
7. Who was Julius Caesar?
8. Why was the age of Augustus called the golden age?
9. Why did the Romans persecute the early Christians?
10. Who was Constantine?
11. Describe life in ancient Rome.
12. What contributions did Rome make to civilization?

Use Your Reading Skills

You learned in Unit 4 that many of our words come from Greek words. Many also come from Latin. Look at the words and their Latin origins below. Using the information given, answer the questions that follow.

agriculture [from *ager* ("field") and *cultura* ("tending")]
civil [from *civis* ("citizen")]
literature [from *litteratura* ("writing")]
science [from *scire* ("to know")]
social [from *socius* ("partner, ally")]
study [from *studium* ("eagerness")]

1. From what Latin word did our word *science* come?
2. What was the meaning of the Latin word *litteratura*?
3. From what Latin word did our word *social* come?
4. What did the Latin word *civis* mean?
5. Which of our words was made up from the Latin words meaning "tending a field"?
6. What was the meaning of the Latin word *studium*?

Use Your Time Skills

Historical time is divided into the centuries before Christ (B.C.) and the centuries after Christ (A.D.). One century is a period of 100 years. Look at the time line at the beginning of Part Two. The 1st century A.D. spans the years from the birth of Christ to the year 100. The 1st century B.C. spans the hundred years before Christ's birth back to 100 B.C. Find the date when the Romans overthrew the last Etruscan king and established a republic. This event took place in 510 B.C., or in the 6th century before Christ. Find the date when the last Roman emperor was forced off his throne. This event took place in A.D. 476, or in the 5th century after Christ.

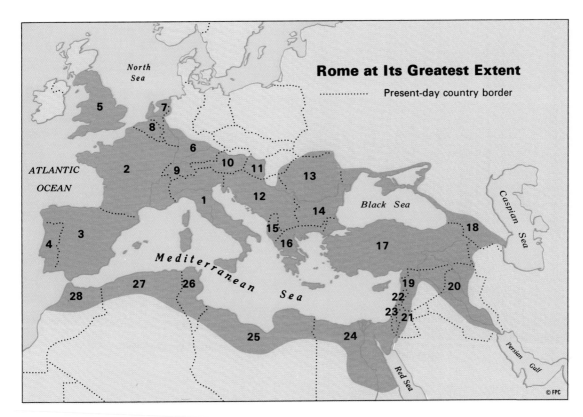

Rome at Its Greatest Extent

.... Present-day country border

In what centuries before or after Christ do the following dates fall?

1. 753 B.C. the founding of Rome
2. 334–323 B.C. Alexander the Great conquers an empire
3. 27 B.C. Augustus becomes the first Roman emperor
4. A.D. 312 Constantine makes Christianity the religion of the empire
5. A.D. 380–450 Barbarians overrun the Roman Empire

Use Your Map Skills

Number 1 to 28 on a piece of paper. Look at the map above. Identify the number which stands for each of the present-day countries that was once a part of the Roman Empire.

Learn by Doing

Many of our months were named after Roman gods or leaders. Use an encyclopedia to find out about the origins of the names of the months listed below.

January   May   July
March   June   August

Read to Learn More

Find the topics listed below in the card catalog of your library. Read all or part of a book listed under one of the topics. Share what you learn with your classmates.

GLADIATORS   AENEID
COLOSSEUM   CLEOPATRA

The Civilization of Kush

These ruins are all that is left of the palace at Meroë, the third and last capital of Kush.

167

The Kingdom of Kush

As You Read

1. Think about these words.
   sakia   wadi   oasis   caravan
2. Look for answers to these key questions.
   a. Where was Kush located?
   b. How did the people of Kush make a living?
   c. Why was the location of Kush good for trade?
3. Use this reading skill.

   After reading a chapter, you sometimes may want to find one of the terms or topics mentioned in it. You can locate the exact page or pages on which this term or topic appears by using the Index pages at the back of this book. Use the Index to find the page numbers in this chapter for the following topics: cataracts of the Nile, shadoof, and trade in Kush.

South of Egypt, in what is today the Sudan, there was once the kingdom of Kush. No one knows exactly when Kush began. We know only that it lasted for thousands of years. Look at the time line on pages 108–109. What other civilizations existed during the time of Kush?

Kush became a center of trade and culture—a crossroads of the African continent. Kush showed how people could overcome natural barriers and use them to their own advantage. Because of its location, Kush also was able to spread its civilization south and west into Africa.

The Land of Kush

Kush was the first African kingdom to develop and thrive south of the Sahara. Like Egypt, Kush was protected from in-

vaders by natural barriers. Look at the map on the next page. Find the Sahara to the northwest of Kush and the Nubian Desert to the northeast. Find the grasslands to the south. Only small groups of nomads were able to live in these regions. Kush was located along the Nile, which flows from the center of Africa. Travel from the source of the Nile, however, was difficult. Look at the map again. Find the marshlands to the south of the grasslands. Here reeds and other plants grow so densely on the Nile that the river cannot be navigated.

Like their Egyptian neighbors, the people of Kush worked the land nearest the Nile River and built their villages and cities beyond its banks. Look at the map of Kush again. Find Kerma (ker′mä) and

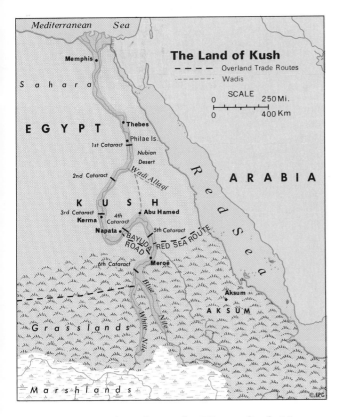

The Land of Kush

- - - - Overland Trade Routes
.... Wadis

SCALE
0   250 Mi.
0   400 Km

How far is this cataract from Memphis? from Meroë?

In ancient times the cataract was a barrier to river travel. Up to this point the Nile was a good water highway that carried people and goods. Rafts, barges, and sailboats glided easily up and down the river north of the rapids. However, the cataract stopped all river traffic. Travelers had to leave their boats, barges, or rafts and take an overland route to continue their journey. Today, as you have read, this cataract is covered by the waters of Lake Nasser held back by the Aswan High Dam.

Long ago river travelers met other cataracts on their journeys south. The Second Cataract was even more of an obstacle than the First Cataract. Travelers again had to travel overland around it. But once back on the river, travelers watched the Nile narrow for the next hundred miles. As it narrowed, the nearby lands became drier. The desert reached right up to its banks. The sandy, dry soil was poor for farming.

Farther upriver, the lands near the Third Cataract and the Fourth Cataract were better for farming. At the Fifth Cataract, the Nile Valley became even greener. Here the river flowed through an area with rich soil, good rainfall, and natural irrigation. This area was especially good for farming. In these upriver areas the civilization of Kush began.

The people of Kush. Wandering hunters and gatherers were probably the earliest people to live in what became Kush. They probably came to the area about

Meroë (mer′ə·wē′). Next, find Napata (nap′ə·tə). These were the three major cities of ancient Kush. Notice that these cities grew up along the Nile River, just as Memphis, Thebes, and other Egyptian cities did. However, the three main cities of Kush were located in areas very different from where the Egyptian cities were. Kush, in many ways, was a land of great contrasts.

As you know, the Nile was a busy waterway. Traders sailed south from Egypt. About a hundred miles south of Thebes, the level valley of Egypt suddenly narrows. Gray granite cliffs enclose the river. Beyond the cliffs is the First Cataract, where the once-peaceful waters of the Nile tumble over jagged rocks. Find the First Cataract on the map above.

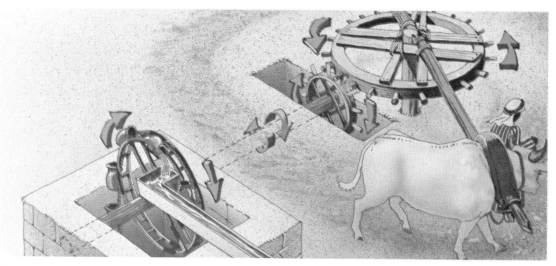

The Kushites harnessed animals such as cattle and camels to the wheels of the sakia to draw water from wells or basins.

5000 B.C. from the west, as the land there became drier and drier. These people lived in the Nile Valley south of the Third Cataract. They hunted and fished along the banks of the Nile. They gathered the fruits, nuts, berries, and grains that grew wild there. In time, these people settled into farming villages along the Nile. Eventually, these villages became leading cities of Kush.

The people of early Kush lived in reed huts. The doorways of the huts were arched, and the reeds were gathered together on the roof to keep the houses from falling apart. Even today, in modern Sudan, some people still live in houses that look much like those of ancient Kush. However, as the cities of Kush began to grow, the style of houses changed. Many people began to build houses from dried mud. Such houses were often built with a number of rooms around an open courtyard. The larger the courtyard, the larger the house.

The Way of Life in Kush

Farming was the foundation of the kingdom of Kush and the source of much of its wealth. The yearly flooding of the Nile brought rich new soil to the farmlands of Kush. Rainfall watered the crops. Later, sometime after 2000 B.C., farmers in Kush learned from the Egyptians how to irrigate their lands. As in Egypt, they used the shadoof. Farmers in Kush also borrowed the **sakia** (säk'ē·yə), a type of waterwheel the Egyptians had later developed. Look at the illustration of the sakia above. How did it help the farmers in Kush?

The early farmers of Kush raised enough food for themselves and their families. Later on, farmers in Kush learned how to raise enough food to store and to trade. Farming near Meroë was especially productive. There the heavier rainfall filled streams and rivers that flowed into the Nile. As soon as the rains stopped, the farmers would leave their villages and walk along the muddy **wadis** (wäd'ēz), or streambeds which carry off the rain in dry regions. Using pointed sticks called selucka (səl'o͞o·kə), they planted grain in the still-wet streambeds and along the Nile's wet banks. The wadis usually remained wet throughout most of the growing season, so irrigation was not needed.

Farmers of Meroë and other areas of Kush grew many kinds of crops. They grew millet and other grains, as well as vegetables and date palms. Millet, which grows well in dry areas, is still the main crop in this region.

Millet was probably the most valuable crop in Kush. It became the basis of trade between the farmers of Kush and people from other lands. The farmers of Kush traded millet with the Egyptians for furniture, jewelry, weapons, and linen. The people of Kush traded millet for cattle with the nomads who lived on the grasslands to the south. Trade, based on farming, became the main source of the wealth of Kush.

The Rise of Trade

The people of Kush lived at a crossroads of Africa. The Nile River served as a water highway. It connected the center of Africa with the southern shore of the Mediterranean Sea. Despite the cataracts, many people used this waterway, carrying with them goods and ideas.

Because boats, barges, and rafts could not travel the entire length of the Nile, overland trade routes were used. These routes cut across the desert. Look at the

The early Kushites lived in reed huts. The reeds were gathered at the top to hold the hut together.

map on page 169. Find the overland routes that connected Kush to other areas. Many overland routes followed rivers or streams or crossed the desert at points where there were water wells. These areas were called **oases** (ō·ā'sēz). Overland routes often connected oases. Water was very important to the desert travelers.

171

Then and Now

Getting Around in Northern Africa

Travel through the kingdom of Kush was often difficult, usually dangerous, and sometimes impossible. Traders, thieves, and priests traveled across Kush thousands of years ago. Today people still cross the deserts, marshes, grasslands, and the Nile River, and for many of the same reasons. Travel in modern-day Sudan, where Kush once flourished, is safer, faster, and more comfortable than it was for the travelers of Kush.

Kushite travelers on the Nile went by boat or raft. Boats and rafts used sails and wind power to move up and down the river. Sometimes, however, rowers had to pull their longboats by rope from along the shore.

Overland travel for Kushite traders was even more difficult. There was very little water during the trip. To make matters worse, the temperature in the desert was often unbearably hot during the day and nearly freezing at night. In the early centuries of Kush, goods were carried by caravans of horses and mules. Much later in their history, the Kushites used camels, often called "ships of the desert." The rolling motion of camels, so

Sailboats like this one carried traders and their goods on the Nile.

similar to that of ships at sea, made the traveler sick. Camels were also known for their ill tempers. They often bit riders they did not like.

Today roads and railroads carry people and goods across many of the ancient caravan routes. The "ships of the desert," though still used, are used less often. Many people now ride in automobiles, jeeps, and buses. Besides greater speed and comfort, automobiles and buses have one other advantage. They do not bite their riders.

Kushite traders traveled by caravan over land routes, crossing grasslands and deserts to bypass the cataracts of the Nile.

In the days of the kingdom of Kush, it was not easy to travel overland. For traders, however, the trip across the dangerous desert to the Red Sea was worthwhile. Look at these routes on the map. Find the route to the Red Sea. At Red Sea trading ports, Kushite traders could buy goods that had been shipped from faraway lands. For example, spices from India, and incense from Arabia were shipped to seaports on the western shore of the Red Sea. These were then carried overland to Kush for trade with people from other parts of Africa. The cotton plant may also have been introduced to Kush over this trade route from India.

Early traders used pack animals such as donkeys and horses to carry their goods across the desert. Much later, nomads from the western desert introduced camels to the traders of Kush. Camels were well suited to desert travel. They could carry heavy loads for many miles in great heat without needing much water. Soon camels were used in **caravans**. These were trains of pack animals that carried traders and their goods overland.

Look again at the map of the trade routes. People from the desert to the west and from the tropical lands to the south came to Kush to trade for food, cloth, and weapons made of iron. They brought with them such prizes as camels, hard woods, elephant ivory, leopard skins, and ostrich feathers. These goods were then sent on to Egypt and to other African lands to the east. As this trade increased, Kush became the center of trade south of the Sahara. Here the three major cities developed.

Centers of trade. Kush is remembered most as a center of trade. Its main cities grew up as trade centers. Kerma was the first large city of the kingdom. It began as a trading outpost. From about 3000 B.C., Kerma was a trading partner with Egypt. Later other cities of Kush, especially Napata and Meroë, took over most of this trade. The location of these cities put them at the center of the trade routes of Kush.

Meroë was especially well located for trade. It was not far from the Red Sea. By way of an overland route, it was possible to travel to the First Cataract, the gateway to Egypt. Its location attracted traders from many lands. It also became a center for ironworking. Because of the importance of iron at this time, Meroë became well known throughout the ancient world.

Checking Up
1. How did the people of Kush irrigate their lands?
2. What cities were the trading centers in Kush?
3. What goods did the people of Kush trade?
4. What answers would you give to the key questions at the beginning of this chapter?
5. *Why did the people of Kush settle south of the cataracts?*

Kush and Egypt in the Ancient World

As You Read

1. Think about these words.
   fortress   royal   tradition   succession
2. Look for answers to these key questions.
   a. In what ways did Egypt influence the civilization of early Kush?
   b. How did Kush conquer Egypt?
   c. Why did the queen mother of Kush have great power?
3. Use this reading skill.
   As you read each chapter in this book, you should look for the main ideas. You should also read to find specific information that supports those ideas. For example, we can summarize the main idea in this chapter as follows: During most of the history of Kush, there were strong ties between Kush and Egypt. What specific information can you find to support this idea?

For many centuries Egypt was the main trading partner of Kush. For the most part, contacts between the two civilizations were peaceful and prosperous. The vast wealth of Kush, however, tempted the powerful kings of Egypt. Slowly at first, the Egyptians pushed their control south beyond the First Cataract. Later, in the 16th century B.C., soldiers from Egypt burned Kerma, the main trading city of Kush. Quickly, then, the Egyptian army fanned out across the kingdom. The Egyptians built large **fortresses,** or strongholds, along the Nile to control the area. They set up a new Egyptian-led government to rule over the kingdom of Kush. For about 500 years, Kush became a part of the Egyptian Empire.

The Influence of Egypt

The pharaohs of Egypt sent many officials to Kush. They also let members of the **royal** family, the family of the king of Kush, help rule. Sharing power led to cooperation between the Egyptian invaders and the conquered Kushites.

The Kushites worshiped both Egyptian and local gods, such as this lion god.

These pyramids, the tombs of the rulers of Kush, stand above Meroë.

During the period of Egyptian rule, many people in Kush learned how to write Egyptian hieroglyphics. They adopted Egyptian styles and customs. Children of the ruling families of Kush traveled to Egypt to study. When they returned, they brought with them a taste for Egyptian styles of clothing, furniture, and housing and even for the Egyptian religion. Temples were built for the worship of Amon-Ra, the later Egyptian sun god, and for other gods of Egypt.

The ruling group of Kush became more and more like the Egyptians. The common people—the farmers, craftworkers, and laborers—had little contact with Egyptian customs and ideas. They continued to keep alive the customs, language, and religion of Kush.

Religion of the people. In many ways the religion of Kush was like that of the Egyptians. The people of Kush believed in an afterlife. Many of the kings of Kush were buried in stone pyramids like Egyptian pharaohs. Buried with the kings of Kush were their belongings because it was believed that the dead king would

need what he had owned in this life. The early people of Kush also believed in many gods and goddesses. They believed such gods held power over rain, the yearly flood of the Nile, and the abundance of wildlife.

As contact with Egypt increased after 1500 B.C., the gods of Kush were often replaced by Egyptian gods—at least among the people of the ruling class. Many Kushite burial sites contained statues, drawings, or carvings of such Egyptian gods as Osiris and Amon-Ra.

Hieroglyphics and art. The people of Kush used Egyptian hieroglyphics to record the great deeds of their kings. They also developed symbols from the hieroglyphics to write their own language. In

The Kushites developed their own hieroglyphic writing about 300 B.C.

their system of writing, these symbols stood for sounds.

Some monuments in Kush have writing in both Egyptian hieroglyphics and Kushite symbols. Because archaeologists know the names of the kings on the monuments, they have been able to learn which sounds were made by which symbols. Archaeologists have not, however, been able to understand the meanings of the words. They can pronounce them, but they cannot translate the language.

The art of Kush also followed the Egyptian style, but a Kushite style gradually developed. Kushite art tended to show people as they really looked. The Egyptians had usually painted people—especially members of the ruling family—as slender and good-looking.

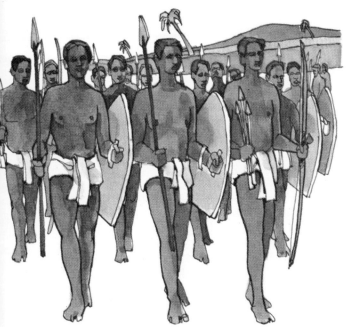

These Kushite warriors served in the Egyptian army.

The Conquered Conquer

For hundreds of years, Egypt dominated Kush completely. Look at the time line on pages 108–109 for East Africa. When did Kush become independent of Egypt? At this time the Egyptian Empire was beginning to decline. A number of weak Egyptian rulers lost distant lands of the empire. Eventually, outsiders took over Egypt itself.

The Egyptians often paid soldiers from Kush and Libya to serve in the Egyptian army. About 750 B.C. the Libyan warriors seized most of Egypt. Somewhat later, Piye (pi′yə), the king of Kush, claimed the Egyptian Empire for himself. He brought together a large army and pushed northward against the Libyans in Egypt. As Kushite warriors advanced down the Nile, they attacked Libyan forces.

The fighting lasted for almost twenty-five years. When it ended, the armies of Kush held the entire Nile Valley from the Mediterranean Sea to the area south of the Sixth Cataract. Rule by Kush lasted only about seventy years. In 656 B.C. Assyrian warriors from Mesopotamia swept into the Nile Valley. The Assyrian army fought fiercely. Kushite and Egyptian forces could not stop them. As a result, Kushite control of Egypt ended, and a new period in the history of Kushite civilization began.

The Flourishing of Kushite Civilization

Safe behind the cataracts of the Nile River and the hot sands of the Sahara, the civilization of Kush continued to thrive. A number of powerful empires took control of Egypt, but none of them was able to win control of Kush. Twice during the history of Kush, its kings moved their capital farther south to protect it from invaders from the north. After Kerma had declined, Napata became the second capital. Later the capital city was moved still farther south to Meroë.

The capital city. Kush was the crossroads of African trade and Meroë was at its center. This capital city became very important for two reasons. First, it was a center of ironworking south of the Sahara. Second, it was here that the civilization of Kush reached its peak. In this period the Kushites developed their writing system and their own style of art.

The kings of Kush kept many Egyptian beliefs and customs that were not preserved in Egypt. They continued to worship the Egyptian god Amon-Ra. They maintained the old temples and built new ones. The kings of Kush also kept the strong form of government they had learned from the pharaohs.

The royal family. The kings of Kush also kept alive the **traditions**, or customs and beliefs, of ancient Kush. They continued to worship their own gods. Another of their traditions involved the **succession** of the king, or who became the new king after the old king died. In Kush kingship passed from older brother to younger brother. However, to the people of Kush *brother* meant any male in the queen mother's family. If a king had no direct male relatives, such as a son or a younger brother, kingship was then

Rule by kings ended in the later days of Kush, when queens held power.

passed to another male in the queen mother's family. Because of this custom, the queen mother had great power as long as she lived. In general, only sons of the royal family could become leaders of the kingdom. This tradition faded with time. In the later days of Kush, some queens ruled outright.

Checking Up
1. Who drove the Kushite soldiers from Egypt?
2. What was the difference between the hieroglyphics of Egypt and the symbols of Kush?
3. For what two reasons did Meroë become important?
4. What answers would you give to the key questions at the beginning of this chapter?
5. *Explain the following statement: Although Kush conquered Egypt, Egypt had permanently conquered Kush.*

177

The Final Days of Kush

As You Read

1. Think about these words.
   ore   protectorate   culture   smelt   slag
2. Look for answers to these key questions.
   a. How did Kush get along with the Roman Empire?
   b. Why did Kush decline as a kingdom?
   c. What contributions did Kush make to the civilizations of Africa?

After the armies of Kush were driven from Egypt by the Assyrians, the once-great empire of the pharoahs fell, in turn, to other armies, including those of Persia and Alexander the Great. Nevertheless, trade between Kush and Egypt went on. Kush continued to prosper.

Sometime after 500 B.C., Meroë became a major center of ironworking south of the Sahara. Kushite workers took iron **ore**, or the rock containing iron metal, from the mines near Meroë. Other workers then removed the iron from the ore and made weapons and tools. In addition to wealth from farming and trade, ironworking brought even more riches to the kingdom.

The Romans Come to Kush

It was probably the great wealth of Kush that first attracted the attention of the Romans about 30 B.C. Roman soldiers in Egypt first encountered Kushite warriors near Philae (fī′lē). Philae was a city on an island in the Nile, just north of the First Cataract. Find Philae on the map on page 169. Philae was on the southern border of Egypt. The Romans demanded that Kush become a **protectorate**. This meant that Rome would defend Kush and Kush would pay a tribute.

Not long after this meeting, the Roman armies were sent eastward to Arabia. The Kushite warriors used this

This temple on the island of Philae was part of the Roman outpost.

This column is from the ruins of Aksum, the main trade rival of Kush.

chance to attack Philae. They even carried off a large bronze statue of Augustus, the Roman emperor. Archaeologists recently found the head of this statue in the ruins of Meroë.

When the Roman army returned from Arabia, it was swift to counterattack. The Romans invaded Kush. Roman legions stormed Kushite forts and captured the old capital of Napata. They burned and looted the city.

The Roman army was far stronger than the forces of Kush. Rome soon controlled the rich African kingdom. Even Rome, however, understood it was better to trade with Kush than to crush it. Once again, because of trade, Kush and its people prospered.

New threats to the kingdom. About the second century A.D., people began using camels in the Sahara. For trading people like the Kushites, the camel was a better means of bringing goods across the desert.

For nomadic desert tribes, however, the camel meant a means of increasing power. Until then, the nomads had been weak. They traveled with their herds from one watering spot to another. Now they became powerful warriors. Riding camels, the nomads raided farming villages. With the camel, the desert raiders could also ride great distances over the desert to attack caravans and trading posts. At the same time, a new power was growing near the Red Sea.

End of a Kingdom

The year was A.D. 325—about 3,000 years after Kushite civilization began. Neighbors of Kush—the people of Aksum, who lived near the Red Sea—had become powerful. Find Aksum on the map on page 169. For years soldiers of Aksum blocked overland trade routes to Kush. Over many years, Aksumite traders took over almost all the trade that had once passed through Kush.

The people of Meroë and Napata fought back. They sent out raiding parties to attack Aksumite camps and caravans. However, Kushite warriors were no match for the armies of King Ezana, the king of Aksum.

Aksumite soldiers burned the cities of Kush. They tore down sacred temples. They robbed Kush of its grain, gold, and other valuables. Kushite civilization was destroyed. Kush had survived other attacks in the past. Never before, however, had Meroë and the area near it been

179

taken over by outsiders. The attacks of the desert nomads, the rise of Aksum, and the cutoff of trade were too much for the old kingdom to bear.

Kush never recovered. Its people, their language, and their civilization were no longer important in the Nile Valley. Other groups speaking other languages took their place. Today only the ruins of once-great Kushite cities, temples, and pyramids remain.

Contributions to African Civilization

No one knows what happened to the people of Kush after the Aksumite invasion. Kushite **culture**—the skills and customs of its people—continued to live. When the first European explorers and traders came to Africa, they found that the Africans knew how to make iron from iron ore. Europeans also discovered other African kingdoms that Kushite civilization had probably influenced. These kingdoms had strong kings like the kings of Kush. Their governments were also well organized.

Ironworking, however, was probably the greatest achievement of Kushite civilization. Sometime after 500 B.C., craftworkers in Kush began to **smelt**, or separate, iron from iron ore by heating the ore in a fire. They probably learned this skill from the Egyptians. Archaeologists have discovered a complete smelter at Meroë. They have also found large **slag** heaps there. Slag is the waste that is left over after the iron has been taken out of the ore. The great size of the slag heaps shows that Meroë was a major center of ironworking south of the Sahara.

Careers

Ironworkers

In ancient times people smelted iron in a simple way. They placed iron ore in a hot fire, where it became soft. Impurities, or the other materials in the ore besides the iron, were carried off as gas or were pounded out in the form of slag. The iron was heated over and over to remove the impurities.

The workers then hammered the soft iron into the shape of the tool or weapon they were making. The fire never grew hot enough to melt the ore. The iron produced in this way is known as wrought iron, or iron that is hammered into shape.

Today iron is still important. Its major use is to produce two other forms of the metal, cast iron and steel. Workers use

Blast furnace workers use a computer to oversee operations.

blast furnaces, or ovens through which blasts of air help increase the heat of the fire. The iron is melted and then cast or set in a mold. Workers also know better ways of removing the impurities. They can produce steel, a purer and stronger form of the metal than cast iron.

Kushite ironworkers heated the fire with a bellows. They pounded the iron into shape on an anvil, using a hammer and tongs.

Most of the iron was used to make weapons and small tools. Because of the strength of iron weapons, the people of Kush had a great advantage over other African groups for many years. They tried to keep the art of ironworking a secret. In time, however, the skill probably spread from Kush throughout central Africa and helped other African kingdoms become powerful.

Checking Up

1. Why did the Romans become interested in Kush? Why did they decide not to crush Kush?

2. How did the nomads of the Sahara increase their power about the second century A.D.?

3. Why did the people of Kush try to keep ironworking a secret?

4. What answers would you give to the key questions at the beginning of this chapter?

5. *How might Kush have influenced other African kingdoms?*

Unit 6 Summary

- Kush was a powerful African kingdom along the Nile south of Egypt.
- Farming and trade were the foundations of Kushite wealth and power.
- Kush was a major center of ironworking in Africa south of the Sahara.
- Natural barriers such as the Sahara, the marshlands to the south, and the cataracts of the Nile protected Kush from invaders.
- The location of Kush helped it become a trade center.
- Because Kush was a rich trade center, Egypt conquered it.
- Kush was strongly influenced by Egyptian civilization.
- Kush ruled Egypt for a short time.
- Kush blended Egyptian and local African traditions.
- Kush had a well-organized government, its own system of writing, and its own style of art.
- Kush declined because of the attacks of desert nomads and the loss of trade to Aksum.

Maps and Diagrams Tell a Story of Landforms

As you read, think about these words.

landform   plain   mountain   rift valley
local relief   plateau   continental drift

Africa is the world's second largest continent. Only Asia is larger. Africa features a range of landscapes that include vast plains, high plateaus, rolling hills, and towering snow-covered mountains. These landscapes reflect **landforms**, or shapes on our earth's surface.

The Landforms of Earth

Movement of the earth's crust and the forces of weather and erosion have been shaping the face of the earth for millions of years. Together, these forces have created four basic landforms found on earth today. These landforms are plains, plateaus, mountains, and hills.

Elevation and local relief. Geographers classify these four landforms by elevation and **local relief**. Elevation is the height of the land above sea level. Local relief is the difference, or change, in elevation from one place to another in the same area.

The diagram below illustrates the four basic landforms. **Plains** are almost flat or gently rolling areas. They have low elevation and low local relief. **Plateaus**, like plains, are generally flat but they are usually higher than nearby areas. Local relief can be great if rivers have carved deep valleys in a plateau area. **Mountains** have both high elevation and high local relief. As you can see on the diagram, they have the highest elevation, and the local relief can rise or fall sharply within a small area. Hills are often worn-

Elevation and Relief of Landforms

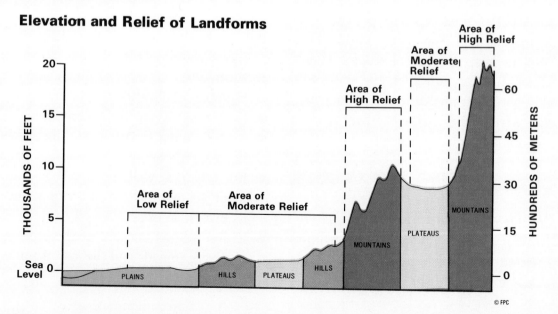

182

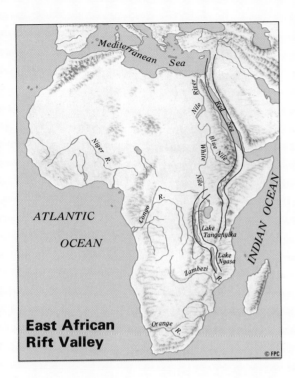

East African Rift Valley

with the same areas on the landform map. How are these maps the same? How are they different? The landform map shows the basic landforms. The physical map reflects more accurately how the land looks today. For example, Africa's great plateau is no longer flat. It has been carved by winds and rivers. Other forces may be at work too.

Continental drift. Many scientists think that our continents are actually moving and have been for millions of years. This idea is called **continental drift**. Such movements could explain changes in the earth's surface. For example, in southeastern Africa long, deep trenches called **rift valleys** split the vast plateau. These valleys are as wide as 30 miles (36 km). Some scientists think these changes could have been caused by the forces of continental drift. Look at the pattern of rifts on the map on this page. The great lakes in southeastern Africa, with the exception of Lake Victoria, lie in rift valleys. The lakes make travel easy along a north-south route. The steep walls of the rift valleys, however, make east-west travel difficult.

down mountains, eroded by wind and water. The shape of hills is often more gently sloping than that of mountains. The local relief is also less than that in mountain areas.

Landforms of Africa

As you learned in Unit 4, the color and shading on physical maps reflect the landforms of our earth. Turn to the Atlas map on pages 12–13 and find Africa. Which areas have the highest elevation? Which areas have the lowest? You can tell many things about Africa from studying this map. However, it doesn't tell you everything about landforms.

Look now at the landform map in the Atlas on pages 14–15. What landform covers the greatest area of Africa? the least? Compare Africa's areas of high and low elevation on the physical map

Checking Up

1. What forces have shaped the face of the earth?
2. How do geographers classify the four landforms?
3. How does the idea of continental drift explain the presence of the rift valleys in southeastern Africa?

Unit 6 Review Workshop

What Have You Learned?

1. What natural barriers protected Kush from invaders?
2. What crops and animals were raised by the people of Kush?
3. What trade routes cut through the land of Kush?
4. What goods did Kush trade?
5. Who was the chief trading partner of Kush?
6. In what ways did Egypt influence Kushite civilization?
7. What type of writing system did the people of Kush develop?
8. What style of art did the people of Kush have?
9. Why was Kush called the crossroads of Africa?
10. Where was the center of ironworking in Kush?
11. What did Kush contribute to the civilization of Africa?

Use Your Reading Skills

When you read, you find details that support or explain general statements. Find the details needed for the following statements. Choose your answers from the list of words below.

Egypt	oases
elephant ivory	ostrich feathers
India	rivers
Kerma	sakia
leopard skins	selucka
Meroë	shadoof
Napata	tropical Africa

1. The people of Kush farmed by using irrigation and wadis. The three devices they used were the _____, _____, and _____.
2. Kushite traders often had to use overland routes. These routes usually followed _____, or crossed the desert where there were _____.
3. The people of Kush carried on trade with several places. Three of these places were _____, _____, and _____.
4. Traders brought goods to Kush from tropical lands farther south. Three of the items they sought were _____, _____, and _____.
5. For safety, the rulers of Kush moved their capital city up the Nile. Their three capital cities were _____, _____, and _____.

Use Your Map Skills

Turn to the map of overland African trade routes on page 169. Find the cities of Kerma, Napata, and Meroë. Notice how these are connected by overland trade routes. On a separate piece of paper, answer these questions.

1. How did traders travel from Meroë to the Red Sea? What two types of routes did they take?
2. What kind of route connected Meroë to Napata? What was its name?
3. What is the distance from Meroë to the Red Sea? to Napata? to the First Cataract?

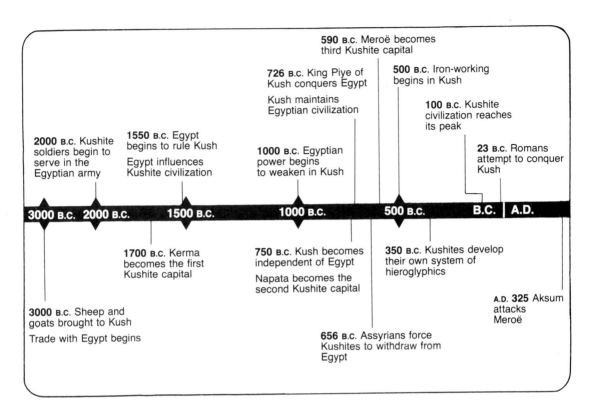

590 B.C. Meroë becomes third Kushite capital

726 B.C. King Piye of Kush conquers Egypt

Kush maintains Egyptian civilization

500 B.C. Iron-working begins in Kush

100 B.C. Kushite civilization reaches its peak

2000 B.C. Kushite soldiers begin to serve in the Egyptian army

1550 B.C. Egypt begins to rule Kush

Egypt influences Kushite civilization

1000 B.C. Egyptian power begins to weaken in Kush

23 B.C. Romans attempt to conquer Kush

3000 B.C. 2000 B.C.   1500 B.C.   1000 B.C.   500 B.C.   B.C. | A.D.

1700 B.C. Kerma becomes the first Kushite capital

750 B.C. Kush becomes independent of Egypt

Napata becomes the second Kushite capital

350 B.C. Kushites develop their own system of hieroglyphics

A.D. 325 Aksum attacks Meroë

3000 B.C. Sheep and goats brought to Kush

Trade with Egypt begins

656 B.C. Assyrians force Kushites to withdraw from Egypt

Use Your Time Skills

Look at the time line above. Use it to find the answers to the following six questions.

1. Did Kerma become the capital of Kush before or after the period of Egyptian rule?
2. Did ironworking in Kush start before or after the people of Kush conquered Egypt?
3. Was Napata the capital of Kush before or after Meroë?
4. Did Kushite civilization reach its peak under Napata or Meroë?
5. Did the Romans invade Kush before or after Meroë had become the capital city?
6. Did Aksum attack Meroë before the Romans invaded Kush?

Learn by Doing

Imagine you were a trader from Kush who traveled by caravan from the Red Sea to Meroë in 300 B.C. Use the information in this chapter as well as its maps, pictures, and time line. Then write an imaginative diary of your experiences and travels. For example, you could describe the trip a caravan made from the Red Sea to Meroë.

Read to Learn More

Find the topics listed below in the card catalog of your library. Read all or part of a book listed under one of the topics. Share what you learn with your classmates.

SUDAN   AKSUM (AXUM)
SAHARA   NUBIA

Unit 7

Early Civilization in China

A Chinese emperor had the Great Wall built to protect China against the invasions of nomads from the north.

Maps Tell a Story of China

As you read, think about these words.
revolution   axis

The People's Republic of China is almost exactly the same size as the United States. Although China is half a world away, it has other physical similarities with our country.

The Land and the Climate

Turn to the world physical map on pages 12–13 in the Atlas. Compare the physical features of the United States and China. The eastern and southern coasts are bordered by large bodies of water. In both countries the lowlands lie in the eastern areas. Great highland areas rise in the west. Both countries are also in the middle latitudes.

Latitude regions. Look at the globes below. Geographers divide the earth into these three temperature regions. In the high latitudes, or polar regions, temperatures are always cold. The sun is never overhead. In the low latitudes, or tropical regions, temperatures are warm. The sun is almost directly overhead all year. In the middle latitudes temperatures vary from season to season. In the middle latitudes, areas closer to the polar regions have cooler winter temperatures. Areas closer to the tropical region have warmer winter temperatures.

Temperatures fall into these patterns because of the way the sun shines on the earth. As the earth makes its yearly **revolution**, or trip around the sun, the direct rays of the sun fall on the region between the two tropic lines. Look at the diagram on page 189. The earth is always tilted on its **axis**, the imaginary line connecting the North and South poles. This tilt causes the seasonal changes in some regions. It also causes differences in hours of daylight as seasons change.

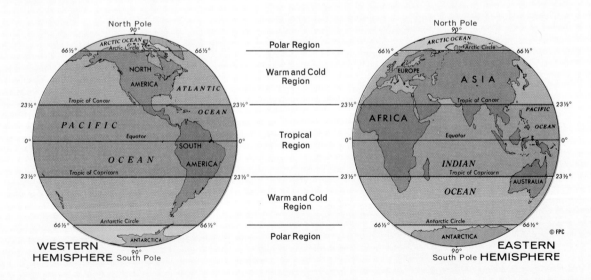

188

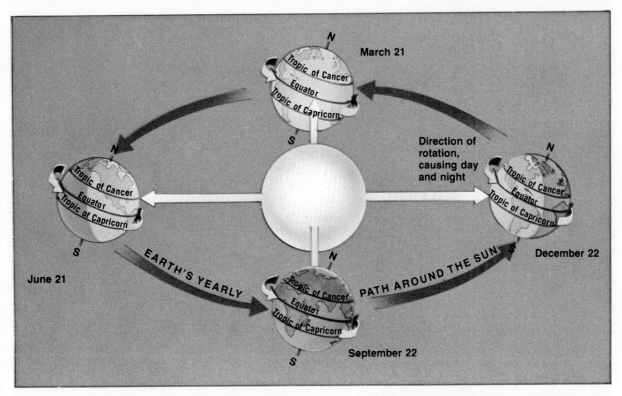

March 21

Direction of
rotation,
causing day
and night

December 22

June 21

EARTH'S YEARLY PATH AROUND THE SUN

September 22

Landforms and climate. Look at China on the landform map on pages 14–15 in the Atlas. What are the major landforms in Western China? The mountains and plateaus have such great elevation that they have a special climate. Turn to the climate map on pages 16–17. What kind of climate do you find in these mountain and plateau areas?

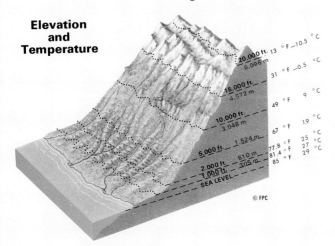

Elevation and Temperature

20,000 ft.
6,096 m — 13 °F — 10.5 °C

31 °F — 0.5 °C

15,000 ft.
4,572 m — 9 °C

49 °F

10,000 ft.
3,048 m — 1.9 °C

67 °F

5,000 ft. — 1,524 m — 25 °C

77.8 °F — 27 °C

2,000 ft. — 610 m — 81.4 °F — 29 °C

1,000 ft. — 305 m — 85 °F

SEA LEVEL

© FPC

By looking at the map of China on page 190, you can see that the mountains are steep and rugged. What is the name of the mountain range along China's southwestern border? The Himalayas are the highest mountains in the world. Temperatures are quite cool. With each 1,000 feet (300 m) increase in elevation, the temperature drops 3.6 °F (2 °C).

The diagram on this page shows how temperatures change if it is 85 °F (29 °C) at sea level. What is the temperature at 10,000 feet? at 20,000 feet? Mount Everest, the tallest mountain in the world, is in the Himalayas just south of China's border. Find Mount Everest on the map. What is its elevation? About what would the temperature be there?

These highland areas are little used by people. They are too steep or too cold or both. Turn again to the climate map on

189

pages 16–17. What climate region lies just north of the highland area? What climate regions does eastern China have?

People and the Land

Landforms and climates greatly influence how people can use the land. The maps on these pages will help explain land use patterns that have existed in China for centuries.

Land use. Look at the land use map on this page. How would you explain the limited land use in western China? What is the major land use in eastern China? How do the physical map and the precipitation map help explain this pattern?

People have farmed in China for thousands of years. Like other places you have read about, farming began in river valleys. China's three main rivers flow from their sources in the western high-

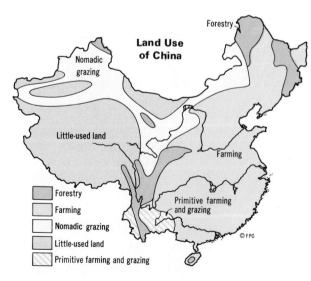

Land Use of China

Forestry

Nomadic grazing

Little-used land

Farming

Primitive farming and grazing

Legend:
- Forestry
- Farming
- Nomadic grazing
- Little-used land
- Primitive farming and grazing

© FPC

190

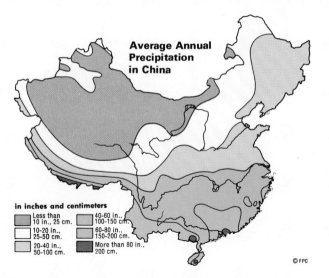

Average Annual Precipitation in China

in inches and centimeters

- Less than 10 in., 25 cm.
- 10-20 in., 25-50 cm.
- 20-40 in., 50-100 cm.
- 40-60 in., 100-150 cm.
- 60-80 in., 150-200 cm.
- More than 80 in., 200 cm.

©FPC

Four Agricultural Regions of China

Dry China

Wheat China

High China

Rice China

©FPC

lands to the eastern shore. What are these three rivers? Follow the course of each one.

The map of four agricultural regions in China quickly points out two basic crops raised. What are they? Southeastern China is warm and wet enough that farmers in some areas can produce two crops of rice every year. Between plantings they can also grow a wide variety of vegetables. Many farmers in this area also grow tea. As you can see on the map at the top of page 190, this area is quite hilly. In order to create level land for farming, people have carved terraces or steps into the slopes. North of the Yangtze, both rice and wheat are grown. As precipitation and temperatures drop farther to the north, wheat and other crops such as barley, millet, soybeans, vegetables, tobacco, and cotton can be grown.

Population. Although China is almost the same size as the United States, about one billion people live there. This is over one fifth of all the world's people. Using

what you have learned about landforms, climate, and land use, in which areas would you expect to find most of the people? Look at the population map on pages 22–23 to see if you were right. Find the cities of Canton and Shanghai. They are at the mouths of which rivers? Find Peking. It is the capital city. Like the United States, the population of China is concentrated in the eastern areas. However, the number of people per square mile (sq. km) is much greater in China. Using the population map, compare China's population with other areas around the world.

Checking Up

1. Why does the temperature of a region depend on its latitude and elevation?
2. What are the similarities in geography between China and our country?
3. What are the four agricultural regions of China?
4. What is China's population?

The Chinese Civilization Begins

As You Read

1. Think about these words.
   dike   bamboo
2. Look for answers to these key questions.
   a. What barriers kept China isolated from other countries?
   b. Why was the valley of the Hwang Ho good for farming?
   c. How did the early people of China control the Hwang Ho?
3. Use this reading skill.
   Sometimes you want to find answers to questions without reading every word. Skimming, or looking at something quickly, is one way to find such information. You are skimming when you look up a word in the dictionary or a telephone number in the directory. When you skim, keep in mind the question you want to answer. Look for the kind of answer that suits the question—a date, a number, or a name. Skim the material in this chapter to find the following: Yu the Great, "China's Sorrow," and the date the Chinese reached the Yangtze Kiang.

No one knows for sure how old Chinese civilization is. We do know that the Chinese became farmers about 4,000 years ago. No longer having to move from place to place for their food, these farmers were able to settle. Villages began to appear in the fertile river valleys.

The Chinese built a lasting civilization. It spread in many directions and had great influence in East Asia. It lasted for thousands of years.

The Land and the People

The official name of China today is the People's Republic of China. Most Chinese, however, call it by its old name—the Central Country, or Middle Kingdom. The Chinese have always thought their country was the cultural center of the world.

Look at the map on page 190. Notice that China is almost surrounded by natural barriers. What seas border China on the east and the southeast? what mountains on the west? what desert on the north? In the past, these barriers were very difficult to cross. For most of China's history, its only neighbors were hunters and nomadic herders. Because the ancient Chinese had little contact with other people, they believed their nation was the most civilized on earth.

The Cradle of Chinese Civilization

China's civilization, like those of Mesopotamia, Egypt, and India, developed along the banks of a river. This river was the Hwang Ho (hwäng hō), or Yellow River.

The Hwang Ho. Find the Hwang Ho on the map on page 190 and trace it from its source to its mouth.

The Hwang Ho is named for the yellow loess the river carries in its waters. As you may remember, loess is deposited by melting glaciers. The Hwang Ho flows through an immense loess plateau, which was formed of dust blown from the dry lands of Mongolia. As the river flows through this area, it picks up a tremendous quantity of the yellow loess. During floods the river deposits loess on the floodplains. Loess is quite fertile. Its texture is so fine that the first farmers did not even need plows. They could turn the soil with hoes.

The Hwang Ho is said to be the cradle of Chinese civilization. This is the area where the people first settled. For many thousands of years, China was a land where people moved from place to place. Some groups moved as they searched for seeds and fruits of wild plants. Others hunted in forests and on grassy plains for wild animals. Gradually the people learned how to grow millet and other grains. They began to keep animals for food instead of hunting wild ones. They were China's first farmers.

Because the farmers no longer traveled from place to place for their food, they were able to settle in groups. Even-

Ancient Chinese peasants had many agricultural chores.

tually, these settlements became villages. The people built homes from sun-dried mud and covered them with roofs of bundled grasses. Next to their homes, they dug storage pits to hold food.

The Legend of Yu the Great. The first villages the people of China settled were near the Hwang Ho. The ancient Chinese believed the river was controlled by a spirit called the Dragon King. Some years the Dragon King was in a good mood. He kept the Hwang Ho filled with water, which the farmers used to irrigate their fields. However, when the Dragon King was in a bad mood, he blew the rain clouds away.

One year the Dragon King got very angry indeed. He swished his tail back and forth so hard that the Hwang Ho flooded most of the land. Towns and villages and people were swept away. When the waters finally went down, the entire valley was filled with yellow mud where only water birds could live.

193

The Chinese built dikes to keep the Hwang Ho from flooding their land.

However, it is true that the Chinese have always had difficulty controlling the Hwang Ho. As a result, the river has been called "China's Sorrow."

For many thousands of years, the Hwang Ho flowed wherever it wished. It cut channels where the ground was lowest. As the loess carried by the river built up the land, the river found a lower place and cut a new channel. Over the years the river changed its course many times.

The early Chinese found it difficult to farm in a valley where the river kept changing its course. So on each side of the Hwang Ho they built a wall of earth, called a **dike**. The dikes kept the river within its banks. The farmers could again grow crops.

The dikes brought a bad result as well as a good one. Before the dikes were built, the floodwaters spread out and deposited the loess over a broad area. However, after the dikes were built, the mud the river carried quickly filled the river bed. The bed of the river kept rising until the river could no longer stay between the dikes. For hundreds of years, the farmers struggled to build higher and higher dikes to contain the ever-rising river. Today the bed of the Hwang Ho is 10 to 40 feet (3–12 m) higher than the land beyond the dikes!

The rise of Chinese civilization. The need to control the Hwang Ho explains why an engineer like Yu is considered a great Chinese hero. It also helps explain how the Chinese civilization probably started. Building the dikes in the Hwang

The farmers could not plant and harvest their crops. So the emperor sent for a young engineer named Yu. He ordered Yu to survey the great river and to work out a plan for controlling it.

Yu worked for eighteen years on his task. Finally, the Hwang Ho flowed through a new channel, wider and deeper than the old one. Once again the farmers could work in their fields.

The emperor was so grateful to Yu that he asked him to rule China. That is how Yu the Great became the first emperor of the Hsia (shē′ä) dynasty. As in Egypt, a dynasty was a series of rulers from the same family.

Controlling the Hwang Ho. Neither historians nor archaeologists have found evidence that the Hsia dynasty actually existed. Only legends about it remain.

Ho Valley was a tremendous task. A few people working on their own could never have accomplished it. Leaders were needed to organize the people. The leaders, such as Yu, told people what to do and how best to do it. Organizing the people to work together became the job of the government.

From the valley of the Hwang Ho, the Chinese spread out to the east and south. By about the year 1000 B.C., they reached China's other great river valley, the valley of the Yangtze Kiang (yang′sē kē·ang′), or Yangtze River. Find the Yangtze on the map on page 190 and trace it from its source to its mouth.

Farming in China's River Valleys

Farming patterns today are much like those in ancient China. Look at the maps on page 191. What has been the main crop grown in the valley of the Yangtze? As you can see from the precipitation map, the Yangtze valley has much more rain than the Hwang Ho valley.

The valley of the Hwang Ho has sometimes been called "the Brown North."

You can see below why the Yangtze valley is called "the Green South."

That is because the land is brown and dusty during much of the year. It turns green only in late spring and summer, when crops are growing. Trees are scarce in the Brown North. Here people grow wheat and millet.

The valley of the Yangtze has sometimes been called "the Green South." Crops can grow there ten months out of the year. Willow and mulberry trees line the banks of rivers. **Bamboo** covers the hillsides. Bamboo is a treelike grass that grows as high as 40 feet (12 m). The Chinese have always used bamboo to make many things, including houses, furniture, chopsticks for eating, fishing poles, and baskets.

Checking Up

1. Why did the people of China call their country the Central Country?
2. How did building dikes along the Hwang Ho help control the flooding? How did it create a problem?
3. What legend do the Chinese have to explain the beginning of their earliest dynasty?
4. Why is the Hwang Ho Valley also known as the "Brown North"? Why is the Yangtze Valley also known as the "Green South"?
5. What answers would you give to the key questions at the beginning of this chapter?
6. *Why do you think that early civilizations tended to develop in river valley locations?*

195

Government and Thought in Early China

As You Read

1. Think about these words.
   mandate   philosophy   ancestor
2. Look for answers to these key questions
   a. What was the Mandate of Heaven?
   b. Why were old people in Chinese families treated with such great respect?
   c. What were the teachings of Confucius?
3. Use this reading skill.
   In some parts of this chapter, you will be asked to follow directions. Sometimes following directions means only that you have to turn to a certain page to look at a map, a time line, or a picture. Take the time to do this. Following such directions will increase your understanding of the chapter.

The civilization that developed in China lasted, in many ways unchanged, until the 20th century. According to legend, Chinese civilization began with the Yellow Emperor, who ruled for almost a hundred years. The legend says that he gave the Chinese silk, trade, writing, arithmetic, medicine, and government.

The Yellow Emperor was followed by other emperors, including Yu the Great. Look at the time line on this page. When did the Yellow Emperor and Yu the Great rule? The legend says Yu the Great started the dynasties in China. The oldest son of an emperor always became emperor when his father died.

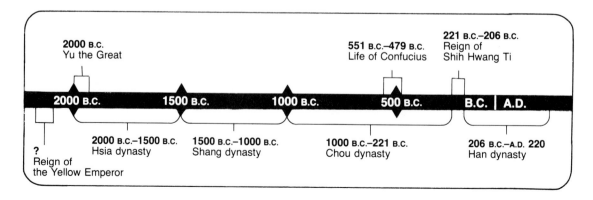

2000 B.C.
Yu the Great

551 B.C.–479 B.C.
Life of Confucius

221 B.C.–206 B.C.
Reign of
Shih Hwang Ti

2000 B.C.   1500 B.C.   1000 B.C.   500 B.C.   B.C. | A.D.

?
Reign of
the Yellow Emperor

2000 B.C.–1500 B.C.
Hsia dynasty

1500 B.C.–1000 B.C.
Shang dynasty

1000 B.C.–221 B.C.
Chou dynasty

206 B.C.–A.D. 220
Han dynasty

This painting shows a victorious new emperor, who has received "the Mandate of Heaven," entering the gates of the capital.

The first dynasty for which historians have found evidence other than legend is the Shang dynasty. Find the Shang dynasty on the time line on page 196. The Shang was followed by the Chou (jō) dynasty, which ruled until 221 B.C.

The Mandate of Heaven

China under the Chou dynasty was centered on the valleys of the Hwang Ho and Yangtze River. It was a collection of small areas, or states, that spent much of their time fighting one another. The princes who headed these states were supposed to obey the Chou emperor. However, the emperor did not really have enough power to control them.

It was during the Chou dynasty that the Chinese developed one of their most important beliefs about government. This belief was called "the **Mandate** of Heaven." The word *mandate* means "order" or "command." From that time, the Chinese believed that the world was controlled by heaven. An emperor was known as the son of heaven. He needed heaven's permission in order to stay on the throne. To obtain it, he had to be honest, just, and kind. If he was not, heaven would no longer favor him. The people would then have the right to revolt and put a new emperor on the throne.

The Mandate of Heaven served several purposes. It helped later emperors gain the respect of the people so that they could establish peace and order. It encouraged the emperors to care for the people's well-being. It also explained why dynasties changed.

197

The Teachings of Confucius

It was also during the Chou dynasty that two important **philosophies**, or ways of thinking, developed in China. The philosophy that most influenced the Chinese way of life was developed by a man named Kung Fu-tzu, or Kung the Master. People who speak English call him Confucius (kən·fyo͞o′shəs).

Confucius was interested in the relationships among people, their families, and their government. He gave people a set of rules to live by. He taught that people would enjoy good fortune when they followed rules of good behavior. Rulers should be wise and honest in order to set good examples. Citizens should obey their rulers, just as children should obey their parents. If both the emperor and his subjects behaved the way they were supposed to, Confucius believed that the country would enjoy good fortune. The emperor would keep the Mandate of Heaven.

The importance of the family. Because of the teaching of Confucius, the family became important in the Chinese way of life. All the members of a family, including grandparents, aunts, uncles, and cousins, helped one another. Often they farmed land together and lived in the same household.

The Chinese believed that people became wiser as they grew older. Older people were treated with great respect. Children supported and cared for their parents.

The Chinese also worshipped their **ancestors**, or dead relatives. The Chinese believed that ancestors took an interest in their families even after they died. If ancestors were remembered, they would help their families. If they were forgotten they would harm their families.

Confucianism in state exams. Confucius taught that government officials should be well educated and honest. In order to find such people, the Chinese set up a system of exams based on Confucius's works. The sons of rich and poor alike could take these exams. Whoever passed became a government official.

Confucius wrote, "Making cloth is women's most important work."

The Taoist symbol shows seemingly opposite things in actual harmony.

People Who Made a Difference

Confucius

Confucius was born in 551 B.C. After working his way through school, he held several offices in the government of his state. Then he opened his own school. For about twenty-five years, he taught government and history to people from all over China.

While he was teaching, however, Confucius kept thinking about government. He did not like the fact that the Chinese were always fighting with one another. He believed that people could learn how to live together in peace.

Eventually, Confucius closed his school. He traveled around the country, explaining to the princes of the Chinese states how they could become better rulers. However, the princes paid no attention to Confucius. After thirteen years he returned to his home state and reopened his school. He died in 479 B.C. at the age of 73.

After Confucius's death, his ideas gradually became more and more popular. About 300 years later, Confucianism was made the official philosophy of China. It held this position for about 2,000 years.

The Teachings of Lao-tzu—Taoism

The second important philosophy developed in China during the Chou dynasty is Taoism (dou′iz′əm). The Chinese believe it was developed by a man named Lao-tzu (loud′zə′), or the Old Master.

Taoists believed it was important to live close to nature. There, alone, an individual could gain glimpses of the Tao, or the harmonious way in nature. Taoists thought all things in nature were closely related. Understanding nature would help a person understand life.

Taoism was for individuals only. Confucianism, on the other hand, helped people get along with one another in groups. Chinese people often followed both philosophies at the same time. These two philosophies took the place of religion for the Chinese. Confucianism gave them a code of conduct. Taoism gave them a respect for the harmony in nature.

Checking Up

1. Why did the Chinese worship their ancestors?
2. What did the Taoists believe about nature?
3. Why were the Chinese able to follow both Confucianism and Taoism at the same time?
4. What answers would you give to the key questions at the beginning of this chapter?
5. *What was China like during the Chou dynasty?*

199

The Ch'in Dynasty

As You Read

1. Think about these words.
   central government   dialect   canal
2. Look for answers to these key questions.
   a. What were the achievements of Shih Hwang Ti?
   b. How has the Chinese writing system helped unite China?
   c. Why did the Chinese dislike the rule of Shih Hwang Ti?

When the Chou dynasty ruled, China was not really a united country. As you learned in the last chapter, China was a group of small states that were ruled by princes. These princes, in turn, were supposed to obey the emperor of China, but they did not. The last years of the Chou dynasty are known as the period of the "warring states." Everyone seemed to be fighting all the time.

China Becomes United

Gradually, a state called Ch'in, the westernmost Chinese state, grew more and more powerful. It conquered other states, one after another. Finally, by 221 B.C., it controlled most of the central part of what is China today. Its prince became known as Shih Hwang Ti (shə hwäng dē). He united China. The name *China* comes from *Ch'in*.

Achievements of Shih Hwang Ti. Shih Hwang Ti gave China a **central government**, in which all officials were brought under the direct control of the emperor. He began by dividing China into forty provinces. Each province had three officials. They were chosen by the emperor for their ability rather than for their family background.

While organizing the government, Shih Hwang Ti realized that Chinese people in one area often did things differently from Chinese people in another area. For example, there was no common

Development of Chinese Writing

Meaning	Picture-Writing	Changes Through the Centuries	Present-Day Character
Light			明
Mountain			山
Horse			馬
Wagon			車

The picture symbols of the ancient Chinese became the characters used today.

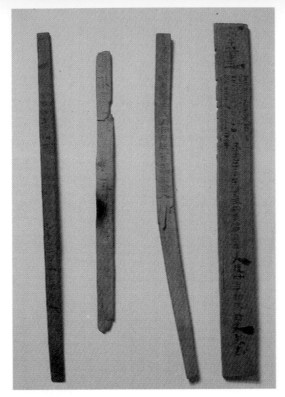

Before the Chinese invented paper, they wrote on tied sticks of bamboo.

writing system. Shih Hwang Ti ordered everyone to use the same system of writing. To make sure they did, he sent official word lists to all parts of China. These lists became the beginning of the Chinese dictionary.

A common writing system. Shih Hwang Ti's change had lasting importance. China was becoming a large country. As the Chinese settled in the southern part of the country, groups began speaking different **dialects**, or forms of the same language. After many centuries, people from the north of China could not understand people from the south of China.

Nevertheless, they could communicate by means of their common writing system. Chinese then, as now, was not written in letters that stand for sounds. It was written in characters, or symbols which represent things and ideas. From the time of Shih Hwang Ti, all Chinese have learned the same characters. In each province, however, people pronounced the characters according to their own dialect. Chinese who spoke different dialects could still communicate by means of the same characters they all used in writing.

Roads and canals. In addition to the common writing system, Shih Hwang Ti made other improvements. He had a system of roads built. The roads were lined with trees and were wide enough for fifty people to walk side by side. He also had people dig **canals**, or waterways. The canals were used for transportation and irrigation.

The Great Wall of China. Nomadic tribes to the north of China often attacked the Chinese. To protect China, Shih Hwang Ti carried out his most im-

Canals are still important in China. One canal connects the Hwang Ho and the Yangtze.

201

Workers struggled to build the Great Wall. It became the world's longest barricade.

portant building project, the Great Wall. Look at the photograph at the beginning of this unit on page 187. The Great Wall runs for 1,400 miles (2,250 km) along China's northern frontier. Legend says that the emperor himself marked out the line of the wall by riding his horse across the countryside. Architects followed behind, putting markers in the ground wherever the horse's hooves had left prints.

Parts of the Great Wall consisted of older walls that had been built by people of other states that Shih Hwang Ti had conquered. Some parts of the Great Wall were built to link these sections. All in all, the project took seven years to complete. One million people worked on the wall. Thousands of workers lost their lives from cold and exhaustion.

Look at the map on page 205 and find the Great Wall. Where is its easternmost point? Where is its westernmost point? Through what kind of land does it run?

The Great Wall kept the nomadic tribes out of China. Among these tribes were the Huns. Many historians believe the Great Wall was one reason for the Huns' eventually moving westward. The Huns were one of the barbarian groups who invaded the Roman Empire.

Burning of the books. Shih Hwang Ti liked uniformity. He wanted the Chinese to use the same characters in writing, to follow the same laws, and to pay the same taxes. He also wanted them to think alike. He thought people got too many ideas from books. People should not waste their time thinking.

Shih Hwang Ti ordered that all the books except those on war, farming, medicine, and fortune-telling be burned. Anyone who objected was either killed or sent away.

Shih Hwang Ti believed that the well-being of the state was more important than the well-being of the people. He felt that the people should work hard, pay taxes, and obey the emperor without question.

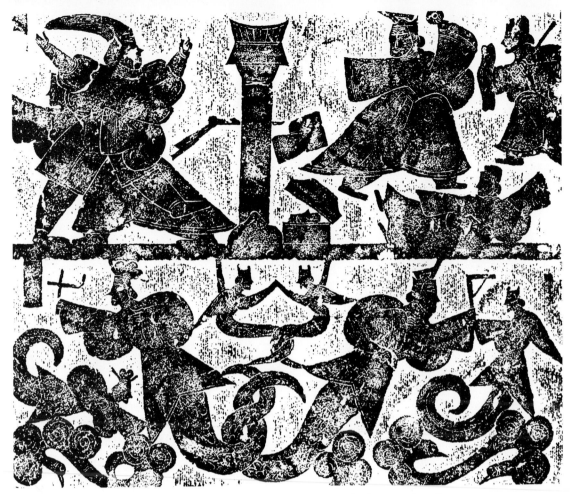

The Chinese disliked Shih Hwang Ti because he tried to make them all think the same way and he burned many books with ideas other than his own. Assassins even tried to kill the emperor.

A New Dynasty

Although Shih Hwang Ti strengthened China in many ways, most Chinese hated him. They did not like having to work on the Great Wall. They did not like paying heavy taxes on such everyday items as salt and iron. They also did not believe that everyone should think the same way. Four years after Shih Hwang Ti died, a peasant named Liu Pang (lē·ü päng), led a revolt against the Ch'in dynasty and set up a new dynasty, the Han. The Mandate of Heaven no longer rested with the sons of Shih Hwang Ti.

Checking Up

1. How did China get its name?
2. Why was the Great Wall of China built?
3. Why did Shih Hwang Ti order the burning of the books?
4. What answers would you give to the key questions at the beginning of this chapter?
5. *Do you think the Mandate of Heaven should have passed from the Ch'in dynasty to the Han dynasty? Why or why not?*

The Mighty Han

As You Read

1. Think about these words.
   civil service   import
   export   technology
2. Look for answers to these key questions.
   a. What were the accomplishments of the Chinese under the Han dynasty?
   b. How did contact with central Asia and India affect Chinese civilization?
   c. What were the practical inventions of the Chinese?

The Han emperors accomplished much in the 400 years that they ruled China. The Han dynasty accomplished so much that the Chinese proudly called themselves "people of Han."

This bronze statue may be one of the horses Chang Ch'ien found to the west of China.

The Han Dynasty

The Han dynasty set up the **civil service** system, under which Chinese government officials took exams to achieve their rank. The Han made the teachings of Confucius the law of the land. The system of exams for choosing people to run the government lasted until 1911, when the last emperor was overthrown. It was used in China for centuries before it was adopted in European countries and the United States.

The Han extended China's boundaries to the east and to the far south. To the west, they sent explorers, soldiers, and traders. Look at the time line on page 108. In what century did this early Chinese empire come to an end?

The travels of Chang Ch'ien. In spite of the Great Wall, China was still troubled by the Huns. The nomadic tribes were constantly trying to break through and raid China's rich farmlands. So a

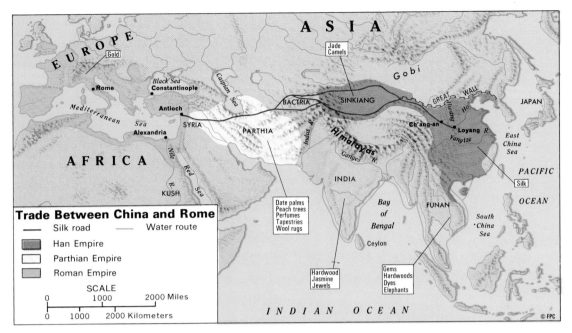

Caravans crossed 5,000 miles (8,000 km) along the Silk Road. The Parthians, who ruled Persia, grew wealthy from duties on the silk.

Han emperor sent an officer named Chang Ch'ien (cháng chē'en') on a journey to find other nomads who might help China fight the Huns. The officer traveled west 2,500 miles (4,000 km).

Although Chang Ch'ien was unsuccessful in finding allies for China, he brought back valuable information. He told the emperor where to find strong, swift horses that could outrun the ponies of the Huns. He brought back new plants such as grapes and alfalfa. He also told the emperor about the wealth that might be gained through trade with India, Parthia, and the Roman Empire.

The Silk Road. Ch'ien's journeys established contact with central Asia. Soon trade began over a caravan route that became known as the Silk Road. Look at the map above and trace the Silk Road.

Chinese workers picked mulberry leaves to feed silkworms.

The Chinese carved these giant Buddhist statues in the cliffs above the Hwang Ho.

About how many miles long was it? Through what countries did it run? Where was the point farthest west?

The camel caravans that plodded westward from China carried mostly silk for trading. Silk making was an ancient Chinese art that had been kept secret for over a thousand years. In exchange for silk, the Romans sent the Chinese gold. What other goods were traded?

Buddhism comes to China. The Chinese were also interested in trade with India. They developed several roads between the two countries and also set up a sea route. Find India on the map on page 205. Silk was **exported**, or sent out for sale, to India. Jewels, jasmine, and beautiful hardwoods were **imported**. They were bought in India to send back to China.

The most important import from India, however, was not a product but a religion. Traders brought Buddhism to China about the middle of the Han dy-

nasty. Its influence gradually spread, and Buddhism became one of China's three main systems of belief, along with Confucianism and Taoism.

Buddhism had a great influence on Chinese art. Sculptors carved statues of Buddhas right in the cliffs along the trade routes. Some cave shrines contained hundreds of these statues of Buddha and his helpers.

Other Accomplishments of the Early Chinese

The Chinese made great contributions to the practical ways in which science can help people. As you have learned, they were outstanding engineers and builders. During and following the Han dynasty they also invented many practical things. Until about 1400, Chinese **technology**, or the tools and methods the Chinese used, was more advanced than that of any country in the world.

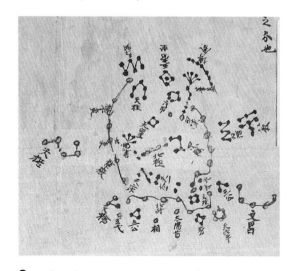

Court astronomers mapped constellations. Find the Big Dipper on this sky map.

Then and Now

Astronomers

Like other ancient peoples, the Chinese studied the stars to predict the future. They believed that knowing about the stars and the planets meant having power over people and nature. Only members of the emperor's court were allowed to do this kind of study.

Astronomers studied the stars and planets. They mapped many constellations, or groups of stars. They even searched for dragons in the patterns of the constellations. They recorded the paths of the planets and were able to predict eclipses. They observed sunspots, comets such as the one now called Haley's comet, and the appearance of supernovas, or new stars that suddenly exploded in the sky. They kept records of what they saw. They knew that it took the earth 365 1/4 days to revolve around the sun.

Chinese astronomers used an instrument that was a sphere containing hoops. The hoops stood for imaginary circles that divided up the sky. By using this tool, Chinese astronomers could find out many things about the stars and planets.

The Chinese built this astronomical clock tower to keep accurate time.

Today astronomers still study the stars and planets. They use high powered telescopes as well as many other advanced techniques. They also check the records of the ancient Chinese astronomers to find out where the stars were centuries ago.

Paper. Paper was first invented in China during the Han dynasty. Earlier the Chinese wrote on either bamboo or silk. However, bamboo books were very bulky and silk books were very expensive. An official named Ts'ai Lun ((t)sī lōōn) invented a writing material that would be easy to hold and less costly. He mashed bits of tree bark, hemp, rags, and a fishnet together. Then he squeezed out the water and hung up the sheets of paper to dry.

Medicine. The Chinese believed the body was sacred and should not be cut. As a result, surgery, or the treatment of injuries through operations, was almost unknown in China. The Chinese found other ways to cure sickness and pain.

Perhaps the most successful way was acupuncture. Acupuncture is a method of puncturing certain points of the body with special kinds of needles. The Chinese believed there were 365 points, each of which influenced a particular

The Chinese invented printing centuries before the Europeans. They used both block print and movable type.

part of the body. The needles might be pushed in a little way or a long way. Sometimes the needles were left in for a few hours or for as long as a week.

Chinese doctors, like ancient Greek doctors, thought that sickness meant that the body was out of balance. To get the body back in balance, they used medicines made from plants. Many of the plants that the Chinese used did help people get better. Doctors today who read the ancient Chinese writings about medicines have discovered that the Chinese used many of the same medicines that doctors still use.

The harness. The Chinese developed several things that help make farming easier and more productive. Perhaps the most important was a new kind of harness for horses.

Before the harness, farmers used only oxen to pull plows and other heavy loads. They could not use horses because the neck collar they used strangled the horse. The Chinese invented a harness that enabled a horse to pull a plow. Since horses move much faster than oxen, the new harness meant that farmers could plow more land in the same amount of time.

Nomads who lived along the Silk Road learned the use of the new harness from the Chinese. They carried the knowledge to Europe.

The compass. The Chinese first made compasses during the Han dynasty. They put some lodestone, a magnetic rock, in a

208

piece of wood and floated the wood in water. The wood pointed north.

At first the Chinese used compasses in building. They lined up town walls and palaces and tombs of emperors with the main compass directions. Later the Chinese used compasses for navigation. Arab traders may have brought the compass from China to European countries.

The Han dynasty marked the height of ancient Chinese civilization. Look again at the time line on page 108. When the Han dynasty flourished in China what was happening in other areas of the world? During the 400 years following the Han dynasty China fell into disunity while barbarian nomads, invaded the northern part of the country.

Chinese painting showed Taoist influence in its interest in nature.

Checking Up

1. How long did the Civil Service system in China last?
2. What was China's main export to the Roman Empire and India? What did the Chinese receive from the Romans in exchange? What did the Chinese import from India?
3. How did the harness make farming easier?
4. What answers would you give to the key questions at the beginning of this chapter?
5. *Both ancient Chinese and Romans were concerned with practical matters about governing and defending empires. What kinds of contributions did each make in these areas?*

Unit 7 Summary

● Chinese civilization developed along the banks of the Hwang Ho, or Yellow River.
● The ancient Chinese built dikes to control the Hwang Ho.
● The Chinese believed that a dynasty could stay in power only if it had "the Mandate of Heaven."
● The family was very important in the Chinese way of life.
● The teachings of Confucius were used in an examination system for choosing people to run the government.
● Other systems of belief that became important in China were Taoism and Buddhism.
● China became united under the leadership of Shih Hwang Ti.
● Under the Han dynasty, China expanded its boundaries and traded with the Roman Empire and India.
● The Chinese invented many things, including silk, paper, printing, the harness, and the compass.

Unit 7 Review Workshop

What Have You Learned?

1. What natural barriers isolated China on the north, the east, the south, and the west?
2. How did the people of China control the flooding of the Hwang Ho?
3. How did the idea that a dynasty held the Mandate of Heaven help the dynasty stay in control?
4. Name three things that Confucius thought were important.
5. What did Taoists believe?
6. How did Shih Hwang Ti help unite China?
7. Why did Shih Hwang Ti have the Great Wall built?
8. What were some results of the travels of Chang Ch'ien?
9. Why do the Chinese call themselves "people of Han"?
10. Name four contributions in technology that China made to the world.

Use Your Reading Skills

When you read, it is important to be able to distinguish fact from myth, legend, and other imaginary accounts. Below are pairs of statements about ancient China. Which is fact? Which cannot be historically proven?

1. a. The Chinese learned how to build dikes to control the flooding of the Hwang Ho.
   b. The Hwang Ho was controlled by the Dragon King who caused floods when he was angry.

2. a. The Hsia dynasty was founded by Yu the Great who built a new channel for the Hwang Ho.
   b. The Shang dynasty is the first dynasty for which historians have found evidence.

3. a. The Chinese learned writing, arithmetic, medicine, and silk making early in their history.
   b. The Yellow Emperor, who ruled for almost a hundred years, taught the Chinese writing, arithmetic, medicine, and silk making.

Use Your Map Skills

Much of China's past lies buried in the earth. Archaeologists and their helpers are working to uncover remains that were buried hundreds of years ago. The map on page 211 shows a few of the hundreds of sites, or places, that have been unearthed in the People's Republic of China. Use the map to answer the following questions.

1. What is the number of the site where the oldest fossils of people were found? Near what present-day city is this site?
2. Near what present-day city were the fossil remains of Peking man found?
3. At what two sites was New Stone Age pottery found?
4. At which of these sites has New Stone Age pottery decorated with animal drawings been found? This site is near what present-day city?

China's Buried Treasures

1. The place where the oldest fossils of people have been found in China.
2. The place where Peking Man lived in caves. Peking Man is a fossil of a person from the Old Stone Age.
3. Villages where pottery was made during the New Stone Age about 6,000 years ago.
4. Another place where New Stone Age pottery was found. Some of the pots were decorated with animal drawings.
5. The burial place of Shih Hwang Ti. Armies of soldiers made from clay were found buried with the emperor.
6. The place where the tombs of Han emperors were discovered. A mummy suit of jade and gold was found there.
7. The place where bronze horses, chariots, and attendants were found buried with the emperor.

5. Near what present-day city was Shih Hwang Ti buried?
6. Near what present-day city was the jade mummy suit found?
7. Near what desert is the site where bronze horses were found?
8. What river is close to all of the sites?
9. Why do you think all of the sites are located in the northern part of China?

Use Your Writing Skills

The Chinese showed great respect for older people. Children made great efforts to care for their parents. Families showed this same regard for the spirits of their ancestors as you may remember from reading the unit. Write a paragraph explaining how you think this respect for older people helped preserve traditional ways in China. How can such an attitude also prevent change and discourage new ideas?

Learn by Doing

In this unit you have learned that the officials in China had to take an exam to qualify for a job in the government. Suppose the mayor of your local community had to take an exam in order to hold office. Write four questions that you think might appear on such an exam.

Read to Learn More

Find the topics listed below in the card catalog of your library. Read all or part of a book listed under one of the topics. Share what you learn with your classmates.

ALCHEMY (CHINESE)   JADE

CHINESE DYNASTIES   SEISMOGRAPH

Unit 8

The World of the Mayas

The ruins of an important Mayan ceremonial center rise from the savanna in the Yucatán Peninsula.

Maps Tell a Story of the Mayas

As you read, think about this term.
urban hearth

The first Americans may have migrated from Asia across a land bridge that then connected Asia and North America. During the thousands of years that followed, these people settled throughout the Americas. One of these groups became the Mayas. They settled in an area that is today part of Mexico and Central America.

The Land

Look at the map below. Notice that the inset map shows what part of Middle America the Mayas settled. Compare this map with the Atlas map on page 10. Name the five present-day countries where the Mayas lived. What body of water borders the northern coast of this area? the southern coast?

Landforms. The Mayan civilization covered a variety of landscapes. Find the

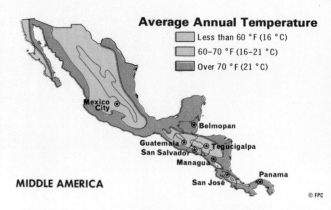

Average Annual Temperature
- Less than 60 °F (16 °C)
- 60–70 °F (16–21 °C)
- Over 70 °F (21 °C)

MIDDLE AMERICA

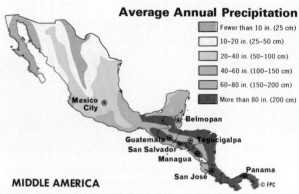

Average Annual Precipitation
- Fewer than 10 in. (25 cm)
- 10–20 in. (25–50 cm)
- 20–40 in. (50–100 cm)
- 40–60 in. (100–150 cm)
- 60–80 in. (150–200 cm)
- More than 80 in. (200 cm)

MIDDLE AMERICA

Yucatán Peninsula. Why is this area called a peninsula? Check the Atlas world physical map on pages 12–13. How would you describe the land and the elevation of the Yucatán? of the area to the south? Mayan cities developed in both the lowlands and the highlands. Find three lowland cities on the map. Find two highland cities.

Climate. The climate in this area ranges from wet tropical lowlands to the cooler highlands. Look at the maps above. Which areas have the warmest temperatures? the coolest? Which areas have the greatest rainfall? the least?

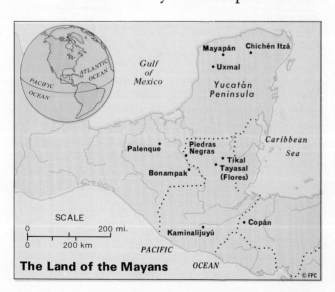

The Land of the Mayans

SCALE
0 — 200 mi.
0 — 200 km

214

Mesopotamia
3500 B.C.

Nile
Valley
3200 B.C.

Indus
Valley
2200 B.C

Hwang Ho
1500 B.C.

Middle
America
100 B.C.

The World's Five Urban Hearths

© FPC

What can you guess about the length of the growing season in this area?

The World's First Urban Areas

The map above shows the five areas in the world where most historians believe that cities first developed. These areas are called **urban hearths**. What are these five urban hearths? The dates on the map show about when each of these urban hearths developed. Which of these five is the oldest? the most recent? The Mayan civilization was one of the urban areas in Middle America.

You have already read about thousands of years of history and about many groups of people. As you have learned from this map, not all groups settled and developed at the same time. Nor did they settle and develop in the same ways. Think about the four urban hearths in Africa and Asia. What did each of these locations have in common? How was this kind of location important

to the way of life of the people? The urban areas in Middle America did not center on river locations. Year-round precipitation provided enough water for farming. As a result, some aspects of their lives were quite different from the river-valley civilizations.

What had happened in the four earliest urban areas by the time urban life was beginning in Middle America? Look at the time line on pages 108–109. What power was expanding in the Mediterranean world? What civilization was reaching its peak in Africa? Had China become an empire?

Checking Up

1. How may the first people have arrived in the Americas?
2. What are the landforms and climate like in Middle America?
3. What is an urban hearth?

The Rise of the Mayan Civilization

As You Read

1. Think about these words.
   slash-and-burn   draft animal   fallow   maize   tortilla
2. Look for answers to these key questions.
   a. When and where did the Mayas develop their civilization?
   b. What were the special farming methods the Mayas used and the different crops they raised?
   c. What kinds of work did Mayan women do? What kinds of work did Mayan men do?
3. Use this reading skill.
   As you read this chapter, it will be helpful to make comparisons between the information you learn about the Mayas and what you have learned about other early civilizations. For example, ask yourself how the area in which the Mayas developed was different from the kinds of areas where other civilizations began. How were the methods and crops of Mayan farmers different from those of the farmers of the early civilizations of the Middle East, India, and China?

Early people in Mexico and Central America were hunters. They trapped such animals as jack rabbits, wild pigs, and deer. Sometimes they killed their game with stone-tipped spears.

Later people began to plant crops. By 6000 B.C. they had started growing squash. By 3500 B.C. they had begun to grow corn. These people had become farmers.

By 3000 B.C. the people in Mexico and Central America were living in small villages. They domesticated a few animals such as dogs, turkeys, and ducks. They also started to make pottery and to weave cloth.

By 1000 B.C. people known as the Olmecs (ôl'meks) started to build ceremonial centers. These were places where the farmers in an area met at certain times of the year. Here they held their religious ceremonies. They also started markets to trade food and other goods.

Mayan Civilization Develops

Other people in Mexico and Central America learned much from the Olmecs. The Mayas were one of these groups. The Mayas began to develop their own civilization about A.D. 100. Mayan civilization reached its peak during the Middle Period, which lasted about 600 years.

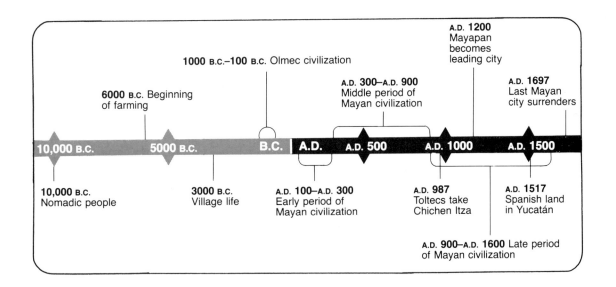

A.D. 1200 Mayapan becomes leading city

1000 B.C.–100 B.C. Olmec civilization

6000 B.C. Beginning of farming

A.D. 300–A.D. 900 Middle period of Mayan civilization

A.D. 1697 Last Mayan city surrenders

10,000 B.C.   5000 B.C.   B.C.   A.D.   A.D. 500   A.D. 1000   A.D. 1500

10,000 B.C. Nomadic people

3000 B.C. Village life

A.D. 100–A.D. 300 Early period of Mayan civilization

A.D. 987 Toltecs take Chichen Itza

A.D. 1517 Spanish land in Yucatán

A.D. 900–A.D. 1600 Late period of Mayan civilization

Look at the time line above. What dates are shown for the Middle Period?

At this time the core of the Mayan world was the central area. It covered present-day Belize, northern Guatemala, and the small part of Mexico west of the Yucatán Peninsula. Study the map on this page. Find the northern, central, and southern areas in which the Mayan world developed.

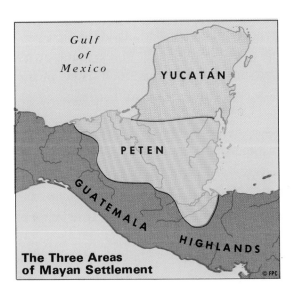

Gulf of Mexico

YUCATÁN

PETEN

GUATEMALA

HIGHLANDS

The Three Areas of Mayan Settlement

© FPC

Why did the Mayas first develop their civilization in the central area? It was a hot and wet rain forest. However, this area had several advantages. The soil was very fertile, and crops grew quickly. The people were able to spend less time farming. They could work on their buildings. This area also had plenty of the limestone they used for building.

After A.D. 900, during the Late Period, many Mayas settled in the northern area of the Yucatán Peninsula. Here it was much drier. Here, too, there was plenty of limestone for building. The soil of the Yucatán was good for growing cotton.

Trade. The Mayas carried on much trade, especially in items from the Yucatán. Cotton was an important trade item, as was salt from nearby sea marshes. Another important trade item from the Yucatán was sisal, which was used to make rope. The Mayas also traded items from more mountainous areas to the south. There the Mayas found jade for their jewelry. There they were also able to get brightly colored bird feathers for the clothing of their priests and nobles.

Farming

Throughout their history, the Mayas were a farming people. The fields around each village were owned by the village as a whole. Each family farmed a field large enough to feed itself. Families also gave a part of their crop to the priests and nobles.

Special farming methods. Many archaeologists believe Mayan farmers used the special method of farming called **slash-and-burn**. Early in the dry season, in December or January, the men cleared the land for their cornfields. Using stone axes, they cut down trees and brush. They spread the cuttings over the ground to dry. Toward the end of the dry season, in March or April, they burned the wood and brush cuttings. The air was filled with a smoky haze throughout the Mayan lowlands at this time of year. The ashes fertilized the soil.

The Mayas did their planting at the start of the rainy season, in May or June. They did not plow the land because they had no **draft animals**. At this time there were no oxen, horses, donkeys, or any other animals in the Americas that could have been domesticated to pull plows. Instead, the Mayas poked holes in the ground with wooden digging sticks. They dropped in seeds of corn, beans, and squash and covered the holes with dirt. Then they prayed for rain.

The plants grew during the rainy season. The farmers weeded the fields once or twice. The different crops ripened at different times. Beans and squash were the first crops to ripen. These the farmers harvested, dried, and stored. Corn was harvested differently. When it was ripe, the farmers bent the stalks. Then they left the corn to dry for a month.

Heavy rain caused tropical soil to lose its fertility quickly. Sometimes the Mayas farmed a cornfield for only one year. Then they let it rest for four years. At other times they let it lie **fallow**, or unused, for seven years. In the meantime, they cleared new fields elsewhere.

Slash-and-burn farming is a good way to use the soil of a tropical rain forest. However, this method requires a large amount of land. As a result, the Mayan population was scattered. People lived in hundreds of small villages that were far apart.

Many different crops. Mayan farmers had only a few domestic animals. However, they grew many different kinds of plants. The most important crop was **maize**, or Indian corn. In fact, the Mayas believed the gods had made the first people out of corn dough. Maize made up 80 percent of the Mayas' food. Next in importance came beans and squash.

The Mayas also grew tomatoes, pumpkins, sweet potatoes, avocados, guavas, vanilla beans, chili peppers, plums, papaya, and cacao. Chocolate comes from the cacao bean. However, the cacao tree grows only in certain areas. Thus, chocolate was a luxury among the Mayas. It was probably eaten only by the priests and nobles.

Mayan families lived in houses at the edges of their fields. Usually five to twelve families lived in a village surrounded by farmland.

Ix Tok's Day

Ix tok (iks täk), a Mayan woman, began her day before sunrise. First she started the cooking fire and began making tortillas (tôr·tē′yəz). These were round, thin, flat pancakes made from corn dough. After each tortilla was baked, Ix Tok put it in a bowl near the fire to keep it hot.

When about thirty tortillas were ready, Ix Tok placed the bowl before her husband and two sons. She also put out a plate of crushed chili peppers to add taste to the tortillas. For drink, she poured pozole (pō·sō′lä) into a clay pitcher. She made pozole by boiling corn dough in water until it was hard. Then she mixed the hard dough with cold water until it looked like milk.

The Mayas built houses of stone and wood and used palm leaves to thatch the roofs.

Mayan women wove all the clothing, blankets, and baskets their families needed.

Ix Tok ate breakfast after her husband and sons were finished. Then she prepared a batch of corn dough for the following day. The corn had been soaking in limestone water since the previous day. She did this to soften the kernels. After she boiled the kernels, she washed them. Then with a long stone, she ground the kernels into a mushy paste.

For the second, or main, meal of the day, Ix Tok planned to serve black beans and meat along with the tortillas. The meat would come from a rabbit her husband had trapped the day before.

By now morning was over. Ix Tok still had several things to do before the men came back from the fields. She fed the turkeys and dogs. Both of these animals provided meat for the family. Next she washed the family's second set of clothes. While they were drying in the sun, she bathed herself and her baby daughter. Ix Tok then worked at her loom. Some days she made clay pots.

By late afternoon Ix Tok's husband and two sons came back from the fields. Ix Tok had water ready for their baths. While they were washing themselves, she baked the tortillas, beans, and meat for the day's big meal. Again, Ix Tok ate only after the men were finished. Then she cleaned out the hut. Before going to bed, she put corn in limewater to soak for the following day.

Ah Kuat's Day

Ah Kuat (äh koo·ät′), a Mayan man, had married Ix Tok when he was twenty years old. By custom, the marriage had been arranged by his parents. Ah Kuat had been very pleased with his bride. He had often seen Ix Tok in the village. He had even spoken with her while she was at the river getting water.

Like most Mayan men, Ah Kuat farmed. He also hunted and fished. He made the stone axes and digging tools that he and his sons used in the fields. He had built his family's house. He played with his children as they were growing up.

Also like most Mayan men, Ah Kuat had a craft. His father worked with leather. His older brother made blowguns. Ah Kuat was a skilled papermaker. Sometimes the parents of boys in the village brought their sons to him, along

Mayan men made paper from the bark of fig trees, which they softened by soaking and coated with lime.

with a gift of food. The boys would learn papermaking from Ah Kuat.

Ah Kuat spent most of his other time on construction work. He and other Mayan men built the stone cities that dotted the Mayan world.

Checking Up

1. Who owned the Mayan farmlands?
2. Why was the Mayan population scattered in small settlements?
3. What foods did the Mayas eat?
4. What answers would you give to the key questions at the beginning of this chapter?
5. *Why is slash-and-burn farming often a wasteful way of using land?*

Mayan Civilization at Its Height

As You Read

1. Think about these words.
   reservoir   barter   causeway
2. Look for answers to these key questions.
   a. What was a Mayan city like?
   b. What was the religion of the Mayas?
   c. What did the Mayas believe about happenings in the sky and about the passage of time?

Mayan cities were ceremonial centers where only priests and their attendants lived. Mayan farmers came to a city either to observe religious ceremonies or to sell their goods at the city marketplace.

A Mayan City

Like all Mayan ceremonial centers, the city that Ah Kuat helped build stood on top of a hill. There were a hundred or more such cities in the Mayan area, one for every fifty to a hundred villages. No village was more than fifteen miles from a ceremonial center. People could walk to a city, conduct their business, and walk home within the same day.

Some cities, such as Copán, were built with a pale green volcanic rock. Most, however, were built with limestone. The blocks of limestone were cemented together with mortar. Sometimes they were carved. They shone dazzling white in the tropical sun.

Pyramids and temples. Each city was built around a central square. The most impressive structure on this square was a flat-topped pyramid between ten and twenty stories high. Each side faced one of the four directions: north, south, east, or west. On top of the pyramid stood a temple. Steep steps ran up each side. They were so steep that it was difficult to climb them without using one's hands. However, when the priests climbed the stairs to offer gifts of flowers and food to the gods, they had to walk erect.

Neither Ah Kuat nor Ix Tok had ever been inside the temple. Only priests could enter the small room with wall paintings in red, yellow, blue, black, and green.

The rooms were roofed with a corbel vault, or arch. The Mayas invented this vault. Mayan architects laid stones one on top of another on facing walls. Each stone extended past the stone beneath. Gradually the distance between the two walls grew smaller until the architects could bridge them with a single stone or wooden beam.

Compare this Mayan arch with the Roman arches shown on page 160.

The temple stood at one corner of the central square. Along the sides of the square were several large buildings with small rooms in which the priests lived. There were **reservoirs** (rez′əv·wärz′), or pools for storing rainwater during the dry season.

Playing Pok-a-Tok. After the pyramid, Ah Kuat's favorite structure in the city was the ball court. It was near the temple. Shaped like the capital letter I, it measured about 25 feet (7.6 m) by 75 feet (22.8 m) and had sloping walls along its sides. Pok-a-Tok, the name of the Mayan ball game, was played by two teams of two to eleven men. A player scored a point in one of two ways. He could hit a rubber ball through a small, upright stone hoop placed 25 feet above the playing field. Or he could force the ball into the other team's end zone. Players could not use their hands, their feet, or even their heads. They had to hit the ball with their hips, elbows, or shoulders.

Because the ball was small and very hard, players wore leather equipment to keep from being hurt. This included a helmet, gloves, a wide belt, and pads for the hips and knees. Players had to be excellent athletes to play Pok-a-Tok. The game was fast and dangerous.

Going to market. Near the ball court stood the city's marketplace. Every twenty days, it bustled with activity when the people came to buy and sell. White cotton awnings protected people from the burning sun. Ix Tok, who sold cloth she had woven, sat in one section of the market. Ah Kuat, who sold the paper he had made, sat in another. One child accompanied each parent to help. Often the Mayas **bartered**, or traded goods, with each other. Sometimes they used cacao beans to pay for their purchases.

Many articles were sold in the market. There were separate sections for vegetables, fruit, and spices. Jewelers sold jade and amber and, once in a while, great white pearls from the Caribbean. The makers of clay images were especially busy. Mayan farmers bought images of Chac, the rain god, or Yum Kaax, the

The Mayas used a tumpline, or strap, to carry goods on their backs.

Players hit the ball through a stone hoop placed sideways in the wall.

corn god, to place in the soil. They believed this would help bring about a good crop. In another part of the market slaves were sold.

Slaves. The Mayas usually punished people who had committed crimes by making them slaves. For example, the first time a person stole, that person was allowed to pay back what had been stolen. If a person stole a second time, the person was punished by being sold as a slave. Thus, the Mayas had no need for jails.

Slaves were usually bought by long-distance traders. They used the slaves to paddle canoes on trading expeditions along the coast. These canoes were large enough to carry forty passengers as well as goods. Slaves were used to carry goods overland.

Roads and transportation. Some Mayan cities were connected by **causeways.** These were raised roads of stone and were paved with white gravel. In most cases, however, people went from city to city by paths cut through the rain forest. The Mayas did not transport goods by cart. They did not have draft animals.

Furthermore, they never made use of the wheel.

The Mayan Religion

Chac, the rain god, and Yum Kaax, the corn god, were only two of the many Mayan gods. Each was more or less related to a force of nature.

The Mayas believed a god named Hunab Ku had created thirteen heavens and nine underworlds. They believed he had also created the sun, moon, stars, and planets. His son, Itzamná ("Lizard House"), was the sky god. The Mayas thought he had invented writing as well as astronomy and mathematics.

The Mayas believed that, like the gods, people's souls lived forever. After death a good soul went to one of the thirteen heavens. A bad soul may have gone to one of the nine underworlds.

The most important religious holiday was the celebration of the new year. The Mayas believed that each year had a god protecting it. Therefore, the people carved a statue of the god of the coming year and took it to the city. There the priests, dressed in masks and feathered robes, placed the statue in the temple. The priests burned incense and called on the people to make offerings.

Then the priests and the people danced. The men and boys danced in one line; the women and girls in another line. Round and round the temple square, they moved. They danced to the sounds of drums, trumpets, bells, and flutes. After a game of Pok-a-Tok and a feast, the ceremony was over.

People Who Made a Difference

The Mayan Priests

The Mayan priests made many of the achievements for which the Mayas are remembered. Mayan priests developed mathematics, two calendars, and a way of writing.

The number system of the Mayan priests was much like our own. It had a symbol for zero. The zero was unknown in Europe until the A.D. 1200s. The zero made it possible for the priests to develop their way of writing numbers. They made the value of a number depend on its place. For example, the symbol we use for the number one means number one only when written alone. When it is written to the left of a zero, it becomes a ten. When it is written to the left of two zeros, it becomes a hundred. A number system based on place value is much less clumsy than a system like the Romans used.

There are two differences between the Mayan number system and our own. We write our numbers from left to right. The Mayan priests wrote their numbers from top to bottom. Our number system is based on ten. Theirs was based on twenty. Look at the diagram of Mayan numbers. Notice that the Mayan numbers up to twenty were not shown by single symbols. They were made up of dots and bars.

The Mayan priests also kept records of events. They counted back more than 3,000 years to when they thought their own civilization had begun. Every twenty years the Mayas built a new stela, or stone column, with inscriptions that began with this Long Count date.

The inscriptions that covered these "talking stones" were in the hieroglyphs of the Mayan priests. Their picture writing system contained about 700 symbols. Historians believe that by the Late

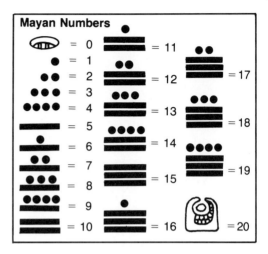

Mayan Numbers

= 0		= 11		= 17	
= 1		= 12			
= 2		= 13		= 18	
= 3		= 14			
= 4		= 15		= 19	
= 5		= 16		= 20	
= 6					
= 7					
= 8					
= 9					
= 10					

The many dates inscribed on stelae show the Mayan priests' concern with time.

Period many symbols had begun to stand for syllables. The writing system of the Mayan priests was the most highly developed in the Americas.

This colorful Mayan wall painting shows a Mayan religious procession.

Measuring Time

Leading religious rituals was the first duty of the priests. They also learned much. The priests studied the sky. They kept records of the movements of the sun, moon, and planets. They knew when eclipses of the sun and the moon would take place.

The priests did not observe the sky, however, to learn about science. They believed that happenings in the sky showed the will of the gods. An eclipse of the moon, for instance, was a warning that some disaster would take place. Knowing about the eclipse in advance enabled the priests to order special sacrifices to try to prevent the disaster from happening.

From the knowledge they gained, Mayan priests developed two calendars. One was a solar calendar of a little over 365 days. It told farmers when to plant and harvest their crops. The second calendar was a ritual calendar of 260 days. It told the Mayas when to perform religious ceremonies. It also told them which days were lucky and which were unlucky. Mayas would not start a journey or get married on an unlucky day.

Every fifty-two years, the first day of the solar calendar and the first day of the ritual calendar were the same. As a result, the Mayas looked at time as a series of fifty-two-year cycles.

It was not just dates that repeated themselves every fifty-two years, however. The Mayas believed events repeated themselves too. For example, if a hurricane occurred, the Mayas were convinced there would be another hurricane on the same day fifty-two years later. In other words, they used the past to predict the future.

Checking Up

1. What goods were sold in a Mayan market?
2. Why did the Mayas carry their goods rather than transport them by cart?
3. Who were the Mayan slaves?
4. What answers would you give to the key questions at the beginning of this chapter?
5. *How were Mayan cities different from the cities of the ancient Middle East, the Mediterranean world, and China?*

The Decline and Disappearance of Mayan Civilization

As You Read

1. Think about these words.
   theory   cenote
2. Look for answers to these key questions.
   a. What explanations do historians suggest for the disappearance of the Mayas?
   b. Who were the Toltecs? How were they different from the Mayas?
   c. In what ways did the Toltecs and Mayas use cenotes?
3. Use this reading skill.
   Sometimes you will read about problems that have not been solved. The decline of the Mayas is such a problem. Explanations have been suggested but not proven. Try to judge the various explanations according to their strengths and weaknesses. As you read the different explanations offered, ask yourself how each partly helps shed light on the problem, but why none completely solves it.

About A.D. 900 something strange happened to the Mayas. Except in the Yucatán and Guatemala highlands, they abandoned their cities to the rain forest and vanished. Even today, the central area is sparsely populated.

Historians do not know why the Mayas left. They have suggested a number of **theories**, or possible explanations.

Why Did the Mayas Leave?

One theory for the disappearance of the Mayas is that the farmers revolted against the priests and nobles. If this is so, however, why did the winning farmers leave the area? A second theory is that the soil became exhausted and could

no longer produce enough food to feed the large number of people. However, scientists are not yet able to prove this theory.

Still another possible theory is the rise of warlike tribes in Mexico. These tribes may have interfered so much with Mayan trade that the people could no longer support the cities. However, even if the cities had to be abandoned, why did the farmers also move away? And why was there a great drop in population?

Perhaps one day archaeologists and historians will discover the answer to this mystery. However, they do know what happened to the Mayas in the Yucatán Peninsula.

A Mayan Town

Today Ah Guy lives in the town of Flores, which used to be called Tayasal. Flores is on an island in Lake Petén Itzá in Guatemala. From the airstrip at the edge of the lake, planes carry out forest products from which the people earn a living. These products include lumber, rubber, and chicle for chewing gum. The planes bring in tourists and manufactured goods.

Life in Flores is a mixture of old and new. Despite the airstrip, there are no automobiles in the town. Some of the houses are built in the Mayan style, with wood walls and thatched roofs. There is still Mayan sculpture in the town's central square.

Ah Guy mixes the old with the new in his work. He brings tourists from the airstrip to the island. He uses the same sort of dugout canoe his Mayan ancestors used in the past. His boat, however, is powered by an outboard motor instead of slaves.

Ah Guy speaks both the Mayan and Spanish languages as well as English. He is a Christian. Ah Guy also follows, however, some ancient Mayan beliefs. Each spring at corn-planting time, he buries a statue of Yum Kaax in the ground. Ah Guy likes to tell tourists the legend of the horse of Hernando Cortes.

Cortes was the Spanish conqueror of Mexico. In 1524 he visited Flores on his way from Mexico City to Honduras. Because his horse was injured, he left it behind. The Mayas had never seen a horse before. They believed it was the god of thunder. They brought it offerings of flowers, fruits, and birds. When the horse died, the Mayas made a statue of it and worshiped it. Years later, a Spanish missionary smashed the statue and threw the pieces into Lake Petén Itzá. The Mayas believe that on a clear day you can still see the thunder god walking about beneath the water of Lake Petén.

The Coming of the Toltecs

In A.D. 987 the Mayan city of Chichén Itzá (chə·chen′ ət·sä′) in the Yucatán was conquered by Toltec (tōl′tek) warriors from Mexico. For about the next 400 years, a mixed Mayan and Toltec civilization flourished in the peninsula.

The Toltecs differed in many ways from the Mayas. They were much more warlike. Their leaders were powerful fighters rather than scholarly priests.

The Toltecs also built temples and ball courts. The Toltecs, however, used new building forms such as columns and beams. Their priests did almost no writing, and they stopped using the Long Count. They did bring the belief in a plumed serpent god to the Yucatán.

The sacred cenote. The Toltecs combined the Mayan cities into an empire. Its first capital was Chichén Itzá. This name means "the mouth of the well of the Itzá." The Itzá was one of the ruling families of the empire. The well was a cenote (si·nōt′ē), or natural underground water source.

Cenotes are formed when soil caves in and uncovers water under the ground.

What two new features in Mayan architecture can you identify at Chichén Itzá?

Toltecs believed the plumed serpent god taught them farming and the calendar.

There are hundreds of cenotes in the Yucatán. The limestone surface of the land is so porous that there are no streams. All the rainwater sinks into the ground. They are the main source of water. The Mayas in the Yucatán used the water from cenotes for drinking, washing, and irrigating. They built all their cities next to cenotes.

The main cenote at Chichén Itzá was very important. Carved stones from the time of the Toltecs show their chief priest making offerings of jewelry and incense at such a well. The Toltecs declared the main cenote sacred. People came from all over the Mayan world to throw offerings into it.

The main cenote was also a well of sacrifice. In times of drought or war when people wanted to ask the gods important questions, they would throw a person into the well. It was hoped the person would rise to the surface of the water. Then the priests would interpret what the person said as the answer from the gods. If the person did not come back to the surface, the priests believed it meant bad fortune.

From the Toltecs to the Spanish

Around A.D. 1200 Chichén Itzá began to lose its power. Control of the Mayan-Toltec empire moved to a city called Mayapán. Mayapán was very different from Chichén Itzá. It was a walled city and not just a ceremonial center. The people lived there throughout the year.

Mayapán kept its power for about 200 years. Then its civilization also declined. Palaces and pyramid temples were not built well. Its pottery was poorly made.

The cenote at Chichén Itzá was 95 feet (29 m) deep and 200 feet (60 m) across.

By A.D. 1400 most of the Mayan cities had revolted against Mayapán. Instead of a united empire, the Yucatán was now a collection of independent city-states. They spent much of their time warring among themselves.

In 1517 the Spanish explorers landed. They had guns and killed many of the Mayas. They brought smallpox, which killed even more people. By 1547 most of the Yucatán was under Spanish control. Some Mayas, however, fled to the forests of the central area. It was 150 years later when the last Mayan town of Tayasal finally surrendered to the Spanish.

Hernando Cortes, the Spanish conqueror of Mexico, also led an expedition through Central America.

Checking Up
1. What changes did the Toltecs bring to the Yucatán?
2. What were the differences between Chichén Itzá and Mayapán?
3. What helped the Spanish conquer the Mayas?
4. What answers would you give to the key questions at the beginning of this chapter?
5. *How are the theories about the disappearance of the Mayas from the central area like the reasons explaining the decline of Kush? How are they different?*

Unit 8 Summary
- By 1000 B.C. the ancestors of the Mayas had changed from hunters to settled farmers.
- Mayan civilization reached its peak in the central area during the Middle Period, between A.D. 300 and A.D. 900.
- Mayan farmers owned land in common, practiced slash-and-burn farming, and grew such crops as corn, beans, and squash.
- The Mayas held religious ceremonies and set up markets in cities built with stone and mortar.
- The Mayas believed in gods of nature and of time.
- Mayan priests developed writing, a number system, and two calendars.
- About A.D. 900, for unknown reasons, the Mayas abandoned their cities in the central area.
- About A.D. 1000 the Toltecs invaded the Yucatán from Mexico and established a Mayan-Toltec empire.
- In the 1500s most of the Mayan world was conquered by the Spanish.

Unit 8 Review Workshop

What Have You Learned?

A. Choose the letter of the item that correctly completes each statement.

1. Mayan civilization developed in (a) a river valley (b) grasslands (c) a tropical rain forest.

2. The most important Mayan crop was (a) beans (b) maize (c) squash.

3. In farming the Mayas used (a) draft animals (b) the plow (c) the slash-and-burn method.

4. The Mayan priests developed all the following except (a) calendars (b) a number system (c) ironworking.

5. The Mayas believed all the following except (a) that people's souls lived forever (b) that the gods could send messages through people thrown into cenotes (c) that it was impossible to predict events or to know lucky or unlucky days in advance.

6. The most important building in a Mayan city was (a) a temple-topped pyramid (b) a ball court (c) a marketplace.

7. When the Mayas did not barter, they paid for goods with (a) gold (b) cacao beans (c) jade.

8. Mayas became slaves if they (a) fell into debt (b) committed a serious crime (c) had been born on unlucky days.

9. The Mayan-Toltec Empire had its first capital at (a) Tayasal (b) Mayapán (c) Chichén Itzá.

10. Cenotes were important in the Yucatán because they (a) were a source of salt (b) provided shelters (c) were a source of water.

B. On a separate sheet of paper, fill in the word or words from the list below that best complete each statement.

beans	flutes
bells	hips
corbel arch	limestone
corn	new year
dogs	shoulders
ducks	squash
drums	syllables
elbows	trumpets
fifty-two	turkeys

1. The three main crops of the Mayas were _____, _____, and _____.

2. Among the animals the Mayas domesticated were _____, _____, and _____.

3. The Mayas built their cities with _____.

4. The Mayas invented the _____ _____ for use in their buildings.

5. In playing Pok-a-Tok, athletes could hit the ball with only their _____, _____, and _____.

6. The most important religious holiday of the Mayas was the _____ _____.

7. Mayan musical instruments included _____, _____, _____, and _____.

8. The first day of the solar calendar and the first day of the ritual calendar were the same every _____ years.

9. Historians believe that most of the symbols in Mayan writing came to stand for _____.

Use Your Reading Skills

Arrange the following events in their proper time order.

1. The Mayas abandoned their cities in the central area.
2. The Toltecs invaded the Yucatán.
3. Ancestors of the Mayas began to domesticate corn.
4. The Mayas started making pilgrimages to the cenote at Chichén Itzá.
5. The Mayan cities revolted against Mayapán.
6. The Mayas developed their own civilization.
7. The Spanish invaded the Yucatán.
8. The Olmecs built ceremonial centers.

Use Your Thinking Skills

Look at the Mayan temple painting above. What does it tell you about each of the following?

a. the type of houses in which Mayas lived
b. the way they transported goods across land
c. the way they traveled by water
d. their everyday activities

Learn by Doing

Use the chart on page 224 to solve the following problems. Write your answers in Mayan numbers.

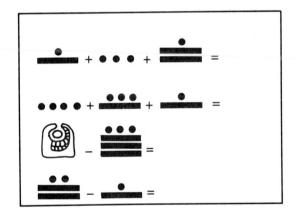

Read to Learn More

Find the topics listed below in the card catalog of your library. Read all or part of a book listed under one of the topics. Share what you learn with your classmates.

MEXICO (ANCIENT)   MAYAS

HERNANDO CORTES

SPANISH CONQUESTS

Part Three
The Middle Period of the World's Civilizations

Throughout history, periods of time can be described by the kinds of changes that occurred. The period between the 600s and 1400s was marked by the rise of new empires and the spread of new religions. This period saw both population and trade increase.

New civilizations and empires developed in the world. Some became powerful, and then declined. Others remained strong. These empires were in Asia, the Middle East, Europe, the Americas, and Africa.

While strong empires flourished, people in some parts of Europe and in Japan lived without much central government. Conquests, trade, and travel brought many parts of the world into contact with one another for the first time. More contact led to more trade between different regions. Cities grew as trade increased.

Two of the world's great religions, Islam and Christianity, spread during this period. Conflicts over territory and trade also took place.

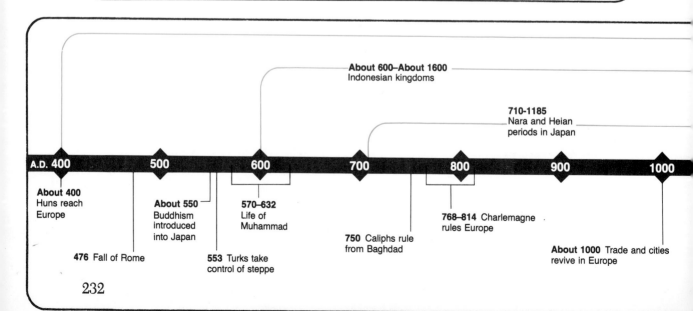

About 600–About 1600
Indonesian kingdoms

710-1185
Nara and Heian
periods in Japan

A.D. 400   500   600   700   800   900   1000

About 400
Huns reach
Europe

About 550
Buddhism
introduced
into Japan

570–632
Life of
Muhammad

768–814 Charlemagne
rules Europe

476 Fall of Rome

553 Turks take
control of steppe

750 Caliphs rule
from Baghdad

About 1000 Trade and cities
revive in Europe

232

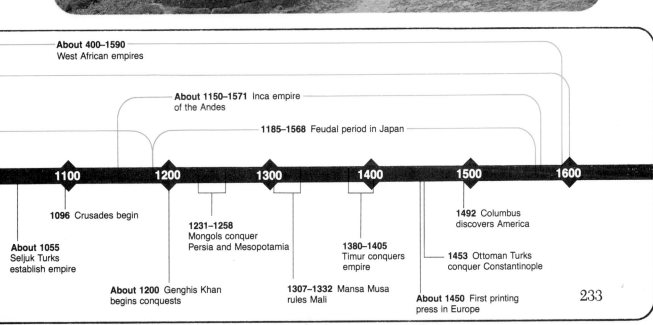

About 400–1590
West African empires

About 1150–1571 Inca empire
of the Andes

1185–1568 Feudal period in Japan

1100   1200   1300   1400   1500   1600

1096 Crusades begin

About 1055
Seljuk Turks
establish empire

1231–1258
Mongols conquer
Persia and Mesopotamia

About 1200 Genghis Khan
begins conquests

1307–1332 Mansa Musa
rules Mali

1380–1405
Timur conquers
empire

1492 Columbus
discovers America

1453 Ottoman Turks
conquer Constantinople

About 1450 First printing
press in Europe

233

Unit 9

Empires of the Nomads

These horsemen are Mongol nomads, who conquered China and central Asia. They are using falcons to hunt.

Maps and Photographs Tell a Story of Grasslands

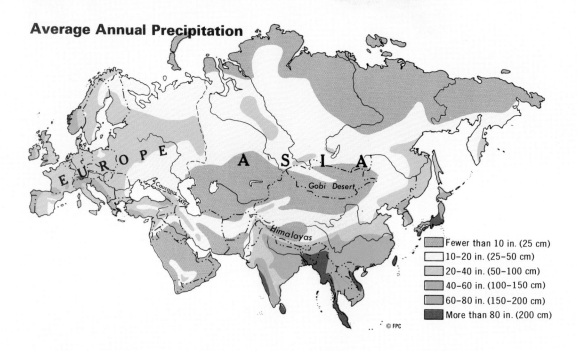

Average Annual Precipitation

Fewer than 10 in. (25 cm)
10–20 in. (25–50 cm)
20–40 in. (50–100 cm)
40–60 in. (100–150 cm)
60–80 in. (150–200 cm)
More than 80 in. (200 cm)

© FPC

The empires of the people you will read about in this unit covered much of what is now Europe and Asia. This great expanse included many climates and landforms. The people were nomads from the grasslands of central Asia.

By looking at the natural vegetation map in the Atlas on pages 18–19, you can see that there are two kinds of grassland areas. Which kind do you find in Europe and central Asia? What kind of vegetation borders the grasslands to the north? to the south? Which of these areas would you expect to receive the most rainfall? the least? Check your answers by comparing the Atlas map with the rainfall map on this page. The photographs below show these two regions.

Much of the steppe is now farmed. Forest borders the steppe on the north.

The central Asian and Gobi deserts border the steppe on the South.

236

Herders and Nomads of the Steppe

As You Read

1. Think about these words.
   steppe   clan   khan   yurt
2. Look for answers to these key questions.
   a. What were the three main areas of the Eurasian steppe?
   b. Why was the horse important to the nomads?
   c. What was the life of the steppe nomads like?
3. Use this reading skill.
   Recognizing generalizations, or statements about what certain groups may have in common, is an important reading skill. Few generalizations are true of all people, in all places, or at all times. Generalizations need to be limited by such words as many, few, some, usually, and nearly. Look carefully for generalizations as you read about nomads in this chapter.

Thousands of years ago nomads traveled the grasslands of Europe and Asia. Skilled at riding horses, they became warriors feared for their raids on settled communities. During the time of the Romans, some rode out of the north and east to attack cities of the empire.

The Romans called the nomads "two-footed beasts." The nomads were small people, and to the Romans they seemed to be a part of their horses. They ate and even slept on their horses.

The Romans thought the nomads were barbarians. The nomads had no great cities. They had no written language. They wore strange clothes. Yet these nomads conquered many lands, learned from other people, and built great empires of their own.

The Eurasian Steppe

The **steppe** region of Europe and Asia was home to the nomads. Because it covered parts of Europe and Asia, it has often been called the Eurasian steppe.

Nomads made their home on the flat, grassy Eurasian steppe.

The steppe was a huge, rolling grassland where few trees grew. This vast area stretched east from the plain of present-day Hungary almost to China's Yellow Sea. Find the steppe area on the map on page 238. Using the map scale, find the distance from its eastern edge to its western edge.

The steppe received little rainfall. The rain that did fall usually came in the spring. When the hot, dry winds of summer blew, the grasses turned brown and brittle. In winter northern winds brought cold and snow.

North of the steppe were thick forests. To the south were drier areas that merged with the great deserts of Asia. Find the Gobi Desert on the map on page 238. This desert forms part of the southern boundary of the steppe.

Mountain ranges and seas made up the rest of the southern steppe border. Find the Altai (əl'tī'), Tien Shan (tē·en' shän'), and Himalaya mountains on the map. The Black Sea, the Caspian Sea,

and the Aral Sea, together with the rivers that emptied into them, were sources of water in a dry land of grasses.

The steppe area was divided into three smaller areas. Use the map on page 238 to locate these regions as you read about them. One part, Mongolia on the east, was separated from China by the Gobi Desert and from central Asia by the Altai Mountains. Between the Altai and the Tien Shan mountains was the Dzungarian ((d)zən·gar'ē·ən) Gap. This was a pass between mountains to the second part of the steppe, central Asia. South of Central Asia were the deserts of Persia and Afghanistan. A gap between the Ural Mountains and the Caspian Sea led to the third part, the Russian steppe. It opened onto the Hungarian plain and all Europe. Locate the three areas of the Eurasian steppe on the map on page 238.

The Early People of the Steppe

The ancestors of the nomads may have been hunters and farmers who lived

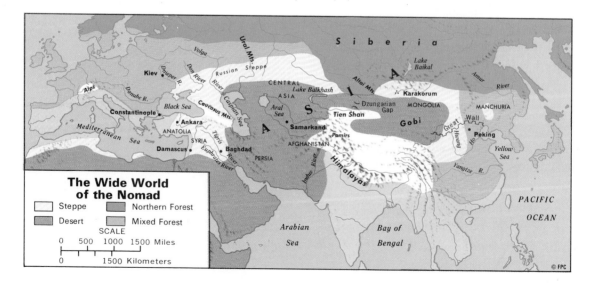

Ancient nomads, like those of today, moved across the steppe looking for pasture. At night they herded their animals together.

along the rivers of the steppe. The summer droughts brought wild animals to the rivers in search of food and water. These hunters and farmers learned to capture and herd cattle, sheep, and horses.

North of the steppe in the forests lived hunters who depended on forest animals and on animals that roamed the steppe for food. Sometimes these hunters joined groups who were already raising herds on the steppe.

The Steppe Nomads

Horses lived on the steppe, along with antelope and bison. The early people on the steppe kept horses and used them for food. They also used them to pull carts.

People tending herds moved from place to place to find pastures. They did not settle in one place. Once they domes-ticated horses, they could travel even greater distances. They were able to move with their herds to places where the grass was greener and the winds were warmer.

The nomads' horses had to be sturdy to survive the harsh steppe climate.

Then and Now

Mongols

Many hundreds of years ago, the nomads of Mongolia attacked the rich and settled empires of the Eurasian world. Under the leadership of Genghis (jeng′gəs) Khan and his successors, they conquered an empire from the Pacific Ocean to eastern Europe and the Middle East.

Now, however, the Mongols live a very different life. No longer do they rule the steppe or the lands beyond. They live divided among three countries. These are the People's Republic of Mongolia, the Soviet Union, and China.

In Outer Mongolia, their homeland, the Mongols help govern themselves. The government, with the help of the Soviet Union, has tried to begin industries and teach farming. Some people, however, are still herders.

In the Soviet Union most of the Mongols have been forced to give up herding. Some have become farmers. More than half of these Mongols have moved to towns and cities to work. They work in mines and factories. Only a few Mongols who herd still live in yurts. Their yurts now have wooden floors and electric lights.

The Mongols in China live in a region known as Inner Mongolia. Many still herd livestock. They do not, however, own their herds. These have become the property of the government.

Thus, some people in all three regions still follow the old ways of nomads. Dressed in long coats called dels, they move over the long-familiar grasslands. They live in yurts and remember the heroes of the past.

These Mongol horsemen are herders who live in the region of Inner Mongolia in northern China.

This nomad camp is in present-day Afghanistan.

Clans and tribes. The nomads traveled in groups made up of a few families. Each of these family groups was a **clan**. When clans joined together, they formed a tribe. The leader of a tribe was called a **khan** (kän). When one tribe conquered other tribes, or when a number of tribes joined together, their ruler was called a khakhan, or king of kings.

Homes. As the clans and tribes moved from place to place, they carried all their possessions with them. They put their household goods in chests. Then they loaded the chests onto carts with wheels so high that the goods stayed dry even when the carts crossed rivers. As many as twenty oxen may have pulled the long line of carts. Herds followed the caravan. A nomad group crossing the steppe looked like a city on wheels!

Some of the carts carried the nomads' tents, called **yurts**. The yurts were round and had wooden doors. Animal skins and felt covered the collapsible wooden framework of the yurts. Paintings of birds and animals brightened the inside walls of the tents.

Nomad men. Nomad boys learned to become skillful riders. They learned to make and shoot bows and arrows. The young boys knew that someday they would raid villages for food or fight other nomads for grazing land. As men, they became fierce and feared fighters.

Yet the men did not spend all their time fighting. Their animals were important to them. Animals were a sign of

Nomads still use yurts, which are easily assembled and taken apart.

Jewelry was sewn on clothing or belts. Valued items had to be portable.

wealth. The nomad men spent much of their time tending their herds.

Nomad women. Women were in charge of the carts and the yurts. Often a young girl would drive twenty or thirty carts, all fastened in a line behind the lead cart. When the group camped, the women set up the yurts, cared for the herds, made butter and cheese, and prepared the skins of animals for use.

The nomad women often had more freedom than women in other parts of the world at that time. They were in charge of the family property. They traded goods and took charge when the men were away. To protect the herds, the women also learned to ride and to shoot with bows and arrows. When needed, the women rode into battle.

Clothing. Men and women dressed alike. Both wore sheepskin boots and wide coats made of animal skins. The coats were fastened with silk sashes. To be comfortable while they were riding horses, both men and women wore pants.

Beliefs. Nomads believed that there were spirits in all natural things—grass, trees, mountains, the Great Sky. They thought it best to stay on friendly terms with these spirits. You will recall from Unit 1 that shamans were people who were thought to have magical powers that enabled them to speak to spirits. So the shamans of the nomads prayed, danced, and sang for rain to fall, for grass to grow, and for herds to multiply.

For centuries the nomads lived on the Eurasian steppe. While the Chinese Han Empire and Roman Empire were flourishing, nomads were tending their herds. Some fought other nomads and raided villages and cities in China and Europe. Some nomadic groups began conquests that took them over large parts of Europe, Asia, and the Middle East.

Checking Up

1. Who probably were the ancestors of the steppe nomads?
2. What kinds of homes did the steppe nomads have?
3. What were the beliefs of the steppe nomads?
4. What answers would you give to the key questions at the beginning of this chapter?
5. *Why do you think the Eurasian steppe made a good homeland for the nomads?*

Conquests of the Nomads

As You Read

1. Think about these words.
   treaty   diplomat
2. Look for answers to these key questions.
   a. Who were the Huns? the Turks? the Mongols?
   b. How did the Mongols conquer their empire?
   c. Why did the empires of the nomads decline?
3. Use this reading skill.
   Remembering time order will help you better understand as you read. Use the time lines when you are asked to. Other important dates are given in the chapter. After you read this chapter, put the following into time order: Genghis Khan conquers empire, Turks settle in Anatolia, Timur conquers empire.

The Huns, the Mongols, and the Turks were three of the most powerful groups of nomads. They conquered other nomads as well as people who lived in towns and cities. Although these groups left few written records, we know their stories from records left by the people they conquered.

The Huns

You will recall from reading Unit 7 that nomads and the people of China fought one another for centuries. One of the tribes most feared by the Chinese was the Huns. The Huns lived to the north of China on the steppe of present-day Mongolia.

The Chinese built the Great Wall to protect their country from the Huns. Look at the time line on pages 108–109. Find the reign of Shih Hwang Ti, during which the Great Wall was built. The Chinese even made **treaties**, or agreements between themselves and the Huns to keep these nomads on the steppe and out of China. In exchange for peace, the nomads got the right to graze their herds on good pasture land.

Later, tribes of Huns went west across the Russian steppe to Europe. Look at the time line on pages 232–233. When did the Huns reach Europe? Led by Attila (at′əl·ə), they defeated many other nomads. Then they attacked cities of the Roman Empire. Rome paid the Huns gold and gave them valuable gifts to keep them away. The Romans feared Attila the Hun and his army of nomads. Attila was long remembered as the person who conquered much of Europe.

The Turks

With the death of Attila, the army of the Huns weakened. Yet other groups of Huns continued to rule the steppe in central and eastern Asia. Another group of nomads, the Turks, eventually defeated them. Look at the time line on pages 232–233. About when did the Turks take control of the steppe?

Before they migrated south to the steppe, the Turks had lived in the forests of Siberia. A strong leader, Bumin (boo′min), organized the Turks into a powerful fighting army. Together with his brother, Bumin ruled an empire that stretched from the Caspian Sea to the Khingan (shing′än′) Mountains. Find this area on the map on page 245.

As so often happened, the empire of the Turks broke up after the deaths of Bumin and his brother. Some Turks who lived near the Silk Road settled down and became traders and merchants. One of these groups, the Uighur (wē′goor) Turks, settled around the five oases of the Tarim Basin. Locate the Tarim Basin on the map on page 245.

There, the Uighurs encouraged trade between the Middle East and China. Like other nomads, they learned from the people they met. The Uighur Turks became Buddhists. They developed a written language and, in time, became scribes and record keepers for other nomad tribes.

Other Turkish clans moved into the dry grassland and desert of central Asia. There they met the Arabs, who were spreading the religion of Islam. These Turks adopted Islam. In time, they be-

These Hun horsemen are carrying off treasure from the home of a rich Chinese family.

244

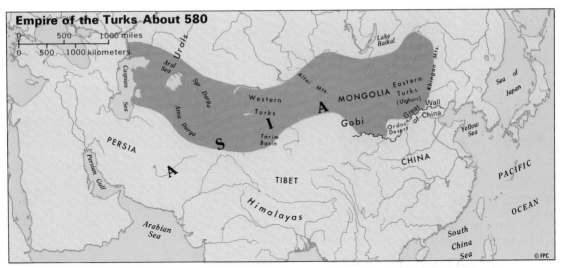

Empire of the Turks About 580

Many groups of Turks still live in eastern China and central Asia, an area called Turkestan.

came more powerful than the Arabs. Known as the Seljuk Turks, they conquered Persia, Mesopotamia, and Syria. In 1071 a group of Seljuk Turks defeated

The Turks became powerful rulers in the Middle East.

the Christian ruler of the Byzantine Empire. The Byzantine Empire was the name given to the remaining lands of the eastern part of the Roman Empire—mainly Greece and Anatolia. These Seljuk Turks then settled in Anatolia, which became known as Turkey. Find Turkey on the map on pages 10–11.

Genghis Khan and the Mongol Empire

The Mongols were yet another group of fierce nomads. From their homeland in Mongolia, they rode across Asia, conquering everything in their path. Genghis Khan, the remarkable leader of the Mongols, organized one of the most powerful armies in history. Look at the time line on pages 232–233. About when did Genghis Khan begin his conquests?

The Mongols defeated the Uighur Turks who had controlled the area southwest of Mongolia. Many of the Turkish tribes then joined with Genghis Khan.

245

Mongol armor was strips of metal sewn onto leather coats. The Mongols fought with spears, bows and arrows, and curved swords.

An ambitious leader, he was eager to increase the number of his followers. He saw himself as ruler of the entire steppe—and beyond.

Genghis Khan, as other nomads before him, wanted the riches of China. In 1211 a new emperor came to the throne of China. Genghis Khan warned that only the spirit of the Great Sky knew what would happen if the emperor decided to be his enemy. The new emperor of China did just that.

The Mongols then swept into China, where they defeated the Chinese army. Even the Great Wall did not stop Genghis Khan!

People Who Made a Difference

Timur

Just when the Mongol empire of Genghis Khan was falling apart, a new Asian conqueror gained power. He was Timur. Look at the time line on pages 232–233. About what time did Timur conquer his empire?

Timur was a central Asian Turk. His tribe had been one of those Turkish groups that joined the Mongols. As a young man, Timur was wounded in the leg by an arrow. He became known as Timur the Lame. That is why his name often appears as "Tamer-lame" or "Tamberlaine."

Timur was brave and often lucky. He used his skill in battle to defeat the Mongols in central Asia. Then he led armies into Turkey and India. He became one of the most feared conquerors in history.

Timur wanted his capital city of Samarkand to be the greatest city in all Asia. Locate Samarkand on the map on page 249. He brought artists and scholars to Samarkand. However, he himself spent little time there. He was almost always off conquering more lands. Timur died in 1405. His empire broke up less than a hundred years later.

Mongol methods of conquest. At first the city walls in China stopped the invading Mongols, who were used to fighting in the open. Genghis Khan returned to the steppe without capturing the capital of northern China near present-day Peking. Before Genghis Khan returned the next year, the emperor fled. He left few soldiers to defend the city. It was easily taken. The Mongols killed those they captured and then burned the city to the ground. The way the Mongols dealt with the defeated people frightened the other cities of northern China into surrendering.

Genghis Khan next turned his attention westward. He led his great army into central Asia, conquering city after city. His astonishing weapons, adapted from weapons invented by the Chinese, terrified cities into surrendering. Some weapons pitched rocks and flaming liquids over walls. Rockets, made by filling bamboo tubes with gunpowder and attaching them to long arrows, shot through the air. Genghis Khan shielded his own warriors by forcing captured people to march in front of them. No wonder cities feared the Mongol army.

In just three years, Genghis Khan and his army gained control of central Asia. Genghis Khan called himself "the emperor of all people."

Mongol rule. Genghis Khan learned from the people he conquered. In China he first considered destroying all the farms and using the land for herding. Soon, however, he gave up that idea. Genghis Khan learned that taxation

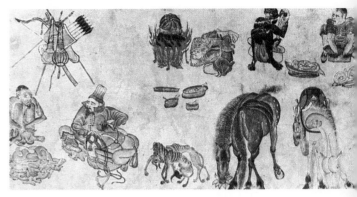

Mongol camps have always been busy places. Can you tell what activities are going on?

would help support his army. So he left a loyal general to rule China and to collect taxes from the Chinese people.

To the Mongols themselves, Genghis Khan gave laws to follow. These laws, called the Yasa (yä´sə´), forbade lying, treachery, and stealing. The old, the sick, the poor, and the wise were to be treated with respect. No one was to be harmed because of religion. The laws were strictly kept. Punishment for not following them was severe.

Karakorum (kər·ə·kōr´əm) in Mongolia was the capital city of the vast empire. People from all over the empire came to live there. Genghis Khan believed that the Mongols could learn from all people. So the city of yurts was filled with craftworkers from many lands. The government included advisers from China, Persia, and other conquered lands. **Diplomats,** or representatives of other countries, traveled to Karakorum from western Europe. Buddhists, Muslims, and Christians were allowed to practice their religions freely.

Genghis Khan united the Mongols and led them to conquer a large empire.

Genghis Khan died in 1227. Under his sons, the empire continued to expand. It reached the Middle East, Russia, Hungary, and Poland. Mongols conquered lands as far west as the Carpathian Mountains, as far south as the Himalaya Mountains, and as far east as the Pacific Ocean. Find the Mongol empire on the map on page 249.

The Decline of the Empires of the Nomads

About thirty-five years after the death of Genghis Khan, the empire began to break up into khanates, or states ruled by khans. Kublai Khan, the grandson who ruled China, moved the capital to the site of Peking. There he ruled as a Chinese emperor, not as a Mongol khan.

Khans in Persia, central Asia, and southern Russia began to go their own ways too. In areas such as China and Persia, the Mongols gradually became more like the people they had conquered. The Mongols adopted the local religion.

Swift horses and skillful fighting had made the nomads masters of the lands they conquered. The world changed, however, as did the lives and influence of the nomads. The use of firearms, for example, made it easier for other people to protect themselves from the nomads.

At one time the nomads had controlled the central Asian trade route that closely followed the route of the earlier Silk Road. Oceangoing ships and sea trade changed that. Ships could travel faster and were less expensive than caravans on overland routes. Travel through the steppe declined. The nomads lost their control over trade.

Marco Polo, an Italian merchant, traveled to China during Mongol rule.

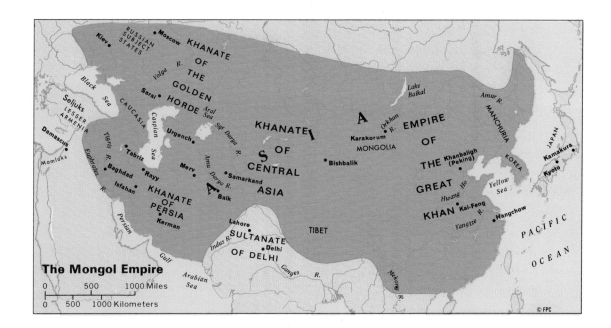

The Mongol Empire

0 500 1000 Miles
0 500 1000 Kilometers

Within a hundred years after his death, the great empire of Genghis Khan fell apart. Left behind were tales of great fighters, conquests, Mongol laws, and a vast empire that nearly covered the known world.

On the steppes the nomads kept the old Mongol ways. Many continued to live as their ancestors had until the 20th century.

Checking Up

1. How did Turkey get its name?
2. Describe Mongol rule in China.
3. What was the Yasa?
4. What answers would you give to the key questions at the beginning of this chapter?
5. *Why do you think Genghis Khan thought of himself as "the emperor of all people"?*

Unit 9 Summary

● The Eurasian steppe, a vast grassland, covered parts of Europe and Asia.
● The Eurasian steppe was the homeland of three nomadic groups: the Huns, the Turks, and the Mongols.
● The steppe nomads were skillful fighters and hunters. They raided settled areas for goods. With horses, the nomads could travel great distances.
● The Huns and Turks had great empires on the steppes. The greatest of all was that of the Mongol leader, Genghis Khan.
● Without strong leaders, the empires of the nomads often broke up.
● Two changes brought the influence of the steppe nomads to an end. Settled people began using firearms against the nomads. Trade shifted from an overland route to a sea route.

Maps Tell a Story of Distance

As you read, think about this term.
map scale

You have had a lot of practice locating different places on maps. You can also use maps to measure distances.

Map Scales

Most maps have a **map scale**. The map scale states the relationship between distance on the map and distance on the earth. Find the map scale for the map on page 251 in the upper left column.

Understanding map scales. Scale can be shown in many ways. This map scale is given in two ways. First, the scale is stated in words: One inch equals 2,000 miles. The map user knows right away that inches refer to distances on the map and miles refer to distances on the earth. If the distance between two places on the map is one inch, the actual distance on the earth between the same two places would be about 2,000 miles.

The map scale is also shown by a line or bar. The line is a special ruler for that map. The units on the line refer to distances on the map. The numbers above and below it refer to distances on the earth. The scale on the map on page 251 shows both miles and kilometers. The distance between marks above the line shows miles. The distance between marks below the line shows kilometers.

Now look at the Atlas map on pages 14–15. Find the map scale. How many miles on the earth does one inch on this map represent? Now turn to the Atlas map on pages 12–13. Notice that the scale on this map is also shown in a third way—1:105,000,000. This scale means that one unit of any measurement on the map (one inch, or one centimeter) would equal 105,000,000 of the same units on the earth.

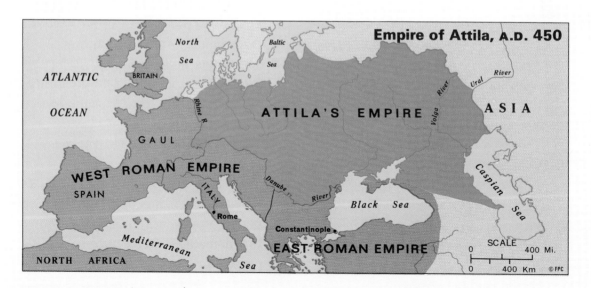

Empire of Attila, A.D. 450

250

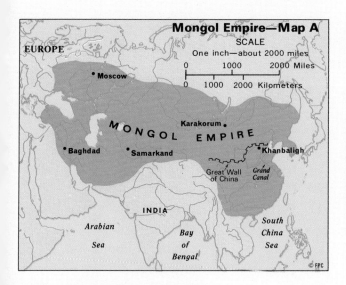

Mongol Empire—Map A

SCALE
One inch—about 2000 miles

0   1000   2000 Miles

0   1000   2000 Kilometers

EUROPE
• Moscow
MONGOL EMPIRE
Karakorum •
• Baghdad   • Samarkand   • Khanbaligh
Great Wall of China   Grand Canal
INDIA
Arabian Sea
Bay of Bengal
South China Sea
© FPC

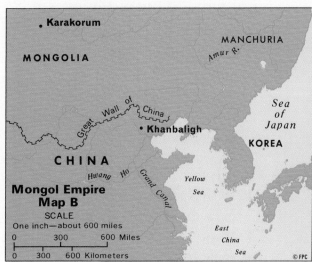

• Karakorum
MANCHURIA
MONGOLIA
Amur R.
Great Wall of China
• Khanbaligh
Sea of Japan
KOREA
CHINA
Hwang Ho
Grand Canal
Yellow Sea
Mongol Empire Map B
SCALE
One inch—about 600 miles

0   300   600 Miles

0   300   600 Kilometers
East China Sea
© FPC

Using map scales. As you know, the empires of the nomads covered vast areas of Eurasia. The map on page 250 shows the extent of the empire of Attila the Hun. Using the map scale, measure the distance across the widest part of the empire. About how many miles did you measure? how many kilometers? Now, using the Atlas map on pages 14–15 and its scale, measure the same distance. Is your answer about the same? Differences occur because the map scales are different. Distances on maps in which a short distance represents many miles can be only approximate.

Now look at Map A at the top of this page. It shows the Mongol empire following the reign of Genghis Khan. This empire was the largest the world had known. What is the scale of this map? Using the scale, measure the distance across the widest part of the empire. Notice that the empire included Moscow, a city in what is today the Soviet Union. Princes from this area once traveled to the Khan's court at Karakorum. How many miles did they travel? Kublai Khan later moved the capital from Karakorum to Khanbaligh, now the site of Peking. How far apart were the two capitals?

Now look at map B. It shows part of Kublai Khan's empire. What is the scale on this map? Using this scale, measure again the distance from Karakorum to Khanbaligh. Is your answer close to your earlier one? Your answers may differ because the map scales are not the same. Use the word *about* when you state distances measured on small-scale maps. The larger the map scale, the more accurate measurements can be.

Checking Up

1. What is the purpose of a map scale?
2. Using map A, measure the distance from Khanbaligh to Samarkand. About how many miles is it? how many kilometers?

Unit 9 Review Workshop

What Have You Learned?

1. Describe the land and climate of the Eurasian steppe.
2. How did the people of the steppe become nomads?
3. How were the nomadic groups organized?
4. What kind of homes did steppe nomads have?
5. What did nomads think shamans could do?
6. Who was Attila?
7. What were the names of two Turkish groups? Why were these groups important?
8. Who was Genghis Khan? How did he conquer an empire?
9. What made Karakorum an important city?
10. Who was Timur?
11. Why did the influence of the nomads decline?
12. In what three countries do the Mongols live today?

Use Your Reading Skills

In this unit new words have been introduced. Words that you learned in earlier units were also used in this unit. The first column below lists both old and new words. The second column lists definitions. Write the letter of the correct definition next to each vocabulary word.

1. clan
2. diplomat
3. empire
4. khan
5. migrate
6. nomad
7. shaman
8. steppe
9. treaty
10. tribe
11. yurt

a. a leader of a nomad tribe
b. a grassland
c. a person who moves from place to place
d. a group of families under one leader
e. a group of many families and their leaders
f. many countries ruled by one person
g. a type of home
h. an agreement between countries
i. to move from one place to another
j. a religious leader
k. a representative of a country

Use Your Map Skills

Look at the map on this page. It shows the three main parts of the Eurasian steppe. Using this map and your Atlas map on pages 10–11, answer the following questions.

1. What present-day country is located on the Russian steppe?
2. What other countries in eastern Europe does the steppe cover?
3. What country includes the largest part of the Eurasian steppe?
4. What other two Asian countries does the steppe penetrate?
5. Through what present-day countries in Asia and the Middle East did the trade route from China to the Middle East run?

The Eurasian Steppe

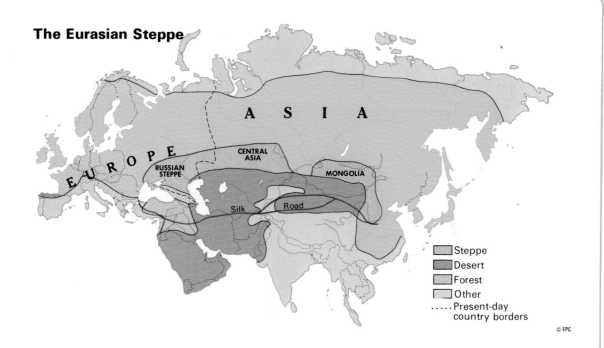

Use Your Writing Skills

Historians have noted that the use of the compass, printing, and gunpowder appeared in Europe in the 1300s and 1400s. The Chinese had invented all three before 1200, about when the Mongols began to unite Eurasia. Write a paragraph explaining why you think the Mongol conquests did or did not help spread their use. Use the maps and time line on pages 232–233 to help you.

Learn by Doing

1. Each of the people listed below was important in the history of the nomads. Find out more about one of them. In a report for your class, include why this person was important, and when and where he lived.

   Attila   Genghis Khan
   Kublai Khan   Timur

2. The horse was important to the nomads' way of life. Find out more about the horse. When was the horse probably first domesticated? How was the horse introduced into the Americas? How did the Plains Indians of North America use the horse? What were the similarities between the ways the Plains Indians and the steppe nomads used the horse? What were the differences? Make a chart showing the information you find.

Read to Learn More

Find the topics listed below in the card catalog of your library. Read all or part of a book listed under one of the topics. Share what you learn with your classmates.

GENGHIS KHAN   MARCO POLO
ATTILA   MONGOLS

Unit 10

The World of Islam

Islam is both a religion and a civilization. Followers of Islam pray in mosques adorned with examples of the art of Islam.

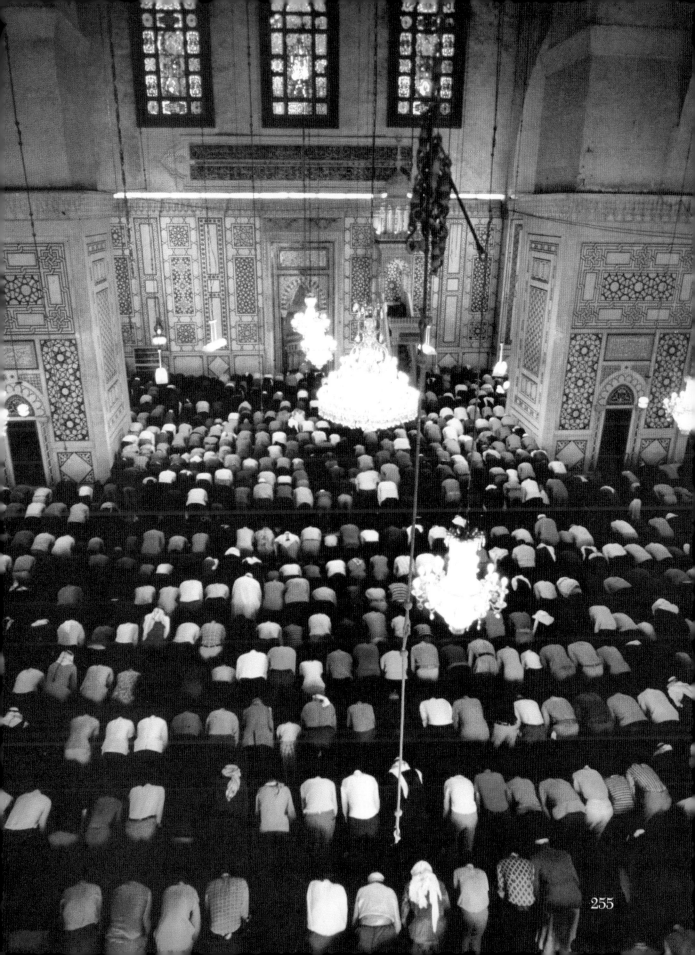

The Beginnings of Islam

As You Read

1. Think about these words.
   pilgrimage   Islam   Muslim
2. Look for answers to these key questions.
   a. What was the climate of Arabia like? How did it affect the way people lived?
   b. What were the religious beliefs of the early Arabs?
   c. What are the beliefs and practices of Islam?
3. Use this reading skill.
   As you read, it is important to interpret, or explain, the meaning of facts. In this chapter, for example, you will read about Arabia, a hot, desert region away from the centers of civilization. Because of its climate and geography, Arabia would not seem to be an important place. Yet Arabia had great importance for world history. How can you explain this fact? Why was it possible for the religion of Islam to begin there?

Most of Arabia is a hot, desert land. For centuries, Arabia's dry land and hot climate have protected it from outsiders. In the summer, temperatures climb to 130 °F (54 °C) during the day. They drop to near freezing at night. However, Arabia has had great influence on the world. Islam, one of the most important religions, started there. A civilization based on this religion later flourished in many other parts of the world.

The Land, Climate, and People of Arabia

Arabia is a peninsula that is surrounded on its three sides by the Red Sea, the Arabian Sea, and the Persian Gulf. It is a large area that covers more than one million square miles (2,590,000 sq km). Look at the Atlas map on pages 12–13. Find the Arabian peninsula. Now find this peninsula on the map on pages 16–17. Notice that much of the peninsula is a desert. It gets only three or four inches (7.6 or 10 cm) of rain a year. What area receives the most rainfall? There are no permanent rivers and few streams on the peninsula. Lack of water makes farming almost impossible.

Now look at the land use map on pages 20–21. In what ways is the land in this area used? What is the main use of Arabian land? Even though these maps show the land today, the patterns have lasted for centuries.

People. In spite of the harshness of the climate, three groups of people made their homes in ancient Arabia. Some were herders. Large groups of desert nomads called Bedouin (bed'ə·wən) herded sheep, goats, and camels across the desert from one grassy area to another. The Bedouin were divided into many tribes. Each tribe was then divided into large family groups, or clans. Often clans fought for valuable grazing land.

A few people farmed. Most farmers lived in mountains near the seacoasts, where farming was possible because of the available water. Other farming groups lived near desert oases, where there was water, and plants could grow. Farmers grew melons, figs, and dates.

Arabian Peninsula
- —— Extent of Byzantine Empire
- - - - Extent of Persian Empire
- —— Trade Route

The third group of people who lived in Arabia were merchants. They sold food, water, weapons, and clothing to the Bedouin and farmers and to people from other lands. The merchants lived in oasis villages or in one of Arabia's few towns.

Trade routes crossed a mountainous area called the Hejaz (hej·az'). Locate these mountains on the map on page 257. West of the Hejaz lay the Red Sea. On the east stretched the great desert of the Arabian peninsula. The rich oasis of Yathrib (yath'rab), later called Medina (ma·dē'na), was located in the middle part of the Hejaz.

At the foot of the mountains in the Hejaz rose the most important of Arabian cities—Mecca (mek'ə). Mecca was located at the bottom of a rocky valley about 50 miles (80 km) from the Red Sea. Since the ground was rocky and uneven, no one could farm there.

However, Mecca did have one important thing in its favor—water. The rains that fell in the winter filled streams in the area, especially the big stream called Zamzam. Because of its water, Mecca became a busy trade center. Caravans stopped there on their way to Syria or Persia. Merchants traded for the gold, silver, silk, perfumes, and slaves brought from faraway places. People of many other lands—Africans, Persians, Syrians, and Greeks—visited and lived in Mecca.

The ways of life of the Bedouin, farmers, and merchants were different. Yet all three groups shared the same culture. Each spoke a form of the Arabic language. Thus, they were called Arabs.

Muslims have made the pilgrimage to Mecca since Muhammad's time.

Religion of the Early Arabs

The people of ancient Arabia believed in many gods and spirits. They believed that spirits lived in trees, water, and stones. They considered one god, however, to be more powerful than all the others. The god's name was Allah (ä′lä).

There was also one object that was especially important to the ancient Arabians. It was a large black meteorite that had fallen to earth about 1,500 years earlier. The meteorite was in the city of Mecca. The Arabs built a box-shaped temple called the Kaaba (käb′a) around the meteorite. Every year, many Arabs made a special trip, or **pilgrimage**, to visit the Kaaba. The yearly pilgrimage brought many people to Mecca. The merchants, who sold the pilgrims goods, became rich. Merchants belonging to the Quraish (kə·rīsh′) tribe became especially rich and powerful.

The Birth of Islam

Muhammad (mō·ham′əd) was born in A.D. 570 in Mecca. He belonged to the Quraish merchant tribe. Because his parents died when he was young, Muhammad was raised by his grandfather and later by an uncle. When he was a young man, he worked as a merchant for his family. Later he worked for a rich businesswoman. It was his job to lead trading caravans of camels loaded with goods from Mecca to Syria.

It is believed Muhammad first met Christians on his trips to Syria. He also knew Jews who lived in Arabia. Thus, Muhammad knew of Jesus and his teachings, of the Hebrew prophets, and of the idea of one God.

Muhammad later married his wealthy employer. He no longer had to work to earn a living. He spent much of his time thinking about religion. Often he went to a quiet place in the desert where he thought about his beliefs.

One night Muhammad believed an angel appeared before him. The angel told him that he was to become the messenger of the one and only God, Allah. It seemed to Muhammad that Allah had chosen him for special work. Later Muhammad claimed he received other messages from Allah. Muhammad's friends wrote down these words of Allah. These writings became the Koran. The Koran was a holy book that told people how to live. Muhammad called his religion **Islam**, which means "submission to the will of Allah." Believers in Islam became known as **Muslims**, "those who have sub-

Muslims pray by kneeling and bowing their heads toward Mecca.

mitted themselves to the will of Allah." Muslims of today practice Islam in the same way as the first Muslims of Muhammad's time.

The Faith of Islam

The religion of Islam is based on the set of beliefs and duties described in the Koran. These beliefs and duties form what are known as the Five Pillars of Islam. The five pillars are having faith, praying, giving money to the poor, fasting, or not eating and drinking at certain times of the year, and making a pilgrimage to Mecca at least once in a lifetime.

Muslim worshipers believe the following: "There is no God but Allah, and Muhammad is his prophet." Every person who wishes to accept the religion of Islam has to repeat that sentence. By custom, the words are the first whispered into the ear of a baby born of Muslim parents. They are also the last words spoken to a dying Muslim. Muslims also believe the Koran is the word of Allah.

Muslims accept many of the same teachings as Jews and Christians. In fact, Muhammad respected Jews and Chris-

tians, calling them "the people of the book," meaning the Bible. He accepted the Jewish prophets as real messengers from Allah. He also respected Jesus as a prophet of God. However, he saw himself as the last of Allah's messengers.

Faithful Muslims pray five times each day—at sunrise, at noon, in the afternoon, after sunset, and at night. They also give money for the needs of poor Muslims. Healthy Muslims fast during certain times of the year. All members of the faith try to travel to Mecca at least once during their lives to pray there.

In addition to the Five Pillars, the Koran also has rules for the daily lives of Muslims. Believers do not eat pork or the meat of an animal that has died because of sickness. They do not drink alcohol. These rules make Islam a way of life.

Checking Up

1. How did Mecca become an important trading center?
2. Who was Muhammad? What was his importance to Islam?
3. Why is the Koran important to the Muslims?
4. What answers would you give to the key questions at the beginning of this chapter?
5. *What are the similarities among Judaism, Christianity, and Islam? What are the differences? Think about the following ideas in your comparison: God, prophets, Holy Book, religious duties.*

The Spread of Islam

As You Read

1. Think about these words.
   idol   caliph   sect   emir   mosque   sultan
2. Look for answers to these key questions.
   a. How did Muhammad establish his religion in Arabia?
   b. How did rule by caliphs develop in Islam?
   c. What was Muslim civilization like outside the Middle East?
3. Use this reading skill.
   If you do not know the meaning of a word, you know you can look it up in the Glossary of the book or in a dictionary. Sometimes, however, you can understand what an unfamiliar word means from the way it is used in a sentence. For example, read this sentence: "He ruled like a powerful sultan." From the way *sultan* is used, you know it means a powerful ruler. Try to learn the meaning of unfamiliar words this way.

Muhammad did not immediately begin to spread his new faith. He was afraid of the enemies he was making. Many people of Mecca worried that Islam would end the pilgrimages to the Kaaba. If people no longer came to Mecca, the city's merchants feared that they would lose much business. Even members of Muhammad's own Quraish tribe were against him.

The Spread of Islam in Arabia

Muhammad decided to leave Mecca. In 622 he fled north to the rich oasis called Yathrib. There he gradually built up a strong group of believers. Within eight years Yathrib was changed from an oasis village to a city. The new city was called Medina, or Medinat al-Nebi ("the city of the Prophet"). From Medina in 630, Muhammad led an army of 10,000 followers in an attack on Mecca, the city of the holy Kaaba.

After much fierce fighting Mecca fell to the warriors of Islam. Muhammad then returned to the Kaaba. As his enemies had feared, he destroyed the **idols**, or statues worshipped there as gods. However, he left the Kaaba itself untouched. From Mecca Muhammad took his faith first to his own Quraish tribe and then to the Bedouin tribes of the desert. The Bedouin became an important part of the army of Islam. Muhammad died in 632, two years after his victory at Mecca. His followers continued spreading his faith far beyond the Arabian peninsula.

Beyond Arabia

Muhammad had not named anyone to take his place after his death. Muslim leaders decided that power should be given to someone who had been close to Muhammad in some way. They chose Abu Bakr, the first convert of Muhammad, to become the leader of Islam.

Abu Bakr became the first of the **caliphs** (kā′ləfs), or successors to the prophet Muhammad. Under Abu Bakr's leadership, Muslims began to spread Islam beyond Arabia.

Abu Bakr sent Arab warriors northward into territories of the Byzantine and Persian empires. The Byzantine Empire was the name of the eastern part of the Roman Empire. It included Anatolia and Greece and extended to Syria and Egypt. The Persian Empire extended from present-day Iraq and the Persian

Muhammad's face was not shown so it would not be worshiped.

Gulf to central Asia. Look at the map on page 257 and find these two empires. Within twenty years of Muhammad's death, Muslims had defeated the Persian Empire and taken Syria and Egypt from the Byzantines.

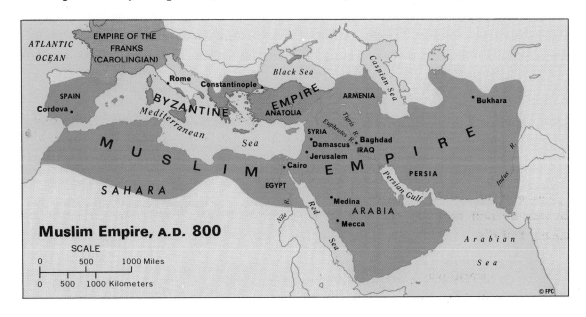

Muslim Empire, A.D. 800

SCALE

0 — 500 — 1000 Miles

0 — 500 — 1000 Kilometers

The most important reason for the Muslim victories over their enemies was the faith of Islam's soldiers. With Allah on their side, they believed they could not lose. Their leaders also told them that any soldier who died fighting a "holy war" would be rewarded by going to heaven. Allah, they said, would welcome any soldier who had fought to spread Islam. The Muslims were also helped in their victories because the Byzantine and Persian empires had been weakened by wars between them.

Dynasties of Caliphs

As Muslim armies were winning victories in other parts of the Middle East, trouble arose in Arabia. The third caliph was killed by enemies. Ali, the fourth caliph, was opposed by several groups. Great unrest spread across the land. War broke out because of the dispute over the succession to the office of caliph. Ali was defeated. His followers became members of a rival Muslim **sect**, or religious group.

The victor in this dispute became the new caliph. He made the city of Damascus (də·mas′kəs) in Syria the capital of Islam. For the next ninety years, members of his family ruled as caliphs. Look at the timeline on this page. When did the caliphs begin to rule from Damascus?

New Conquests. Toward the end of the 600s, Muslims conquered North Africa. They brought Islam to the people who lived there. North African Muslims became known as Moors. In the year 711, Arabs and Moors moved north from Africa into Spain. Turn to the map on page 261. In which directions did Islam spread? What natural barrier did the Moors have to cross to enter Europe?

The Muslims treated people they conquered with greater fairness than other conquerors of the time. They did not force everyone to become Muslim. They even allowed Jews and Christians to keep their own religions. Those who did not convert to Islam had only to pay a special tax.

The Caliphs of Baghdad. As Islam expanded, the caliphs in Damascus became very worldly, or interested in the riches they had won. Their Arab army turned

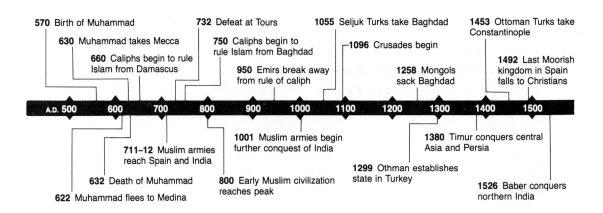

570 Birth of Muhammad

630 Muhammad takes Mecca

660 Caliphs begin to rule Islam from Damascus

732 Defeat at Tours

750 Caliphs begin to rule Islam from Baghdad

950 Emirs break away from rule of caliph

1055 Seljuk Turks take Baghdad

1096 Crusades begin

1258 Mongols sack Baghdad

1453 Ottoman Turks take Constantinople

1492 Last Moorish kingdom in Spain falls to Christians

A.D. 500   600   700   800   900   1000   1100   1200   1300   1400   1500

711–12 Muslim armies reach Spain and India

632 Death of Muhammad

622 Muhammad flees to Medina

800 Early Muslim civilization reaches peak

1001 Muslim armies begin further conquest of India

1299 Othman establishes state in Turkey

1380 Timur conquers central Asia and Persia

1526 Baber conquers northern India

against them. Members of the sect that was formed by the followers of Ali also joined this uprising. In 750 the leader of a new family became the caliph. He moved the capital of Islam to Baghdad (bag'dad'). Look at the time line on page 262. When did early Muslim civilization reach its peak?

The power of these Baghdad caliphs began to weaken after two hundred years. **Emirs** (i · mirz'), or local commanders in North Africa, Persia, and central Asia, still declared their loyalty to the caliphs. The caliphs, however, had little power.

Islam Outside the Middle East

Muslim civilization has thrived in areas distant from the Middle East and in periods long after the first three centuries of Islam. Spain, India, and Africa have all been centers of Islam.

Muslims in Spain. When the Moors crossed the Strait of Gibraltar into Spain, they conquered almost all the country within seven years. After their victory the Moors then crossed the Pyrenees into France. Their advance into Europe was stopped in 732 at the Battle of Tours. Nevertheless, the Moors remained in Spain for almost 800 years.

The Moors began many towns and cities in Spain. The greatest city of them all was Cordova (kôrd'ə · və), the Moorish capital. By 960 Cordova had a population of 250,000 people. The city was dotted with palaces, public baths with hot and cold running water, and **mosques**, or Muslim places of worship. Fountains and

Cordova's Great Mosque had slender columns and horseshoe arches.

flower gardens added to the city's beauty. Cordova grew to be the greatest center of learning in all Europe. Europeans from many countries came to the city to study in its great libraries and to trade at its rich markets.

Farms surrounded Cordova. Farmers grew olives, grapes, and vegetables. The Moors irrigated their fields and used mules and donkeys for plowing instead of slower oxen. They also grew new crops such as rice, cotton, sugarcane, oranges, and lemons. Moorish craft wares such as silk, paper, rugs, leather, and glass had no equal throughout Europe.

Muslims in India. Muslims gained a foothold in the Indus Valley in India in

263

712, a year after the Moors entered Spain. Muslim armies did not begin a full-scale invasion, however, until three centuries later. They then settled down to enjoy the wealth of this rich land. Soon India was filled with many Muslim kingdoms.

Early in the 1500s, another Muslim army overran India. A Turk named Baber (bäb′ər) led it. Because Baber claimed he descended from Genghis Khan, his dynasty is known as the Mogul, which means "Mongol." The Mongols were the conquerors you learned about in Unit 9. At first the Mogul emperors controlled only the north of India. However, by 1690, they had taken over most of the Muslim and Hindu kingdoms farther south. The wars between Muslims and Hindus left much bitterness in India. This ill feeling has lasted into the 20th century.

The Moguls were great builders. They left mosques, palaces, forts, and tombs that can still be seen in India today. A palace at Delhi, the Mogul capital, is one of the largest palaces on earth.

Muslims in Africa. In the 900s and 1000s, Muslim traders and missionaries began to travel south into Africa. They crossed the Sahara into the west African empire of Ghana. The Muslims mainly converted the rulers of the people they met. Many Africans continued to worship spirits in their traditional ways. Islam only gradually reached a larger number of people. Several Muslim empires later arose in the grassland region along the southern edge of the Sahara.

As Islam spread, Africans began to study the Arabic language. They read and enjoyed Arabic poetry. They were especially interested in the Koran, which they studied in schools such as the uni-

The Taj Mahal, the most famous Mogul building, is a tomb for a Mogul queen.

The empire of Mali extended to the starting point of Saharan caravan routes. Mali's mosques blended African with Muslim forms.

versity at Timbuktu in the Empire of Mali. This site became a center of learning in Africa. There Muslim scholars studied history, law, mathematics, and Islam. Because Timbuktu was attacked many times, it eventually declined as a center of trade and learning.

Turks and Crusaders

About the year 1000, the Turks began to take over many lands of the Middle East. The Turks were one of the groups of nomads you learned about in Unit 9. Named after their early leader, Seljuk (sel'jōōk'), these Turks conquered Baghdad in 1055. The Seljuks allowed the caliphs to stay in Baghdad. The Seljuk rulers, however, held real power. They took the title of sultan, or ruler.

Jerusalem also fell to the Seljuks. For centuries Jerusalem had been a city of special religious meaning to Jews, Christians, and Muslims. After Jerusalem was taken, the Seljuks next threatened Con-stantinople, the capital of the Christian Byzantine Empire. To save the city and the empire, the Byzantine emperor asked for help from Christians in Europe. A series of wars were begun by the Christians to try to drive back the Turks and to capture Jerusalem. These wars lasted hundreds of years.

Checking Up

1. Why did Muslim soldiers fight so bravely in the name of Islam?
2. How did Muslims treat the people they conquered?
3. Why were the caliphs in Damascus overthrown?
4. What answers would you give to the key questions at the beginning of this chapter?
5. *What influence did the Moors have upon the way of life of people in Spain?*

Muslim Love of Beauty and Learning

As You Read

1. Think about this word.
   minaret
2. Look for answers to these key questions.
   a. What did the Muslims learn from the Greeks?
   b. What contributions did Muslims make to mathematics? What contributions did they make to medicine?
   c. Name some Muslim accomplishments in the fields of literature and architecture.

The Muslims learned much from earlier civilizations and from the people they conquered. From the writings of the Greeks, Romans, Persians, and Indians, the Muslims learned about art, science, mathematics, astronomy, and farming. They drew upon this knowledge to create new forms of art, architecture, and literature. They also made many scientific discoveries of their own. Just 200 years after Muhammad's death, the Muslim world was alive with a new interest in art, building, and science. From Muslim outposts in southern Europe, such as Spain, the new interest in learning spread northward.

The Importance of Learning

Muslim leaders encouraged their followers to learn to read. Muslims read the Koran because it was believed to contain Allah's own words. People who could read could study what Allah had said, and Muhammad had taught.

Muslims discovered books written by the ancient Greeks. From these writings the Arabs learned about medicine and the human body. They learned about philosophy from books by Plato and Aristotle. From Euclid they learned mathematics. From Ptolemy they learned to study the stars.

Great Schools and Scientists

Muslims led the world in learning from the 800s through the 1300s. Islamic universities and libraries were started in such widely separated cities as Baghdad, Cordova, Cairo, and Timbuktu.

Mathematics. In Baghdad Muslim mathematicians developed algebra, a branch of mathematics that uses symbols to solve problems. The word *algebra* comes from the Arabic word *al-jabr*, which means "the joining of broken parts." From India Muslims borrowed the numbers that we use today. We still call our numbers arabic numerals. The

266

Muslim sailors used the astrolabe to fix their position at sea.

Indian number system was based on ten and included the idea of zero. Our word *zero* comes from the Arabic word *sifr*.

Muslims used their mathematical skills to help them understand the movements of the stars and planets. Muslim astronomers charted the orbit of the moon around the earth. They worked out a highly accurate calender that was based on the twelve revolutions of the moon around the earth every 355 days. These Muslim scientists believed that the earth was round at a time when some folk stories of Europe still thought that the earth was flat.

Medicine. The Muslims also made great progress in medicine. They pre-pared medicines from different plants to treat many kinds of illnesses. Muslim doctors, for example, used strong herbal teas to treat fever and infections. Salves were used to treat sores and ulcers. Stronger drugs made from some plants were used to control pain.

Muslims understood the importance of cleanliness in preventing illness. They even built hospitals in large cities. They also tested doctors before allowing them to practice medicine. Baghdad once had 860 doctors with licenses to practice medicine. One of these doctors wrote over 200 books on medicine, astronomy, and chemistry, or the science that studies the makeup of matter. This doctor explained the difference between measles and smallpox, and studied how infections spread among people. These books were later translated into Latin. They helped doctors in western Europe learn more about disease and the human body.

Art and Architecture

Beauty interested Muslims. They developed their own style of art. Because

Muslim geographers drew maps to help merchants in far-off lands.

267

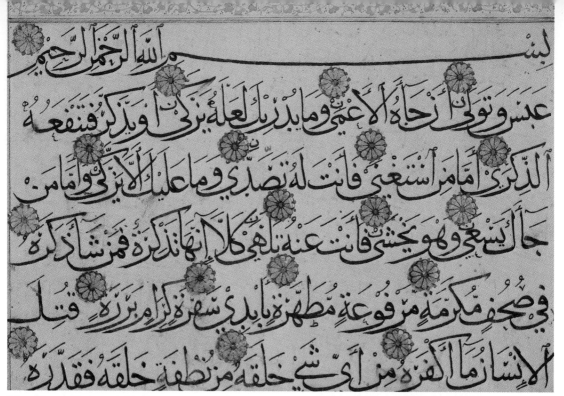

Muslim artists perfected the art of calligraphy, or beautiful writing, for the verses of the Koran.

Muhammad did not believe in idols, he asked Muslims not to show the forms of people or animals in art. He feared the people might worship these images. Muslim artists, therefore, developed an art that usually did not show living creatures. Instead, the artists painted beautiful, complicated designs of flowering vines and connecting lines. They used bright colors to give life to their artwork. The artists also developed beautiful styles of writing. They created works of art using quotations from the Koran and from poetry. With these quotations, they decorated swords, fine rugs, and tiles on the walls of buildings.

Storytelling. Before writing, storytellers from each Arab tribe provided entertainment by telling stories—stories people had already heard many times before but which they loved to hear time and again. *The Arabian Nights* is a collection of such stories. They were first told in Persia and later written down in Egypt during the 1300s. They tell of a caliph and of the brave sailor Sinbad, of Ali Baba and the forty thieves, and of Aladdin and his magic lamp. These stories are still popular today, nearly 1,000 years after they were first told.

Architecture. Muslims also contributed a great deal to architecture. Muslim architects studied the rich churches and palaces of the Byzantines and Persians. The type of dome that topped Byzantine churches also appeared on the first great mosque, the "Dome of the Rock" mosque in Jerusalem. It was built in 691. Look at the picture of the dome of this mosque on page 77. Early Muslims had prayed in simple, undecorated mosques. Later, caliphs decided that Muslims

In one story from the *Arabian Nights*, Aladdin finds a genie inside a lamp.

should have large and richly decorated houses of worship. To do this, they called in craftworkers and stonecutters from all over the Muslim world.

From corners of the outside walls of mosques rose tall, slender towers called **minarets.** From the tops of these minarets, criers called muezzins (moo·ez′ənz) called believers to prayer five times each day. Muslims bowed down on prayer rugs in the direction of Mecca and prayed. They answered the call to prayer both in mosques and at home.

Some buildings were constructed to do more than honor Allah. The caliphs also raised great palaces for themselves. One of the finest of these palaces is the Alhambra in Spain, built for the Moorish rulers of Granada, the last Muslim kingdom in Spain. Look at the picture on page 270. The graceful columns and arches of the Alhambra have dazzled visitors for centuries. At first the Muslims may have imitated Byzantine and Persian architecture. However, in the Alhambra we see that they became masters of this art in their own right.

From the top of tall, slender minarets, muezzins call believers to prayer.

Muezzins have been called the church bells of Islam.

Then and Now

The Arab Nations

Muslims once influenced most of the known world. Muslims were leaders in many areas, such as astronomy, mathematics, medicine, sailing, and trade. However, the Muslim world lost its lead centuries ago. After about 1500, Arab nations did not continue to progress in developing science and technology. Stronger European powers such as England and France could control weaker Arab countries such as Egypt and Algeria. Today, however, there seems to be a new feeling of nationalism, a firm belief in a country and way of life, among the Arabs.

The wealth many Arab countries have earned from oil over the last 50 years has increased the importance of the Arab world. Several Arab countries in the Middle East and Africa are now the world's largest suppliers of oil, one of the earth's basic sources of energy. In-

Oil wealth has brought great changes to the Middle East.

dustrialized countries of the West need the oil for transportation, heating, and manufacturing. These countries have paid higher and higher prices to get it. As a result, Arab countries are once again holding power in the world. For the first time since the days of the early caliphs, Arab countries have influence in world affairs.

The fountain spouts in the Alhambra, a famous Moorish castle, look like lions.

The Decline of Early Islam

As Muslims were making great progress in the arts and sciences, the power of the caliph was slowly beginning to decline. The final blow came in 1258, when Baghdad fell to Mongol invaders. The Mongols killed the last caliph. They destroyed many cities and irrigation networks in Persia and Iraq. It took centuries for this region to recover.

A new Muslim power, centered in Turkey, reunited much of the Muslim Middle East in the 1400s and 1500s. Named after their first leader, Othman (ōth·män'), the Ottoman Turks con-

In 1453 Mehmet, the Ottoman sultan, conquered Constantinople.

quered Syria, Iraq, Egypt, North Africa, and southeastern Europe. The Ottoman Empire, the last great Muslim power in the Middle East, lasted until the 20th century.

Checking Up
1. Why did Muslims study the Koran?
2. Why did Muhammad forbid Muslims to show the forms of people or animals in art?
3. How did the world state of the caliph decline?

4. What answers would you give to the key questions at the beginning of this chapter?
5. *Why were Muslim outposts in southern Europe, such as Spain, important in reawakening an interest in learning in Europe?*

Unit 10 Summary
● Arabia, a harsh, dry land, supported three groups of people: nomads, farmers, and merchants.
● The prophet Muhammad built up a group of believers in Medina. He then took Mecca, where he converted members of his own tribe and other Bedouin tribes.
● Muhammad called his new religion Islam, which means "submission to the will of Allah."
● Muslims, or "those who have submitted themselves to the will of Allah," base their lives on the Five Pillars of Islam.
● Muslims believe the Koran contains the actual words of Allah.
● A short time after Muhammad's death, Muslim armies spread Islam from Spain to India.
● The Arabs learned from the people they conquered. They contributed to medicine, mathematics, art, and architecture.
● Rule by the caliphs ended when the Mongols seized Baghdad in 1258. The religion of Islam, however, has followers in most parts of the world today.

271

Maps Tell a Story of the Spread of Islam

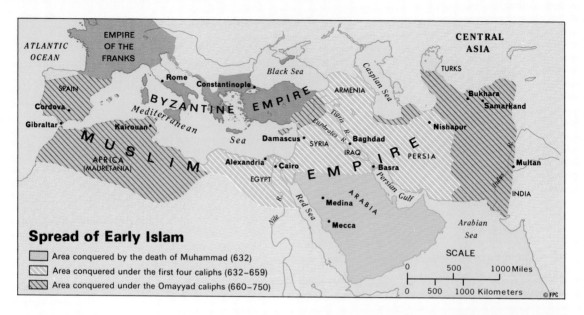

Spread of Early Islam

Area conquered by the death of Muhammad (632)
Area conquered under the first four caliphs (632–659)
Area conquered under the Omayyad caliphs (660–750)

In Unit 8 you learned about urban hearths, areas where cities developed. The growth of many civilizations took place in these urban hearths. Throughout history, however, civilizations have often spread. Looking at Islam shows how such a spreading has taken place.

Look at the map above. It shows you two things. First, it tells you the periods in which early Islam spread. Second, it shows the areas into which Islam spread. Islam began in the cities of Mecca and Medina. Use the map key to find the name of the area in which these two cities are found. Use the map key to find the territory that Muslims had conquered by Muhammad's death in 632.

Islam continued to spread under the first four caliphs who ruled between 632 and 659. What five areas did Muslim armies conquer during this period? Remember that these armies were traveling overland, often by camel. What was the overland distance from Medina to Damascus? to Cairo? to Basra? to Nishapur?

Islam spread even greater distances in the period after the capital was moved to Damascus. Look again at the above map. What four areas were conquered by Muslim armies between 660 and 750? What is the overland distance from Damascus to Kairouan? to Gibraltar? to Bukhara? to Multan? What is the distance from Gibraltar to Multan?

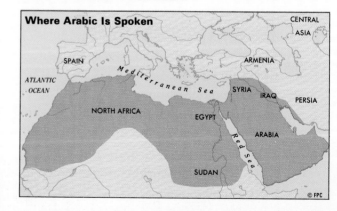

Where Arabic Is Spoken

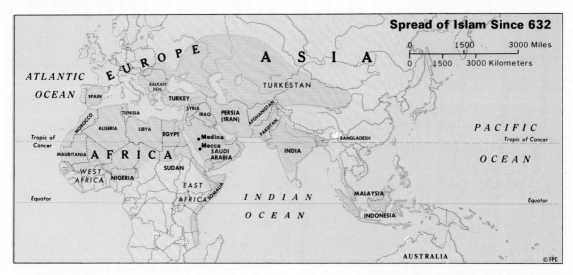

Spread of Islam Since 632

The soldiers in the first Muslim armies that spread Islam were Arabs. They brought their customs and language with them. As the conquered people became Muslims, many learned Arabic so they could study the Koran. In time these people began to use Arabic as their own language. Look at the second map on page 272. It shows the spread of the Arabic language. Compare it with the earlier map. In what four areas that the early Muslim armies conquered did Arabic become the language of the people? Not all people who were conquered by the Muslim Arabs took up the use of Arabic as their own language. Again look at the map on the spread of Arabic. Compare it with the earlier map. In what four areas conquered by the early Muslim armies was Arabic not adopted?

Remember that Islam began in Mecca and Medina. After 660 the development of Islam took place in the older centers of the Middle East, especially in the cities. Look at the first map on page 272. What are the names of two important cities in Iraq? in Egypt? What major city is in Syria? in North Africa? in Spain? in Persia? in central Asia?

Muslim civilization used the art and science of many other groups of people in the lands of the caliph. Islam, however, produced a new civilization of its own. This new civilization grew in the areas conquered by the early Muslim Arabs. In later periods of history, the religion and civilization of Islam was spread by other Muslim groups. Look at the map on this page. It shows the areas over which Islam has spread at different times since the beginning of Islam. Name five areas of the world that became a part of Islam after its early years of growth.

Checking Up

1. Where did the civilization of Islam develop?
2. How did Islam continue to spread long after its early years of growth?

273

Unit 10 Review Workshop

What Have You Learned?

1. How did Arabia's land and climate protect its people from invasion?
2. How was Islam different from the religion of the Arabs before the time of Muhammad?
3. Why did some members of Muhammad's own Quraish tribe oppose his new religion?
4. What is the Koran?
5. Where did the caliphs establish their capitals?
6. How was Islam spread to the region of Africa below the Sahara?
7. What were the Moguls famous for?
8. What contributions did Muslims make to mathematics and science?
9. Who were the Moors, where did they come from, and what area of Europe did they invade?
10. Why did many people from western Europe travel to Cordova in Spain?

Use Your Reading Skills

On a separate sheet of paper, fill in each blank with the word from the following list that best fits the definition.

pilgrimage	minaret	caliph
muezzin	Bedouin	sultan
emir	mosque	

1. Trip taken by a believer to visit a holy place: _____
2. Name given to successors of Muhammad: _____
3. Mosque crier who calls believers to prayer: _____
4. Name given commanders over whom the caliph had little power: _____
5. Muslim place of worship: _____
6. An Arab nomad: _____
7. A powerful Muslim ruler: _____
8. Slender tower rising from the walls of a mosque: _____

Use Your Research Skills

Do research on one of the following Muslim countries today.

Afghanistan	Algeria	Iran
Saudi Arabia	Lebanon	Libya
Morocco	Pakistan	Iraq
Jordan	Oman	Kuwait
Somalia	Sudan	Syria
Tunisia	Turkey	Yemen

Find out about the country's climate, landforms, natural resources, and people. Describe its government and industry, and include events that have happened there in the last five years. Use at least three sources to find your information: year books, magazines, encyclopedias.

Use Your Time Skills

Use the time line on page 262 to help you rearrange the following six events in the order in which they happened.

1. Arabs and Moors enter Spain.
2. Caliphs begin to rule from Baghdad.
3. Muhammad takes control of Mecca.
4. Baber conquers northern India.
5. Moors are defeated in the Battle of Tours.
6. Muhammad flees to Medina.

274

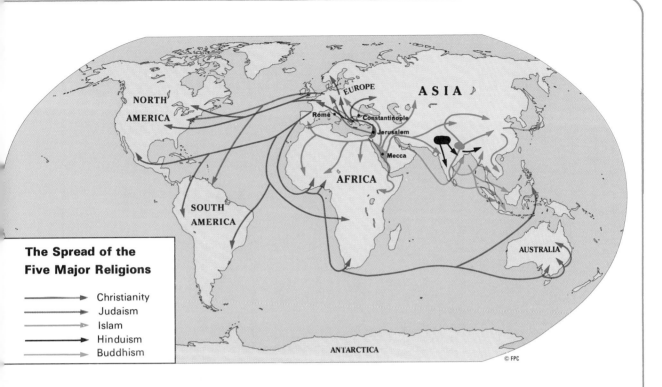

The Spread of the Five Major Religions

→ Christianity
→ Judaism
→ Islam
→ Hinduism
→ Buddhism

Use Your Map Skills

Like Islam, other important religions have spread over the world. Using the map above, answer these questions.

1. What two religions have spread mainly in Asia?
2. What two religions have spread into Africa?
3. What three religions have spread to Europe?
4. What religion has spread to all six continents where people live?

Learn by Doing

People measure the passage of time from the year of an important event. In many countries the years are counted from the birth of Jesus Christ. However, there are other chronologies, or time measurements. Muslims have a separate chronology. They count years from the time Muhammad fled from Mecca to Medina in A.D. 622. This event is called the Hegira (hi·jī′ra). Thus, on Muslim calendars our year A.D. 622 would be the year 1 of the Hegira.

On a separate piece of paper, write down these years according to our calendar: 711, 750, 1258, 1453, 1492. How many years after the Hegira did each of these important dates occur?

Learn to Read More

Find the topics listed below in the card catalog of your library. Read all or part of a book listed under one of the topics. Share what you learn with your classmates.

ISLAM   TURKEY

PERSIA   ARAB COUNTRIES

Unit 11

The European Middle Ages

The twin towers of Notre Dame in Chartres, France, rise above the city today. This 12th-century cathedral is an example of Gothic architecture.

277

A New Order in Europe

As You Read

1. Think about these words.

   noble   clergy   monastery

2. Look for answers to these key questions.

   a. Who were the important leaders who helped build the Frankish kingdom?

   b. How did Charlemagne rule his empire? What did he do to help learning?

   c. What factors helped unite Charlemagne's empire? What factors helped tear it apart?

3. Use this reading skill.

   People speak and write from their own points of view. Your outlook on school subjects, for instance, might be different from your classmates' outlooks. In the same way, people in history have recorded their own points of view. In this chapter, on page 284, you will read a passage about the Vikings' invasions of Europe. The passage was written by a member of another group. When you reach the passage, think of why the writer feared the Vikings. What might have been the Vikings' point of view? When you finish the chapter, write one paragraph, as if you were a Viking chief.

For about 1,000 years after the fall of Rome, western Europe entered a period we call the Middle Ages. European history is often divided into three parts. You have already read about the early civilizations of Greece and Rome, which make up the first, or ancient, part. The Middle Ages fall between these early civilizations and modern times. For convenience, historians often mark the year 1500 as the beginning of modern Europe. The dates and lengths of time for each part are not exact. The three-part division is simply a helpful way for us to organize historic events.

The fall of Rome in 476 brought many changes to western Europe. For a few hundred years, there were no powerful emperors with vast empires. Instead, many barbaric groups fought one another. Look at the map on the next page. Who were some of these groups?

Trade and travel began to suffer because of the unsafe conditions. Learning declined because there were few schools and books. The government, scholarship,

Europe After the Fall of Rome
About A.D. 500

and artistic life of western Roman civilization seemed to be lost.

Gradually, however, a new way of life developed. By the 8th century, there were once again powerful kingdoms with

Even their jewelry often reflected the barbarians' warlike spirit.

strong leaders to help establish order. More important, Christianity united nearly everyone in western Europe. The church became especially important. The Christian faith guided the daily lives of rich and poor alike.

The Frankish Kingdoms

The Franks were one of the strongest barbarian groups to emerge after the fall of Rome. The Franks invaded Gaul, the area just northwest of Italy that had been part of the Roman Empire. Gaul then became the center of a new kingdom for the Franks. The modern country France is named for the Franks.

Clovis. The Frankish king who led the invasion of Gaul was a young man named Clovis. Only fifteen years old when he became king in 481, Clovis invaded Gaul a few years later with his armies. In the following years, Clovis defeated rival barbarian groups.

Clovis's kingdom was the first important political, or governmental, organization of the early Middle Ages. The king unified his land further when he became a Christian. Many of Clovis's subjects in Gaul were already Christians, and his action pleased the people.

Clovis ruled for about thirty years. After his death the kingdom was divided and began to decline. Over the next two hundred years, rival kings competed for power.

Charles Martel. A leader named Charles Martel inherited power in a small Frankish kingdom in 715. The name *Martel* comes from the French word for "hammer." Charles was nicknamed "Charles the Hammer" because he defended Gaul from invading Muslims. He stopped them in the Battle of Tours that you learned about in Unit 10. Charles became a hero to the Franks. He was a strong leader who helped extend the Frankish kingdom. Charles was never officially king because that title was kept for the descendants of Clovis. Yet Charles was powerful and famous enough for his descendants to become Frankish kings.

Charlemagne and the Empire

Charles's grandson ruled the greatest European empire of the early Middle Ages. He was known as Charlemagne (shär′lə·mān′), which means Charles the Great. Charlemagne became king of the Franks in 771. He was constantly waging

Note how bold and strong Charlemagne looks in this statue. Why was he a successful emperor?

war against barbarian groups and against Muslims. As his armies defeated one enemy after another, Charlemagne brought more and more of Europe under his control. With each victory, Christianity spread. Charlemagne forced the conquered people to accept this faith.

Look at the map on the next page. What stages of growth are shown? How did the boundaries in western Europe change from the time of the Roman Empire to the height of Charlemagne's rule?

After the split of the Roman Empire, emperors continued to rule the Eastern, or Byzantine, Empire. Charlemagne's

280

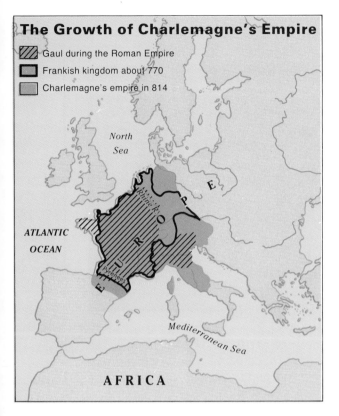

Gaul during the Roman Empire

Frankish kingdom about 770

Charlemagne's empire in 814

North Sea

ATLANTIC OCEAN

Mediterranean Sea

AFRICA

Religious and political leaders were powerful during the Middle Ages.

territory included much of the western part of the old Roman Empire. To many, Charlemagne seemed to have remade the Western Roman Empire. On Christmas Day in 800, Charlemagne went to church in Rome. During the service the pope, head of the Christian church, placed a crown on Charlemagne's head and proclaimed him emperor. The crowds roared their approval.

Managing an empire. Charlemagne knew it would be difficult to rule his huge empire alone. So he worked out a special system of government. Charlemagne divided the empire into smaller parts and put one of his **nobles** in charge of each part. Nobles were high-ranking officials of the empire. They were often related to a ruler. Charlemagne kept

careful check on each of the parts of the empire. The emperor also made frequent tours of inspection.

Revival of learning. Unlike the Romans, Charlemagne did not have many educated people to help him run his empire. During the early Middle Ages, few Europeans knew how to read and write.

Charlemagne loved learning. He gathered together teachers and scholars from all over Europe. He set up a school in his palace for the sons of the nobles. The emperor made frequent visits to the classroom too. He would personally punish students who had not learned their lessons.

281

Careers

Printing

The printing process has changed drastically since the time when scribes hand-produced their beautiful manuscripts in the monasteries. Think of all the printed materials there are today. Books, newspapers, magazines, labels, tickets, advertisements, signs, and package instructions are only some. Printing is one of the biggest industries in our country.

There are many different kinds of jobs in the printing field. Here are just a few.

Typesetters. People who first arrange the type, or letters, as they will look when printed are the typesetters. Typesetters usually work at electronic composing machines. The machines make an image of the type.

Proofreaders. Proofreaders carefully read the words that have been set. They look for mistakes and give the typesetter directions for correcting them.

Press operators. When the product is ready for the final printing of many copies, operators turn on the huge press.

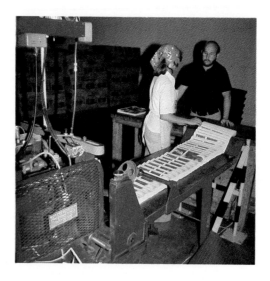

The material to be printed is on inked plates. These plates then press the type onto the paper fed into the press. The press can print hundreds of copies in minutes. Operators watch to see that the press is working properly. They also regularly check samples of what is being printed to be sure that the copies look all right.

Other schools were set up throughout the empire. Teaching was usually done by members of the **clergy**, the priests and others who chose a religious way of life. They were the only well-educated people of the time. The schools were usually in a **monastery**. Monasteries are separate communities of religious people. Scribes, or clergy members who were able to write, helped keep learning alive in the early Middle Ages. Working in monasteries, they patiently copied parts of the Bible and the works of Roman scholars. Most Roman writings we

Thousands of colorful manuscripts from the Middle Ages still exist.

282

Why do you think the scribes could be called artists of the Middle Ages?

know today have come to us through copies made by the scribes. The scribes' writings were known as manuscripts (man'yə·skripts') and were often highly decorated.

The Decline of Charlemagne's Empire

Charlemagne's great empire began to fall apart after his death in 814. The kings who came after Charlemagne were not as strong as he had been. Rivalry began when the empire was divided among Charlemagne's three grandsons.

Two other important factors led to the breakup of the empire. Although it was united in religion, the empire remained a collection of people with different customs and languages. In addition, new barbarian invasions began in the 9th century and lasted for about 100 years. The Magyars (mag'yärz), a group of nomads traveling on horseback, came from the east. Along the southern coast of Europe, Muslim pirates took control of the seas. From the north came the most feared people of all—the Vikings.

The Vikings. The Vikings were a seafaring people from northern Europe. They were adventurous sailors and fierce warriors. With their quick, long ships they raided the coast of Europe and sailed inland along rivers. Look at the

The Vikings traveled far and wide in ships like these.

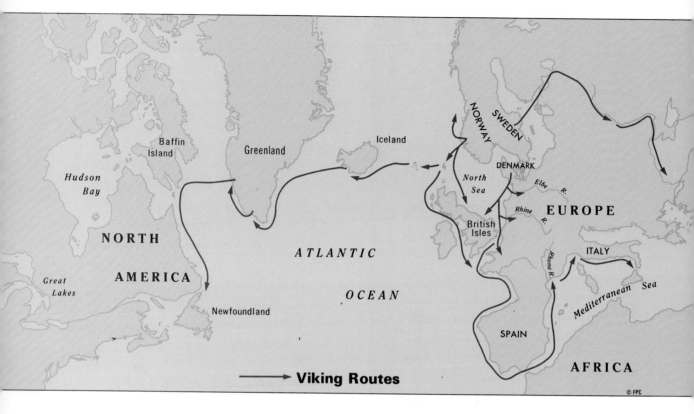

Hudson
Bay

Baffin
Island

Greenland

Iceland

NORWAY SWEDEN

DENMARK

North
Sea

Elbe R.

Rhine R.

EUROPE

British
Isles

ITALY

Rhone R.

NORTH

AMERICA

ATLANTIC

Great
Lakes

OCEAN

Newfoundland

Mediterranean Sea

SPAIN

AFRICA

© FPC

→ Viking Routes

map above. From what present-day European countries did the Vikings sail? To what places besides Europe did they travel?

Later, the Vikings settled some areas they conquered. First, however, they were raiders. About 860 a fearful Frank wrote, "The number of ships grows. The endless stream of Vikings never ceases to increase. Everywhere the Christians are victims of massacres [killings], burnings, plunderings. The Vikings conquer all in their path, and no one resists them."

By about 1000, many parts of Europe had been overrun by these raiders. The order and scholarship established by Charlemagne declined. Much of Europe was divided. Thousands of small communities formed. A very different form of

government arose, one more suited to such small areas.

Checking Up
1. What do we mean by the European Middle Ages?
2. Who were the Franks?
3. Who were the Vikings? Where did they come from, and why were they feared?
4. What answers would you give to the key questions at the beginning of this chapter?
5. *Why was Charlemagne the greatest European leader of the early Middle Ages? Name three of his different accomplishments.*

Knights, Nobles, and Castles

As You Read

1. Think about these words.
   feudalism   vassal   fief   knight
2. Look for answers to these key questions.
   a. What is feudalism?
   b. Why were castles often built on hills?
   c. Why were knights so important in the feudal system?
3. Use this reading skill.
   Not all the information in this book is in words. You can learn a great deal from the pictures. Study them carefully and read the captions. Look especially for what the pictures in this chapter tell about the life of the nobles of the European Middle Ages. Be able to make two conclusions about their life. Here is an example of one conclusion: Warfare was an important part of the nobles' way of life.

The period after Charlemagne's death was a time of fear and worry. Wars raged among the nobles of western Europe. At any moment people could expect their village to be surprised by Vikings or other invaders.

The Feudal System

To get the protection they needed, the nobles began to form personal agreements. The political system known as **feudalism** (fyo͞od′əl·iz′əm) was based on these agreements. Here is how the system worked. Landholding nobles called lords gave the use of parts of their lands to lesser nobles. The lesser nobles were called **vassals**. A vassal promised to oversee the land, pay taxes to the lord, and fight for the lord when necessary.

The lord-vassal relationship did not stop with a single agreement. A great lord had much land to give out. He turned the land over to high nobles. A piece of land controlled by a noble was a **fief** (fēf). The nobles, in turn, could split up their fiefs into small ones, making agreements with lesser nobles. A noble, then, might be vassal to a higher lord. At the same time, this noble might also be a lord to other vassals.

The feudal contract. A lord did not give away his land. He gave the vassal only the use of it. Control of the fief passed down from father to son. A vassal's oldest son would become the vassal of the lord who owned the land. If a vassal had no sons, his oldest daughter might be married to a vassal who would

Many castles of the Middle Ages still exist. How is Conway Castle in Wales different from the one on page 233?

height gave a lord's soldiers a better position to fight off attackers. Because of the protection castles offered, villages usually grew up nearby. The castle became the center of village government.

No two castles were exactly alike. Some were surrounded by deep, water-filled ditches called moats. Others were protected by fence-like barriers which were arranged in a circle around the castles.

Usually a castle had a great hall where the lord's family ate and entertained. Castles had many other uses. Part of a castle was often used as a prison. The prison, called a dungeon (dən'jən), was a dreary chamber where criminals were often tortured.

The knight. Feudal society was organized for war. One of its most important members was the trained soldier, the **knight**. Training for knighthood began early. When a boy from a noble family reached the age of seven or eight, he entered service at the castle of another lord. For several years he served as a page, a kind of castle errand boy.

About the age of fourteen or fifteen, the boy became a squire. He cared for the horses, learned to care for equipment, and helped serve at the lord's table. Much of his time was spent learning how to ride and fight with many kinds of weapons. The training continued until the youth was about twenty and ready to become a knight.

Becoming a knight was the young man's coming-of-age ceremony. As you read in Unit 1, each culture has a differ-

take over the fief. If the vassal had no children, control of the fief would return to the lord.

There were many taxes and services that vassals owed their lords. The vassals kept soldiers. When the lord called for help, the vassals and their soldiers came to his aid. Vassals were required to house, feed, and entertain lords who traveled through the fief. A lord also had the right to call all the vassals together for advice or to settle arguments between vassals. The lord and vassals gathered together to form a court.

The castle. Feudal lords lived in castles. Castles were often built on hills, looking down on the countryside. The

286

THE·KNIGHT

HELMET

SHIELD

MAIL

SPURS

Before they wore armor, knights wore a covering of metal rings called mail.

ent way to note a child's coming of age, or passage to adulthood. In his knighting ceremony, the young man received his sword and promised to be brave during battle. He also promised to defend his lord and to fight for the church.

As a knight, a young man was ready to rule a fief of his own. If he was the eldest son, he could inherit his father's fief. By doing a good job in battle, he might be given a fief of his own by the lord he served. There were more knights than there was land, however. Many knights, therefore, became castle guards. Others became soldiers for hire, roaming from place to place offering their skills as soldiers wherever needed.

Women of the castle. Women, especially in the early Middle Ages, did not have as much freedom as women in late Roman times had had. Women could and did hold land, however. A woman's husband or brother often provided the knights to protect her land.

A girl from a noble family, like a boy, was often sent to another castle at an early age. There she learned about household duties from the lord's wife. Marriage came early. Most girls were married by the time they were fourteen years old. A girl's father or her father's lord often chose a husband for her. After marriage the woman was under her husband's control. He could do as he pleased with any property she brought into the marriage. A woman who did not

Sewing clothes took up much of the women's time.

marry might go off to a convent, a place where religious women lived and worked.

Later in the Middle Ages, women's responsibilities increased. When the men were away at wars for long periods of time, wives took over the duties of the lord around the castle.

Castle Life

The castle day started before sunrise with religious services in the chapel. Then came breakfast and the day's business. The lord, if he were home at the castle, might tour the fief or meet with his vassals.

The main meal was usually served at midday. Many of the daily castle chores involved food preparation. Meat and bread were the most important foods. Meats frequently included rabbit, lamb, and deer, known as venison. If the lord's land held a pond or a river, fresh fish might be served. At great banquets birds such as swan and peacock were offered. Onions, peas, and cabbage were common vegetables.

People usually drank wine or beer with their meals. These drinks took the place of water, which in most places was too polluted to drink. The people knew little about how to keep the water safe to drink.

Another very time-consuming chore was dressmaking. All the women in the castle, from the lord's wife to the lowliest servant, helped. They spent long hours spinning thread, weaving cloth, and making clothes for the whole household.

The jousts were colorful and exciting, but also very dangerous, contests.

When not working or warring, people of the castle loved games and other entertainments. Chess and backgammon were popular games. Large organized hunts were common. Most exciting, however, were the jousts and tournaments.

A tournament was a contest in which groups of knights practiced fighting. There were two teams of knights, each

The castle banquet was the high point of the evening. Besides a feast, the banquet was also a form of entertainment.

charging against the other on horseback. All the knights were completely outfitted in heavy metal armor. They would use shields to protect themselves. With lances the knights tried to pierce the opponents' armor and knock them off their horses. Jousts were smaller versions of tournaments. Just two knights opposed each other in a joust.

In the evening, especially if there were guests, there might be a great banquet (bang′kwət). A banquet was a combination of feasting and entertainment. Trumpeters sounded the call for the meal. The lord's family and guests took their places at long tables in the great hall. Servants filed in with the various courses of food. During the long feast minstrels, or traveling musicians, strolled through the hall entertaining the diners. Most guests probably agreed that a banquet was a perfect ending to the long and active day at the castle.

Checking Up
1. What did a lord give to a vassal? What did a vassal give to his lord?
2. How was the castle used?
3. Describe the training of a knight.
4. What answers would you give to the key questions at the beginning of this chapter?
5. *Why did the feudal system develop? Why do you think it was necessary?*

Living in the Age of Faith

As You Read

1. Think about these words.

   peasant freeholder serf manor tithe Crusade

2. Look for answers to these key questions.
   a. How did the manor system work?
   b. How did agriculture change during the Middle Ages?
   c. What were the Crusades?

Most people of the European Middle Ages did not live in castles. Nobles made up only a small part of the population. The clergy, the second major class, or group, of people, were also few in number. By far the largest group of people were **peasants** (pez'ənts). Peasants were the hard-working farmers who labored on the land for their living.

Some peasants farmed their own land. They were called **freeholders**. Freeholders still needed a nearby lord's protection. They paid him a fee or rent. Most peasants were too poor to own land, however. They farmed a small part of a lord's land. These poorer peasants were called **serfs**. In exchange for the lord's land and protection, the serfs performed many services for the lord and gave him much of their harvest.

The Manor System

Trade between cities and countries was not highly developed in the first part of the Middle Ages. Much of western Europe was a land of small farming vil-

lages, each of which had grown up near a powerful lord's castle. The peasants needed the lord's land and protection. The nobles needed the peasants' labor for food and other services. Thus, the **manor** system began. The manor was the district under the rule of one lord. The lord's castle was known as the manor house.

The peasants' day was filled with chores from morning until evening.

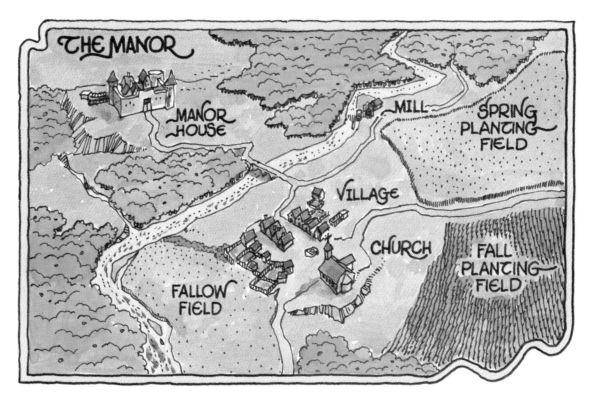

THE MANOR

MANOR HOUSE

MILL

SPRING PLANTING FIELD

VILLAGE

CHURCH

FALL PLANTING FIELD

FALLOW FIELD

Land and people both were part of the manor. Much of the manor land belonged to the lord. His serfs had to work that land. The rest of the land was divided among the village freeholders.

The manor included a pasture where livestock grazed. The serfs took care of the lord's farm animals as well as their own. The mill, where grain was ground into flour, belonged to the lord. The peasants had to pay for the use of it. In fact, the peasants had to pay the lord for almost everything they used. If they gathered wood for a fire, they gave some of it to the lord. Some of the fish they caught in the manor's pond or stream would also be given to the lord.

In addition, peasants had to work a certain number of days for the lord. Freeholders worked a few days in the plowing and harvesting seasons. Serfs, however, worked two or three days a week all year long. A lord could demand the services of a serf at any time for some special work, such as road repair or bridge building.

Often serfs could not even leave their village. They belonged to the manor. They might buy their freedom from the lord, but the price was usually impossibly high. Unlike slaves, serfs could not be bought and sold. Still, serfs had little more freedom than slaves.

Peasants had to produce nearly everything they needed. They made their own clothing, their own tools, and their own furniture. Peasant children worked with their parents. As soon as the children were old enough to walk, they had jobs to do.

The horse collar was an important agricultural advance. Do you remember where the harness came from?

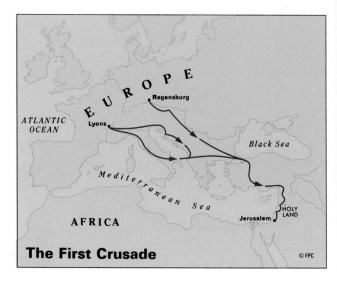

The First Crusade

Sometimes peasants did have relief from their hard labor. In the later Middle Ages, especially, there were village fairs, which were fun for all. Sundays were free because the church did not allow work on Sunday. Also, there were many religious holidays throughout the year. The Christmas holiday alone lasted a full twelve days!

Changes in agriculture. By the 11th century, farming had improved and had become more productive. One important change was in land use. Grain was the most important farm product in western Europe. Because grain crops wore out the soil quickly, farmers began to use a two-field system. Half of the manor's farmland was planted in grain. The other half was left fallow, or unplanted. The unplanted soil had a chance to rest and renew itself. The next year the farmer would plant it, and leave the other half to lie fallow.

Later, farmers switched to a three-field system. One field was planted in winter grain such as wheat or oats. In spring a second field was planted in vegetables such as peas and beans. The vegetables added nitrogen (nī′trə·jən) to the soil, making it more fertile. The third field was left fallow for a year.

The horse-pulled plow was another important development in agriculture. Earlier, plows had been pulled by oxen. With a harness, one strong horse could plow land faster than two oxen. With horses, farmers could work more land and grow more crops.

In time, some peasants produced more food than they needed to pay their lord and support themselves. They could trade or sell what was left over. They began to have a little more money for themselves. Some were able to buy their freedom from serfdom.

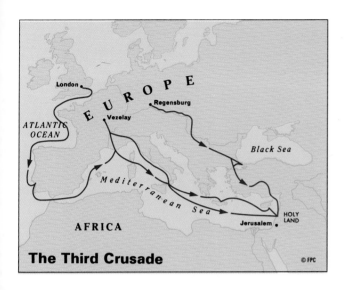

The Third Crusade

The Church

People looked to the church for order in their lives. They hoped for a better life not only on earth but especially after death. The church was so much a part of people's lives that this time is often called the Age of Faith.

Most church leaders were nobles. Led by the pope in Rome, they held great power. By the 12th century, the church held much land, and powerful church leaders controlled it. The church also had great wealth. All members of the church had to pay 10 percent of their yearly earnings to the church. The tax was called a **tithe** (tīth) and was collected at village churches or manor chapels. Parish priests led these services. Often parish priests came from the peasant class. Becoming a priest was one way for a peasant to better himself. Of course, he had to get his lord's permission to become a priest.

The Crusades. Late in the 11th century, the Muslim Seljuk Turks seized lands on the eastern shore of the Mediterranean Sea. This area was known as the Holy Land because many events recorded in the Bible had taken place there, including the birth of Jesus Christ. The most important city in the Holy Land was Jerusalem. Fighting among the Seljuks disrupted the Christians' visits to the Holy Land. Then the Seljuks marched against the Eastern Roman, or Byzantine, Empire. The emperor there asked the pope in Rome for help.

In 1095 the pope asked the people of western Europe to go to war against the Turks. The First **Crusade** resulted. The Crusades were a series of Christian invasions of the Holy Land. Eight major Crusades took place for about 200 years, between 1095 and 1300.

Thousands of European men, women, and children from all classes answered the pope's call. Great armies of knights were raised, and all set out for the Holy Land. European Crusaders clashed with Muslim forces on and off for the next 200 years. Crusaders captured Jerusalem at one point and established control over nearby lands. Find this area on the map of the First Crusade on page 292.

Look at both Crusade maps. How did the routes differ? Crusading knights had horses and supplies. What problems might they have had traveling on land? on sea?

The Children's Crusade. One Crusade was made up almost entirely of children. Urged on by priests, the children believed God would help them take back the Holy Land from Muslim control. Un-

293

The children set out on their crusade filled with hope. Most never returned from the harsh journey.

fortunately, few lived long enough to complete the journey. Hunger and disease killed many. Others were victims of criminals. Some drowned at sea. Many who did survive were sold into slavery in the eastern lands.

Results of the Crusades. In 1187 Muslim armies retook Jerusalem. The clashes between Christians and Muslims continued for another 100 years. Finally, in 1291, the Muslims drove out the last of the Christians.

In many ways the Crusades were a failure. Thousands of people died. The lands fought over remained in Muslim control. Even so, the Crusades had some positive effects. Europeans traveled to distant lands. They learned about different people. Europeans were introduced to cane sugar and to spices such as cinnamon and nutmeg. They grew to like the silks and other fine fabrics that were common in eastern lands. They learned of inventions such as the astrolabe, an instrument to help sailors find their way. You can see a picture of an astrolabe on page 267. A desire for these new products grew. In time, increased trade would help to put an end to the manor system in Europe.

Checking Up

1. Into what two groups were the peasants divided?
2. What were some of the duties of peasants to their lord?
3. Describe the three-field system of farming.
4. What answers would you give to the key questions at the beginning of this chapter?
5. *How was the feudal contract between lords and vassals like the agreement between peasants and nobles of the manor? How were the two agreements different?*

The Later Middle Ages

As You Read

1. Think about these words.

   middle class   apprentice   cathedral

   guild   master   journeyman

2. Look for answers to these key questions.

   a. What was the difference between the middle class and the peasant class?

   b. What was the purpose of the guilds?

   c. What were four important kingdoms that arose in the later part of the Middle Ages?

   d. Why was art an important way to teach about religion in the Middle Ages?

In the second half of the European Middle Ages, after about 1000, feudalism slowly began to decline. Strong kings began to build new kingdoms. Trade and manufacturing increased. Some villages became towns. New towns were built. Some towns grew into cities. A new interest in learning grew.

The Rise of Towns

Early trading towns were a little larger than the manor villages. However, they differed from manor villages in important ways. First, trading towns were free from the control of feudal lords. Second, their purpose was not agricultural. They were established as places in which to do business. For this reason, they were usually built along trade routes—at the crossing of two roads, for instance, or on a river that could be navigated.

Town life offered variety and choice. What are the people doing here?

295

Parts of the walled French city of Carcassonne (kär·kə·son′) date back to the fifth century. Walled cities were designed as fortresses.

Most townspeople were either merchants or craftworkers. Most villagers did not produce their own food. They bought farm products from nearby farm villages.

Most early towns had walls with heavy gates that were locked at night. People needed protection from robbers. As a town grew larger, the old wall was torn down to provide more room for houses. A new wall was built farther out.

Trading towns developed with the help of powerful feudal lords. A lord provided the land for a town. In exchange for the land, he was usually given money. The manor provided a lord with the labor of the peasants and with farm produce. Yet labor and farm produce could not buy fine clothing or spices from Asia. Money was needed for these things.

Many nobles willingly freed peasants from manor duties in return for a yearly payment of money. The nobles were often less willing to give up control of the towns. Nevertheless, by the end of the 12th century, most towns had charters giving them some self-government. They elected their own officials, passed their own laws, held their own courts, and collected taxes. Many towns had rules saying that a serf who lived in the town for a year and a day without being claimed by a lord would become a free person.

The townspeople added a new class of people to the society of the Middle Ages. They became the **middle class** between the landholding nobles and the land-working peasants.

Guilds

The leading members of a town were the merchants and craftworkers who controlled the **guilds**. Guilds were associations of special groups of workers. Each

See if you can pick out the different kinds of goods here.

group of workers who followed the same occupation had its own guild. There were guilds for traders, bakers, shoemakers, blacksmiths, and weavers, to name a few. There were even guilds for merchants who worked together.

The purpose of a guild was to protect its members and to check the quality of their products. Guild members agreed on the hours of work, the quality of materials, and the quality of the final products. The guild also set the prices for the finished products.

The craft guilds had their own way of training new members. **Master** craftworkers were the most knowledgeable and experienced people in their field. A young person was sent to work as an **apprentice** (ə·prent′əs) to a master craftworker at an early age. Apprentices were given food and a place to stay by the master during training. They did not receive any payment.

Around the age of nineteen an apprentice became a **journeyman** worker. The journeyman took on more responsibility and was paid a small salary. After about three years, a journeyman could become a master if there was an opening in the guild and if the young person had enough money to start a business.

Membership in some guilds was open to women as well as men. A Paris tax list from the year 1292 showed five guilds that were made up of women only. About 80 of the more than 120 guilds listed had some women members.

Kingdoms of the Later Middle Ages

Certain kings began to gain power over competing feudal lords in the later Middle Ages. Usually kings were glad to see the rise of towns and the decline of the manors. As their manors shrunk in population and wealth, the local nobles grew less powerful. Kings could not rule effectively if they did not have the nobles under their control. Some of the kingdoms that arose in the later Middle Ages include England, France, the Holy Roman Empire, and Spain.

England. In 1066 a noble named William, Duke of Normandy, invaded England. Normandy was an area of northern France that had been settled by Vikings. William and his Norman descendants became the rulers of the powerful English kingdom. Known as William the Conqueror, the first Norman ruler strengthened his power by taxing landowners and keeping track of England's population and resources.

297

Then and Now

Disease Control

In the middle of the 14th century, a terrible disease struck Europe and wiped out nearly one-fourth of the people. The bubonic plague (bōō·bon'ik plāg) was feared by all and came to be known as the Black Death.

The plague was spread by bacteria (bak·tir'ē·ə), tiny particles of living matter that live in animals and people. Harmful bacteria can cause disease and even kill an animal or a person. Plague bacteria were spread by fleas that were carried by rats.

Rats were common in the crowded and dirty towns of Europe during the Middle Ages. They also lived on the many ships that were sailing to and trading with distant lands. The ever-present rats carried the plague to people. Few people struck by the plague recovered. Even worse, one sick person could quickly infect anyone else nearby. It was important to close off the house and burn the clothes of any victim.

We still have many diseases today, of course. Even the bubonic plague still exists. The important difference is that we can *control* contagious (kən·tā'jəs) diseases much better today. Contagious diseases are those that spread from one person to another.

Rat control and cleaner conditions could have protected Europe in the 14th century. Today cleaner standards, food inspections, rodent and insect control, and bacteria-fighting medicines all help prevent such tragedies as the Black Death.

France. When the Normans were establishing control over England, French leaders were unifying France into one large kingdom. By the early 14th century, King Philip IV was ruling a large country. Philip challenged the church's power as well. He taxed the clergy and saw that a French pope was elected in 1305. Under Philip's rule the church headquarters moved from Rome to France, where it remained for nearly seventy years. While in France the church leadership was controlled by the French government. All the popes during this time were French.

The Hundred Years' War. The English and French kingdoms began to compete with each other. Each one wanted more land in France. In the late 1330s, a long series of wars began. They are usually grouped together and called the Hundred Years' War. By 1453 France had won. The English were left with very little French territory. At the end of the war, feudalism was further weakened, and both countries were more strongly unified.

Holy Roman Empire. Even before 1000, German kings were exercising strong control over other nobles. King

Otto I worked closely with the church to strengthen his rule. In 962 the pope crowned Otto emperor of the Holy Roman Empire, which included German and Italian territory. In later years, when French and English kingdoms were growing more powerful, the German Empire became less so.

Spain. Early in the Middle Ages, the North African Muslims, or Moors, took over Spain. During the next several hundred years, the Spanish fought to drive the Moors out. Spain became more strongly unified in the process. In 1479 King Ferdinand and Queen Isabella merged their territories, creating a single and powerful Spanish Kingdom.

Education, Art, and Architecture

Formal education was usually limited to the monasteries during the first part of the Middle Ages. In the later Middle Ages, learning moved from the monasteries to the cities. Schools were started at **cathedrals** (kə·thē′drəlz), the great churches. The subjects remained those that had been taught in Roman times. Grammar, speech, writing, and debate were the chief subjects. The students also studied religion, arithmetic, geometry, music, and astronomy.

The first universities of western Europe were started in the 12th and 13th centuries. At first they were gathering places for students and teachers. As universities developed, however, they became more permanent. Universities such as Oxford in England had their own buildings and campus grounds. Students

Artists painted many pictures of the Christ child during the Middle Ages.

began to live together in or near the buildings in which they studied. Such buildings were called colleges.

Most of the art of the Middle Ages focused on religion. At a time when most people were still unable to read, art became a way to teach about religion. Paintings were often based on scenes from Bible stories. Statues were of saints.

Architecture was usually modeled after Roman buildings during the early Middle Ages. In the 1100s a new style of architecture called Gothic became popular. The grand cathedrals of the late Middle Ages are Gothic. The cathedrals are famous for their towering steeples, beautiful stained-glass windows, and curved beams that support the heavy stone walls. They are great artistic achievements of the European Middle Ages.

299

Flying buttresses, the curved beams of the cathedrals, support the building enough to leave wall space for the great windows.

Checking Up

1. Why were lords willing to give the peasants freedom?
2. How did a young person train to become a member of a guild?
3. How did learning change between the early and late Middle Ages?
4. What answers would you give to the key questions at the beginning of this chapter?
5. *How did town life differ from manor life for most people? Why do you think serfs and other peasants would be attracted to town life?*

Unit 11 Summary

- The Middle Ages lasted in Europe for about 1,000 years after the fall of the Western Roman Empire.
- Frankish kings built an empire that included much of western Europe. Charlemagne was the greatest Frankish leader.
- The Christian church became especially powerful during the European Middle Ages.
- Society of the early Middle Ages was made up of three groups of people: nobles, clergy, and peasants. Peasants included freeholders and serfs.
- After Charlemagne many nobles formed feudal contracts with one another. Feudal society was organized largely for war.
- Peasants usually lived on a manor and supported themselves, their families, and their lord by farming.
- Later in the European Middle Ages, trade and town life developed. With the rise of towns came a new middle class and more freedom and mobility for the peasants.

Maps Tell a Story of Trade

As you read, think about this word.
textile

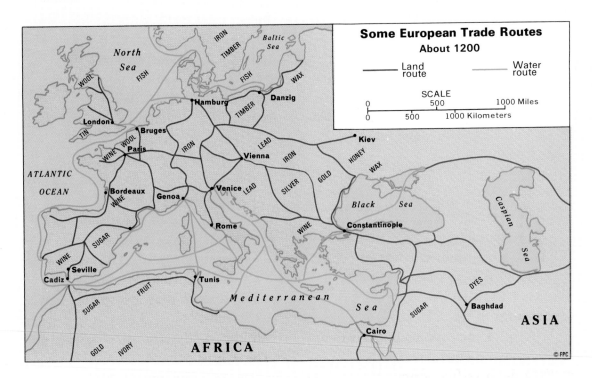

Some European Trade Routes
About 1200

In the later part of the Middle Ages, European trade increased greatly. The people wanted goods such as silks and spices from Asia. The craftworkers in the European towns were producing goods to be sold. Glass and **textiles**, or cloth, were some important products.

Minerals and other **raw materials** were also important to trade. Raw materials are used to make products. Wool, for example, is a raw material used in making woolen textiles.

Venice. Venice was the most important European trading center of the Middle Ages. The people were successful shipbuilders, sailors, and fishers. They developed strong trade ties with other lands when most European trade was very weak.

Checking Up

1. Name some European towns shown on the map other than Venice.
2. What are some of the European trading products shown?
3. Use the map scale to compare the lengths of land and sea routes. Which is the shorter route between the following cities?
   a. Venice to Constantinople
   b. Bruges to Bordeaux
   c. Cádiz to Tunis

Unit 11 Review Workshop

What Have You Learned?

1. Why was western Europe disorganized after the fall of Rome?
2. Who was Charlemagne? Why did some people think he had remade part of the Western Roman Empire?
3. What did Charlemagne do to help spread Christianity and education in his empire?
4. What was the feudal agreement? Who made feudal agreements?
5. Who were the knights? What was their main job?
6. What were three activities of people who lived in castles?
7. What was the manor? What did the peasants of the manor do?
8. How did improvements in agriculture help the peasants?
9. Which religion did most Europeans follow during the Middle Ages?
10. What lands did the Crusaders want to free from Muslim control?
11. Why did towns begin to grow during the later part of the European Middle Ages?
12. How did the rise of towns change life during the later Middle Ages?
13. Who were the middle-class people? How were they different from peasants and nobles?
14. Name four powerful European rulers in the later Middle Ages.
15. What are Gothic cathedrals? Use the pictures in this unit to describe Gothic cathedrals.

Use Your Reading Skills

Fill in each blank with the best word from the following list.

fief	craftworkers
Franks	pope
manor	Crusades
universities	Vikings
Muslims	towns

1. Clovis was king of the _____.
2. The _____ were defeated by Charles Martel at Tours.
3. The _____ were seafarers from northern Europe.
4. The land a feudal lord turned over to a vassal was called a _____.
5. The district that a lord ruled over was called a _____.
6. In the Middle Ages, the leader of the church was the _____.
7. The _____ were a series of wars against Muslims in the Holy Land.
8. In the later part of the European Middle Ages, many peasants left the manor for the greater freedom of the _____.
9. Merchants and _____ belonged to guilds.
10. Learning moved to _____ in the later European Middle Ages.

Use Your Thinking Skills

Look at the two pictures on the next page. Why is the subject of each special to the European Middle Ages? Write a good caption for each picture. Compare your captions with others in the class.

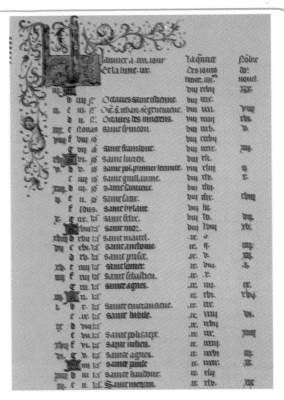

Use Your Writing Skills

Write paragraphs for two of the topic sentences listed below. Use examples and facts.

1. Peasants of the manor had very little freedom.
2. European education was usually poor during the early Middle Ages.
3. Castle life could be interesting and entertaining.
4. The Christian church was wealthy and powerful during the European Middle Ages.

Learn by Doing

1. Make a model of a manor. Use the diagram on page 291 and information from other books for help. Place labels on the different parts of the manor.

2. Form small groups in class. Make up a short skit about one of the following people.
   a. a young squire setting out on a Crusade with his lord
   b. a young noble woman about to become lady of the castle
   c. a newly freed serf leaving the manor for the first time

   Present your skit to the class.

Read to Learn More

Find the topics listed below in the card catalog of your library. Read all or part of a book listed under one of the topics. Share what you learn with your classmates.

MIDDLE AGES   CRUSADES

CHARLEMAGNE   CASTLES

FEUDALISM   KNIGHTS

Unit 12

Japan:
An Island Civilization

Landscape gardening in Japan is a highly developed art form.

Maps Tell a Story of Japan

As you read, think about this word.

monsoon

Japan is made up of 4 main islands and 500 smaller ones. These smaller ones are not inhabited. Many of the small islands are so tiny that they cannot be seen on a map like the one below. Look at the map. The large island farthest north is called Hokkaido (hō·kī′dō). Notice that the island name is shown in a different kind of lettering from that used for cities or bodies of water. Find the names of the other large islands. Which is largest? Which is farthest south? Which enclose the Inland Sea?

Location

Look at the shape of the four main islands of Japan. Find them on the world map on pages 10–11. What other countries are closest to Japan? Which of these neighbors are smaller than Japan? Which are larger? What country do you think most strongly influenced Japan?

Japan is located along the same lines of latitude as most of the United States. What ocean separates the two countries? The map on page 307 shows how Japan would look if it were moved eastward and placed over the East Coast of the United States. How do the two nations

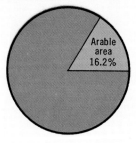

Arable Land in Japan

Arable area 16.2%

306

Size and Latitude Comparison of U.S. and Japan

Montreal •
45°N

Hokkaido

Boston •

New York •
40°N

Philadelphia •

⊕ Washington, D.C.

Honshu

Yokohama • • Tokyo
35°N

Kobe • • Kyoto
Hiroshima •
Atlanta • • Osaka

Shikoku   Inland Sea

Kyushu

ATLANTIC
OCEAN   30°N

Gulf   of
Mexico

SCALE
0   200   400 mi.
0   200   400 km

© FPC

compare in size? Which of Japan's large islands is as far north as the New England states? Which island is as far south as Alabama? What United States city is at the same latitude as the island of Shikoku (shē·kō′kōō)?

Land

Look again at the physical map of Japan. Notice the key to the colors used on the map. What does the dark brown color indicate? the lighter brown? How would you describe the land of Japan?

About four-fifths of Japan is covered with hills and mountains. The largest plain is the area around Tokyo. Find it on the map. Even this plain stretches only about 120 miles (193 km) in its longest direction. Other coastal plains are

smaller. There are also many small inland river valleys. Each is separated from the others by hills and mountains. What other area have you studied that contains many small plains separated by hills and mountains?

Japan's hills and mountains are mostly steep and rugged. The hills are heavily forested. Farming is difficult if not impossible in these highland areas. Less than 20 percent of Japan's land is flat enough to farm or settle. The entire population of Japan, almost half the size of the population of the United States, lives in an area half the size of Iowa!

Water

Japan is similar to Greece in another way. Both countries have many islands. Both have large areas of seacoast. No part of Japan is more than 70 miles (112 km) from the sea. The coastal areas contain many small but excellent natural harbors. What does this closeness to the sea suggest about the way many Japanese people can make a living? How do you think it might affect the kinds of food the people eat?

Japan's steep mountains contain swift-moving streams and rivers. These are excellent sources of waterpower. The river waters can be controlled by dams and used to generate electricity. Japan's industries use so much power today, however, that water sources provide only about 5 percent of the nation's power. Most of the other power sources, especially coal and petroleum, must be imported.

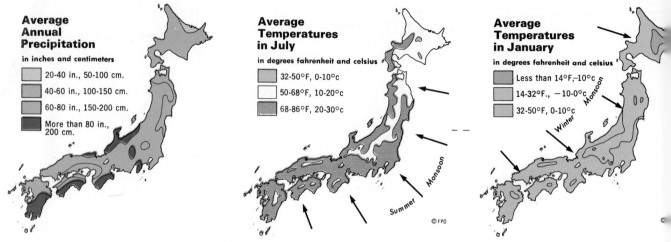

Average
Annual
Precipitation

in inches and centimeters

☐ 20-40 in., 50-100 cm.
☐ 40-60 in., 100-150 cm.
☐ 60-80 in., 150-200 cm.
■ More than 80 in., 200 cm.

Average
Temperatures
in July

in degrees fahrenheit and celsius

☐ 32-50°F, 0-10°c
☐ 50-68°F, 10-20°c
☐ 68-86°F, 20-30°c

Average
Temperatures
in January

in degrees fahrenheit and celsius

■ Less than 14°F,–10°c
☐ 14-32°F., –10-0°c
☐ 32-50°F, 0-10°c

Winter Monsoon

Summer Monsoon

©FPC

Climate

Because Japan is small and surrounded by water, its climate is greatly influenced by the oceans. Look at the map of ocean currents. How might the Japan Current influence the climate? What parts of Japan are influenced by the cold current? Which current might influence the area around Tokyo?

Look at the two temperature maps. What are the average summer temperatures in the largest part of Japan? How do these compare with the summer temperatures where you live? Which areas of

Japan have the coldest winters? Do you think Tokyo has much snow in winter?

Compare the temperature maps with the physical map of Japan. Are the coolest areas in the highlands or in the lowlands?

The oceans influence Japan's climate in another way. They provide plenty of precipitation. As winds pass over the water, they pick up moisture. Much of this moisture is released as rain or snow when the winds pass over land. Summer wind systems in Asia are called **monsoons**. Look at the temperature maps. From which direction do the winds come in summer? in winter?

Look at the precipitation map. In general, does the most precipitation fall inland or along the coasts? What part of Japan gets the least rain or snow?

Ocean
Currents

Japan
Current
Warm

Oyashio
Current
Cold

Japan
Current
Warm

©FPC

Checking Up

1. Where is Japan located?
2. What land forms does Japan have?
3. How do sea currents influence the climate of Japan?

308

The Early Japanese

As You Read

1. Think about these words.
   Caucasian   Mongoloid   isolation   paddy   shrine   Shinto
2. Look for answers to these key questions.
   a. From what continent did the early Japanese people come? What ways of life did they follow?
   b. What was clan society in early Japan like? Into what three classes was it divided?
   c. What are the beliefs of the Shinto religion?
3. Use this reading skill.
   An important reading skill is distinguishing fact from fantasy. Fantasy is something that is not true. Legends are often fantasy. As you read this chapter, identify some early Japanese legends.

As you learned in earlier units, we know only a little about people who lived before writing was used. Writing was introduced into Japan much later than in many other parts of the world. There are, therefore, still many mysteries about what happened in Japan in early times.

Early Settlers

Some scientists think people have lived on the Japanese islands for at least 11,000 years. The first people to settle there may have been the Ainu (ī′nōō). The Ainu were members of the **Caucasian** race, the race to which most Europeans and Middle Easterners belong.

Later migrations to Japan by people of the **Mongoloid** race, the race most East Asians belong to, gradually drove the Ainu northward. Several thousand Ainu

Hunters, fishers, and gatherers, the Ainu believed the bear was sacred.

still live on the northernmost island of Hokkaido today. The present-day Japanese, however, are the descendants of the later migrants, not of the Ainu.

Isolation. The migrations that first brought people to Japan probably took place at the end of the last ice age. In Unit 1 you read about the land bridges that connected islands and continents during that time. Japan was connected to the Asian mainland during these times. After the ice melted and the sea level rose, Japan became an island country, as it is today. This **isolation**, or separation, cut off Japan from the rest of Asia, until people became experienced sailors.

Isolation had advantages and disadvantages. Japan did not fall under the control of the more powerful Chinese that you read about in Unit 7. On the other hand, the Japanese did not gain any of the advantages of contact with the more advanced civilization in China. While farming, animal raising, and village life were developing in China, Japan remained a land of hunters, fishers, and food gatherers.

Agriculture. Some basic farming may have been practiced in Japan quite early. It was not until the 200s B.C., however, that wet rice farming was introduced into Japan. It probably came from China. About the same time, the knowledge of ironworking also spread from China to Japan.

Growing rice in **paddies**, or flooded fields, spread through most of Japan, except for Hokkaido, where the growing season was too short. Rice soon became Japan's most important food. Along with fish and other seafoods, it made up the main part of the Japanese diet.

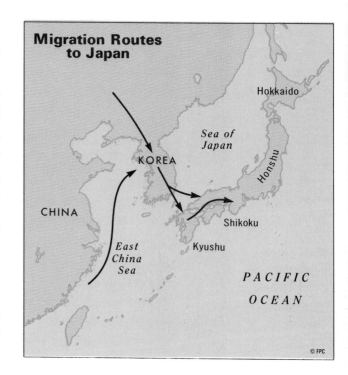

Migration Routes to Japan

Life in Early Japan

The early Japanese had no writing of their own. Much that we know about this period comes from the writings of Chinese visitors to Japan. Much later the Japanese wrote their own histories of this period. These histories often contain more legend than fact.

Clans. Between about the 200s B.C. and the A.D. 300s, Japanese life centered around clans. Clan members were the upper class of early Japan. Each clan included a large number of related families. Because Japan is made up of many small valleys and coastal plains separated by hills and mountains, clans were isolated from one another. Chinese travelers who visited Japan during this time described it as a land of "a hundred or more countries" ruled by women.

tant parts as leaders. In later times, especially as warfare began to increase, male leaders became more important.

The leader, or chief, of each clan also served as a religious leader. Each leader was thought to be the descendant of some god or goddess. The clan members believed they had a common ancestor. This ancestor was also considered a god and was worshiped by all clan members.

Below the clan members were the common workers. These people were associated with a clan but were not clan members. The common workers farmed the land, producing food for themselves

The Japanese use about half the farmland in their country to grow rice.

In those early days, some clans were indeed ruled by women. Others had male leaders. It is possible that in even earlier times *most* of the clans had women leaders. Many legends trace the Japanese people back to the sun goddess Amaterasu (ä·mä·tä·rä·sōo). Although they are only legends, they do seem to indicate that women once played impor-

Clan members set statues of warriors in front of tombs to guard them.

This later painting shows the great respect the Japanese have for nature.

included a variety of gods and spirits. It was given the name **Shinto**, which means "the way of the gods."

Shinto gods included both real and imagined people. Ancestors who were especially admired were worshiped. Every clan had its own special ancestor god or goddess.

In Shinto, people also worshiped natural objects and objects made by people. Any natural object that impressed people could become an object of worship. A waterfall, a large tree, or a strangely shaped stone might be worshiped.

The most important objects of worship made by people were the mirror, the sword, and the necklace. These three objects were said to have been brought to earth by the sun goddess Amaterasu. They were thought to contain her spirit. Other objects were believed to contain a spirit that had special powers over a certain area. The spirits worshiped by a clan protected the clan's territory. One spirit, the rice spirit, was worshiped throughout Japan.

The Japanese built **shrines**, or special places of worship. If something like a waterfall became a shrine, a gateway was built to mark the spot. Japanese families also set up simple shrines in their homes. There they could worship the family god, a real or imagined ancestor. People worshiped by praying and carrying out special ceremonies.

The Yamato. For a long time, each clan was independent of all others. Gradually, some clans grew in strength. They began to gain control over other

and the clan members. Some specialized in occupations such as fishing, weaving, or pottery making. Others provided military service for the clan. The workers worshiped the same gods as the clan members.

At the bottom of early society were the slaves. They made up about 5 percent of the population. Most slaves performed household duties for clan families.

Shinto. The earliest religion in Japan was a simple form of nature worship. Later it became more complicated and

Gateways such as this one mark the sites of Shinto shrines.

neighboring clans. Sometimes control was gained through warfare. At other times it was gained through peaceful means, such as an arranged marriage between members of two clans. Eventually, one clan, the Yamato (yä·mä·tō), managed to gain control over much of Japan.

The Yamato are thought to have originated on the island of Kyushu (kē·ōō′shōō). Later they moved to the Yamato Plain, the area east of Osaka. Find these places on the map on page 306. From there they began to extend their influence to most of central and western Japan and even, for a time, into southern Korea. The Yamato expansion, or conquest, probably took place during the A.D. 200s and 300s.

The conquered clans were not forced to give up their right to rule themselves. They did, however, have to agree to follow the leadership of the Yamato. They also agreed to worship the Yamato gods, including the main one, the sun goddess Amaterasu. Thus, the chief of the Yamato, who was also the clan's highest priest, became the priest of most Japanese people. The Yamato conquest became the first step in unifying, or joining together, the Japanese people.

Checking Up
1. Who were the Ainu?
2. What do people worship in the Shinto religion?
3. What was the importance of the Yamato to Japan?
4. What answers would you give to the key questions at the beginning of this chapter?
5. *In what ways was the Shinto religion similar to shamanism?*

313

Japanese Civilization Develops

As You Read

1. Think about these words.
   regent   scroll
2. Look for answers to these key questions.
   a. In what ways did China influence Japan?
   b. What important political developments took place between the 700s and the 1100s?
   c. What were the achievements of Japanese culture during the Heian period?

By the middle of the A.D. 500s, the Roman Empire had fallen apart. Western Europe was entering a period of disorder. China, on the other hand, was nearing the end of the troubled times that followed the fall of the Han dynasty. China was still far more advanced than Japan. Over the next few hundred years, a new dynasty, the T'ang (618–906), would again lead China to great heights. It was during this time that Japanese contact with China began to increase.

New Ideas from China

The year 552 is often given as the date when Chinese influence on Japan began. In that year visitors from Korea came to the Japanese court. These Koreans had close ties with China.

Many Japanese saw that there was much to learn from the Chinese. They studied Buddhism, a religion that was already almost a thousand years old. Through Buddhist monks who traveled to Japan, the Japanese learned more about China. They were impressed by the government, art, and learning of this ancient country.

During the next few hundred years, contact between Japan and China increased. Traders traveled between the two countries. Bright young people from

Work on this Buddhist monastery pagoda began in A.D. 607.

important Japanese families were sent to China to be educated. Buddhist monks from Japan went to China to study. The Japanese eagerly accepted new ideas from China.

Buddhism. At first, Chinese influence was felt only among the upper classes. The noble families of Japan were the first to accept Buddhism. The common people still worshiped their Shinto gods. Many nobles practiced Shinto along with Buddhism. A leading Buddhist monk in the mid-700s approved this practice. He said Shinto and Buddhism were simply different forms of the same religion.

Architecture and art. Many Buddhist temples and monasteries were built in Japan. The Japanese followed Chinese forms in architecture. Japanese palaces were also built in the Chinese style. The Japanese, however, built mainly in wood instead of the stone and brick that the Chinese used.

This bronze statue of Buddha shows strong Chinese influence.

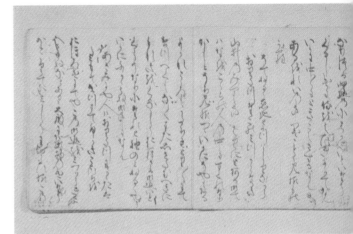

Japanese writing is also an art form, as this example of calligraphy shows.

Statues and paintings of the Buddha and of other subjects related to Buddhism were brought to Japan from China. Japanese artists began to use the style of the Chinese.

Writing. Writing was one of the most important contributions to Japan from China. The Japanese took over many Chinese characters and for a period of time also wrote in Chinese. Upper-class people used Chinese in much the same way that educated Europeans used Latin during the Middle Ages. Over time, the Japanese developed a system for writing the syllables of their own language. Both Chinese characters and Japanese signs are used in Japanese writing today.

Government. Even the government of Japan was influenced by China. Most of Japan was still under clan rule at the time. The clans followed the Yamato emperor and worshiped his gods, but the emperor had little influence on local affairs. Clan leaders still controlled their own regions.

315

Prince Shotoku

In the late A.D. 500s, Prince Shotoku (shō·tō·kōo) was made regent. As regent, he did not have the title of emperor, but he had all the powers of one. Look at the time line on page 232. What was happening in central Asia and the Middle East at this time?

Prince Shotoku proved to be one of early Japan's most important leaders. As a devout Buddhist, he encouraged the spread of the new religion throughout Japan. He also introduced other Chinese ideas.

The prince sent the first Japanese embassy to the Chinese court. He adopted the Chinese system of weights and measures. He brought the Chinese calendar to Japan. He had many Buddhist monasteries and temples built, and he invited Buddhist missionaries to Japan.

Prince Shotoku gave Japan its first written constitution. Yet his "Seventeen-Article Constitution" did not set up a government or explain laws. It was instead a code of behavior, with ideas borrowed from Buddhism and Confucianism. One of the articles told the people that they should honor the emperor as their ruler. Prince Shotoku wanted to weaken the clan leaders. His work helped strengthen the role of the emperor and unite the Japanese people.

The Yamato emperor saw that China had a strong central government and a well-organized civil service to run that government. Japan did not even have a capital city from which to run a central government. The Japanese tried to follow the Chinese example. They set up a new government under the emperor and built a new capital city.

Nara and Heian

The new capital city was called Nara (när′ə). The emperor moved there in A.D. 710. The city was laid out in the style of the Chinese capital. It had straight streets in a checkerboard pattern. A number of Buddhist temples were also built at Nara, making it the center of Japanese Buddhism.

Nara period. Nara remained the capital of Japan until A.D. 794. During this period Chinese influence on Japan reached its peak. Also during this time, the first Japanese histories were written. They traced the Yamato emperors back to the year 660 B.C., when the legendary Jimmu (jē·mōo) became the first emperor. Jimmu, according to legends, was the great-grandson of the sun goddess Amaterasu. Thus, the emperors traced their family back to a goddess. This family became known as the "sun line." The present-day emperor of Japan is the 124th in that line.

At Nara the Japanese attempted to set up a central government with a civil service similar to that in China. This central government, however, never worked as well as the Chinese system. Clans, especially those far away from the capital, refused to give up the right to govern themselves.

The civil service, too, was mostly a failure. In China tests were given to choose the best people for government jobs. In Japan more attention was given to family background in choosing officials. Clan leaders simply appointed their own people to office.

In order to weaken the power of the clans, all land was declared the property of the emperor. A plan was drawn up to redivide the land among the farmers so everyone would have the same amount. The powerful clan families who owned much land did not accept this plan.

Another problem arose in the capital at Nara. Buddhist monks controlled the temples and much monastery land around the city. They were in charge of education. It seemed the monks would soon control the government. The emperor Kammu (kä·mōō) decided, therefore, to move the capital away from this center of Buddhism.

Again the Japanese built a new city in the Chinese style. In 794 the emperor moved to the new capital at Heian (hā·än). It later became known as Kyoto, which means "capital city."

Heian period. Heian remained the center of Japan's government from 794 to 1185. Look at the time line on page 232. What was happening in Europe and the Middle East during this time? During the last 300 years of the Heian period, the Fujiwara (fōō·jē·wä·rä) family managed to control Japan's government.

The Fujiwara was one of the leading noble families in Japan. They did not try to make one of their own members em-

On this screen showing a festival in Heian, clouds cover much of the city.

peror. This would have broken the sun line of emperors that was thought to stretch back to Amaterasu. Instead, the Fujiwara controlled the emperors. The Fujiwara became **regents**, or rulers, for the emperors while they were children. As soon as an emperor became an adult, the regents retired him and brought a new child emperor to the throne.

These child emperors were kept busy with ceremonial and religious tasks. They served as Shinto high priests, and they headed the busy life at court. Meanwhile, the Fujiwara regents ran the government. Very seldom from this time on did a strong emperor try to take control of Japan.

317

What does this scroll of *The Tale of Genji* tell you about the Heian period?

Life at Heian. The new capital was the center of Japan's cultural life. The nobles who flocked around the emperor lived a rich life. They dressed in costly robes, wearing colors that indicated their rank at court. Formal codes of behavior told them how to conduct themselves.

During this time Chinese influence began to decline. The Japanese had borrowed many ideas from China. Now they began to change these ideas to fit their own way of life.

The first important Japanese literature appeared at this time. Much of it was written by women. The men of the time continued to write in Chinese. The women, who were less educated and who had not learned Chinese, wrote in Japanese. The writing of diaries, poems, and stories became a favorite pastime of many upper-class women.

One of these women, Murasaki Shikibu (moo·rä·sä·ke shi·ki·boo), wrote an important novel. This was *The Tale of Genji* (gen'jē), written in the early 1000s.

Lady Murasaki, a noble woman, served in the court at Heian. *The Tale of Genji* is a long story about an imaginary emperor's son named Genji and his search for love. In addition to being an important work of literature, the book tells its reader much about life among the Japanese upper classes a thousand years ago.

It was during this period that some artists began to paint **scrolls**. These were very long paintings that could be rolled up. A scroll told a continuous story as the picture was unrolled. One of the most famous of these picture scrolls illustrated *The Tale of Genji*.

The Heian period marked the beginning of Japan's refined civilization. That civilization would continue. However, Heian, like Nara, was to be replaced as the center of Japanese life.

Checking Up

1. For what reason did the emperor Kammu move the capital from Nara to Heian?
2. Why was the attempt to set up a strong central government in Japan unsuccessful?
3. How do you explain the fact that women were the first to write in the Japanese language?
4. What answers would you give to the key questions at the beginning of this chapter?
5. *Compare the influence China had upon Japan with that of Rome upon Europe.*

Feudal Japan

As You Read

1. Think about these words.
   shogun   samurai   meditation
2. Look for answers to these key questions.
   a. How was the rule of shoguns established in Japan?
   b. What caused the development of feudalism in Japan?
   c. Why did the central government collapse at the end of the feudal period? How was a new central government set up?
3. Use this reading skill.
   This chapter offers a good opportunity to compare and contrast two quite different societies. As you study Japanese feudalism, remember what you learned about European feudalism in Unit 11. How were the two forms of feudalism alike? How were they different?

By the late 1100s, the power of the Fujiwara family was declining. Other families began to struggle for power in Japan. At the same time, Japanese society was changing. A feudal system was developing.

Struggles for Power

While some nobles were involved in the social life at the emperor's court, others remained on their large estates away from the capital. These landholding families began to grow in importance.

Two especially strong families began to compete for power. Both had great military strength, far more than the Fujiwaras. By 1185 one of these two families had defeated the other. The name of the leader of the winning family was Yoritomo (yō·rē·tō·mō).

Shogun rule. After his victory Yoritomo was the strongest leader in Japan. Like other strong Japanese leaders, he did not try to make himself emperor. Instead, he had the thirteen-year-old emperor give him the title of **shogun** (shō′gən), which means something like "chief commander." As shogun, Yoritomo became the military and political leader of Japan.

Yoritomo decided to keep his headquarters away from the emperor's court at Heian. He did not want his loyal warriors to fall into the easy life of the court. His military government was moved to Kamakura (käm′ə·kŏŏr′ə), a small town near present-day Tokyo. Find Tokyo on the map on page 306. Kamakura became a second capital, with far more influence than Heian. Yoritomo took over all the powers that had belonged to the regents who ruled for the emperor.

During the next 300 years, shoguns headed the government of Japan. The military-style government continued. In time, however, the power of Yoritomo's line of shoguns weakened. Regents from a different clan ruled for the shoguns. Later a new family of shoguns came to power. Although there was a central government in Japan, it had little control over the important landholding families.

Japanese Feudalism

Feudalism in Japan developed as a result of the lack of a strong central government and of the power of local landholding families. Important lords held large amounts of land. The government could not force them to pay taxes on their land. Many small farmers sought the protection of a powerful lord and turned over their land to him. The farmers continued to work the land, but it belonged to the lord. The position of these small farmers was similar to that of European peasants who worked a lord's manor.

When Yoritomo defeated his rivals, he took their land. Some of his soldiers were given parts of this land as a reward. Others were made protectors of lands seized by Yoritomo. They became vassals of the new shogun and looked after his land.

Important landholders throughout Japan also turned over their land to loyal followers. Before long, there was a large class of these warrior-managers. They took care of a lord's lands and pledged

The samurai wore armor in battle. Can you name this warrior's weapon?

loyalty to the lord in return. They fought for their lord when needed. These people were called **samurai** (sam′ə · rī′).

The Samurai. Most of the samurai were warriors famed for their fighting skill. A samurai fought on horseback. He was armed with a bow and arrow and two steel swords, one long and one short. These swords were among the finest in the world. Swords were prized possessions passed down from father to son. A samurai would boast of the number of soldiers his sword had killed in battle.

The samurai were similar to the European knights of the Middle Ages. Like those knights, they wore armor to protect themselves in battle. Their armor, however, was lighter and less clumsy than that of the Europeans. They moved quickly swinging their curved swords.

The samurai had their own code of behavior, called bushido (bŏŏsh'i·dō'), or "the way of the warrior." Bravery during battle was highly important. A samurai would fight to the death rather than surrender to an enemy. Most important of all was loyalty to a lord. The bushido code said that "death is lighter than a feather, but duty is weightier than a mountain." Loyalty to one's lord was even more important than loyalty to one's family. A samurai simply could not surrender or accept disgrace. The samurai would rather die.

Zen Buddhism. By the time Buddhism came to Japan in the A.D. 500s, the religion had split into a number of different sects. More Buddhist sects spread to Japan during the feudal period. Zen began to be popular during the 1100s and 1200s. Zen became associated with the Samurai.

Zen monks meditated in order to achieve enlightenment.

Zen stressed self-control, or discipline, and self-concentration, or **meditation**. People studying Zen had to obey their teacher, or master, without question. They spent many hours sitting in a rigid position, trying to empty their minds of all thought. Zen taught that the truth finally became known in an instant flash. Only after a long period of training could a person see the truth like a sudden burst of light. Zen Buddhism was especially attractive to the samurai because of its emphasis on discipline.

Changes in the arts. The arts changed in both content and style during the feudal period. As the samurai grew in importance, paintings of warlike scenes began to replace those of stately court life. Scroll pictures told stories of wars and important battles.

Other paintings were influenced by Zen. Many pictures of landscapes were drawn. Instead of using bright colors, the painter often used only shades of black and gray. These paintings suggest the quiet meditation of the Zen Buddhist.

Japanese temples and houses usually had carefully designed gardens. These gardens were also works of art. Gardens, too, were influenced by Zen. The Zen garden is amazingly simple, with little more than an area of raked pebbles and a few large stones.

Feudal Warfare

In the late A.D. 1200s, the military government at Kamakura faced a strong threat from outside Japan. This threat brought about its downfall.

In a Zen garden, moss-covered rocks rise like islands from a sea of pebbles.

Warfare marked the last century of feudalism in Japan.

The Mongol attacks. As you remember reading in Unit 9, the Mongols had conquered much of Asia. Kublai Khan, the Mongol ruler of China, wanted to add Japan to his territories. In 1274 and again in 1281, he sent fleets carrying armies to invade Japan. The Japanese fought bravely, but they were outnumbered by the huge number of Mongol invaders.

Luckily, great storms at sea came to the aid of the Japanese both times. The second Mongol invasion attempt made up the largest sea-borne force until modern times. Thousands of Mongols were drowned when the storm destroyed the fleet carrying them between two Japanese islands. The Japanese called this storm kamikaze (käm′i·käz′ē), or "divine wind." They believed the storms proved that their gods were protecting them. However, the Mongol attacks did weaken the regents who ruled from Kamakura. A new line of shoguns took over the government.

Civil war. The new shoguns never completely controlled all of Japan. Finally in 1467, there was an argument over who would become shogun. The ruling family split into rival groups, and ten years of civil war resulted. By the end of that war, there was no central government left in Japan. During the next 100 years, leaders of powerful families ruled over their local areas. Warfare among these local leaders continued off and on. No one was strong enough to rebuild the central government.

A new family of shoguns. Finally in 1568, one of the powerful lords managed to conquer a large part of central Japan, including the capital. He was killed before he could bring all of Japan under his control. However, one of his generals, Toyotomi Hideyoshi (tō·yō·tō·mē hē·de·yō·shē), seized leadership in 1582 and completed the conquest of Japan. Hideyoshi had himself appointed regent for the emperor. After Hideyoshi's death one of his generals, Tokugawa

Then and Now

Social Classes

When Hideyoshi took power in 1582, he ruled that all people had to remain at the rank where they were. No one could change occupations or rise to a higher class. Japanese society was divided into four classes. At the top were the samurai, or the warriors. Craftworkers, merchants, and peasants made up the other three classes. They counted for almost nothing compared with the samurai.

The idea of a privileged class was not new in Japan or elsewhere in the world. The idea that a person could not rise to a higher class was also widespread. Although there were some exceptions, this was the case in Europe during the Middle Ages.

It was not until modern times that rigid class systems began to break down. Today there are few class barriers in most of the world. In modern Japan, as well as in our own country, poor people have the same rights as the rich. A person born poor can, through talent and effort, rise to become wealthy and powerful.

Ieyasu (tō·kōo·gä·wä ē·ə·yä·sōo), took the title of shogun.

Ieyasu had himself named shogun in 1603. He set up a new, strong government for all of Japan and ruled from his new capital city, Edo (e·dō). Edo was later named Tokyo. The Tokugawa family, which ruled Japan for the next 250 years, tried to close off Japan to the outside world. It was not until 1867 that government by shoguns ended in Japan. It was then that Japan opened itself to modern influence and rapidly became an industrial country.

Checking Up

1. Why did Yoritomo move his capital to Kamakura?
2. Who were the samurai? What was bushido?
3. What was the goal that the Zen Buddhist sought?
4. What answers would you give to the key questions at the beginning of this chapter?
5. *Compare the position of the emperor in Japan with that of the emperor in China. How do they greatly differ?*

Unit 12 Summary

- Japan is a mountainous country made up of four main islands.
- The Ainu may have been the first people to come to Japan. Later invasions by Mongoloid peoples from Asia drove the Ainu northward.
- Early life in Japan centered around clans. The Yamato clan took power in the A.D. 200s and 300s, setting up a line of emperors.
- In the 500s, Buddhism and other influences from China spread to Japan.
- Japan developed its own cultural forms during the Heian period when regents controlled the emperors.
- Shoguns headed the government of Japan through the feudal period.
- During the feudal period, small farmers worked the land of powerful lords. The Samurai fought for the lords.

323

Unit 12 Review Workshop

What Have You Learned?

A. Choose the letter of the item that correctly completes each statement.

1. The largest of Japan's islands is (a) Kyushu (b) Honshu (c) Hokkaido.
2. According to legends Japan's emperors are descended from (a) the Ainu (b) the Fujiwara (c) Amaterasu.
3. The earliest religion of Japan was (a) a form of nature worship (b) Buddhism (c) Zen.
4. China influenced Japan in all the following except (a) ideas on government (b) the Shinto religion (c) art and architecture.
5. Which of the following is correct? Zen Buddhism (a) was not associated with the Samurai (b) taught that truth became known in an instant flash (c) had little influence on painting or landscape gardening.
6. The first important shogun was (a) Yoritomo (b) Prince Shotoku (c) Hideyoshi.
7. Bushido has to do with (a) Zen Buddhism (b) government by shoguns (c) the way of life of the samurai.
8. Feudalism in Japan saw (a) many small farmers working on the lands of the lords (b) a strong central government (c) little warfare among rival families.
9. The samurai were (a) the sons of lords (b) mainly warriors (c) relatives of the shogun.
10. The Tokugawa shoguns (a) ruled Japan for 250 years (b) established their capital in Kamakura (c) opened Japan to modern influence.

B. On a separate sheet of paper, fill in the words from the list below that best complete each statement.

Ainu	Nara
Buddhism	regent
discipline	Shinto
meditation	sword

1. The _____ were probably the first people to come to Japan.
2. The two important religions in early Japan were _____ and _____.
3. Prince Shotoku's title was _____.
4. The first Japanese histories were written during the _____ period.
5. The most important possession a samurai had was his _____.
6. Zen Buddhism stressed _____ and _____.

Use Your Reading Skills

A. What does the Japanese painting on page 325 tell you about the geography of Japan? What two activities does it show the Japanese involved in? Notice how small the people are against the landscape. What do you think the artist wants to tell you about the Japanese regard for nature?

B. Match each of the following words with the correct definition below.

1. Mongoloid
2. paddy
3. shrine
4. scroll
5. regent
6. shogun
7. samurai
8. meditation

a. a ruler for a child emperor
b. self-concentration
c. a warrior for a landholding lord
d. a chief commander
e. the race to which most East Asians belong
f. a painting that can be rolled up
g. a flooded field for growing rice
h. a monument containing objects of worship

Use Your Time Skills

Put the following into time order. Review the unit to find the dates.

1. Fujiwara regents
2. introduction of Buddhism
3. introduction of wet rice farming
4. Kamakura shoguns
5. Nara period
6. Tokugawa period
7. Yamato expansion

Learn by Doing

Working with a group of your classmates, prepare a report on one of the following topics. Use reference books to find out about each.

Commodore Matthew Perry
Meiji Restoration
Japan and World War II
Japan today

Read to Learn More

Find the topics listed below in the card catalog of your library. Read all or part of a book listed under one of the topics. Share what you learn with your classmates.

TEA CEREMONY (JAPANESE)   HAIKU
WOODCUT (JAPANESE)   KARATE

Unit 13

The World of the Incas

An archaeologist first discovered the remains of this
Inca city in the early part of the 20th century.

Maps Tell a Story of the Inca Empire

As you read, think about these words.

guano   snow line   basin

When Christopher Columbus set sail across the Atlantic, he hoped to reach Asia. He never knew that he had reached the Americas. Nor did he know that the Western Hemisphere contained one of the greatest empires the world has ever seen. The Inca Empire was named after the Indian people who founded it. The Incas date back to about 1150. The last emperor of the Incas died in 1571.

The Inca Empire covered what is now all or part of five countries. Look at the map below on the left and name these countries. About how many miles did the empire extend from north to south? Into what present-day country did its northern boundary extend? Where was its southern boundary? What large lake is shown on the map? The area of the Inca Empire was about 380,000 square miles (988,000 sq. km). It was larger than Spain and Italy combined.

As you can see, the Inca Empire contained two main geographical regions: the narrow strip of desert along the Pacific Ocean and the Andes. The eastern border of the empire almost reached the rain forest.

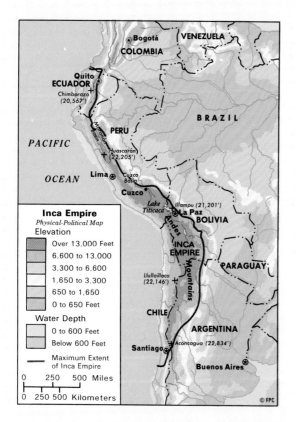

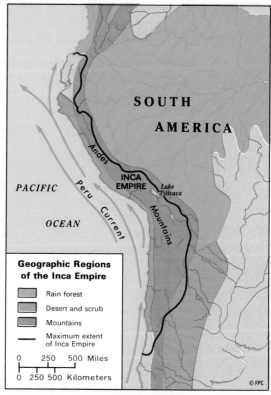

The Desert Region

Look at the precipitation map on this page. Which geographical region of the area that the Inca Empire once covered receives the least rain? This desert coast is almost barren. There are occasional oases formed by streams that flow westward from the Andes. In some places there are cactuslike plants and shrubs that do not need much water. Most of the coast, however, consists of long stretches of barren soil.

It seldom rains in this region. Sometimes years go by without a rain cloud in the sky. When the clouds do form, however, they bring rain in torrents. The Incas who lived in the oases were afraid of these storms. The floods they brought often washed away houses, bridges, and roads.

The reason that the coast is so dry is that a cold ocean current, the Peru Current, flows just off the shore. Find this ocean current on the map on page 328 on the right. The Peru Current, flowing northward from the Antarctic, is much colder than the water through which it flows. As a result, winds from the west that blow across the cold current become chilled. The air is actually colder at the bottom, next to the ocean, than it is aloft. Cold air is dense and heavy. Air must rise for precipitation to begin. There is almost no opportunity for this to happen along the Pacific coast.

At the same time the Peru Current prevents rain, it also keeps coastal temperatures cooler than temperatures in many other desert regions of the world.

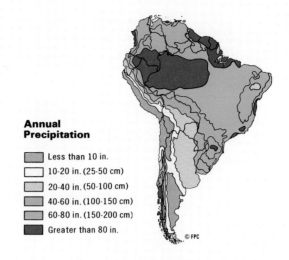

Annual Precipitation

Less than 10 in.
10-20 in. (25-50 cm)
20-40 in. (50-100 cm)
40-60 in. (100-150 cm)
60-80 in. (150-200 cm)
Greater than 80 in.

© FPC

The average yearly temperature in Lima (lē′mə), for example, is 64 °F (17 °C).

You might think that the dry air would hurt farmers. In fact, it was a great help to Inca farmers. The offshore islands are inhabited by millions of cormorants and other fish-eating birds. These birds leave their droppings, called **guano** (gwän′ō′), on the islands. The dry air keeps the droppings from spoiling. Inca farmers used the rich guano as fertilizer.

The Mountain Region

Look at the population density map on page 330. Which geographical region of the area that the Inca Empire once covered has the greatest population? The central highland region was also the most densely populated part of the Inca Empire. Look again at the map on page 328 on the left. About how many miles above sea level do the Andes rise? What peaks are named on the map?

As you know, the higher the land is above sea level, the colder it gets. The **snow line** is the level above which it is so

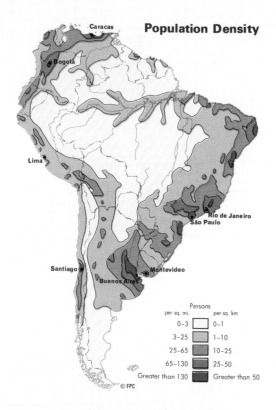

Population Density

Caracas
Bogotá
Lima
Rio de Janeiro
São Paulo
Santiago
Montevideo
Buenos Aires

Persons
per sq. mi.   per sq. km
0–3   0–1
3–25   1–10
25–65   10–25
65–130   25–50
Greater than 130   Greater than 50
© FPC

however, the basins turn bitterly cold. The Indians sleep under wool capes and animal skins. The higher a basin is, the greater its daily range of temperature is. The annual temperature range, however, is small. There is little difference between summer and winter seasons. The reason the annual temperature range changes so little is that these regions, in spite of their high elevation, are close to the equator. The sun is almost directly overhead all year. The river basins receive plenty of rain, between 20 and 60 inches (51 to 152 cm) a year, and sometimes more.

The Rain Forest

To the east of the Inca Empire lay the hot, dense rain forest. The rivers that wound their way through this region were broad and slow moving. The Incas obtained tropical foods from this area. Look at the population density map on this page. Notice that this area has an extremely low population. Few Indians lived in the rain forest in Inca times. Today it still remains almost uninhabited.

cold that there is always snow, even in summer. At the equator the snow line is about 18,000 feet (5,486.4 m) above sea level. Usually, the snow line is lower the farther away you travel from the equator. At the North and South poles, the snow line is at sea level.

As you can see from the map on page 328, many of the Andean peaks are high above the snow line. The Incas did not live there. Rather, they lived in the **basins**, or deep valleys, that the eastward flowing rivers formed. The most important basin was Cuzco (kōō′skō), where the Inca Empire started. What other basin is shown on the map?

The basins are hot during the day when the sun is shining. Indian farmers work stripped to the waist. At night,

Checking Up
1. What three geographical regions did the Inca Empire contain?
2. What did Inca farmers along the coastal strip use for fertilizer?
3. How did the climate in the mountain region affect the clothing Inca farmers wore?

An Empire in the Andes

As You Read

1. Think about these words.
   ambassador   rebellion
2. Look for answers to these key questions.
   a. What significance did the legend of Manco Capac have for the Incas?
   b. What was the religion of the Incas?
   c. How did the Incas build their empire? How did they hold it together?

The first Indians to live in the Andes probably migrated there about 11,000 years ago. They were hunters and food gatherers. They built villages along the coast, where there were plenty of fish, shellfish, and sea birds to eat.

By about 2800 B.C., the people had learned to grow lima beans, cotton, and other crops. By about 1500 B.C., they were growing corn and making pottery.

The Incas used llamas to carry packs and as a source of wool and meat.

They domesticated the alpaca (al·pak′ə) and the llama (läm′ə), animals related to the camel. Both animals provided wool and meat.

Between 1000 B.C. and A.D. 1000, several Indian civilizations developed in the Andes region. Some existed during the time of the Romans, the Han Chinese, and the Mayas. Each Indian civilization lasted a few hundred years before it disappeared. Then came the Incas.

The Legend of Manco Capac

The Incas believed that their rulers, called Inca, were descendants of their sun god. According to an Inca legend, the sun god sent two of his children to earth to help the people. The children were Manco Capac (mäng′kō käp′äk) and his wife, Mama Ocllo (mä′mə ō′kyō). As they rose out of the water of Lake Titicaca (tit′i·käk′ə), the sun god gave them a stick made of gold. He told them to find the place where they could push

331

the stick all the way into the ground. There the land would be fertile. There they should stay and build a nation.

Manco Capac and Mama Ocllo found that place in the Cuzco basin. They started the town of Cuzco, which became the capital of the Inca Empire.

The son of Manco Capac and Mama Ocllo became the ruler of the Incas. The other rulers of the Inca dynasty descended from him. Still other descendants populated the valley of Cuzco. All the Incas thought that they were special people because they were descendants of the sun god.

The Religion of the Incas

The Incas believed that the god Viracocha (vir′ə·kō′chä), created the world. The sun god was Viracocha's most important servant and the Inca's main god.

At the sun festival, priests offered gifts to the sun while people celebrated.

The Incas thought of the sun god as the giver of life. Without the sun, crops and animals could not survive.

The Incas believed in life after death. If they were good, they went to live with the sun. There they would be warm and well fed. If they were bad, they went to live inside the earth. There it was cold and dark.

The festival of the sun was the most important Inca celebration. It took place close to the summer solstice. In the Southern Hemisphere, this is the time of the year when the direct rays of the sun are farthest south of the equator. Look at the Atlas map on page 10. Notice that Cuzco is south of the equator. So the summer solstice fell on the longest day of the year in the Southern Hemisphere, December 22.

On the day of the solstice, the Inca watched for the first rays of the sun above the horizon. Then he welcomed the sun and offered it a gold cup filled with chicha (chi′chä′), a drink made from corn. The sun god promised the Inca light, warmth, and good crops.

The Growth of the Empire

From about A.D. 1150 to 1438, the Incas expanded throughout the Andes. Look at the time line on page 232. What was taking place in Europe, Asia, and Africa during this time? In 1438 the new emperor Pachacuti Inca Yupanqui (pä′chä·kōō′ti ing′kə yōō·päng′kē) came to the throne. During the thirty-three years he ruled, he greatly extended the borders of the empire.

From warfare to diplomacy. *Pachacuti* means "earth shaker." Pachacuti was indeed an earth shaker in building a mighty empire. Pachacuti began extending the Inca Empire by conquering one neighboring group after another. The Incas fought skillfully with clubs, spears, and bolas (bō'läz), or slings that threw rocks as big as fists. The Inca fighters became so feared that they did not always have to go to war. Instead, Inca **ambassadors**, people who represented their ruler, appeared before the leader of another group they wanted to take over. They would invite the leader "in the name of the sun" to accept Pachacuti as ruler. In most cases, the leader accepted the invitation. He did not want to fight the Incas. In this way, the Incas were able to add more land to their empire.

Holding the empire together. As the Inca Empire grew, it included more and more groups of people with different languages and different customs. Pachacuti developed ways to hold all these people together and to teach them the culture of the Incas.

For one thing, Pachacuti ordered everyone in the empire to worship the sun god. The people were allowed to continue to worship their own gods, but they had to honor the sun god too.

Pachacuti brought conquered chiefs and their children to Cuzco for their education. Other conquered people learned Inca ideas and customs. Pachacuti also made Quechua (kech'wə) the official language of the Inca Empire, just as the Romans had done with Latin.

The Incas called suspension bridges "little brothers of the road."

The Inca system of roads. Also as the Romans had done, Pachacuti united the empire by a system of roads. Just as "all roads led to Rome," so all roads in the Inca Empire led to Cuzco. The Inca road system was longer than the Romans'.

There were two main roads in the Inca system. Both roads ran north and south. One ran along the Pacific coast. The second, the Royal Road, was inland and passed through Cuzco. East-west roads joined the two main roads.

The two main roads were wide enough in most places for eight people to walk side by side. The roads were smoothly paved with stone.

Suspension bridges crossed canyons and rivers. These hanging passageways were made of braided and twisted fibers, and held together with mud. The bridges swayed from side to side in the wind.

The Incas did not use the wheel and had no carts. There were, however, long-distance relay runners who carried messages to and from Cuzco.

333

People Who Made a Difference

Thor Heyerdahl

The Incas and other Indians in South America built walls and roads. They made pottery and built irrigation systems. Some of these things are similar to those done by people in the Middle East and Asia. In fact, some scholars believe that people from Asia visited the American Indians many years ago. They believe that they taught the Indians arts and crafts.

Others believe that just the opposite occurred. They think that the people in South America sailed to Asia and to islands in the Pacific. One of these people is Thor Heyerdahl (tôr hī′ər·däl′).

Heyerdahl believed that people from what is today Peru sailed west to the Polynesian islands in the Pacific Ocean. These islands include Hawaii, Samoa, and New Zealand. Heyerdahl knew that some Polynesians tell legends about their ancestors from the east. The Polynesians grow sweet potatoes that they call Kumara, which is the same word the Incas used. Could the Indians have sailed from Peru to Polynesia?

Heyerdahl decided to find out. He built a raft of light wood called balsa. The raft was like those used by the Incas. Heyerdahl named the raft *Kon-Tiki* (kon tē′kē), one of the names for the Inca creator god.

On April 28, 1947, Heyerdahl and his crew of eight set sail from Peru. After 101 days and 4,300 miles (6,800 km), the Kon-Tiki landed on the Tuamotu Islands of Polynesia. Heyerdahl proved that the Incas could have made the journey!

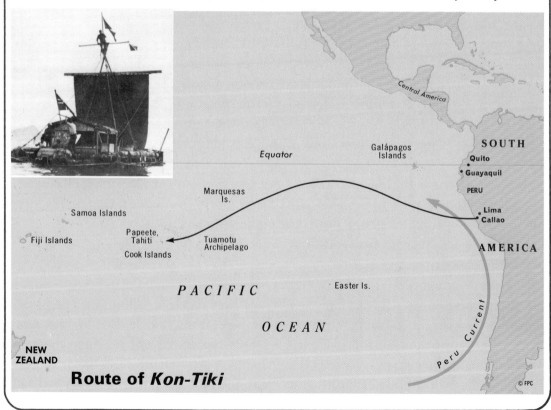

Route of *Kon-Tiki*

The Inca system of control. Pachacuti used the mitimae (mid′ə·mä′) system to control his empire. Here is how the system worked. When a new area was added to the empire, people from villages in the area were moved to other areas. Villagers living in the mountains were moved to another mountainous area. Villagers living on the seacoast were moved to another place along the coast. Wherever villagers were moved, they were put close to loyal Incas.

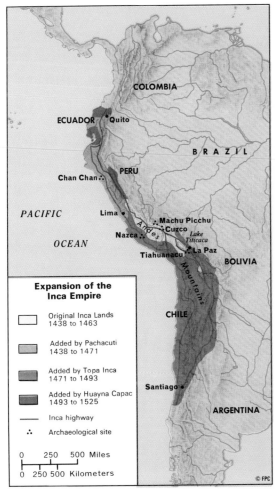

Roads crisscrossed the 2,500 mile (4,000 km) length of the empire.

People who had lived under Inca rule a long time were brought in to replace the people who had been moved. The newcomers taught the Inca religion, language, and customs to the conquered people who had been allowed to stay. They also watched for signs of **rebellion**, or uprisings, against Inca rule.

Expanding the empire. Pachacuti laid the foundation of an empire that his son, Topa (tō′pä) Inca, greatly expanded. Topa Inca died in 1493, just one year after Columbus reached America. At the time of the death of Topa Inca, the Inca Empire included the Andes regions of the present-day countries of Ecuador, Peru, Bolivia, Chile, and Argentina.

Topa Inca's son, Huayna Capac (wī′nä käp′äk), was emperor from 1493 to 1525. He continued his father's strong control of the empire. Look at the map on this page. It shows the greatest extent of the Inca Empire in 1525, the year Huayna Capac died.

Checking Up
1. What crops and animals were raised by early people in the Andes?
2. How did the Incas send messages to the ends of their empire?
3. What was the mitimae system? Why did the Incas use it?
4. What answers would you give to the key questions at the beginning of this chapter?
5. *In what ways was the Inca Empire like the Roman Empire?*

335

Life in the Inca Empire

As You Read

1. Think about these words.
   taboo   extended family   overseer   terrace
2. Look for answers to these key questions.
   a. How was Inca land divided? How did villagers farm?
   b. What were the accomplishments of the Incas?
   c. How was the Inca Empire governed?
3. Use this reading skill.
   An important skill is recognizing main ideas. Read the last paragraph under the section "Farming the Land." Which of the three sentences below gives the main idea of that paragraph?
   a. The main crop of the Incas was the potato.
   b. The Incas grew several crops.
   c. The Incas had a simple but varied diet.

The Inca, or emperor, was powerful and wealthy. He was the leader of a great empire. All the land in the empire belonged to him. Vast sums of gold and silver were also his.

The Emperor

Because the people believed that the emperor was descended from the sun god, he was treated like a god. He lived in great splendor in a palace that was like a town. It was made up of hundreds of large one-room buildings that opened onto beautiful patios, or courtyards. On the floors were beautifully woven rugs. Hangings embroidered with gold and silver decorated the walls. Thousands of servants waited on the emperor.

If visitors went to see the emperor, they first had to take off their sandals.

Archaeologists think Cuzco, the Inca capital, looked like this reconstruction.

Then they had to tie a heavy pack on their backs. The weight of the pack made them appear properly humble before the emperor.

Whatever the emperor touched became **taboo**, or forbidden for ordinary people to use. Thus, if the emperor left any food on his plate, it was destroyed. The dishes the emperor used, the clothes he wore, and the mats on which he put his feet also became taboo. Once a year they were collected and burned as an offering to the sun.

The Land and the People

The Inca's royal court included nobles and priests. They, too, lived in splendor. Most of the Inca people, however, were farmers who lived in the many villages in the empire.

The land. The emperor owned all the land, which he divided into three parts. One part was for the sun, one was for the emperor, and the third was for the people. Of course, the people farmed all three parts.

The crops from the fields for the sun god supported the priests and temples. The emperor's land supplied the royal court, the nobles, and the army. It also supported the architects, craftworkers, engineers, and teachers who worked for the government.

Part of the crop from the emperor's land was stored in warehouses. If there was ever a food shortage anywhere in the empire, the stored food was distributed to the people. The emperor took care of his people.

Farming the land. The land given to the people was divided among the many villages. The Incas believed that everyone in a village was descended from a common ancestor. Each village, therefore, was an **extended family**, or group of related people. The people farmed together, went to war together, and celebrated holidays together.

Each village had an **overseer**, a person who supervised the people. Each year the overseer redivided the land among the families in the village. Each family received enough land to grow its own food. The parents and children all received certain amounts of land.

After dividing the land, the overseer told each farmer when to plant, what to plant, and when to harvest. Before working their own fields, the farmers first cultivated the fields of the sun god and the emperor.

The Incas grew corn for chicha and bread. The main crop, however, was potatoes. There were about 250 different kinds of potatoes. The Incas knew how to freeze-dry potatoes for storage. The farmers also grew beans, pumpkins, tomatoes, and peanuts. Some areas produced strawberries and avocados.

These crops provided much of the Incas' food. There was meat, too, which came mostly from llamas and guinea pigs. This meat was usually cooked in a stew. The Incas who lived along the coast ate fish and shellfish, especially shrimp. Red pepper and salt added spice to the food. The most popular drink was mulberry juice.

337

Like the Egyptians, the Incas moved stone without using wheels.

The people. Most Inca girls grew up to be farmers' wives. Some, if they were beautiful or talented, joined the households of the nobles. A few went to the emperor's household.

Most Inca boys became farmers like their fathers. Some, however, became craftworkers, engineers, or other special workers. The empire needed and used people with special talents.

Crafts and Technology

The Incas were skillful workers in gold, silver, copper, and tin. They made pottery and wove beautiful textiles. Some workers were stonemasons who built the Inca roads and buildings. With-

out using cement, they fitted huge stones together so tightly that even today a knife cannot fit between them. Still other workers were engineers and architects who planned the roads, bridges, and buildings. Some, like Roman engineers, planned thousands of miles of canals and aqueducts that carried water

Terraced farmland did not wash away during heavy rainstorms.

everywhere. Some of the water was used for irrigation. Engineers also cut **terraces**, or level areas, in the sides of mountains. The flat land of the terraces increased the amount of land that could be farmed.

People who knew how to use the quipu (kē′pōō) were especially important. The quipu was made of knotted strings used for counting. From a cord 36 inches (.9 m) long, hung shorter strings of different colors. Each color stood for an item that was being counted. For example, white stood for alpacas, yellow for gold. The knots on each string stood for tens, hundreds, or thousands. A string with no knots, or one with space between the knots, was counted as zero. The Incas used the decimal system just as we do.

The Incas used the quipu for counting everything in the empire, even the number of people. Every year there was a complete census taken in the empire. Those who knew how to use the quipu were important to the Incas.

Only quipu users understood the rows of knots and different-colored yarns.

Remember that the Inca emperor had people brought to Cuzco for an education. Those who taught in the palace school were also important people. They were wise teachers who recited the story of Manco Capac and other Inca legends. They retold the history of the Incas so students could memorize it.

Government in the Empire

No one in the Inca Empire ever lacked food, clothing, or shelter. The government saw to that. The government also saw that all the rules were obeyed. There were rules for everything. Inca life was highly organized.

Overseers and nobles. For every ten farm families, there was an overseer. This person kept track of births, deaths, and marriages. He turned in monthly reports on crops and herds. He gave advice on problems. He also made sure people followed the rules.

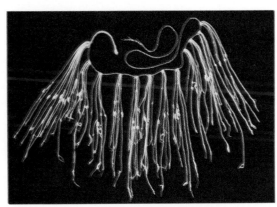

The quipu was a kind of adding machine made of strings.

For example, suppose he looked in a house and found some dirt. He would order the family members to wash their hands and faces in a bucket and then drink the dirty water, in public. This way the people would be shamed in front of their neighbors. They would probably be careful to keep things clean after that.

Above the overseers were nobles who were responsible for 100 families. Still other nobles were responsible for 500 families. These nobles were like judges. They listened to complaints and punished those who broke the rules. People of high rank were punished more severely than common people. Nobles were expected to set a good example. Furthermore, if a person stole food because he was hungry, the noble responsible for him was also punished. The noble had failed in his duty to care for those below him.

Inca women wove colorful fabrics from cotton and llama and alpaca wool.

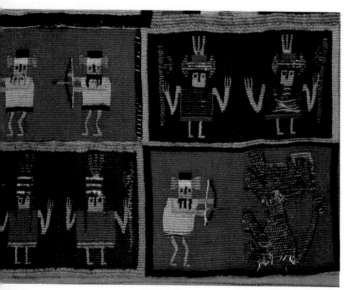

Nobles of increasingly higher rank were responsible for 1,000 families, for 10,000 families, and so on. Above all these people were four high nobles, each of whom governed one-fourth of the empire. These nobles were usually members of the royal family. Over these nobles and all the people was the emperor.

Taxation. You have already learned that the people had to farm the land of the sun god and the emperor. They were also taxed. Because there was no money, taxes were paid in labor. All men were required to serve in the army, build roads, mine gold, or do any kind of work the Inca wanted done. This work often took them away from home. They never had to worry about their families, however. The government looked after their families while they were gone.

The women often worked in the fields. They also wove the textiles each village had to give to the emperor. All this work helped make the empire a mighty one.

Checking Up
1. How did the Inca emperor live?
2. What was the quipu? Why was it important?
3. How did the Incas pay taxes?
4. What answers would you give to the key questions at the beginning of this chapter?
5. *What were the advantages of living in the Inca Empire? the disadvantages?*

The End of the Inca Empire

As You Read

1. Think about these words.
   heir   civil war   ransom
2. Look for answers to these key questions.
   a. Why was there a civil war in the Inca Empire? How did this war weaken the empire?
   b. How were the Spanish able to conquer the Incas?
3. Use this reading skill.
   The ability to summarize is an important reading skill. A summary expresses the main ideas of a reading selection clearly and briefly. To summarize, you must find the main ideas and put them into your own words. Read this chapter and summarize the main idea about the Spanish conquest of the Incas.

In 1525, when Huayna Capac died, there were 10 million people in the Inca Empire. They probably thought the empire would last forever. Yet just a few years later, the Spanish ruled the Incas. The Inca population dropped to about 1½ million. How did this change occur?

The War Between Brothers

A problem arose when Huayna Capac chose two **heirs**, or people to inherit the empire. He chose one son, Huascar (wäs′kär), to be Inca of the south and to rule from Cuzco. He chose his favorite son, Atahualpa (ät′ə·wäl′pə), to be Inca of the north and to rule from Quito (kē′tō). Find Cuzco and Quito on the map on page 335.

For two years there was peace between the two brothers. Then Huascar

After defeating Huascar, Atalhualpa was carried back to camp in a litter.

decided there could be only one Inca. He sent an army north to take Atahualpa prisoner.

341

A terrible **civil war** followed. A civil war is fought between two groups of one country. For five years the fighting continued, and conditions in the empire got very bad. Farmers neglected their fields. Food in the warehouses was stolen. On top of everything else, a plague swept through the empire. It was probably either measles or smallpox. It probably came from Panama, where Spanish explorers had begun settlements. You may remember from Unit 8 that the Spanish had landed in Central America in the early 1500s.

Atahualpa and Pizarro

In 1532 Spanish soldiers entered Inca lands. There were about 180 soldiers with a few "short-necked llamas." The

The Incas called gold "the sweat of the sun." All gold belonged to the Inca.

Pizarro's desire for wealth brought him to the land of the Incas.

strange-looking "llamas" were actually horses, which the Incas had never seen before. Led by Francisco Pizarro (frän·sēs'kō pē·sär'ō), the Spanish fought their way up the Andes to the place where Atahualpa was staying.

Atahualpa accepted Pizarro's invitation to dine with him. On the evening of November 16, 1532, Atahualpa was transported to the Spanish camp. About 5,000 unarmed warriors accompanied him. They had actually entered a trap. The Spanish attacked the Incas. Within half an hour, Atahualpa was a prisoner. The Spanish, their horses, and their guns defeated the Incas.

The Spanish demanded a **ransom** from Atahualpa, or money for the emperor's freedom. The emperor said that he would fill the room where he was being kept—once with gold and twice with silver. The room was 22 feet (6.7 m) long,

17 feet (5.2 m) wide, and 9 feet (2.7 m) high. Within two months the ransom was collected. Historians say it was worth at least $28 million. Nevertheless, Atahualpa did not receive his freedom. Instead, he was charged with trying to start a rebellion. Even conversion to Christianity did not save Atahualpa. Pizarro had the Inca put to death. Ten weeks later Pizarro and his soldiers entered Cuzco.

Why the Empire Fell

The empire had been weakened. First came the civil war. Then the plague had killed hundreds of thousands of people. In addition the Spanish guns were more powerful weapons than any that the Incas had.

The Spanish conquest was also helped by the fact that the Incas always did things in a certain way. They fought for twenty days and then rested for ten. So the Spanish attacked them during their days of rest. The Incas fought only during the day. So the Spanish attacked them at night.

The Incas were used to obeying orders. After conquering the Incas, the Spanish put Huascar's son, Manco, on the throne. They issued orders in Manco's name. The Spanish were so cruel, however, that Manco rebelled. In 1536 he fled Cuzco and led the Incas against the Spanish. The Inca rebellion continued under Manco's son. Finally, in 1571, Manco's son was captured and beheaded. Spain then ruled the people of the Andes for about 250 years.

Checking Up

1. How did the fighting methods of the Incas help bring about their downfall?
2. Why did the Incas continue to fight the Spanish after the Spanish had conquered their lands?
3. What answers would you give to the key questions at the beginning of this chapter?
4. *Why do you think the Spanish killed Atahualpa instead of keeping him prisoner?*

Unit 13 Summary

- By 1500 B.C. the ancestors of the Incas farmed and lived in villages.
- The religion of the Incas was based on worship of the sun.
- Pachacuti established a great empire.
- The Incas were united by both a common language and religion. In addition, their empire was held together by roads and the relocation of conquered groups near loyal villagers.
- The Inca Empire was highly organized and well regulated.
- The emperor owned all the land and ruled all the people.
- The Incas were engineers who built roads and buildings of stone.
- The Incas were conquered by the Spanish in the 1500s.
- Civil war and plague weakened the Incas. The Spanish used guns and horses, and fought differently.

Unit 13 Review Workshop

What Have You Learned?

1. Why did the Incas live in mountain basins?
2. How did the Inca road system help unite the empire?
3. Why was Pachacuti an important Inca emperor?
4. What was the Incas' main crop?
5. Why were some conquered villagers relocated to new areas?
6. Why were the Incas able to add new lands to the empire without fighting for them?
7. Why was the festival of the sun important to the Incas?
8. Why did both Huascar and Atahualpa claim their father's throne?
9. How were the Spanish able to defeat the Incas?
10. What were the achievements of the Incas in engineering and crafts?

Use Your Reading Skills

Recognizing the difference between fact and opinion is an important reading skill. A fact is something known to be true. An opinion is only what someone thinks. Read the statements below. Tell if the statement is fact or opinion. Give reasons for your answers.

1. The Incas were descendants of Polynesians.
2. The Incas thought their emperor was a god and treated him like one.
3. Atahualpa was a more able ruler than Huascar.
4. The Incas were braver than the other Indians.
5. Inca nobles were expected to set a good example for the other people.
6. The Incas were a carefree people.
7. Most Peruvian rivers flow in an eastward direction.
8. The Incas had many rules for people to follow.

Use Your Thinking Skills

After the Spanish conquered Peru, many of the Inca villages were abandoned. The Indians were forced to work on large ranches and plantations or in silver mines. Inca irrigation canals and terraces fell into disuse. An area that had once produced enough food for a much larger population fed fewer and fewer people. Recently archaeologists have suggested that the Inca irrigation canals be repaired and farming villages be revived. Why do you think the restoration of the Inca irrigation network and farming system might benefit Peru?

Use Your Time Skills

Use the time line on page 345 to answer the following questions.

1. How many years do the Incas span?
2. How long was Pachacuti ruler of the Incas?
3. How long did the Inca rebellion against the Spanish last?
4. How long was it from Pachacuti's rule until the last emperor?

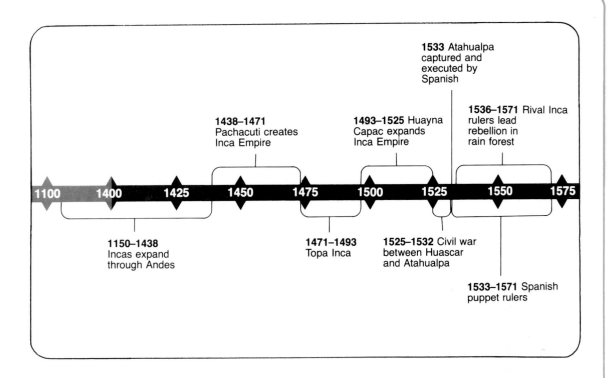

1533 Atahualpa captured and executed by Spanish

1438–1471 Pachacuti creates Inca Empire

1493–1525 Huayna Capac expands Inca Empire

1536–1571 Rival Inca rulers lead rebellion in rain forest

1100   1400   1425   1450   1475   1500   1525   1550   1575

1150–1438 Incas expand through Andes

1471–1493 Topa Inca

1525–1532 Civil war between Huascar and Atahualpa

1533–1571 Spanish puppet rulers

Use Your Research Skills

You have learned that there are five present-day countries in the area that the Inca Empire once covered. Choose one of these countries. Find out about the country today: its size, its population, its government, and the way the people make a living. You may also want to include something in your report about the history of the country under Spanish rule. Use encyclopedias and other reference works. Prepare a report or a talk to give to your classmates.

Learn by Doing

1. You have read about many interesting events in the Inca Empire. Choose three of these events for a mural. Draw or paint each event. Then write a description of what you have shown in the mural. You will want to include dates, names of people, and places.

2. Many of the Indians who live in the Andes today wear the same kind of clothing their ancestors wore during the Inca Empire. Each village, however, has something distinctive about its dress. Find out about the Peruvian and Bolivian Indians who still live in the Andes. Write a report about their clothing. Illustrate your report with drawings.

Read to Learn More

Find the topics listed below in the card catalog of your library. Read all or part of a book listed under one of the topics. Share what you learn with your classmates.

FRANCISCO PIZARRO   MACHU PICCHU

INCA   PERU

Unit 14

West Africa and Indonesia

Early maps were highly decorated. Here the African king Mansa Musa receives an Arab trader.

347

Maps Tell a Story of Africa

Africa is the world's second largest continent. Only Asia is larger. Africa's great deserts, forests, and grasslands have been home to many civilizations for thousands of years.

Before 1500

Look at the map of Africa on this page. It shows some of the early civilizations the people developed. Find those you have already read about. Where are they located? In the next few chapters, you will read about three of the West African kingdoms, also called empires, near the Niger River. These civilizations are sometimes called the merchant empires of West Africa. Their people became wealthy by controlling profitable trade routes with Europe and Asia.

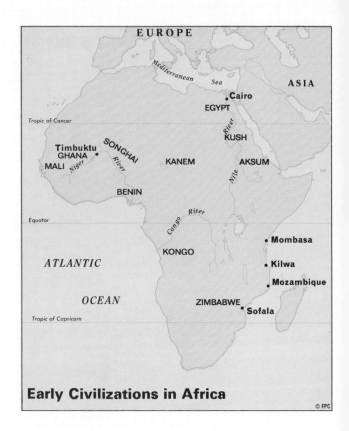

Early Civilizations in Africa

The king of Zimbabwe lived in this structure, known as the temple.

Look at the southeastern coast of Africa on the map. The several cities shown there were flourishing ports as early as 500 B.C. Traders from India and China sailed to Africa's east coast searching for gold, ivory, and iron. They also wanted slaves to bring back to Asia. The Africans exchanged their goods for fine Indian cloth and Chinese pottery.

Find Zimbabwe (zim·bäb'wē), located west of the coastal trade cities. Archaeologists have worked at the ruins of Zimbabwe and have found out about the people who lived there, the Karanga. We have many writings about Zimbabwe from Europeans who visited the east coast of Africa when the Karanga were still living nearby.

The wealthy Karanga controlled the gold supplies of Zimbabwe. They followed the rule of a powerful king, known as the Lion, and considered him to be a god. The Karanga so feared and respected their king that they dared not even look at him directly! They only heard his voice. The Karanga were eventually conquered by another African people, who ruled Zimbabwe after 1500.

European Conquests

About 1500, European explorers began a great search for new world trade routes and came upon many parts of the world that were new to them. Portuguese explorers led the way with the exploration of Africa. They sailed along the west coast of Africa in the 1400s and, by the end of the century, were the first to sail around the southern tip of the huge continent.

Beginning with the Portuguese, the Europeans brought great change to Africa. They divided the continent into colonies. A colony is a territory ruled by another country. Both the land and the people of a colony are subject to the control of the foreign power.

Earlier the Phoenicians, Greeks, and Romans had colonized parts of North Africa. The Arabs had extended their empires into Africa. When the Portuguese began to colonize Africa in the 16th century, however, they began the largest colonizing movement the world had ever seen. Within a few hundred years, nearly all of the huge continent became divided into European colonies. The Europeans

wanted Africa's natural resources. They also rivaled one another to establish great empires. Using treaties, guns, and troops, they seized Africa.

The map below shows how Africa was divided by 1914. How many European powers controlled Africa then? Which two controlled the most land?

Africa Today

Africa is no longer colonized by Europe. From the 1950s to the 1970s, most African countries became independent. Africans fought hard for their freedom. There were some bitter wars. The European countries were weakened by the great world wars of the 20th century. They had economic burdens at home. Colonies were difficult to manage and

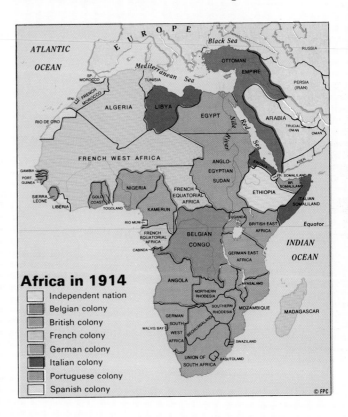

Africa in 1914

- Independent nation
- Belgian colony
- British colony
- French colony
- German colony
- Italian colony
- Portuguese colony
- Spanish colony

Nigeria, once a British colony, has busy outdoor markets.

world opinion about the unfairness of colonization was growing.

There are more than fifty independent countries in Africa today. You can see them on the map above.

Independence has presented Africans with many challenges. These include the search for peaceful government, resource development, and adequate food and education for the people.

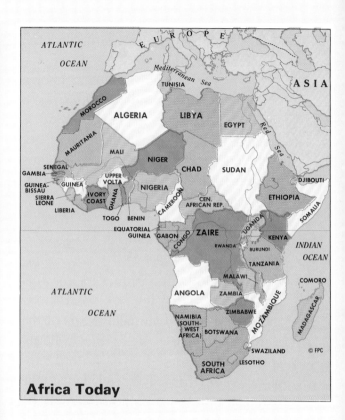

Africa Today

Checking Up

1. What people lived in Zimbabwe? What resource made them rich?

2. In 1914, when most of Africa was still colonized, which two areas were independent?

3. What were three of the Portuguese colonies in Africa in 1914? What were three of the German colonies in Africa in 1914?

4. Use the map "Africa Today" to name five independent African countries. Next, use the map "Africa in 1914" to find out which European powers once controlled each of these five modern African countries.

The Land of Gold: Ghana

As You Read

1. Think about these words.
   ebony   refugee
2. Look for answers to these key questions.
   a. How do we know about the kingdoms of West Africa?
   b. Which products were traded in Ghana?
   c. How were the two parts of Ghana's capital city different?
3. Use this reading skill.
   An important reading skill is the ability to discover cause and effect. In this chapter you will discover why Ghana became a powerful empire in Africa and also why it fell. What were two of these causes? What effects did Ghana's rise to power have upon various groups of people in the land?

Great empires flourished in West Africa from the 700s to the 1600s. Many early African people had no written language. We have learned of these people from archaeological remains, from stories handed down from family to family, and from accounts of Arab travelers. Three of the empires were located south of the Sahara in the grasslands of West Africa. The oldest was Ghana (gä′nə).

The Empire of Ghana

According to the stories handed down in families, the empire of Ghana began around A.D. 200. A group of people from North Africa migrated south across the Sahara to the grasslands along the Niger River. There the newcomers married into the families of the local farmers and fishers. After about A.D. 300, they began to conquer neighboring people.

You can see Ghana on the map below. Find the same area on the map of modern Africa on page 350. What present-day countries are located where the empire was? Notice that today there is an African country called Ghana south of where the old empire of Ghana was. The people of today's Ghana believe their ancestors came from the old empire.

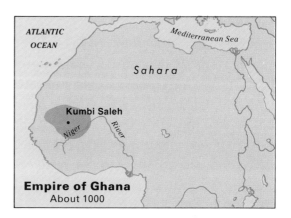

ATLANTIC OCEAN

Mediterranean Sea

Sahara

Kumbi Saleh

Niger

River

Empire of Ghana
About 1000

Then and Now

Salt Gathering

Salt is one of the most common minerals on earth and one of the most important. Our bodies need salt. Many foods contain salt. In addition, salt has many industrial uses.

Salt production has changed, of course, since slaves dug for the solid slabs of the mineral in the Sahara. Those workers had few comforts. There were no shade trees, and the temperature was often more than 100 °F (38 °C). The soil was unfit for farming, and the water was too salty for drinking. The slaves had to depend on food imports, which did not always arrive on time.

Today salt is taken from the ocean, from saltwater lakes, from mines, and from wells. When natural salt water is evaporated, pure salt crystals remain. Solid quantities of dry salt can be mined with power tools and machines.

These windmills in Brazil are pumping salt water into settling ponds, where the water will evaporate.

Most of our country's salt now comes from wells. Wells are holes that people drill into the ground. Fresh water is forced several hundred feet down to a salt deposit. The water, after dissolving some of the salt, is brought up to the surface. This salty water is then evaporated to produce the dry salt.

Ghana's Conquests

The people in Ghana were able to conquer their neighbors because they had superior weapons. They had swords and lances made of iron. Ghana's neighbors fought with weapons made of **ebony** (eb′ə·nē), a hard black wood from tropical trees.

For hundreds of years, the people of Ghana were the only ones who used iron in western Africa. Some scholars believe that the Ghanaians learned the technique of ironworking from the people of Kush. The technique may have been carried westward by the Kushite **refugees** (ref′yŏŏ·jēz′) after Kush was conquered by Aksum. Refugees are people who flee

from a country because of danger. The use of iron weapons enabled the Ghanaians to conquer their neighbors and expand the boundaries of their land.

The Ghanaians also used iron for their farming tools. Better farm tools enabled them to grow more food. The farmers of Ghana grew mainly cotton, as well as grains such as millet and sorghum (sôr′gəm). These are grass crops that are used for cereal and animal feed. Farming was important to the people, but their greatest interest was trade.

Trade in Ghana

For more than 600 years, from about the 5th to the 11th century, Ghana was the greatest trading center in western Africa. Each year thousands of camel and donkey caravans passed through the kingdom. The caravans brought cattle, wheat, sheep, honey, raisins, ivory, pearls, and olives. The most important trade items were salt and gold.

Salt came from mines in the Sahara. There slaves of Moorish states spent their lives digging thick slabs of salt out of the ground. There was so much salt that even the slaves' houses were built of salt blocks.

Gold was mined in an area known as Wangara (wäng·gär′ə). Ghanaian merchants kept Wangara's location a secret. Scholars believe it lay in the forested land southwest of Ghana.

The Wangara gold trade was carried on without words because the traders and miners did not speak the same language. Ghanaian merchants made their way to special trading sites along a river in the gold country. They announced

The Sahara mines still supply salt to Africans.

their presence by beating large drums. They piled salt and other goods in rows at the river's edge. Then they went into the forest to wait.

The Wangara gold miners next appeared at the trading site and examined the salt and other goods. They left the amount of gold they thought was a fair price. The Wangara gold miners then went back into the forest, and the Ghanaian merchants returned to the trading site for the gold.

If the merchants were satisfied with the exchange, they would scoop up the gold and leave, beating drums to show that the trading was over. If the merchants were not satisfied, they would again leave and wait for more gold to be added. Eventually, both sides were satisfied, and the "dumb barter" was over.

Life in the Capital

In 770 the rulers of Ghana set up their capital city. Actually, they built two cities about 6 miles (10 km) apart. A broad avenue lined with houses connected them.

One of these cities, Kumbi Saleh (kŏŏm′bē sä·lā′), was Ghana's commercial center. There the merchants traded cloth, honey, raisins, and other goods that came by camel caravan from Morocco (mə·räk′ō). The craftworkers made weapons, jewelry, cloth, sandals, and pottery.

Many of the merchants in Kumbi Saleh were Muslims. You remember from Unit 10 that the Muslims had extended their empire into parts of Africa by the 700s. Some Ghanaians accepted Islam. There were several mosques in the commercial city.

The second city served as Ghana's political center. A stone wall surrounded the city. Inside stood a palace filled with sculptures and paintings. There the king held his court. It was the custom for Ghanaians to bring their complaints to the king. He had complete power over everyone in the kingdom.

The Decline of Ghana

In 1042 a group of Muslims organized an army in North Africa and started a war against Ghana. They called it a holy war because they wanted to convert all the Ghanaians to Islam. In 1076 they succeeded in conquering the city of Kumbi Saleh. They converted many of the people to Islam.

The Muslims stayed in power for only a few years. Even though they left, however, Ghana was never the same. The people were not able to reestablish the salt and gold trade on which their wealth depended. They couldn't reestablish the boundaries of their kingdom. Ghana became weaker and weaker. Finally, in 1240, Ghana fell to another great empire, Mali.

Checking Up

1. What were the two most important occupations of the people of Ghana?
2. How did the Ghanaian merchants trade with the gold miners since they did not speak the same language?
3. What was the cause of the decline of the empire of Ghana?
4. What answers would you give to the key questions at the beginning of this chapter?
5. *Explain how you think iron gave the Ghanaians power over other people.*

Conquest and Pilgrimage: Mali

As You Read

1. Think about this word.
   inflation
2. Look for answers to these key questions.
   a. Who were the Mandingoes?
   b. Who were two kings of Mali? What did they accomplish?
   c. Why was Timbuktu an important city?

Look at the empire of Mali on the map below. Compare its size and location with that of Ghana, shown on page 351. About how much larger than Ghana was Mali? Use the map on page 350 to find out what present-day African countries are located where the old empire of Mali was. Notice that today there is an African country called Mali.

The people of Mali were called Mandingoes (man·ding′gōz). Their religion was Islam. Ghana had been seriously weakened ever since 1076, when Muslims first conquered Kumbi Saleh. It was not hard for the Mandingoes to conquer the weakened Ghanaians. Before long the new empire of Mali emerged.

A New Empire

The Mandingo leader and founder of Mali was Sundiata (sun·dē·ä′tə). His name meant "hungering lion." He was one of twelve sons of the king of Mali. When he was a boy, his father died and his brothers were killed by a rival for the throne. Sundiata's life was spared. Perhaps the rival king did not feel threatened by a child whose legs were so crippled that he could not walk.

Sundiata surprised the enemy king, however. He was intelligent, ambitious, and determined. Day after day, he exercised his legs until he was able to walk with an iron cane. Then he continued to exercise until he could walk normally. Nor did he stop there. He developed great skill at horseback riding and hunting. He also studied military tactics and leadership.

When Sundiata became an adult, he led a successful revolt against the group

Empire of Mali
About 1240

ATLANTIC OCEAN
Mediterranean Sea
Sahara
Timbuktu
Niger River

that controlled Mali. He then marched his troops westward. By 1240 Mali was the largest and most powerful empire in western Africa.

Sundiata divided the country into provinces and placed one of his generals in charge of each province. Every year the generals sent Sundiata gifts. Arrows and lances showed there was peace and order in the province. Rice and millet showed there was enough food for the people.

In fact, Sundiata did much to make Mali a rich farming area. He put many of his soldiers to work at the same type of slash-and-burn farming that the Mayas used. The farmers grew grains, nuts, and gourds called calabashes. Sundiata sent experts around the country to teach about feeding and caring for animals.

Sundiata reestablished the salt and gold trade across the Sahara. By the time of his death in 1255, Mali was richer than Ghana had ever been.

Mansa Musa

Sundiata started a dynasty that ruled Mali for several hundred years. The most famous king of this dynasty was Mansa Musa, whose name in English means King Moses. This king became famous even in Europe. His fame spread widely because of his great pilgrimage to Mecca. As you learned in Unit 10, Mecca is the holy city to which each Muslim must make a pilgrimage.

Citizenship

Mansa Musa's Leadership

Mansa Musa was more than a political and military leader. The king was interested in the cultural and educational standards of Mali as well.

Timbuktu developed as a result of Mansa Musa's pilgrimage to Mecca. In the holy city, he met a scholar from Spain named Es-Saheli (es sä·hil′ē). Mansa Musa persuaded him to return with his group to Timbuktu. There Es-Saheli built the Sankore (san·kôr′ē) Mosque, to which a university was attached. Mansa Musa brought back many scholars from Mecca. He paid them to teach and study in Timbuktu.

Sankore University soon developed an excellent reputation. Great respect was paid to scholars. Students came to Timbuktu from all over the Muslim

The Sankore mosque still stands in Timbuktu today.

world. As a result, there was a big demand for books and manuscripts. By the 1400s Timbuktu's merchants were enjoying a flourishing book trade. Because of Mansa Musa's leadership and encouragement, Timbuktu became an important center of learning.

Mansa Musa set out on his long journey in 1324. Possibly as many as 60,000 persons made up the caravan! There were court officials and servants. There were Muslim doctors, teachers, and soldiers. The king's followers rode fine horses covered with colorful decorations. In front marched 500 slaves carrying golden staffs. Behind them walked 100 camels, each laden with 300 pounds of gold dust and gifts.

The pilgrimage lasted about fourteen months. At best, a camel caravan can cover about 30 miles (48 km) a day. Mecca was more than 3,000 miles (4,300 km) from Mali!

On his way to the holy city, Mansa Musa stopped in Cairo, Egypt. There he gave presents of gold to court officials and to the city's poor. He gave away so much gold, in fact, that the gold became less valuable. More and more gold was necessary to make purchases. Twelve years after his visit, Cairo was still suffering from **inflation**, or rising prices.

Mansa Musa's prilgrimage spread Mali's fame throughout the Arab world. The nation's trade increased until, by 1400, as many as 12,000 camels a year were crossing the desert between Mali and Egypt.

Whenever Arab merchants settled in a new community, they were either accompanied or soon followed by Muslim scholars, lawyers, and religious leaders. The local mosques were centers of learning. There the students were taught to read the Koran. As a result, many trading cities were also centers of education.

The most famous of these cities in Africa was Timbuktu (tim′bək′tōo′). Look at the map on page 355. Near what river is Timbuktu located?

Timbuktu had a large water supply and fertile soil. Farmers were able to grow enough food to feed a population of about 20,000 people. Timbuktu was twice the size of the average city in Europe at that time.

The Decline of Mali

The kings who succeeded Mansa Musa were less able rulers. Yet Mali was rich and well organized enough that the country flourished for about another century. Little by little, however, groups that had been conquered by the Mandingoes broke away and declared their independence. Desert raiders captured much of Mali's northern area. By 1400 there was a new power emerging in West Africa—Songhai (sông′hā).

Checking Up

1. What qualities enabled Sundiata to become king of Mali?
2. Why did Mansa Musa make a pilgrimage to Mecca?
3. How were education and religion related among the Muslims?
4. What answers would you give to the key questions at the beginning of this chapter?
5. *How might Mali have been different if Mansa Musa had not made his pilgrimage to Mecca?*

The Third West African Empire: Songhai

As You Read

1. Think about this word.
   infantry
2. Look for answers to these key questions.
   a. In which direction did the Songhai conquest of Mali proceed? Why did it follow this direction?
   b. What were some of the main features of Songhai's system of government?
   c. What type of class system existed among the people of Songhai?
3. Use this reading skill.
   An important skill in reading is the ability to use details to support main ideas. A main idea of this chapter is the strong organization of the Songhai government. See how many details you can find in the chapter to support the main idea.

Songhai was the last of the three great trading empires that developed in West Africa. You can see Songhai on the map below. Compare its size and location with those of the two previous African empires you have studied. Use the maps on pages 351 and 355.

The Songhai Empire

In the 1400s the Songhai people began conquering the people of southern Mali. They were led by a warrior king named Sonni Ali. In 1468 they captured Timbuktu, the great religious and learning center. They later captured the city Jenne (je·nā′). Like Timbuktu, Jenne had become a center of learning in Mali. Locate these cities on the map.

As the Songhai armies pushed north, they captured the rich salt mines in the desert. Before long they gained control of the north-south trade routes. Soon Songhai became even larger and wealthier than Ghana and Mali. Its total area was more than 2 million square miles

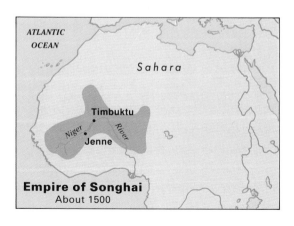

Empire of Songhai
About 1500

(5.2 million sq. km), or about two-thirds the size of the United States.

Like Ghana and Mali, Songhai was ruled by a king. Also like Mali, Songhai was divided into provinces. Each province was headed by a governor appointed by the king. The king often chose loyal friends or family members as governors.

The king also appointed tax collectors for each town or district. The people of Songhai paid a certain percentage of their crops as taxes.

The king appointed inspectors for all important markets. These inspectors supervised trade and enforced a single system of weights and measures throughout the empire.

In addition to this uniform system of weights and measures, Songhai had a uniform legal system. Songhai cases were tried according to Islamic law, which became widespread throughout the land. The king appointed a Muslim judge in each town to administer justice.

In the 1500s Songhai was the most powerful and well-organized empire of West Africa. It was also known for its culture, schools, libraries, banking system, as well as the university located at Timbuktu.

The People of Songhai

Songhai's population was divided into three classes, or groups. At the top were the Songhai people. They were the political leaders. They lived apart from everyone else and married only within their group.

How is this Songhai family paying its taxes?

Next came the workers and soldiers. Some workers made spears and arrows for the army. Others were responsible for the care of all the horses. Another group had the job of ferrying people and goods across Songhai's lakes. Still others worked as servants of the king and royal family.

The army was made up of two kinds of soldiers. The mounted soldiers, who rode on camels or horses, belonged to the Songhai people. They were armed with lances and sabers, or curved swords. The **infantry**, or foot soldiers, came from conquered people or had been prisoners of

Which group of the Songhai army is shown here?

war. They usually fought with bows and poison-tipped arrows.

A third class of people were the slaves. Most of them worked on the farms and took care of the crops and the cattle.

The Decline of Songhai

Although Songhai was the most highly organized of the three great kingdoms of West Africa, it had the shortest life. The empire began to weaken after the great leader Askia Muhammad I died in 1538. As had been true in Ghana, the death blow to the empire came from the north.

In 1589 the ruler of Morocco attacked Songhai. Much of Morocco's economy depended on gold, and Songhai controlled West Africa's gold supply.

Morocco had only a small army of about 4,000 soldiers. Most of them were Europeans who had been captured in war. However, the Moroccan soldiers had a tremendous advantage over the Songhai warriors. They had guns, while the only weapons the Songhai had were bows, arrows, spears, and swords.

In 1590 the Moroccan army easily defeated a Songhai army that was seven times larger. The provinces of Songhai fell away from one another and became separate states. No province was strong enough to capture the others and assume the role of leader. The era of the third great empire of West Africa was over by the end of the 1500s.

Checking Up

1. What four kinds of officials did the king of Songhai appoint?
2. What were two uniform systems in Songhai?
3. Why was a small Moroccan army able to defeat the Songhai army seven times larger?
4. What answers would you give to the key questions at the beginning of this chapter?
5. *Why do you think a strong leader, a Mansa Musa or an Askia Muhammad, is necessary to organize a kingdom and make it strong?*

Early Indonesia

As You Read

1. Think about this term.
   volcanic ash
2. Look for answers to these key questions.
   a. What were the most common religions in Indonesia?
   b. What part did men play in growing wet rice? What part did women play?

Thousands of miles east of Africa is the island country of Indonesia. Find Sumatra, Java, and some of the other large islands of Indonesia on the map below. Besides these islands there are thousands of tiny ones. There are many active volcanoes on the islands. The **volcanic ash** from eruptions has made the soil especially fertile.

Indonesian Kingdoms

About 4,500 years ago, people began moving into Java and the islands nearby.

The people may have migrated from southern China. They settled on the islands and began to hunt, fish, and farm. By about 200 B.C., they were also trading, especially with the Han Empire of China. However, China had little influence on the Indonesian people.

India, on the other hand, did influence the island people. Later, tens of thousands of Indians migrated to these islands. Some were traders, others were farmers, and still others were priests. They took with them the Hindu religion

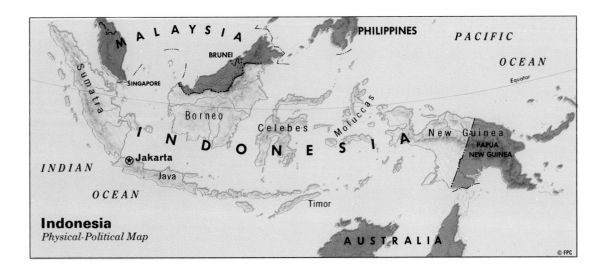

Indonesia
Physical-Political Map

Some Indonesians practice Hinduism, which came from India centuries ago.

you read about in Unit 3. They also introduced writing into Indonesia.

From about A.D. 600 to the early 1600s, several kingdoms flourished in Indonesia. A few were based on Sumatra. The people in these Sumatran kingdoms followed the Buddhist religion, which also began in India, as you read in Unit 3. Many who lived on the coast earned their living by trade. Most of the kingdoms, however, were based on the island of Java. The people followed the Hindu religion and earned their living by cultivating rice.

The most important kingdom in Java lasted from 1293 to 1398. It controlled not only the Indonesian islands but also the Malay (mə·lā′) Peninsula and the Philippines (fil′ə·pēnz′). Locate these places on the map on pages 12–13.

During the time this kingdom existed, Muslim traders brought Islam to the islands. The religion spread rapidly until, by 1500, most of the people were Muslims. The island of Bali, however, remained Hindu.

Making a Living in Indonesia

Most people in Java and Bali practiced wet rice cultivation. Rice farming was a never-ending job. The climate enabled farmers to grow 2½ full crops a year. The paddies, or fields, were irrigated with water from the rivers. Each paddy had a mud dike built around it so the water could not run off.

The men tilled the flooded fields with wooden plows pulled by water buffalo. When the soil was soft and muddy, the women transplanted the rice. They used seedlings that had been growing in small plots. With the forefingers of their left hands, the women poked holes in the

Like many Asian rice farmers, the Indonesians terrace their fields.

The puppet show is a popular tradition in Indonesia today. How did it begin?

wet soil. With their right hands, they put three rice plants into each hole.

Harvesting was usually done by the women, though in some areas of Indonesia it was everybody's job. Each worker cut the rice one stalk at a time, saying a prayer to the rice goddess with each sweep of the knife. They dried the stalks in the sun and then took them home to be threshed and stored.

Religious Entertainment

One of Indonesia's chief forms of entertainment was the puppet show. Instead of looking at the puppets directly, the people watched the shadows of the puppets on a large white screen. The screen was made of cloth stretched on a bamboo frame. A lamp filled with burning coconut oil lit the screen.

The stories told by the puppet masters were Hindu legends. They were religious stories about the struggle between good and evil and the proper ways to behave. The Indonesians believed they were puppets of God. Performing the puppet shows was one way of worshiping God.

Checking Up

1. How many crops could an Indonesian farmer grow each year? Why was this possible?
2. What answers would you give to the key questions at the beginning of this chapter?
3. *How do you think the puppet show could have been used to teach people proper ways to behave?*

Unit 14 Summary

● Between 400 and 1600, three great trading empires—Ghana, Mali, and Songhai—flourished in West Africa.
● Ghana became strong because its soldiers had weapons of iron.
● Mali became famous when Mansa Musa made a long pilgrimage to Mecca. He established Timbuktu as a major center of learning and religion.
● Songhai lasted fewer than 200 years, even though it was the largest and the best organized of the three empires.
● Asians began settling the islands of Indonesia about 4,500 years ago. Arab traders brought Islam to Indonesia.
● Farming has been the main occupation in Indonesia for hundreds of years.

Unit 14 Review Workshop

What Have You Learned?

A. Complete each of the following eight statements with the correct word. Make your choices from these words.

Indians trading Songhai Mali
Ghana farming Morocco iron

1. The chief occupation of the people of Ghana was _____.
2. Indonesians learned writing from the _____.
3. Ghanaian soldiers used weapons made of _____.
4. The main occupation of people in Indonesia was _____, which it still is today.
5. _____ was the earliest and the smallest of the three West African empires you read about.
6. _____ was the most highly organized and largest of the three West African empires.
7. Mansa Musa was the king of the empire of _____.
8. Songhai was defeated by an army from _____.

B. Choose the best answer to complete each of the following statements.

1. Most goods were carried from Ghana and Mali by (a) caravan (b) ships (c) mail.
2. The capital of the empire of Ghana was (a) Timbuktu (b) Kumbi Saleh (c) Cairo.
3. The West African kingdoms were near the (a) Congo River (b) Nile River (c) Niger River.
4. The major religion in Mali and Songhai was (a) Hinduism (b) Islam (c) Christianity.
5. The Mandingoes lived in (a) Ghana (b) Mali (c) Songhai.
6. The king who overcame a handicap was (a) Mansa Musa (b) Sundiata (c) Askia Mohammed.

Use Your Reading Skills

Summarize in outline form the section from chapter 4 headed "Making a Living in Indonesia." The first paragraph has been done as an example.

I. Making a Living in Indonesia
  A. Wet rice cultivation
    1. Practiced by most Indonesians
    2. A year-round job because of long growing season

Use Your Time Skills

Arrange the following events in the order in which they occurred.

1. Ghanaians learn to use iron.
2. Moroccan soldiers use guns.
3. Timbuktu becomes a center of learning and religion.
4. Mansa Musa sets out on his journey to Mecca.
5. Sundiata founds the empire of Mali.

Use Your Map Skills

Monsoons, the seasonal winds you read about in Unit 12, affect Indonesia's rainfall. Much of the country has a wet season from December to March and a

364

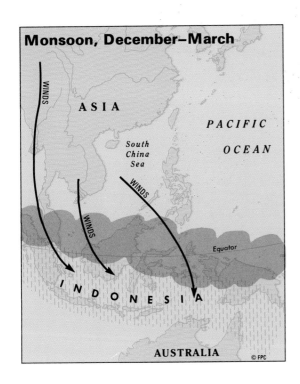

Monsoon, December–March

ASIA

PACIFIC OCEAN

South China Sea

WINDS

WINDS

WINDS

Equator

I N D O N E S I A

AUSTRALIA

© FPC

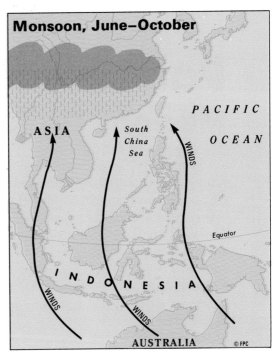

Monsoon, June–October

ASIA

PACIFIC OCEAN

South China Sea

WINDS

WINDS

WINDS

Equator

I N D O N E S I A

AUSTRALIA

© FPC

dry season from June to October. The maps above show how the monsoons work over Indonesia.

1. From which direction do the winds blow from December to March?
2. The dry winter winds of the Northern Hemisphere pick up moisture over the South China Sea. What happens when the air can no longer hold it?
3. From which direction do the winds blow from June to October?
4. The summer winds do not shed their moisture until they have traveled north of Indonesia. What places are receiving rain when Indonesia is having its dry season?

Learn by Doing

Early maps were often highly decorated. The map on page 347 is a good example. Make a colorful map of West Africa, North Africa, and the Middle East. Show the route of Mansa Musa's journey to Mecca. Decorate your map. For example, you may include the following items: mosques, camel caravans, salt slabs, gold nuggets. Label these actual places: the Niger and Nile rivers, the Sahara, Timbuktu, Cairo, Mecca.

Read to Learn More

Find the topics listed below in the card catalog of your library. Read all or part of a book listed under one of the topics. Share what you learn with your classmates.

AFRICA (HISTORY)   MALI

INDONESIA (HISTORY)   TIMBUKTU

Part Four
Modern Times

The late 15th century marks the beginning of modern history. The changes are great enough to separate the modern period from earlier periods you have studied.

One change came as people began to explore lands far away from Europe. Feudal communities had been small worlds. The modern world included the whole earth.

There were major changes in technology. As printing improved, ideas spread quickly to more and more people. The industrial revolution was probably the most important technological change of the modern period. Industrialization changed the way people lived and worked.

There were political changes. Great worldwide empires developed. Major European empires competed fiercely for power and wealth. As the great empires were developing, ideas of democracy and nationalism were spreading. Around the world people fought for independence.

Many modern changes are still going on. We are living in a period of great change today.

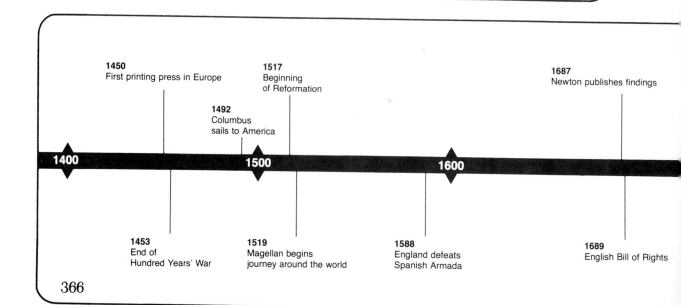

1450
First printing press in Europe

1517
Beginning
of Reformation

1687
Newton publishes findings

1492
Columbus
sails to America

1400

1500

1600

1453
End of
Hundred Years' War

1519
Magellan begins
journey around the world

1588
England defeats
Spanish Armada

1689
English Bill of Rights

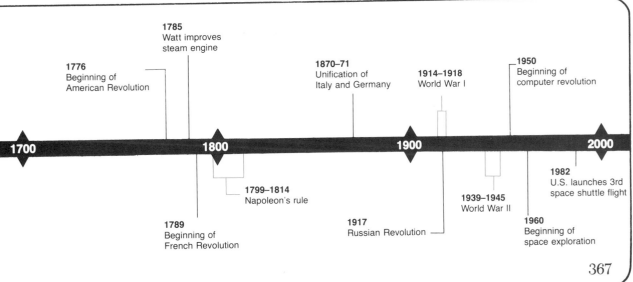

1776
Beginning of
American Revolution

1785
Watt improves
steam engine

1789
Beginning of
French Revolution

1799–1814
Napoleon's rule

1870–71
Unification of
Italy and Germany

1914–1918
World War I

1917
Russian Revolution

1939–1945
World War II

1950
Beginning of
computer revolution

1960
Beginning of
space exploration

1982
U.S. launches 3rd
space shuttle flight

1700   1800   1900   2000

Unit 15

Early Modern Europe

Florence, Italy, became one of the liveliest cities of
early modern Europe. The arts flourished here and in
other cities during the period we call the Renaissance.

Maps Tell a Story of the Americas

The Vikings of northern Europe sailed to Greenland and North America as early as the 900s. You can trace their voyages on the map on page 284. The Vikings explored mainly along the coasts. They made no permanent settlements in North America.

Most people in Europe did not know about the Vikings' voyages. Even by the 1500s, the American continents were almost unknown to the Europeans. As navigation improved, however, the Europeans sailed farther and farther away from their known world. Eventually, they sailed to the Americas. These lands were new and greatly interested the Europeans. What kinds of people were living here?

Before the voyages of exploration, most people believed that the earth was smaller than it is. The voyages helped people to learn about the size of the earth and the shapes of its landforms.

Maps show the changes in what the Europeans learned about the world. Look at the map below. It is a map of the world made in the 15th century. Which continents are shown? Notice how inaccurate the map is. The Europeans still had much to learn!

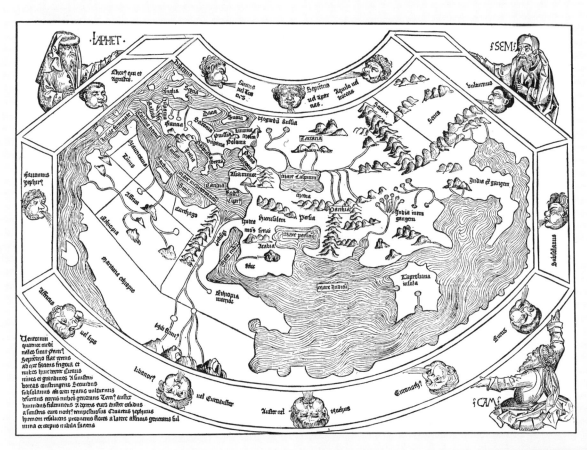

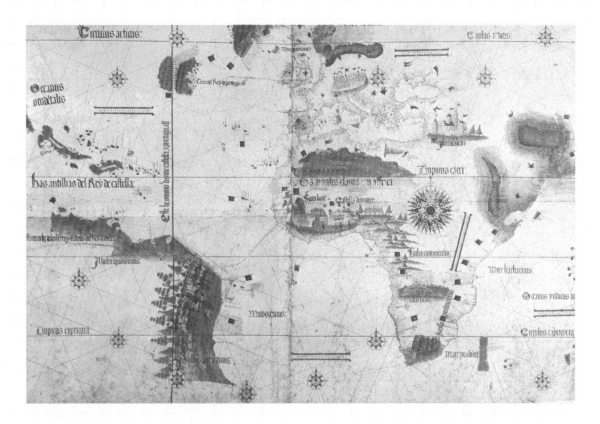

Next look at the map above. It was probably made only about fifty years after the first map. Notice the difference between them, however. How has the Europeans' view of Africa changed? How much of the Americas is shown?

Finally, look at the map below. It is a 17th-century map of the world. How is this map more complete than the first two? Which American continent is shown in more detail? Notice the dragons and sea monsters. Why do you suppose the map maker included them? Find the Americas on the Atlas map on page 10 and compare them with the way they are drawn on this map. In what ways is the 17th-century map still quite inaccurately drawn?

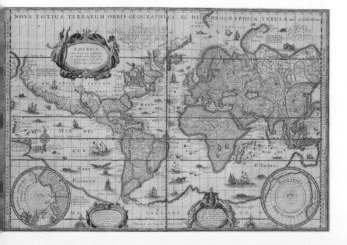

Checking Up
1. Of the seven continents, which ones were little known or unknown to the Europeans around 1500?
2. Find the equator and tropic lines on the second and third early maps. Check in the Atlas to see if they are right.

The Renaissance

As You Read

1. Think about these words.
   solar system   patron   utopia
   movable type   fresco
2. Look for answers to these key questions.
   a. What was the Renaissance?
   b. How did knowledge about the solar system change during the Renaissance?
   c. Who were three of the great artists of the Renaissance?
3. Use this reading skill.
   The artistic period called the Renaissance (ren'ə·sänts') has ties to early Greek civilization. Look at the painting on page 376, lower left. Read the caption to find out the names of the two Greek thinkers pictured. Use the Index to find out where they were first written about in this book. Why are they famous?

Toward the end of the Middle Ages, as you remember from Unit 11, feudalism declined and busy towns began to grow. Great universities were beginning to flourish. Trade between Europe and Asia was increasing. All this bustling activity, along with new inventions and discoveries, led to a period of history we call the Renaissance. The word *renaissance* means "rebirth." It is used to describe the time from the late 1300s to about 1600, when there was a rebirth of interest in the Greek and Roman artistic ideals.

A Time of Change

The Renaissance began in Italy. The Italian cities of Florence, Rome, Milan, and Venice grew into rich centers of trade for the rest of Europe. Some merchants became wealthy through trade. They used part of their wealth for works of art and for education. They helped the Renaissance develop and spread. By the 15th and 16th centuries, the Renaissance had spread into countries of northern Europe.

Changes in business and education. As trade increased, so did the size of the middle class. The middle class included merchants, wealthy craftworkers, and others who worked in business. Some middle-class people became richer and more powerful than the nobles. Business was replacing warfare as a way to achieve power.

People did not always welcome new ideas about the universe. Galileo was tried by the church for his conclusion about the solar system.

There were changes in education too. As business grew in importance, there was a greater need for practical skills. A merchant needed workers who could read, write, and use numbers. There were more and more laws for businesses. People who could understand the laws were needed.

Changes in science. Scholars looked again at the writings of the ancient Greeks and Romans. They rediscovered knowledge that had been forgotten for centuries during the early Middle Ages. They learned about the human body and about medicine. Plato, Aristotle, and others were studied. Renaissance thinkers began to experiment with ideas, especially ideas in science.

One science that especially interested people during the Renaissance was astronomy. A Polish astronomer, Nicolaus Copernicus, believed that the sun was the center of our **solar system**. The solar system is made up of the sun and the planets that revolve around it. Copernicus believed that the earth and the other planets moved around the sun. Most people at this time believed that the earth was the center of the universe. They thought the sun revolved around the earth.

About 1612 an Italian astronomer, Galileo, improved the telescope. He was able to help prove that the earth and the other known planets did indeed revolve around the sun.

Not everyone agreed with these new ideas about the universe. In fact, Galileo was put on trial by the church. Church leaders felt that the earth might somehow be viewed as less important if it were not the center of the universe. In order to save his life, Galileo said that he had been wrong.

The workers at left are setting the separate block letters to be printed.

In early woodblock printing, a whole page was carved on one block. The use of movable type saved time and expense.

Changes in printing. Remember that during the Middle Ages books were written by hand. It took hundreds of hours for a scribe to make one copy of a book. As a result, books were rare and expensive. There were no newspapers or magazines. People had to depend on what they heard from others.

Printing from **movable type** was introduced in Europe about 1450. Using this system, a printer arranged separate wood block letters into words on a large wooden frame. When enough type was set, it was ready to be inked and printed. Later, the printer could separate the type and use the same letters over again. The illustrations above further explain this process.

No one knows for sure who first used movable metal type in Europe. The credit usually goes to Johann Gutenberg. He printed a beautiful Bible in 1456. Books and other printed materials became less expensive and more available. By 1480 there were printing shops in more than 100 towns and cities in Europe. By 1500 more than 15 million books had been printed.

Books spread ideas quickly. People could own their own Bibles. Scholars could learn from one another through books. Galileo, for example, learned from the writings of Copernicus.

Changes in Art and Literature

Wealthy merchants, popes, rulers, and nobles spent money on art and entertainment. They hired musicians to write new music and to play at parties. They hired artists to paint and sculptors to carve statues. People who encourage and pay artists are called **patrons**. Renaissance artists worked for their patrons.

Artists. Some of the most famous Renaissance artists worked in the Italian cities, especially Florence. Leonardo da Vinci was one of these. Leonardo studied and sketched the human body. He made the people in his paintings and sketches look very lifelike. Look at his self-portrait on the next page. How do the details of the face make it look so real?

Leonardo was also a scientist and an engineer. He worked on ideas for engines and even designed a flying machine more than 450 years ago.

Michelangelo painted biblical scenes on the Sistine ceiling. The picture above is only one detail of the huge fresco that covers the ceiling (below).

Leonardo's *Self-Portrait* is one of his many masterful drawings of people.

Albrecht Dürer's *Young Hare* is a well-known northern Renaissance painting.

375

Michelangelo's famous sculpture shows Christ held by his mother.

Northern Renaissance master Pieter Brueghel (pē'tər brōō'gəl) filled his paintings with everyday scenes of ordinary people.

In the *School of Athens,* Raphael showed Plato and Aristotle (center), the two famous Greek thinkers.

One of the world's most accomplished artists, Michelangelo designed the dome for Saint Peter's Church.

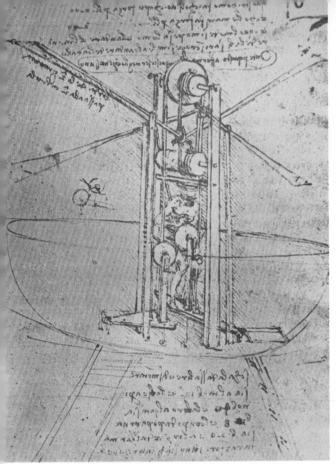

How do you think Leonardo expected this machine to fly?

Raphael (räf′ē·əl) was another important Renaissance artist. In addition to his many religious paintings, Raphael did **frescoes** (fres′kōz) for the pope's residence in Rome. Frescoes are painted directly on plastered walls. They are often grand murals that tell stories.

Michelangelo was yet another great Renaissance artist. He was a painter, sculptor, and architect. Michelangelo painted frescoes for the arched ceiling of the Sistine Chapel in Rome.

Look at and read more about the examples of Renaissance art on pages 375–376. Notice that not all the art is about religious subjects. Artists of northern Europe, especially, painted everyday scenes and objects.

Writers. Some say that William Shakespeare was the world's greatest writer. The works of the English playwright are still read and performed today. Like other Renaissance writers, Shakespeare wrote in the common language of the people rather than in Latin.

Another English writer, Thomas More, wrote *Utopia* (yōō·tō′pē·ə). It is a story about a perfect world. We still use the word **utopia** to describe a perfect place.

The artists and writers of the Renaissance made important contributions to our lives. We can learn about the ways people lived by reading books written during that time. We can still enjoy the paintings, statues, and buildings. Perhaps most important are the ideas and discoveries of the Renaissance that led to other ideas and discoveries. Truly, the Renaissance was the beginning of our modern world.

Checking Up
1. How did wealthy Italian patrons help the Renaissance develop?
2. In what way did education change during the Renaissance?
3. Who was Galileo? Johann Gutenberg?
4. What answers would you give to the key questions at the beginning of this chapter?
5. *In what important way did the development of movable type contribute to the Renaissance? Can you name any later inventions that have helped speed communication today?*

The Age of Exploration

As You Read

1. Think about these words.
   cape   strait   Northwest Passage
2. Look for answers to these key questions.
   a. What was the Age of Exploration? What lands were explored?
   b. What European countries were involved in exploration? Who were some of the explorers?
   c. What were two important results of exploration?
3. Use this reading skill.
   Diagrams and other illustrations can show information in a compact fashion. The chart of explorers on page 383 is a good example. Notice how the maps on pages 380 and 381 show some of the same information. How could a time line show the information?

In the late 1400s, the Age of Exploration began in Europe. You have already learned about the Spanish exploration and conquest of parts of Latin America. Remember, too, that the Portuguese began to explore and colonize Africa in the 15th century. Soon other European countries began to search for new lands.

The Search for Trade

Most of the early explorers were looking for new trade routes to Asia. You will recall that the Crusaders brought back spices, silks, and other products from Asia. People in Europe liked these products. A lively trade developed. However, goods from Asia were expensive because most of the trade routes were overland. The journey was long and difficult. More goods could be carried more cheaply by ship. Many European countries were determined to find new sea routes to Asia.

Portuguese and Spanish Exploration

In the early 1400s, a Portuguese noble, Prince Henry, started a navigation school. By the end of the 15th century, the Portuguese had learned a great deal about navigating the oceans.

A sea route to Asia. Under Prince Henry's direction, the Portuguese sailed south to explore the west coast of Africa. In 1487 the explorer Bartholomeu Dias (bär·thäl'ə·myo͞o dē'as) reached the southern tip of Africa which was later named the Cape of Good Hope. A **cape** is a point of land that extends into the sea. The Portuguese believed that reaching the southern tip of Africa gave good hope of finding a sea route to Asia.

With the good wishes of the king and queen, Columbus set sail west. Although he made four journeys, Columbus never made it to Asia.

In 1498 another Portuguese explorer, Vasco da Gama, sailed around the cape all the way to India. He brought back shiploads of spices. The Portuguese sailors had found a sea route to Asia!

An Italian sailor, Christopher Columbus, looked for a different sea route to Asia. Like most educated people of his time, Columbus believed that the earth was round. He wanted to sail west to reach the Indies, a common name for eastern Asia then.

Columbus asked King Ferdinand and Queen Isabella of Spain for the money to make the trip. Columbus knew that Spain wanted to find new trade routes to Asia. The king and queen agreed to give him the money.

Columbus made four western voyages. He never did reach the Indies, however. As you know, Columbus sailed to islands of the Caribbean Sea. Columbus did not know that two great continents, North and South America, kept him from finding his sea route to Asia.

Other explorers soon followed to explore the new continents. The Americas were named for another Italian who sailed for Spain, Amerigo Vespucci (äm′ə·rē′gō ve·spoo′chē). Vespucci was probably the first explorer to realize that he had reached a new world.

A trip around the world. In 1519 Ferdinand Magellan and his crew began a voyage that was to last two years. They sailed west from Spain across the Atlantic. Next they sailed along the east coast of South America. They passed through the **strait** (strāt), or narrow passage of

water, that is named for Magellan. The explorers then sailed north along the west coast of South America. They found that the continent was enormous!

The adventurers headed west for Asia. They were not prepared for such a long journey. After more than three months, the sailors were almost starving. Finally, they reached Guam, an island in the Pacific. After finding food and rest on Guam, the sailors reached the Philip-

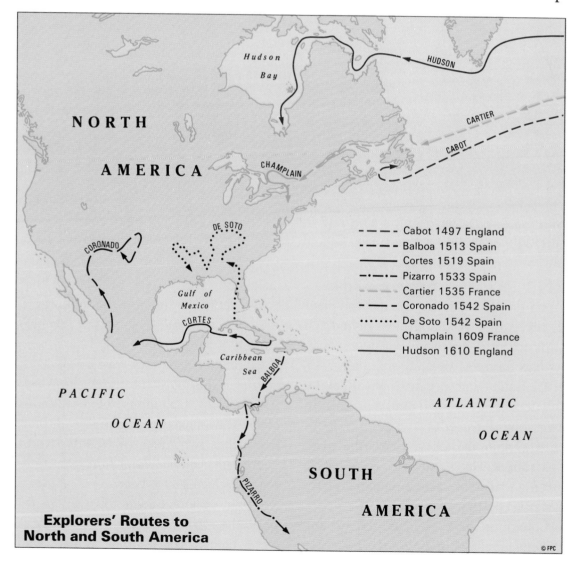

Explorers' Routes to North and South America

– – – –	Cabot 1497 England
– ·– ·–	Balboa 1513 Spain
———	Cortes 1519 Spain
–·–·–	Pizarro 1533 Spain
– – – –	Cartier 1535 France
– – –	Coronado 1542 Spain
··········	De Soto 1542 Spain
———	Champlain 1609 France
———	Hudson 1610 England

© FPC

380

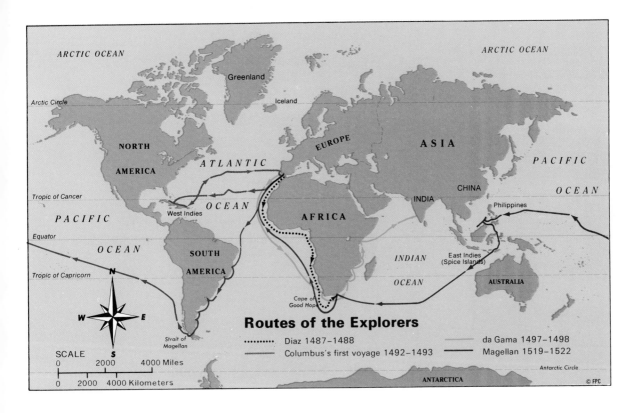

Routes of the Explorers

.... Diaz 1487–1488
——— Columbus's first voyage 1492–1493
——— da Gama 1497–1498
——— Magellan 1519–1522

SCALE
0   2000   4000 Miles
0   2000   4000 Kilometers

© FPC

pines. There Magellan became involved in arguments among the islanders. Magellan was killed. The voyage continued, however. When the sailors returned to Spain in 1522, they had completed the first journey around the world! Trace their route on the map above. Use the scale to figure out about how long their journey was.

Claiming new lands. When Magellan reached the Philippines, he claimed the islands for Spain. Other explorers claimed land for other countries. Claiming land became a regular practice of European explorers. If the people who lived in these places did not want the Europeans to take their land, the Europeans conquered them. Sometimes there were disagreements about claims.

Portugal and Spain, for example, asked the pope to settle their disagreements. The pope declared a Line of Demarcation (dē'mär·kā'shən) to divide land between the two countries. You can

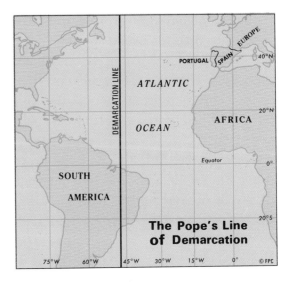

The Pope's Line of Demarcation

© FPC

381

Cortes (upper left) receives Mexican Indians. The woman beside him is Malinche who is serving as a translator.

see the line on the map on page 381. All territory west of the line could be claimed by Spain. Land east of the line could be claimed by Portugal. At approximately what degree of longitude is the line? About how much of South America was left open to Portuguese claim by the pope's line?

Riches from new lands. South America had rich gold and silver deposits. By 1550 the Spanish were mining huge amounts of these minerals to send back to Spain. The Spanish explorers Hernando Cortes and Francisco Pizarro, and others, helped find and claim the gold and silver.

Cortes had heard stories of the great Aztec Empire. In 1519 and 1520 he went in search of Aztec gold. With his army Cortes conquered the Aztecs and took control of their empire. As you read in Unit 13, Pizarro conquered the Incas in

1532. You may remember how the Spanish conqueror tricked Atahualpa, the emperor of the Incas.

There were several other Spanish and Portuguese explorers. Find them on the chart. What lands did they claim?

English Exploration

Other countries paid no attention to the pope's Line of Demarcation. They claimed new lands as eagerly as the Spanish and Portuguese.

English voyages of exploration began as early as 1497. In that year John Cabot, an Italian who sailed for England, made the first of his two voyages. He, too, was looking for a new route to Asia. Cabot explored the northern coast of North America. He was the first to search for the **Northwest Passage**, a supposed water route through the northern part of the Americas.

Selected European Explorers

Explorer	Date of Voyage(s)	Area Explored (present-day name)	Sponsoring Government
Vasco Nunez de Balboa	1513	Panama, Pacific Ocean	Spain
John Cabot	1497–1498	Canada	England
Pedro Cabral	1500–1501	Brazil	Portugal
Jacques Cartier	1535	St. Lawrence River, Canada	France
Samuel de Champlain	1603–1616	St. Lawrence River, Lakes Champlain and Huron	France
Christopher Columbus	1492–1504	Caribbean Islands	Spain
Francisco de Coronado	1540–1542	Southwestern United States	Spain
Hernando Cortes	1519–1521	Mexico	Spain
Vasco da Gama	1498	Sea route to India	Portugal
Hernando de Soto	1539–1542	Southeastern United States, Mississippi River	Spain
Bartolomeu Dias	1487–1488	Cape of Good Hope	Portugal
Sir Francis Drake	1577–1580	Sea route around the world	England
Sir Martin Frobisher	1576–1578	Northern North America (searched for Northwest Passage)	England
Henry Hudson	1607–1611	Greenland, North Atlantic Ocean, Hudson Bay (searched for Northwest Passage)	England
	1609	East Coast of United States, Hudson River, New York	The Netherlands
Sieur de La Salle	1679–1682	Mississippi River	France
Ferdinand Magellan	1519–1521	Led first voyage around world	Spain
Jacques Marquette	1673	Mississippi River	France
Francisco Pizarro	1531–1535	Peru	Spain
Juan Ponce de Leon	1513	Florida	Spain
Giovanni da Verrazano	1524	North America (searched for Northwest Passage)	France
Amerigo Vespucci	1499–1504	Caribbean Islands, South America	Spain

Careers

Space Science

Today explorers look beyond our planet and probe the mysteries of the universe. What are the distant planets like? How do changes on the sun affect temperatures on the earth? Are there any new resources to be found in space? These are some of the questions that face space scientists.

The space science field includes astronomers, technicians, computer specialists, and aerospace engineers. Most jobs in space science require good math and science ability as well as a college degree or more.

The scientists study space from observatories and space labs around the world. Powerful telescopes with cameras produce some information. Scientists also use orbiting spacecraft to find information. The spacecraft have cameras and computers. They can take pic-

At the space center in Houston, Texas, scientists view photos taken from space.

tures and run experiments on the material they find. Through lab computers, ground scientists are in contact with the orbiting spacecraft.

Space scientists probably agree that we know a great deal about the universe today. There is, however, much, much more to explore and learn!

Sir Walter Raleigh was another English explorer. In the late 16th century, Raleigh explored the coast of what is now the southeastern United States. Later he tried to establish English colonies there, but his attempts failed. Jamestown, the first permanent English colony in America, was settled in 1607. Find the other explorers who sailed for England on the chart on page 383. Who else searched for the Northwest Passage?

French Exploration

France, too, had its explorers. Between 1534 and 1542 Jacques Cartier (zhäk kär·tyā′) explored the St. Lawrence River in Canada while looking for

the Northwest Passage. He established France's claim to Canada. Later, in 1608, Samuel de Champlain founded Quebec, the first French colony in America.

Dutch Exploration

The Netherlands was the fifth European power to enter the race for trade and colonies. The Dutch managed to take over much of the Portuguese trade in southeastern Asia. In 1609 Henry Hudson began his search for the Northwest Passage. He came to the river that now bears his name. Later, the Netherlands established a trading post that became the colony of New Amsterdam.

Use the chart to find out for what other government Hudson sailed.

None of the English, Dutch, or French explorers discovered the Northwest Passage to Asia. Look at the world map in the Atlas on pages 10–11. Is there any waterway that spans North America from east to west? Look at the ocean north of the continent. It is usually frozen and impossible to navigate. The explorers of North America did not find treasures of gold and silver, as the Spanish had in South America. They did find riches of furs, fish, and land, however. They explored and mapped parts of North America.

Results of Exploration

The voyages of exploration brought many changes to Europe. There were many new products from the Americas. From the American Indians, the Europeans learned to plant corn, potatoes, squash, and other plants. The potato became part of the European diet.

The growing Asian trade increased the wealth and power of the exploring countries. Each country tried to get as much trade as it could. Each country also tried to establish colonies in the new lands. European culture spread to the Americas and to other places around the world. The world had become large indeed!

American Indians taught the Europeans to use fish as fertilizer.

Checking Up

1. Why did western European countries look for new routes to Asia?
2. What was the Line of Demarcation?
3. What answers would you give to the key questions at the beginning of this chapter?
4. *Do you think the Age of Exploration is over? What are some places that are still unexplored today? What are some changes that may come as a result of further explorations?*

The Reformation

As You Read

1. Think about this word.
   Reformation
2. Look for answers to these key questions.
   a. What were some of the criticisms of the Roman Church?
   b. Who were two important leaders of the Protestant Reformation?
   c. What were the achievements of the Counter Reformation?

For hundreds of years after Christianity began, there was only one church. In 1054 the church split into two parts: the Roman Church and the Eastern Orthodox Church, centered in Constantinople.

The Roman Church stayed united until the 1500s. Then, within a short time, new Christian churches developed. This time of great religious protest and changes in the Christian religion is called the **Reformation** (ref′ər·mā′shən). It was given this name because several people worked to reform, or change, some practices of the Roman Church. The new churches became known as Protestant churches.

Protests and Reformers

The Roman Church was very wealthy. Part of the wealth came from the tithes people paid. The church also owned vast areas of land. Not all religious leaders were honest people. Some used the church's wealth for themselves.

Nobles, always interested in more land, looked hungrily at the church's land. Many resented the power of the pope and other church officials. Discontent with the church began to grow.

There were other problems too. The church often sold its high offices to wealthy people. You may remember from Unit 11 that bishops and other important church officials usually were wealthy nobles. The church sold forgiveness for sins too. People who did something wrong could pay the church for forgiveness. Many people did not like the ways the church used to get money.

Martin Luther. One of the people who saw the problems in the church was Martin Luther. Luther became concerned about some of the practices of the church. He did not believe that people should have to pay for forgiveness. He did not believe that people had to fast, make pilgrimages, or do other special things to show they believed in God.

Eventually, Luther made up a list of ninety-five statements about some of the practices of the church. He nailed the list to a church door in Germany in 1517.

Putting lists and messages on church doors was a common practice at the time. It was a way of spreading ideas and information to other people.

Of course, officials in the church did not like Luther's statements. The pope criticized him. Finally, the pope expelled Luther from the church. He was not allowed to attend church services.

By this time, however, Luther had many followers. Nobles who wanted to weaken the power of the church agreed with Luther's ideas. So did many members of the middle class who lived in towns and cities. Lutheranism became the official religion of much of Germany, Denmark, and Sweden.

John Calvin. John Calvin was another reformer who helped start a new church. Calvin agreed with many things Luther said. Calvin began to speak out in favor of Protestantism. Because of his teachings, he had to leave his home in France. Calvin went to Switzerland. In time, many people left their homes to start or follow the new Protestant religions.

Calvinism was different from Lutheranism, however. Calvin believed that religious services should be very simple. Church services should include Bible reading, psalm singing, and sermons. In addition, he believed that people did not need priests to tell them what God said. He also believed that only certain people would be saved by God.

Calvin's ideas spread quickly. In France his followers were called Huguenots (hyōō′gə·näts). In England they were called Puritans.

An early drawing shows Luther writing his protests. Notice that Luther's pen stretches all the way to Rome.

The Church of England. Protestantism spread to England in a different way. About 1527, Henry VIII wanted the pope to annul, or dissolve, his marriage to his wife Catherine. The king wanted to marry another woman.

The pope did not know what to do. Catherine's nephew was Charles V, the powerful emperor of the Holy Roman Empire you read about in Unit 11. Henry VIII, too, was powerful. The pope did not want to make either ruler angry. So he did not make a decision.

Henry VIII grew tired of waiting and decided to act. He had laws passed that separated the church in England from the Roman Church. He appointed an archbishop to the new Church of England. The archbishop granted Henry a divorce. Later Henry VIII became head of the Church of England. At that time he made the Church of England the official church of the land.

The Puritans were one of many groups that fled Europe for the New World in the 17th and 18th centuries.

Results of the Reformation

The number of Protestants grew. New churches began in many European countries. Yet many people remained with the Roman, or Catholic, Church. Some of these people, however, worked to reform and strengthen the Catholic Church.

The Counter Reformation. The efforts of people to reform the Catholic Church are known as the Counter Reformation. To counter something means to be against it. The counter reformers were against the Protestants. Nevertheless, they wanted to reform some practices of the Catholic Church.

Ignatius Loyola. The Society of Jesus was one of the most effective programs of the Counter Reformation. The organization was started by Ignatius Loyola in 1534. The Society of Jesus was run like an army, with Loyola as its general. Its members were called Jesuits. The main purposes of the Jesuits were to teach and to spread the word of God. They set an example for other Catholic priests.

The Jesuits established and taught at some of Europe's most successful schools. Jesuits often served as advisers to nobles and rulers. Jesuit teachers went to Protestant countries to convert people to Catholicism. They also went to the Americas and other places to convert people.

Religious struggles. Because people believed strongly in their religion, they often refused to accept the beliefs of others. Often there was fighting about religious beliefs.

Some people left their countries to find religious peace. Some settled in European countries that protected their religion. Others left for America and started new settlements where they could worship freely.

Checking Up

1. What was the purpose of Luther's ninety-five statements? What was their effect?
2. Why were there religious struggles in Europe?
3. What answers would you give to the key questions at the beginning of this chapter?
4. *What main point did both the Protestant Reformation and the Counter Reformation have in common?*

The Rise of Nations

As You Read

1. Think about these words.

   nation   monarchy   Parliament
   nationalism   absolute monarch

2. Look for answers to these key questions.
   a. How did rulers strengthen their powers?
   b. What is nationalism?
   c. Name three strong European monarchs. List one event that occurred during the rule of each.

Strong political organizations developed in Europe in the late Middle Ages. Kings and queens became more powerful. Through marriages, wars, and clever politics, they extended their control over wider territories. Modern **nations** were developing. In a nation a large group of people are united under one central government.

Nationalism

People within the nations were becoming more aware of their own national identities. People in France began to think of themselves as French rather than as members of some town, city, or feudal community. The same thing happened with people in other nations. People within each nation came to realize how much they had in common. They spoke the same language. They shared customs, and they had a common history. Many of them followed the same religion. This strong feeling for one's own nation is called **nationalism**. Because of nationalism, people supported their government.

France, England, and Spain became three of the most powerful nations in western Europe by the end of the 1500s. All three had developed strong central governments. They usually had powerful kings or queens.

France

As you remember from Unit 11, France eventually won the Hundred Years' War against England. Find the war on the time line on page 366. The war increased feelings of nationalism in France. France's territory grew secure.

The French monarchy. In 1594 Henry IV became king of France. He was the first of a new family of rulers, the Bourbons. Henry IV did several things to strengthen France. Although he was a Protestant, he became a Catholic. Since most of the French were Catholic, the

389

Seventeen-year-old Joan of Arc helped the French in the Hundred Years' War.

word is law. Louis XIV believed in "divine right." He said that God gave him power to be king and no one could take that power away.

The Bourbons ruled France without interruption until the late 1700s. From time to time, some monarchs tried to extend the territory of France, and wars were fought. France also tried to extend its power and influence by establishing colonies in the New World.

Estates General. The common people in France had little say in the government. There was a council of advisers for the monarch called the Estates General, but the advisers in the council were nobles and clergy. Eventually, the Estates General also included members of the middle class. However, the organization was not very powerful. The king seldom called it into session.

king wanted to please the people. At the same time, he passed laws giving religious freedom to Protestants. He did not want France weakened by religious struggles.

Henry IV also strengthened the **monarchy**. A monarchy is a government by a royal ruler, usually a king, a queen, or an emperor. Henry limited the powers of the nobles. He reformed the government by choosing well-qualified people from outside the nobility for high office. The king gave help to French industry, business, and agriculture. The wealth of France increased. The middle class became strong supporters of Henry IV.

Henry's grandson, Louis XIV, became king when he was only four years old. After he grew up, he became an **absolute monarch**. Absolute monarchs hold complete power in their governments. Their

With the Magna Charta, powerful English nobles forced the king to guarantee them certain rights.

390

Queen Elizabeth

Elizabeth I of England was the daughter of Henry VIII and Anne Boleyn, the second of Henry's wives. During her childhood she received a good education. She could read and write Latin.

Elizabeth became queen of England after the death of her half-sister, Mary. Mary was Catholic and was not liked by many of the English people who were members of the Church of England. Mary had tried to make the English people become Roman Catholics.

Elizabeth made the Church of England powerful again. Like Henry IV of France, she helped business and industry. She sent sailors to explore new lands, especially those in North America. Sir Walter Raleigh sailed for Queen Elizabeth. The Spanish Armada was defeated during Elizabeth's rule.

During Elizabeth's rule, Renaissance art became important in England. England became especially known for its

writers. William Shakespeare wrote his poems and plays during the time of Elizabeth I.

Good Queen Bess, as her people called her, served her country well. She helped England become one of the most powerful nations in the world.

England

England, too, developed a strong central government and a powerful monarchy. England's monarchy, however, never became as absolute as that in France. As far back as 1215, limits had been put on the ruler. At that time, English nobles forced King John to sign the Magna Charta, or Great Charter. This charter limited the powers of the ruler. It also established the rights of a council of nobles who served as advisers to the ruler.

Parliament. Eventually, the English **Parliament**, a group of representatives having the power to make laws, developed. The Parliament in England, unlike the Estates General in France, took the power to tax. With this power, Parliament could somewhat control the ruler. The English monarch had to ask Parliament for money.

The English monarchy. England had many problems after the Hundred Years' War. There were struggles about who would rule the country. Two families, Lancaster and York, fought each other for years. Each family believed that one of its members should become the ruler of England.

The war ended when Henry Tudor defeated the last York king. Henry Tudor, distantly related to both families, was crowned Henry VII of England.

King Henry VII and his descendants strengthened England. You have already read about Henry VII's son, Henry VIII. Henry VIII's daughter, Elizabeth I, became queen and ruled until the early 1600s. She helped make England one of the most powerful European nations.

Spain

Spain became united after Ferdinand and Isabella married and joined their two kingdoms. These were the same rulers who paid for Columbus's voyages.

The Spanish monarchy. Spain became a Catholic nation. The two rulers insisted that everyone in Spain had to be Catholic. They forced Muslims and Jews to leave the country. Spain lost some of its most talented people.

Nevertheless, Spain became a strong nation. Charles, the grandson of Ferdinand and Isabella, became king of Spain and emperor of the Holy Roman Empire. Find the Holy Roman Empire on the map above.

Struggles for Territory

These three powerful nations—France, England, and Spain—often tried to take territory from one another. Not only did the three nations want to claim land in the New World. They also wanted to claim one another's land in Europe. One struggle led to the end of Spain as a great power.

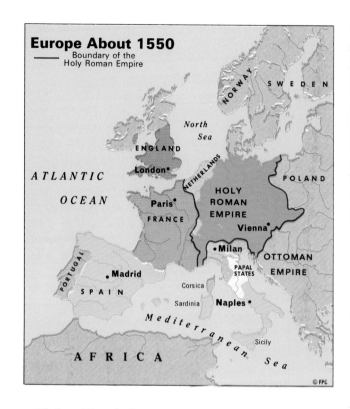

Europe About 1550

Philip II ruled Spain as an absolute monarch until the end of the 1500s. Philip also ruled the Netherlands. The Netherlands was a Protestant nation and rebelled against Spain. England helped the Netherlands.

Philip decided to invade England with a huge fleet of ships. The fleet was called the Spanish Armada. Although the armada had 130 ships and carried more than 30,000 fighters, the English won. The small English ships were far more effective in battle. Also, a terrible storm sank many of the Spanish ships. Spain's power was broken.

Struggles continued among many nations. Although rulers and nobles led the armies, the common people provided most of the soldiers and sailors. Yet the common people had few rights and little

The English cleverly routed the Spanish in the famous Battle of the Armada.

power. Even in England, only a few people could make decisions. In later years many struggled for more rights.

Checking Up

1. What was the important difference between the English Parliament and the Estates General?
2. How did Spain's power decline?
3. What answers would you give to the key questions at the beginning of this chapter?
4. *How might absolute power in a government be dangerous?*

Unit 15 Summary

- The Renaissance was a period of high artistic accomplishment in western Europe. The movement began in Italy in the late Middle Ages and spread to other European countries in the 15th and 16th centuries.
- Europe's Age of Exploration began in the late 15th century. European explorers sailed to Africa and the New World and began to claim lands.
- The search for trade routes to Asia sparked most of the explorations.
- The Roman Church came under serious attack in the 1500s. The Reformation led to the establishment of Protestant Christian churches.
- The Roman, or Catholic, Church began to reform during the Counter Reformation.
- Powerful nations with strong central governments began to emerge in early modern Europe with the decline of feudalism. France, England, and Spain were the major powers.

Unit 15 Review Workshop

What Have You Learned?

Complete each of the statements below with the best answer from the following list.

Northwest Passage   printers
Martin Luther   Jesuits
Ferdinand and Isabella   England
New World   India
Spain and Portugal   Columbus

1. Johann Gutenberg was one of the first _____ in Europe.
2. Ignatius Loyola was the founder of the _____.
3. _____ was a leader of the Reformation.
4. Many religious refugees went to the _____ looking for freedom of worship.
5. Philip II sent the armada to _____.
6. _____ tried to reach Asia by sailing west.
7. The Line of Demarcation divided land claims between _____.
8. Vasco da Gama was the first Portuguese explorer to sail to _____.
9. _____ were the monarchs who defended Catholicism in Spain.
10. Many explorers were unsuccessful in their search for the _____.

Use Your Reading Skills

Remember what you have read and decide if each of the following statements is true or false. If a statement is false, correct it.

1. Renaissance scholars studied the writings of ancient Greeks and Romans.
2. During the Renaissance, education became more religious.
3. Galileo used the telescope to study the solar system.
4. Leonardo da Vinci was an Italian Renaissance artist who also designed a flying machine.
5. Martin Luther and John Calvin were explorers of the New World.
6. One of the most effective reforms of the Counter Reformation was the establishment of the Jesuits.
7. The Hundred Years' War was fought between the houses of York and Lancaster in England.
8. Elizabeth I and Isabella were powerful European monarchs who encouraged exploration.

Use Your Thinking Skills

Following is a list of names that can be divided into four groups. Decide what the groups are and then list each name where it best fits.

Calvin   Loyola
Copernicus   Luther
Elizabeth I   Michelangelo
Galileo   Philip II
Dürer   Brueghel
Leonardo   Isabella

Use Your Map Skills

Look at the map on the next page. It is based on an early-16th-century map of

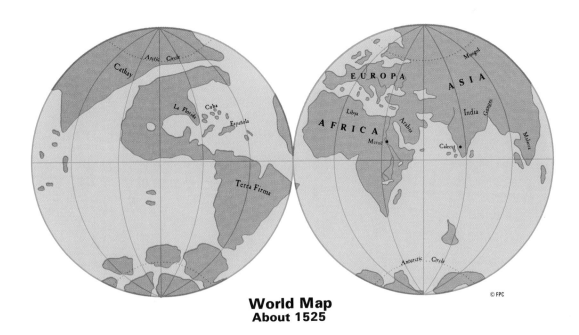

World Map
About 1525

the world. Use a dictionary or encyclopedia to find the meanings of *Cathay* and *terra firma*. Then use the map to answer the following questions.

1. Which continents are shown most accurately?
2. Find the Americas. What is wrong with the shape of each continent?
3. Notice the landmasses near the South Pole of each globe. What do you think these are?

Learn by Doing

1. Make a map of the world with arrows showing the routes of the various explorers. Use the Atlas maps at the beginning of this book as a guide. Label the arrows with the explorers' names. Make each arrow the same color as that explorer's sponsoring country. Make a key also.

2. Take part in group presentations about Renaissance art. Each group is to choose a Renaissance painter, sculptor, architect, or writer. Find out everything you can about your artist. Look for pictures of his work. Tell the class why this artist is important.

Read to Learn More

Find the topics listed below in the card catalog of your library. Read all or part of a book listed under one of the topics. Share what you learn with your classmates.

EXPLORERS   REFORMATION

RENAISSANCE   HOLY ROMAN EMPIRE

Europe:
Reason and Revolution

Royal power was supreme in late 17th-century France. The monarchs lived at the grand palace of Versailles (vər·sī′) near Paris.

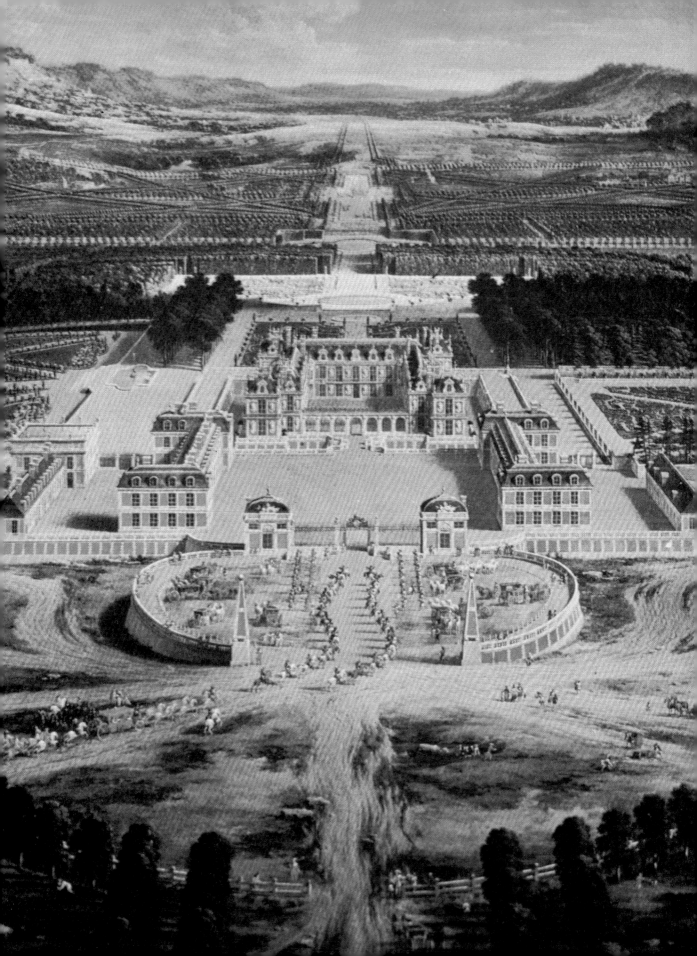

Maps Tell a Story of Europe

Europe is the world's second smallest continent. Only Australia is smaller. Yet people in Europe have greatly influenced the rest of the world. You know that political and religious events in Europe have had worldwide effects. In Unit 16 you will learn about more European events that changed the lives of people in Europe and other places. Before doing so, however, let's look at the geography of Europe.

Landforms
- Plains
- Plateaus
- Hills
- Mountains

© FPC

Land

Look at the landform map. Notice all four major landforms on this small conti-

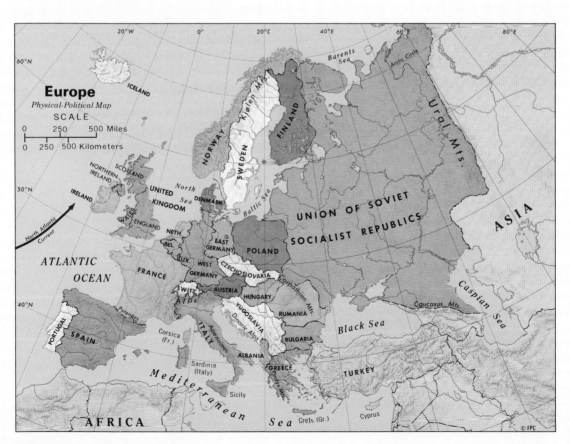

Europe
Physical-Political Map
SCALE

nent. Which one covers the largest area? Plains make good farmland. Check the Atlas land-use map on pages 20–21 to see if there is much farming on the European plains. Which landform covers the smallest area? In what European countries are mountains found? Use the physical map of Europe to find the names of some of the ranges.

Average Summer Temperatures

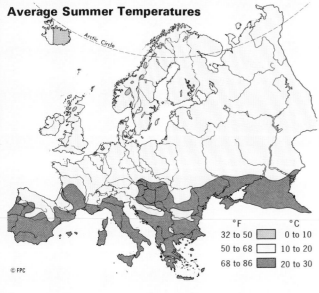

°F		°C
32 to 50		0 to 10
50 to 68		10 to 20
68 to 86		20 to 30

© FPC

Average Winter Temperatures

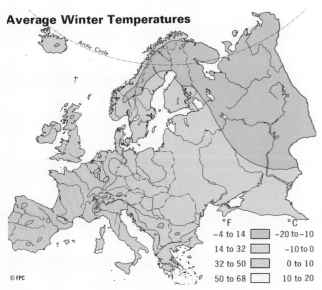

°F		°C
–4 to 14		–20 to –10
14 to 32		–10 to 0
32 to 50		0 to 10
50 to 68		10 to 20

© FPC

Climate

Most of Europe is located in the middle latitudes of the Northern Hemisphere. Thus, there are seasonal changes, much as there are in most of our country. Use the Atlas map on pages 10–11 to compare the latitudes of the United States with those of Europe. How far north does each area extend? How far south?

The European climate is generally milder than that of other places in the same northern latitudes. Notice how much of the small continent is surrounded by ocean. The ocean greatly influences Europe's climate. The warm North Atlantic Current flows toward Europe, warming the winds that blow over the land. This current is shown on the physical map. Which Pacific Ocean country that you have already read about has a climate that is also influenced by an ocean current?

Look at the temperature maps. Which parts of Europe are coldest in winter? How does distance from the ocean affect winter temperatures?

Checking Up

1. Why does most of Europe have a mild climate?
2. How do temperatures vary between northern and southern Europe?
3. Parts of southern Europe are in a climate region you read about in Unit 4. Find the name of this climate on pages 112–115.

399

The Age of Reason

As You Read

1. Think about these words.
   society   despot
2. Look for answers to these key questions.
   a. How did Enlightenment thinkers define *reason*? Why did they think reason was so important?
   b. What was the French *Encyclopedia*?
   c. In what two main ways were Enlightenment scientists alike?
3. Use this reading skill.
   Remember to look for the difference between facts and opinions. Many of the conclusions of the Enlightenment scientists you will read about are facts—they can be proved. Many of the political thinkers expressed opinions—what they believed to be true or best. When you finish this chapter, list two facts of Enlightenment science. Then list two opinions of Enlightenment political thinkers.

The revival of learning that began in the Renaissance continued into the 17th and 18th centuries. During these centuries, many educated people in Europe became interested in the power of reason. The period of the 1600s and 1700s is known as the Age of Reason because its leading thinkers believed that problems could be solved through the use of reason, the intelligence of the human mind. People were not bound by old ideas. They thought that reason would enable people to understand the entire universe.

"Dare to know," wrote a German philosopher, Immanuel Kant. "Have the courage to use your own intelligence." Kant used the term *Enlightenment* to de- scribe the Age of Reason. The knowledge gained by education plus new ways of thinking, many people felt, would enlighten everyone—people would understand the world.

Scientific Advances

The English philosopher Francis Bacon was an early Enlightenment figure. Bacon wrote about science. He urged scientists to observe carefully and to experiment. He urged them to gather evidence, much as a modern detective does to solve a crime. He believed that only when scientists had enough evidence should they form theories, or explanations about how things work. They could experiment to prove their theories.

Scientists learned about the solar system with the aid of the telescope.

There were experiments to test water, air, heat, and air pressure.

Suppose you wanted to find out the best conditions in which to grow green houseplants, for example. If you followed

With microscopes, people could magnify very small objects.

Bacon's scientific reasoning, you would grow several plants under different conditions. You would watch their progress daily and take notes. Not until you had carefully observed them for several weeks would you make a decision about the best conditions for the plants. Your decision would be based on *your own observation and experiment*, not on some rule or idea you had before you began.

Galileo was one who followed this scientific method. In fact, he can be considered an early Enlightenment scientist. He carefully observed the moon and some of the planets. He gathered more evidence for the theory that the planets moved around the sun.

Johannes Kepler was another astronomer of the early Enlightenment. This

German scientist proved that the planets travel in oval-shaped orbits around the sun. He also proved that the closer a planet is to the sun, the faster it moves around the sun.

Kepler and Galileo did much to change people's understanding of the universe. Old ideas change slowly, but the efforts of these two scientists, especially, helped modern astronomy destroy the old idea of the earth as the center of the universe.

Isaac Newton was perhaps the greatest scientist of the Enlightenment. Late in the 17th century, this English astronomer and mathematician developed his law of gravity in the universe. By this time many scientists had accepted the ideas of Copernicus, Kepler, and Galileo. There was still much to understand about the solar system, however. Why didn't the planets fall into one another, for example? Why didn't they crash into the sun or fly off into space? Newton explained that forces of gravity in the universe kept the planets in their own steady orbits.

Not all scientific achievements of the Enlightenment were in the field of astronomy. The brilliant Newton studied light and color extensively. He discovered that white light is actually made up of a spectrum, which is a mixture of the rainbow colors.

Dr. William Harvey was another Enlightenment scientist, as was chemist Robert Boyle. Harvey showed how blood traveled through the human body, pumped by the heart. Boyle experimented with air pressure and proposed theories about the chemical makeup of matter.

These and other Enlightenment scientists had two important points in common. They experimented, and they believed in the power of reason. There were clear explanations for the working of the universe, and reason could discover them.

Political Thought of the Enlightenment

By the beginning of the 18th century, belief in the power of reason had become very important. The use of reason influenced many aspects of human life.

The French philosophers. Many of the leading thinkers of the 18th century were French. Like the scientists, they believed strongly in the ability of people to reason and to think of solutions to problems. They wanted to use reason to improve **society**, or all groups of people in a country. To do so, the philosophers

Newton was the greatest scientist of his time. What were his discoveries?

People loved to gather to discuss literature, politics, or scientific ideas in Paris.

turned their attention to the government of society.

One of the most famous of the French philosophers was the writer Voltaire (vōl·tãr′). As a young man, Voltaire spent some time in England. He studied English government and liked it better than the French government. Finding that people had more freedom in England, he criticized the absolute monarchy in France in his writings.

Voltaire was put in prison several times for his criticism of French government. When not in prison, he was forced to live outside of France for much of his life. Nevertheless, Voltaire continued to write. His plays, poems, and stories were filled with humor. He delighted in poking fun at his enemies.

Jean Jacques Rousseau (rōō·sō′) was another French philosopher. Like Voltaire, he criticized the evils in government. In his book *The Social Contract*, Rousseau said that a government should be built on a common agreement, or contract, between the people and their rulers. He believed a ruler should have certain powers only because the people agreed to give the ruler those powers.

Montesquieu (mänt′əs·kyōō′) was a third leading French philosopher. This French noble took an active interest in government and criticized the power of **despots**, absolute rulers who abused power. Montesquieu held that government power should be divided into three sections. There should be executive, legislative, and judicial (or court) branches.

An earlier English philosopher, John Locke, had expressed ideas similar to those of the French thinkers. Governments, said Locke, should be built on the consent, or approval, of the governed. The people can give the government certain powers so that it can protect them and their interests. If the government does not use this power for the right purposes, the people should have the right to take its power away. In other words, people have a right to replace their rulers.

The ideas of the French philosophers, Locke, and others were not at all the opinions of the absolute monarchs of Europe. The rulers felt that they had a God-given, or divine right to rule. The clash of these ideas led to dramatic changes later in the 18th century.

The spread of ideas. The philosophers and scientists of the Enlightenment did not spread their ideas in universities. Many universities, in fact, fought against the new ideas. Instead, people met in coffeehouses and clubs to discuss their thoughts. Wealthy patrons brought groups of thinkers together in their homes for hours of lively conversation.

Groups of scientists also gathered together to form academies. Two of the most important of these were the Royal Society of London and the Paris Academy of Sciences, both founded in the 1660s. The academies gave scientists an opportunity to meet and discuss their new discoveries. Because their ideas were published in journals, more and more people learned about their work.

The first regular newspapers and a number of magazines began in the late 17th century. More and more people could find out what was going on in the world. Benjamin Franklin's experiments with electricity in America, for example, soon became known all over Europe. The much-admired Franklin was made a member of the Royal Society of London.

The Encyclopedia. One of the greatest achievements of the Enlightenment was the French *Encyclopedia.* A group of French philosophers began to work on the project in 1751. Their goal was to make all human knowledge available to everyone. When the *Encyclopedia* was finished, it included twenty-eight volumes and thousands of illustrations.

Many famous people, including Voltaire and Rousseau, wrote articles for the *Encyclopedia.* Some of these articles criticized absolute monarchs. Besides articles on government, the *Encyclopedia* included information about science, art, and medicine. There was even information on such common trades as weaving, mining, and printing. Almost no part of human life was left out. The French philosophers wanted to make knowledge available to everyone. The encyclopedias you use today are based on the idea of putting all knowledge between the covers of a set of books.

Checking Up
1. What was the Age of Reason?
2. What did each of the following contribute to the Enlightenment: Bacon, Kepler, Newton, Voltaire?
3. How did the political ideas of Locke and Rousseau differ from those of the absolute monarchs?
4. What answers would you give to the key questions at the beginning of this chapter?
5. *Why do you think absolute governments feared the spread of political ideas of the Enlightenment?*

New Empires

As You Read

1. Think about these words.

   mercantilism   monopoly   profit
   economy   tariff
   balance of trade   joint-stock company

2. Look for answers to these key questions.
   a. How did mercantilism work?
   b. What areas of the world did the empire nations of Europe colonize?
   c. How did the nations with empires differ from one another?

The Age of Exploration led to a new kind of empire. Some European nations now controlled lands thousands of miles away. The explorers who looked for trade routes and for gold and silver were followed by soldiers and settlers who conquered vast lands across the Atlantic. Smaller areas were taken over as trading posts in Africa, Asia, and the Pacific. The new European empires were world-wide empires. You can see them on the map below.

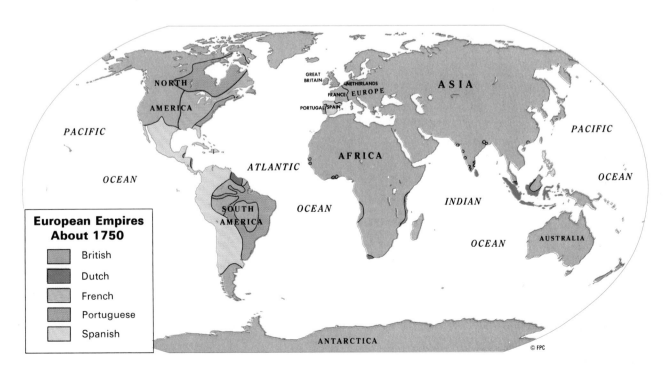

European Empires About 1750

- British
- Dutch
- French
- Portuguese
- Spanish

Mercantilism

People settled the new colonies for many reasons. Some looked for riches, others for a new chance in life. Some wanted religious freedom. Still others went to spread Christianity.

The European governments had their own reasons for starting trading posts and colonies. Each wanted to become as wealthy as possible. Leaders felt that there was only one sure way to build up a nation's wealth. They wanted to bring as much gold and silver into the nation as possible.

Then, as now, people measured wealth in gold and silver, the world's most precious metals. Leaders in western European countries believed that the best way of increasing the amount of gold and silver in a country was to practice the policy of **mercantilism**. Mercantilism was followed by many western European governments in the 17th and 18th centuries. By doing so, the governments controlled their **economies**. A nation's economy includes all its money, goods, and services. Mercantilist governments controlled exports and imports. They established overseas colonies.

Exports, imports. A mercantilist country wanted a favorable **balance of trade**. That is, it wanted to sell more goods to other countries than it bought from them. The other countries would have to pay for the difference in gold and silver. As the exporting country collected more and more gold, it would become richer. Every mercantilist country wanted mainly to be an exporting country.

Tariffs and helpful policies. To get a favorable balance of trade, a mercantilist government did several things. It helped agriculture, business, and industry so enough goods could be produced for a country's needs—and more. Surplus goods could be sold to other countries. Government help could be in the form of money or special treatment.

A business that government considered of great importance to the country was often made a **monopoly** by the monarch. The company given the monopoly was the only one allowed to produce or sell a certain product. Because trade was so important to mercantilist countries, a trading company often had a monopoly on some part of trade. If only one trading company could deal in spices from Asia, for example, people could buy spices only from that company. The company would probably be a great success because of its monopoly.

Governments also placed **tariffs**, or taxes on imports, on some or all goods that came into a country. They wanted to be sure that imports were expensive. They wanted few people to buy them.

Colonies. Overseas colonies were important to mercantilist countries. The colonial areas had or grew raw materials such as lumber, cotton, sugarcane, and tobacco. The colonies shipped these raw materials to the home country, where they were made into finished products.

Mercantilist countries did not want their colonies to compete with them. So they usually stopped the colonies from producing their own goods.

406

The Spanish called their huge colonial estates haciendas
(häs'ē·en'dəz). How is this one like the manor on page 291?

The Colonial Powers

The first important colonial empires, the countries that had overseas colonies, were all in western Europe within easy reach of the Atlantic. They were Spain, Portugal, the Netherlands, France, and England. They were the exploring nations you read about in Unit 15.

Spain. Spain was the first country to build a large overseas empire. You will recall that the Spanish took over large parts of North and South America. Around the same time, Magellan claimed the Philippine Islands in the Pacific for Spain.

The Spanish who settled the colonies in North and South America were mostly soldiers, wealthy landowners, or missionaries. The Europeans forced the Indians of the area to work for them. Later, the Spanish brought over great numbers of black Africans as slaves.

The Spanish were interested mainly in finding gold and silver. Where there was no gold or silver, the settlers set up large farms or ranches to grow crops such as sugarcane or to raise cattle. Sugar became the chief product of the Caribbean islands. In Mexico and South America, the Spanish raised cattle on large ranches.

The voyage to the Philippines was a long and dangerous one. As a result, fewer Spanish people settled there. The islands were used mainly as a place from which to trade with other parts of Asia. Look at the map on page 405. Which European country controlled the largest overseas empire in 1750?

Portugal. The Portuguese empire was mostly a trading empire. Portugal set up trading posts rather than large colonies. There were trading posts in Africa, where Portugal traded slaves. Portuguese

407

sailors were the first Europeans to reach and trade with Japan. The most important Portuguese trading posts, however, were in India and the Spice Islands, now Indonesia. The Portuguese fought and defeated the Muslims who had controlled trade in the Indian Ocean. They took over the valuable trade in spices, silk, cotton, coffee, and other products.

In Brazil, Portugal's only possession in the Americas, the Portuguese set up sugar plantations. They also mined some gold there. Like the Spanish, the Portuguese sent many Catholic missionaries into their territories.

The Netherlands. Through trade, the Netherlands became a rich and powerful country during the 17th century. Even while the Dutch were fighting for their independence from Spain, they built up a strong merchant fleet. They bought and sold everywhere. Dutch merchants even sold supplies to the Spanish armies they were fighting!

The Dutch were clever business people who made enormous profits with relatively few colonies.

The Philippines: From Colony to Nation

The Republic of the Philippines is an island nation in the Pacific Ocean. After centuries of colonial rule, the Philippines became independent in 1946.

As you know, the Philippines were claimed by Spain in the early 1500s. Spanish clergy members greatly influenced Filipino life for much of the colonial period. The clergy converted most of the people to Catholicism and set up schools for the people. Still, the people did not have many rights and resented Spanish rule.

When Spain and the United States went to war in 1898, Filipino fighters joined United States troops against Spain. Spain was defeated, but the Filipinos did not become independent, as many had hoped. Instead, the United States ruled the islands as a territory. Still, the people had many more rights than they had had under the Spanish. After World War II, the islands became completely independent from foreign powers.

Today the rich Philippine farmland and mineral resources still supply the country. Most Filipinos farm. Rice and sugar, an important export, are among the chief crops. The country must im-

Like many other people, the Filipinos gained independence in the years after World War II.

port food, however, to feed the large and rapidly growing population. The tropical forests supply lumber, bamboo, and rattan.

Most of the Filipinos are still Catholic and celebrate many religious festivals. There are other Christian groups and Muslims as well. Spanish and English remain very common languages on the islands, but there is another national language, Tagalog, as well. In addition to the many Philippine public schools and universities, there are still many religious schools, as when the Spanish ruled. Language, religion, education, and customs are still a blend of old and new in the Philippines.

The Dutch government could not follow the mercantile system. There was little industry in the Netherlands. The country was not large enough to produce everything its people needed. The Dutch had to depend on trade with other countries to satisfy their needs. Buying and reselling products from elsewhere became their main business.

The Dutch set up two giant companies: The East India Company and the West India Company. Each was given a monopoly on trade with one half of the world. The East India Company, which had its own fleet of ships, drove the Portuguese out of many of their trading posts. The Dutch then took over much of the trade in spices, silk, and tea.

The West India Company was less successful, but it did manage to take over trade in the Caribbean. It also set up a North American colony called New Netherland around the busy port of New Amsterdam. At first the colony was little more than a trading post. The Dutch traded with the Indians for furs. Later the government encouraged more farmers and workers to settle there. By 1664 about 10,000 Dutch settlers lived in New Netherland, which is now New York.

Joint-stock companies. It took a lot of money to set up a company as large as the Dutch East India Company. Such companies were formed as **joint-stock companies**. A joint-stock company sells shares of a business, or stock, to many people. A person who buys stock in a company owns part of that company and is a joint stockholder in it. If enough stock can be sold, the company has enough money to begin business. Each stockholder shares in the profits, or losses, of the company. **Profit** is the money left after all expenses have been paid. Many trading companies were organized as joint-stock companies.

England. After the founding of Jamestown in 1607, England set up more colonies in North America. Several were founded as joint-stock companies, but eventually the English government took control of them. By 1773 England had thirteen American colonies stretching along the Atlantic coastline between French Canada and Spanish Florida. By 1776 these English colonies had more than 2½ million settlers.

Advertisements urged settlers to sail to the new colonies. What is the message of this poster?

More people came to the English colonies than to those of other European nations. They were attracted by the cheap land and the greater opportunities for poor and middle-class people. Settlers came mainly from England, Scotland, and Ireland. The colonies also attracted Protestants from France and Germany.

Another joint-stock company, the British East India Company, was set up to trade with Asia. Its main trading posts were in India, where the English soon came into conflict with other countries.

France. The French, like the Dutch, were more interested in trade than in settling colonies. France took over some islands in the Caribbean, but its main colony, New France, was in North America. French explorers claimed areas in Canada, around the Great Lakes, and

The British battled the French and the Indians for North America. British general Braddock died in this battle.

down the Mississippi River as far as the port of New Orleans.

French trappers and fur traders did a lively business, but French settlers were few in number. By 1700 only about 20,000 French settlers lived in all of New France. After 1700 the numbers began to grow, but not as rapidly as in the English colonies.

French traders followed the Portuguese route around Africa into the Indian Ocean. The French East India Company established itself at several ports in India and began to compete with the English and Dutch traders who were already there.

English-French Rivalry

England and France competed for land and trade in many areas of the world. This competition led to a series of wars during the 17th and 18th centuries. The last of these was the Seven Years' War, which was fought in North America, the Caribbean, Africa, and India.

In North America the war ended with France's surrender in 1763. England took over many of France's colonial possessions. Canada and all of North America east of the Mississippi became England's, as did nearly all of France's trading posts in India.

England came out of the war as the most powerful nation in Europe. It had the largest empire in the world. Not many years passed, however, before England lost one of its most valuable possessions: its American colonies.

Checking Up

1. Name the five great empire nations of western Europe.
2. What is a favorable balance of trade?
3. What is a joint-stock company?
4. What was the Seven Years' War?
5. What answers would you give to the key questions at the beginning of this chapter?
6. *Why do you think European nations were willing to fight over colonies?*

Democracy in England

As You Read

1. Think about this word.
   Restoration
2. Look for answers to these key questions.
   a. Why did English rulers come into conflict with Parliament?
   b. What was the Glorious Revolution? What were its results?

England was the first modern European nation to develop a democratic government. England still had kings and queens, but over the years more and more of the power of government was taken over by Parliament. Parliament represented many of the English people.

You already read about the Magna Charta, which was signed during the Middle Ages. Most later kings and queens of England paid little attention to the Magna Charta. Nevertheless, it was an important step in the development of England's democracy.

Parliament

The struggle for democracy in England was, in large part, a struggle for power between monarchs and Parliament. Parliament was made up of two groups, or houses. One group was the House of Lords, which was made up of the nobles. The other group, the House of Commons, represented the common people. The people elected members of the House of Commons.

In time, the House of Commons became the more important branch of Parliament because it alone could grant taxes to the king or queen. The House of Commons represented the growing middle class, which included the large numbers of merchants, craftspeople, and other workers.

A monarch could not overrule Parliament after the 17th century.

Struggle for Power

Elizabeth I had been able to get along with Parliament. Later rulers did not do as well. They fought with Parliament often. They quarreled over religion, over politics at home and overseas, and especially over money. Kings tried to raise money on their own, but Parliament insisted that only it could pass tax laws.

In 1628 King Charles I needed money badly. He called Parliament into session to ask for it. Parliament agreed to give the money, but only if the king signed the Petition of Right. Charles had no choice. He signed the Petition of Right, which stated, among other things, that only Parliament had the right to pass English tax laws.

The struggle for power was not over, however, and it finally led to civil war. The king raised an army of supporters. Parliament raised an army of its own. Parliament's army, led by Oliver Cromwell, won the war. Cromwell had the king executed and did away with the monarchy entirely. Together with Parliament Cromwell, and later his son, ruled England for ten years. This was the only time since the Middle Ages that England did not have a monarch.

Citizenship

Common Law

Throughout most of Europe, laws were based mainly on Roman law. They were long, written codes, that told exactly how legal cases should be decided. English laws were different.

These judges used what is called common law. Common law developed as judges decided cases. For example, suppose a person bought a horse that became sick soon after the purchase. Could the new owner get the money back? The decision made by a judge in the case would become common law. Every decision made by a judge became a part of the common law. It would be used as a guide for future cases.

Common law has been called "the unwritten law." In fact, most of it was written down, often in great detail. The importance of common law, though, was not that it was written or unwritten. Its importance was that a decision could serve as a guide for later decisions.

The laws could still change. A judge might decide that earlier decisions were wrong, or that changing times required a change in the law. Each new decision, then, became another part of the common law.

Even though most of our laws are written by our legislators today, courtroom decisions are still based on past ones. Much of a lawyer's training today is based on a study of important legal cases of the past.

How has the artist made Charles I look foolish in this early drawing?

The Restoration. England prospered under Cromwell's government. Nevertheless, there were people who wanted a monarch to rule England again. Cromwell was, after all, a dictator and a very strict Puritan who did not want people to dance, play games, or amuse themselves in other ways. Some people longed for the return of a king.

In 1660, two years after Cromwell's death, Parliament restored the monarchy. The son of Charles I returned from France, where he had gone for safety during the civil war. He became King Charles II. The act of restoring the monarchy and the period that followed it are called the **Restoration.**

The Glorious Revolution. New troubles arose when Charles II died. He left the throne to his brother, James, who was a Catholic. Even though most of the nation was Protestant, James II tried to

Charles II came back to power in England with great celebration. Why do you suppose people were tired of Puritan rule?

Puritans wore plain clothing and did not approve of royal extravagance.

bring the Catholic Church back to England. Protestant leaders in Parliament decided to take action against the king. They turned for help to William, a powerful Protestant prince in the Netherlands. He was the husband of the king's daughter, Mary. Parliament asked William to bring an army to England to save the Protestant religion.

William's army landed in England late in 1688. James II and his few followers fled to France. In the following year, a group of parliamentary leaders declared that James had given up the throne and offered it to William and Mary. The English called this change of government, during which not a single shot was fired, the Glorious Revolution.

The Bill of Rights. Before William and Mary took the throne, they accepted the Bill of Rights that had been passed by Parliament. The Bill of Rights is an important document in English history. It placed limits on the power of the monarchy. No monarch could do away with laws, raise an army, or collect taxes without the approval of Parliament. Parliament was to be free to meet regularly and hold free discussions. The people were granted such rights as trial by jury and freedom from cruel punishments.

While absolute monarchs continued to rule in France and elsewhere, the democracy in England became an example of the kind of political ideas that flourished during the Enlightenment. Bolstered by the writings of Locke and others, these ideas took hold in the English colonies in America during the 18th century. There they led to another kind of democratic government.

Checking Up

1. What was the Petition of Right? the Bill of Rights?
2. Why did Parliament ask the Dutch prince William to invade England?
3. What is the House of Commons? House of Lords?
4. What answers would you give to the key questions at the beginning of this chapter?
5. *Why do you think Parliament was able to become more powerful than the rulers of England?*

The Democratic Revolution

As You Read

1. Think about these words.
   Congress   amendment
2. Look for answers to these key questions.
   a. What were the causes of the French and American revolutions? What were their results?
   b. What influence did Napoleon have on Europe?
3. Use these reading skills.
   Continue to use the reading skills you have learned. Look for main ideas as you read. Find details that support the main ideas. Compare and contrast the French and American revolutions, two main ideas you will read about in this chapter.

Although the Glorious Revolution had been a peaceful one, later revolutions were not so peaceful. Yet they, too, were based on democratic ideas developed during the Age of Reason.

Many colonists felt ready for independence by the late 1700s.

The Revolutionary War

The Glorious Revolution gave more rights and greater freedoms to the English people. Soon people in the American colonies began to demand more rights and freedoms for themselves.

Colonial complaints. People had come to the American colonies looking for land, religious freedom, and better jobs. The American colonists wanted a better life than they had had in Europe. They began to complain more and more about England's control over the colonies.

The English government still followed mercantile policies. The colonies were seen mainly as a way to enrich Great Britain, which included England, Scotland, and Wales. Colonists had to sell their materials to Great Britain. There they were made into products that were sent back to the colonies to be sold. Government rules did not allow the colonists to make products themselves. The colonists wanted the right to develop industries and trade with other countries.

Colonists complained about taxes also. They had to pay taxes to support the British government. Yet there were no representatives of the American colonists in Parliament.

As time went on, the complaints increased. Some colonists decided to act. One group of protesters in Boston threw a shipload of tea into the harbor. Parliament took strong measures to punish the colonists for the "Boston Tea Party." The British government closed down the port of Boston, angering people who depended on the sea for their living.

Independence and revolution. Benjamin Franklin, John Adams, Thomas Jefferson, and other representatives from the thirteen colonies met in 1776. They signed the Declaration of Independence, written by Thomas Jefferson. According to the Declaration, the colonies considered themselves free from Great Britain. When a government does not work for the people, the Declaration said, "it is the right of the people to alter or abolish [ə·bäl′ish] it." *Abolish* means "to get rid of." John Locke had said the same thing a century earlier.

Great Britain sent troops to stop the rebellion in the colonies. The war for independence, or Revolutionary War, resulted. A revolution is a war against a ruling government. After eight years of fighting, the British finally gave up in 1783. The colonies became independent.

The Declaration of Independence reflected ideas of the Enlightenment.

The Constitution. During the Revolutionary War, the thirteen colonies formed a government called the Confederation. The separate colonies, which became states after the war, cooperated to defeat the British. The Confederation left most of the powers of government to the individual states. In many ways the independent states functioned as thirteen separate nations, each with its own government and laws.

In 1787 representatives of the states met and drew up a new constitution. The Constitution of the United States joined the states into a single nation with a central government. This central government would be made up of **Congress**, a group of representatives of the people, which would make the laws for the nation; a president, who would carry out the laws; and the Supreme Court, which would be the nation's highest court.

Ten **amendments**, or additions, were soon written. These are our country's Bill of Rights. They guarantee such rights as

Our Constitution is the oldest written government plan still used.

freedom of religion, speech, and press, and trial by jury.

The United States was established as a democratic republic, a nation in which the people elect representatives to serve in the government. In the early days, however, it was not fully democratic. Not everyone could vote or hold office. Many poor people, all women, and slaves were left out. In later years additional amendments to the Constitution extended the rights of citizenship to more people. Democracy continued to spread in the United States and elsewhere.

Problems in France

The United States Constitution took effect in 1789. In that same year, another revolution broke out, this time in France. Problems had built up over many years and finally forced a change in France's government.

There were three classes of people in France at the time. The clergy were the First Estate. Nobles were the Second Estate. These two privileged classes made

up about 3 percent of the entire French population.

The rest of the people made up the Third Estate. They were the doctors, the lawyers, the teachers, and the workers who ran the farms, factories, and businesses. Even though they paid most of the taxes, people of the Third Estate had little or no voice in the government.

The educated people of the Third Estate knew about the ideas of the Enlightenment. They agreed with those who attacked the government and asked for changes. Voltaire had helped them learn about the freedoms the English enjoyed. They also knew about the Revolutionary War in America. General Lafayette, a leader in the early days of the French Revolution, had helped the Americans during their war for independence. Benjamin Franklin and Thomas Jefferson were special representatives to France and were well liked by the French.

As in America, taxes were a chief complaint in France. There were an income tax, a land tax, a property tax, and a salt

The French nobility lived in splendid style.

tax. Taxes had to be paid on goods that were shipped from one place to another. In spite of these and other taxes, the government never had enough money. Wars, lavish living by the monarchs, and years of poor management had left the government deeply in debt.

The French poor often did not have enough to eat.

To make matters worse, some industries began to close. Many workers were unemployed. Bad weather caused crop failures. The price of bread, the main food of the poor, rose as the wheat crops failed.

The French Revolution

The French king, Louis XVI, was so desperate for a solution to France's money problems that he did something that had not been done for more than 100 years. He called for a meeting of the Estates General, France's parliament. All three estates were represented in the Estates General. Each estate had one vote. The First and Second Estates usually voted the same way—against the Third Estate.

After a few weeks of arguing, the representatives of the Third Estate met separately and declared themselves the National Assembly. The French Revolution began. The Assembly vowed to give France a new constitution and demanded that the king accept it. The king had to give in and approve the National Assembly.

The new Assembly did away with the privileges of the upper classes. It drew up the Declaration of the Rights of Man. This was a document similar to the United States Bill of Rights. Finally, in 1791, the Assembly completed a constitution that set up a constitutional monarchy. The Assembly pledged "Liberty, Equality, and Fraternity" to the people. The slogan became the battle cry of the revolution.

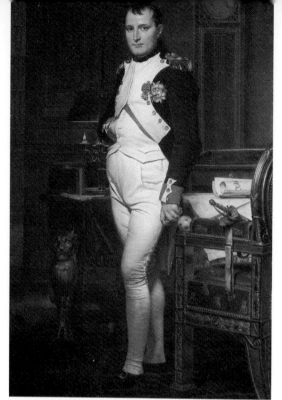

Napoleon blazed through Europe, conquering and then losing an empire in less than fifteen years.

The revolution in France frightened other European rulers. They feared that the unrest in France might spread to other countries. Before long, France found itself at war with other European countries. Leaders of the revolution abolished the monarchy and established a republic. The king and thousands of others, especially nobles, were put to death during a period known as the Reign of Terror. Actually, anyone declared "an enemy of the revolution" was killed or put into prison. A period of disorder followed as rival leaders fought for power. England, the Netherlands, and Spain joined the fight against France.

Napoleon's Rise to Power

During these confusing years, Napoleon Bonaparte rose to power. After holding a series of high offices in the new government, Napoleon finally took control of France. In 1804 he crowned himself emperor. Napoleon changed France and much of the rest of Europe. Even before he became emperor, he worked to reform the French government. He started a system of public education in France. He made it possible for poor and middle-class people to work in public offices. He established a tax system that taxed both rich and poor. Napoleon organized France's money system and set up the Bank of France. He also organized France's laws into a uniform system called the Code Napoleon.

Napoleon's armies conquered more than half of Europe, adding more and more territory to the new French em-

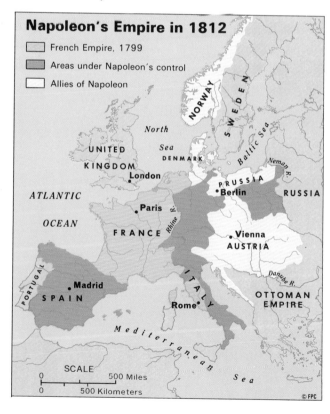

Napoleon's Empire in 1812

- French Empire, 1799
- Areas under Napoleon's control
- Allies of Napoleon

SCALE
0 — 500 Miles
0 — 500 Kilometers

© FPC

pire. Look at Napoleon's empire on the map on page 420. Napoleon's attempt to conquer all of Europe eventually led to his defeat. He invaded Russia in 1812 but could not conquer it. The bitter Russian winter and the lack of supplies for his army helped defeat the general.

Although he tried to hold his power, Napoleon failed. Great Britain and other European nations fought back. In 1815 at the famous Battle of Waterloo the British and their allies defeated Napoleon once and for all.

The leaders of the nations that defeated Napoleon met to restore the old monarchies to power. They wanted to establish peace in Europe by not allowing any one nation to become more powerful than the others. Europe wanted a rest from the ambitions of a Napoleon.

Later in the 19th century, the French again managed to establish a republic. The desire for freedom and participation in government spread from the United States and France to other places around the world. In the 19th and 20th centuries, people throughout the world increased their demands for democratic government.

Checking Up

1. Why did the American colonists object to British taxes?
2. What was the American Declaration of Independence?
3. How did the French National Assembly form?

4. What answers would you give to the key questions at the beginning of this chapter?
5. *What are some examples of freedoms we have in the United States today?*

Unit 16 Summary

- The Age of Reason was a period during which European philosophers believed in the power of reason to discover the workings of the universe.
- Enlightenment science showed that the sun was the center of our solar system.
- European nations competed for colonies, especially in the Americas, and trading posts in other parts of the world. Constitutional monarchy began after the Glorious Revolution in England.
- The American colonists fought for independence from England in the late 18th century. Their leaders set up a new democratic republic in the United States.
- The French Revolution destroyed absolute monarchy for a while in France.
- Napoleon rose to power in France after the Revolution. He reformed French government and extended his rule over much of western Europe.
- Rival European leaders feared and finally defeated Napoleon.
- The demand for democracy grew in the 19th and 20th centuries in many places in the world.

Unit 16 Review Workshop

What Have You Learned?

1. What did Enlightenment philosophers believe about the power of human reason?
2. What was the major Enlightenment conclusion about the solar system?
3. What was Newton's theory of gravity in the universe?
4. Who were the French philosophers? What were two of their ideas?
5. What is common law?
6. Why did the European empires want a favorable balance of trade?
7. How did the European governments try to help businesses succeed?
8. What are the two branches of the English Parliament? Which one had become more powerful by the 17th century?
9. What was the Restoration?
10. Who was Oliver Cromwell?
11. What were the three classes of people in France before the French Revolution?

Use Your Reading Skills

A. Decide which word best completes each of the following sentences.
   1. Bacon said that scientists should perform _____.
   2. Voltaire and Rousseau were 18th century French _____.
   3. A company that has no competition has a _____.
   4. In foreign trade, nations tried to gain a favorable _____.
   5. Nations tried to _____ more products and raw materials than they imported.
   6. A company that sells stock to many people is called a _____.
   7. Judges form _____ as they make decisions in court cases.

B. Look at the incomplete chart on the next page. Notice the three main categories into which it is divided. Review what you have read and complete the chart on your own paper. Compare your answers.

Use Your Group Skills

Participate in a class discussion about the American colonies just before the Revolutionary War. Work in small groups of three or four. About half of the groups should represent the point of view of the American colonists. The rest of the groups should represent that of the English government.

Each group is to concentrate on one particular point. For example, one American group may consider taxes. Another may consider self-government. Another may talk about the desire for home industries. One English group may consider the mercantilist policies. Another may treat the competition for empires among European powers.

First research your arguments carefully in the library. Each person should help present the information.

Review of Historical Events 17th and 18th Century Western Europe		
Philosopher or Scientist	**Important Political Leader**	**Important Political Event**
Name: Francis Bacon *Contribution:* encouraged scientific experiments	*Name:* Oliver Cromwell *Contribution:*	*Example:* American Revolution *Result:* North American colonies became free from England
Name: *Contribution:*	*Name:* Napoleon *Contribution:*	*Example:* French Revolution *Result:*
Name: *Contribution:*	*Name:* *Contribution:*	*Example:* Glorious Revolution *Result:*
Name: *Contribution:*	*Name:* *Contribution:*	*Example:* U.S. Constitution *Result:*

Use Your Writing Skills

Choose a country other than the United States that was a European colony at one time. Use the map on page 405. Compare it with the Atlas map on pages 10–11 to find its modern name.

Find out more about this country. What has happened there since the 18th century? What is it like today? Use library books for help. Prepare a three- or four-page report of your findings. Include a time line, map, or chart.

Learn by Doing

Foreign trade is as important today as it was in the days of the mercantile empires. Find out about the main products and raw materials that our country exports and imports. Make a poster entitled "The United States and the World." Draw a map of the United States in the center. Show export arrows pointing away from the country and import arrows pointing toward the country. Label the various imports and exports.

Read to Learn More

Find the topics listed below in the card catalog of your library. Read all or part of a book listed under one of the topics. Share what you learn with your classmates.

ENLIGHTENMENT   REVOLUTIONARY WAR

NAPOLEON   FRENCH REVOLUTION

Unit 17

Industrialization

Iron foundries such as this one met the greater demand for iron needed to build machinery and railroads during the industrial revolution.

425

The Industrial Revolution

As You Read

1. Think about these words.
   industry   manufacture   factory   market
2. Look for answers to these key questions.
   a. Why did the factory system replace cottage industry?
   b. What part did steam power play in the Industrial Revolution?
   c. Why were transportation and communication important to the Industrial Revolution?
3. Use this reading skill.
   Charts organize information for you. In this lesson, some important information is presented in chart form. Study the chart carefully. Notice how it helps you see connections among different pieces of information.

There have been many kinds of revolutions throughout history. The agricultural revolution you read about in Unit 2 changed the ways people produced their food. The political revolutions described in Unit 16 changed governments. Still another kind of revolution began about the time of the Revolutionary War. This revolution brought about changes in **industry,** or the ways people produce things. It is called the Industrial Revolution.

From Cottage to Factory

The change from the older craft industry to a more complicated form of industry came about in textile, or cloth, production in England during the 1700s. Before the Industrial Revolution began, people **manufactured,** or made, textiles in their homes. Because these workers often lived in cottages, this kind of manufacturing has been called cottage industry. Workers in cottage industry produced goods, or products, that other people needed.

Until the late 1700s, the textile industry in England was mainly a cottage industry.

Cottage industry. Such an industry worked this way. A cloth merchant supplied the raw materials to the cottage workers. Raw materials are goods, such as cotton, that are used to manufacture other products, such as cloth. The workers used spinning wheels to spin the fibers of cotton into thread. Then they wove the thread into cloth on hand-looms. Even though many members of a family helped in some ways, the amount of cloth produced by one family was small. Cottage workers usually made just enough money to meet their basic needs. Some also farmed a little to provide food.

A merchant picked up the finished cloth and paid the workers. The cloth was then sold in England. Sometimes the cloth was exported, or sent, to places in Europe or to England's colonies.

Inventions bring change. Cottage industry worked well until the 1700s. By this time, population had increased greatly. There was a greater demand for goods, including cloth. Cotton, which was cheaper than wool, was especially in demand.

Merchants looked for ways to make more cloth in less time. They found these ways through new inventions. Most of the inventors were people who had little training in science. Yet their machines were of great importance for the future of technology. The chart on page 428 shows some of these new inventions. Such inventions made the industrial revolution possible. Machines did the work that people had done by hand. More goods could be produced in less time by using machines. **Factories** began to take the place of cottage industry. A factory is a building or group of buildings where goods are made.

The factory system. The use of factories was not an entirely new idea. Although many people still worked at home, some merchants had already brought people together in large buildings. Then a merchant did not have to travel from cottage to cottage.

The use and development of spinning and weaving machines, however, spread the factory system. Machines were usually large, complicated, and expensive. Individual workers could not afford to buy them for use in their homes. Eventually, people stopped working in their homes and worked in factories instead. There many workers could use the same machines. Even the best cottage workers could not compete with the fast, efficient machines.

Power for machines. It was power that truly made the industrial revolution possible. Many of the early textile factories were built near rivers to use their waterpower. Fast-moving water turned wheels that made machines run. Then the invention of the steam engine made it possible to build a factory just about anywhere.

The first usable steam engine was built by Thomas Newcomen in the early 1700s. It was used to pump water out of coal mines. James Watt began to work on the steam engine in the 1760s. He continued improving it. He built the first one to be used to provide power for a

Inventions Change the Textile Industry

Date	Invention/*Inventor*	Description	Results
1733	**FLYING SHUTTLE** *John Kay*	Speeded up weaving and allowed weavers to produce cloth twice as wide as the old hand looms did. (Not put into general use until 1860s.)	The shuttle doubled the amount of cloth weavers could produce, and thus created a demand for more thread.
1767	**SPINNING JENNY** *James Hargreaves*	Allowed a single spinner to make six or seven threads at one time (later increased to as many as 80 threads).	By producing thread faster, the jenny helped spinners to keep up with weavers.
1768	**WATER FRAME** *Richard Arkwright*	Used water power to run spinning machines. Spun a much stronger thread than spinning wheels.	The water frame needed a stream or river to provide water power. This took more and more spinning into factories and out of homes.
1779	**SPINNING MULE** *Samuel Crompton*	Combined the spinning jenny and water frame in a machine that produced stronger and finer threads.	Better threads improved the quality of cloth and increased the demand for it. Greater sales led to still more factories.
1785	First spinning mill using **STEAM POWER** *James Watt*	Replaced human- or water-powered machines with steam-powered ones.	The use of steam power allowed factory owners to build factories in locations away from sources of water power.
1785	**POWER LOOM** *Edmund Cartwright*	Replaced human-powered looms with machines that could be powered by horses, water, or steam engines.	Weaving, like spinning, could be carried on in factories rather than in homes. This helped to bring an end to cottage industry.
1793	**COTTON GIN** *Eli Whitney*	Separated cotton seed from fiber by machine rather than by hand. Speeded up the delivery of raw cotton to spinning mills.	The increased supply of raw cotton made cotton cloth cheaper and increased the demand for it. More sales led to greater growth in the textile industry.

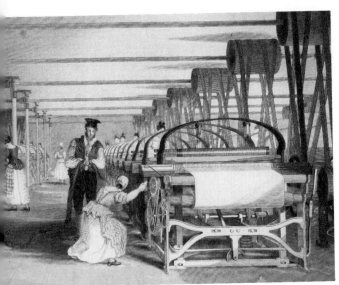

Weaving machines doubled the amount of cloth workers could manufacture.

Spinning machines enabled workers to meet the growing demand of weavers.

spinning mill in 1785. By 1800 factories all over England were adopting the use of steam power. Before long, it became the main source of power everywhere.

England and the Industrial Revolution. Historians trace the beginnings of the Industrial Revolution to England in the late 1700s. At first, English manufacturers used wood for fuel, but the supply was quickly used up. They then began to use the plentiful supply of coal to power their engines. England's many rivers and streams also provided a source of power for the machines. There was iron for making machinery. British colonies around the world were sources for the raw materials needed to feed the factories. The colonies also became **markets** for the manufactured goods, or places where the goods could be sold. There were plenty of workers for the factories because of changes in both cottage industry, and in agriculture.

Transportation and Communication Changes

The textile industry was not the only industry to grow and change. New inventions and new manufacturing methods influenced other industries as well. Changes in one industry brought about changes in others. Steam engines had, in fact, first been used in the mining and iron industries. After the textile industry adopted steam power, inventors soon applied it to trains and ships. As a result, the iron and steel industries grew rapidly. More and more iron and steel were needed to build trains, railroad tracks, ships, and bridges. The need for more steel, in turn, influenced the mining industry because coal and iron ore were needed to make steel.

Other industries depended on transportation. Factory owners needed ways to bring large amounts of raw materials to their factories. They needed to ship

The earliest railroad trains were used for bringing up coal from mines.

finished goods to markets all over England and to other parts of the world.

The English improved many roads, but the horse-drawn wagons that used the roads could not carry heavy loads. There were new canals built to connect different parts of England. Canal boats could carry heavy loads, but they were slow. It was not until railroads were built that the English found a means of transportation that could keep up with the growing needs of industry and trade.

Railroads. Soon after James Watt built a successful steam engine, other people tried to use steam power to move trains. A few train engines, or locomotives, were built and tried out in the early 1800s. It was not until 1830, however, that the first successful railway started. This line connected Manchester, a growing textile city, and Liverpool, a port city about 30 miles (48 km) away.

George Stephenson built the first steam-powered locomotive, which he called the *Rocket*, to pull a train. The *Rocket's* average speed of 14 miles (22.5 km) per hour seems slow to us. Yet it was fast for the time. The line was a success. Stephenson and others continued to improve engines. More railway lines were built. By 1847 there were about 5,000 miles (8,047 km) of track in the British Isles. More than 250,000 people in England (1.4% of the total population) were involved in railroad work.

Steamships. Ships also used steam power. The United States took an early

A steamboat first crossed the Atlantic Ocean in 1819.

lead in developing steamships. Robert Fulton built the first successful one in 1807. Eleven years later, another U.S. ship became the first steamship to cross the Atlantic Ocean. Regular steamship service across the Atlantic began in the 1830s.

Yet sailing ships continued to be used for many years. The sailing ships of the early 1800s were faster and cheaper than early steamships. Not until the late 1870s did the English begin to build more steamships than sailing ships. After that, steam power quickly replaced sails for most of the world's shipping.

Communication. Industry and trade were growing rapidly. Business people needed better communication systems. English cloth makers bought much of their cotton from the southern part of the United States. Messages between cotton buyers and cotton growers had to cross the Atlantic Ocean. Letters, orders, prices, and news about cotton crops could travel no faster then the fastest ship. It could take a month or more for an English buyer to get a message to a seller in the United States and receive a reply. Merchants and factory owners in other industries had the same problem— messages traveled too slowly.

A United States inventor solved the problem. Drawing on his knowledge of recent findings about electricity, Samuel Morse built a telegraph in 1837. The telegraph used electricity to send messages over wires. Morse developed a code using dots and dashes, or short and long bursts of electricity, to stand for the letters of the alphabet. Thus, messages could be flashed over wires in seconds.

Telegraph wires were strung across land and laid in cables across oceans. Cables linked England and France in 1851 and England and the United States in 1866. In later years telegraph cables linked England with its colonies in India and Australia.

In the 1870s another American, Alexander Graham Bell, invented the telephone. The telephone allowed spoken messages to be sent over wires for long distances. Guglielmo Marconi (goo·lyel'mō mər·kō'nē), an Italian, developed the radio in the 1890s. The radio sent messages without wires. By the early 1900s, radio messages could be sent and received all over the world. Even ships at sea had radio connections. By this time the Industrial Revolution had turned western Europe, the United States, and Japan into industrial nations.

Checking Up

1. Why were overseas colonies important during the industrial revolution?
2. How did important inventions change the textile industry?
3. What were the important developments in transportation and communication?
4. What answers would you give to the key questions at the beginning of this chapter?
5. *What, if any, advantages can you find in cottage industry?*

Graphs Tell a Story of Growth

Many causes brought about the Industrial Revolution. One cause was growth in the number of people. As the number of people continued to grow, so did the need for goods and services. More people meant a greater market for cloth and other goods, for food, and for services such as transportation.

Look at the graph of population growth on this page. What was the British population in 1700? How many people lived in Britain fifty years later? Did the population grow more quickly between 1750 and 1800? Which fifty-year period showed the greatest population growth? During which period would you expect to have seen the biggest increase in industrial production? Why?

The graph of cotton production in the upper left column of page 433 shows the growth of one of England's most important industries. During which period did cotton production stay about the same? When did cotton production increase most rapidly?

Look back at the chart of inventions on page 428. During which period were most of the machines invented? What happened to cotton production during that time? after that time?

The third graph in the upper right column of page 433 shows the value of British exports—goods sold overseas. The value is shown in British pounds. (One British pound in the late 1700s would be worth about $25 in United States money today.)

What was the value of British exports in 1700? About what year did exports reach their highest level? During which period did the value of exports rise most quickly?

You will notice that exports dipped slightly about the 1870s. By this time the Industrial Revolution had spread well beyond England. Most of western Europe and the United States were becoming in-

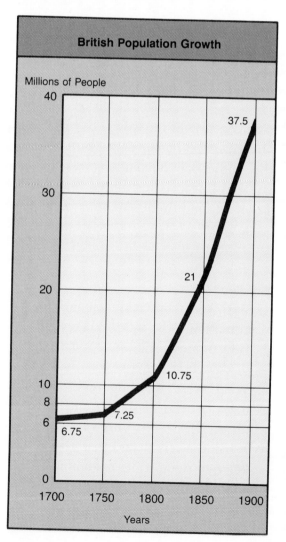

British Population Growth

Millions of People

37.5

21

10.75

7.25

6.75

1700 1750 1800 1850 1900

Years

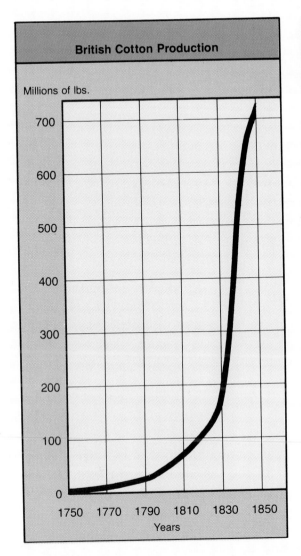

British Cotton Production

Millions of lbs.

700
600
500
400
300
200
100
0

1750 1770 1790 1810 1830 1850
Years

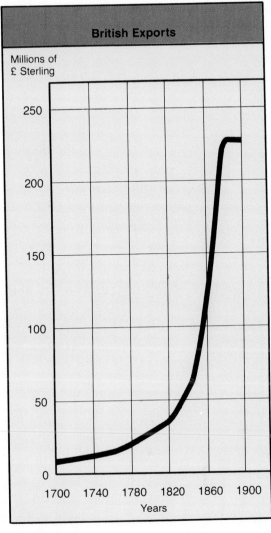

British Exports

Millions of
£ Sterling

250
200
150
100
50
0

1700 1740 1780 1820 1860 1900
Years

dustrial countries by the late 1800s. Governments in these countries began to place taxes on foreign imports. These taxes made the prices for foreign products higher. Governments hoped that higher prices would limit the imports of foreign goods. Reducing imports, they thought, would help their own industries grow. Thus, the British were not able to sell as many of their products to other industrializing countries. By this time, however, the Industrial Revolution had made England one of the world's wealthiest countries.

Checking Up
1. How did population growth help cause the Industrial Revolution?
2. How did new inventions lead to greater cotton production?
3. Why did many governments place taxes on imports in the late 1800s?

The Capitalist System

The Industrial Revolution did not begin overnight. More than inventions were needed to make industries work. People had to build factories, and set up machinery. Systems of production had to be developed. Factory owners had to hire workers. They had to make arrangements for the transportation and sale of finished products. All this and more had to be done before a single product could be sold. Starting a factory or operating a mine required time and a lot of money. A person might have the time, but where was the money to come from?

Capitalism

In some cases an individual had enough money to start an industry. In other cases money for industries came from the sale of stocks. In Unit 16 you read about joint-stock companies. The method that was used to provide money for businesses involved in overseas trade was also used to build new industries. Many different investors bought shares of a company. The money they invested provided the huge amounts of money needed to start a new business or expand an old one.

Capitalism at work. The Industrial Revolution brought about the growth of **capitalism.** Capitalism is an economic system based on private ownership of business and industry. The system began in certain areas of Europe as early as the late Middle Ages. It reached its full de-

434

velopment during the time of industrial revolution.

Capitalism comes from the word *capital*. Capital is anything that can be used to create wealth. Money is one form of capital. Money can be invested in a business to make a profit, or money that is left after all expenses have been paid. Land, factories, tools and machinery, and railways are also capital. They are used to produce goods or services that can be sold at a profit.

Here is an easier example. Suppose someone gave you a lot of money. You could use the money as capital to buy a bicycle and start a delivery service. The bike you bought would then become capital because it would be used as a way of performing a service that you could sell to make a profit. You would then be a capitalist, one who uses capital to make a profit.

Capital can also be used to expand businesses. Suppose your delivery service turned out to be a success. You made a profit of about ten dollars a week. You could simply spend the money and enjoy yourself, or you could put most of that profit right back into the business. You might, for example, save for a second bicycle. Then you could hire another worker to ride it and make even more deliveries. Your business could become larger, and your profits could be greater. With your profits, you could expand your business even more.

This example shows, on a small scale, how businesses began to grow during the Industrial Revolution. Owners of industrial businesses, or **industrialists,** used capital to make more and more profits. Some or all of the profits were used to buy more machines, build more factories, hire more workers, and expand the business. The market for goods and services continued to grow. Industrialists knew that they could continue to produce more goods and find buyers for them. Some industrialists became very wealthy.

The Spread of Industrialization

The industrialization that began in England later spread to other parts of the world. By the end of the 1800s, many countries of the world had been changed by the Industrial Revolution.

Industrialization in Europe. The French Revolution and the wars of Napoleon held back industrial progress in western Europe for a time. After Napoleon's defeat in 1815, countries such as Belgium and France began to industrialize. By the middle of the 1800s, the Industrial Revolution had spread to Germany and the Austrian Empire in central Europe. In eastern Europe, Russia did

It took much capital to build large factories such as this iron works.

435

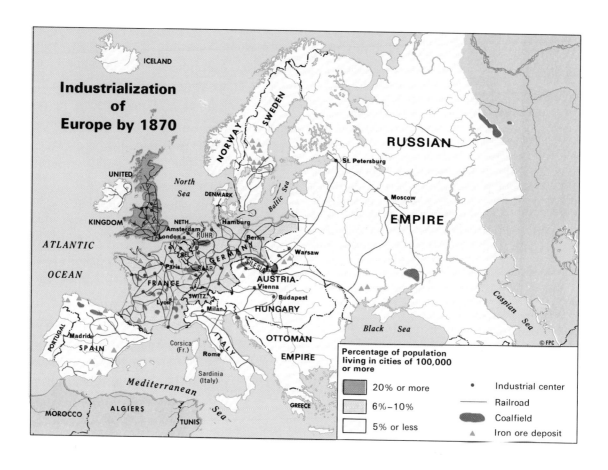

Industrialization of Europe by 1870

Percentage of population living in cities of 100,000 or more

- 20% or more
- 6%–10%
- 5% or less
- • Industrial center
- — Railroad
- Coalfield
- ▲ Iron ore deposit

not become industrialized until the late 1800s and early 1900s.

The pattern of industrialization in other countries was much the same as it was in England. Industries developed. Workers migrated to cities for jobs. Cities grew.

Industrialization in the United States. Although the United States was much larger than England, it had fewer people. Yet it did have an abundance of natural resources, such as timber, coal, and iron ore. This supply of natural resources was a great advantage when the United States industrialized. The United States also produced agricultural products, such as cotton, that industries could use.

Business people in the United States started companies that sold such raw materials. Other United States capital went into shipping and trading companies. At first, little capital went into industry.

Of course, there was some industry in the United States. Iron, for example, was produced as early as the 1600s. However, industrialization did not become widespread in the United States until after the Civil War (1861–1865). Then industries grew rapidly. As industries developed, workers left farms to seek jobs in cities. Millions of people from all over the world also arrived in the United States. Many of them found jobs in industries.

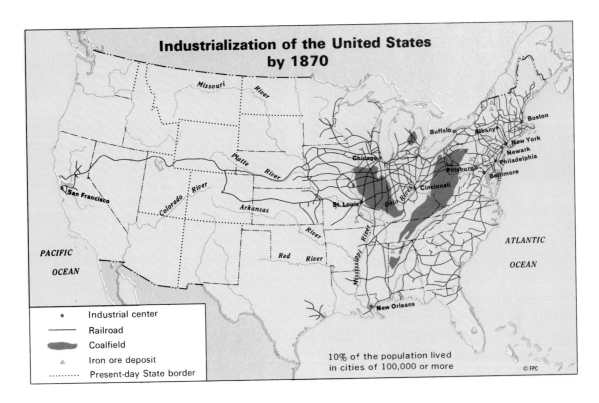

Industrialization of the United States by 1870

Industrial center
Railroad
Coalfield
Iron ore deposit
Present-day State border

10% of the population lived in cities of 100,000 or more

© FPC

Government and Industry

The governments of many countries wanted to increase the wealth of their countries. Industry proved to be one way of producing more wealth. A country that produced more goods could sell these goods to other countries. England, for example, became wealthy by exporting goods made in its factories. English goods were sold in other places around the world.

The English government and other governments favored the growth of industry. Parliament, for example, passed laws that helped industry grow. The government encouraged the building of roads, canals, and railways. The government also helped by establishing colonies overseas. Here English merchants hoped to sell their goods.

The way people thought about economic matters was changing at the time of the Industrial Revolution. In the 1700s the economic thinker Adam Smith claimed that a nation's wealth depended on the amount of goods and services it produced. His ideas opposed the policy of mercantilism, which measured a nation's wealth by the amount of gold and silver in its treasury. Smith's book, *Wealth of Nations*, came out in 1776, when England's Industrial Revolution was beginning. Smith also opposed mercantilist ideas about government control over a nation's economy. The ideas of Smith and those who agreed with him led to a policy known as **laissez faire** (le'sā·fãr').

The French term *laissez faire* means something like "let people do as they

Railroad building in the United States reached its peak after the Civil War.

The first oil wells were built in the United States in the 1860s and 1870s.

choose." The idea was to let business do as it chose. Adam Smith thought that government could help business best by leaving it alone. Government rules, he said, did not help growth.

As the Industrial Revolution spread in England and in other countries, laissez faire became the main idea behind government policies toward business. Industries were allowed to run with little or no government control. This policy lasted during most of the Industrial Revolution.

It was not until the late 1800s and early 1900s that some governments began to feel that businesses were becoming too powerful. It was only then that governments begin to pass laws controlling business.

The Nonindustrial World

In the 1800s only Europe, the United States, and, later, Japan went through an industrial revolution. The rest did not become industrialized. In the nonindustrial world, most people continued to make a living by farming. While industrial countries grew stronger and richer, other countries remained poor and weak.

Many of these areas became colonies of industrial countries. They provided raw materials that fed factories in Europe, the United States, and Japan. They bought industrial products from the developed countries. Because colonies were sources of raw materials and markets for manufactured products, the industrialized countries began a race for colonies around the world. The colonies received few of the benefits of the Industrial Revolution. Some areas of the world became wealthy, while others did not.

Checking Up

1. How did people get money to start or enlarge industries?
2. Into what areas did United States business people first put their capital?
3. What does *laissez faire* mean? Where did the idea come from?
4. What answers would you give to the key questions at the beginning of this chapter?
5. *How did some areas of the world become wealthier than others?*

From Farm to City

As You Read

1. Think about these words.

   crop rotation   commercial   business cycle

   enclosure   illiterate

2. Look for answers to these key questions.

   a. What changes in agriculture took place during the industrial revolution?

   b. How did the growth of industry change cities?

   c. What were the lives of the workers like?

The industrial revolution changed where people worked and how they lived. As industry expanded, changes in country life forced more and more people to leave farms and villages and go to towns and cities to find work. A second agricultural revolution was taking place along with the industrial revolution.

Changes in Agriculture

Changes in agriculture, like those in industry, started in England in the 1700s and later spread to other countries. The growth of population in England influenced farming as well as industry. There were more people to feed, and more of them were working in towns and cities. Farmers needed to produce more food to supply the growing number of urban people.

New methods. Early in the 1700s, such people as Charles Townshend and Jethro Tull urged farmers to use better farming methods. Both men practiced new methods on their own farms. They wrote books telling how farmers could increase their crops.

You will recall that during the late Middle Ages farmers used a three-field system. This system of leaving one field unplanted each year continued. Townshend, however, developed a way of planting all the fields every year.

Townshend recommended **crop rotation** and the use of fertilizers. Crop rotation meant planting a different kind of crop in a field each year. Farmers could grow a crop that wore out the soil, such as wheat or other grains, for one year. Then they could plant the field with something like turnips or clover the next year. These crops helped restore the soil. They also provided winter feed for the cattle or other farm animals.

Tull introduced a way to plant seeds in even rows rather than just scatter them, as farmers had done for hundreds of years. Planting in rows made it easier

	Three-field System	Crop Rotation System
1st year	winter grain	turnips
2nd year	spring grain	barley
3rd year	fallow	clover
4th year	repeat of above cycle	wheat
results	Farmers left ⅓ of their land to lie fallow each year.	Farmers could plant all of their land every year by varying crops; they used turnips and clover as winter feed for their animals.

The chart above shows typical planting systems. The order in which crops were planted might vary from farm to farm.

to care for and harvest the plants. It became easier for farmers to use the new farming tools and machines that were beginning to come from factories.

The iron plow and other improved farming equipment helped farmers grow more crops. Steam-powered farming equipment, such as the harvester, was introduced by the early 1800s. Most farmers, however, did not use such powered equipment until the late 1800s.

Farmers also improved the quality of animals they raised. Better breeding

Reapers opened up the U.S. agricultural heartland in the 1840s.

methods helped farmers raise bigger and healthier animals. Heavier cattle produced more meat. Healthier cows gave more milk. Stronger horses pulled heavier loads.

Enclosure. The new farming methods worked better on large farms than on small ones. A new practice helped the development of larger farms.

Since the Middle Ages, farmers had worked on small pieces of land located near their villages. Just one farmer might have three or four different pieces of land in different locations. This way of farming was not very efficient.

During the late Middle Ages, the practice of **enclosure** began. Enclosure was fencing in the land. Wealthier people bought the land of poorer farmers and increased the size of their holdings. The rich farmers bought up the common land—grazing land that had been used by all the farmers of a village. The poor farmers, not able to buy any of the common land, had no place to graze their animals. They were forced to sell the rest of their land to the richer farmers.

440

The practice of enclosure increased during the late 1700s and early 1800s. In England Parliament passed many enclosure laws, bringing more and more land into the hands of the richest farmers. Farms became bigger and bigger, and the number of farms became smaller.

Earlier, most farmers had grown crops and raised animals to supply their own families with food. They had sold a few of their farm products to make extra money. Now most large farms were involved in **commercial** agriculture. They produced farm products to be sold at a profit. Farming became a business.

Enclosure had several effects. On the positive side, larger farms allowed farmers to make better use of the land. Farmers could use better farming methods and raise more food to feed the growing population. On the negative side, enclosure forced many small farmers to give up farming. Some of these people stayed in the country and became hired farm workers. Others went to towns and cities and looked for work in the factories.

Enclosures created larger fields that were better for farming and grazing.

Cities Grow

Most new factories were built in or near large towns or cities. Towns and cities had plenty of people to work in the factories. These urban areas also had transportation systems for shipping and receiving goods. As industry grew, so did the cities.

Industrial cities. Many cities grew larger and larger as industry increased. In England people driven from their

441

farms by enclosures flocked to the industrial cities to find work. Cities in the north of England, where the textile industry was centered, grew large.

Manchester was near the center of the area that became known for its textile production. Manchester had been a textile-producing town since the late Middle Ages. When the industrial revolution was just beginning in the early 1770s, Manchester had about 22,000 people. By 1790, when steam-powered factories were developing, the population reached 50,000. In 1815, when the industrial revolution was moving rapidly, Manchester was a busy city of 270,000 people.

Other industrial cities grew almost as quickly as Manchester. Many were textile cities. Others had different industries, such as mining, steelmaking, or producing machinery. Whatever the industry, the city sky was usually darkened by the thick smoke of the burning coal that fed the steam engines.

English working families often had to live in cramped quarters.

Layers of smoke made the industrial cities unpleasant places to live.

Conditions in cities. Workers crowded the city streets. The cities expanded with little or no planning for their growth. Workers poured into the cities faster than housing could be built for them. Old buildings were split up into tiny apartments. Many apartments were just small single rooms for entire families. New buildings were built hastily with the cheapest materials.

In 1832, about 20,000 Manchester families lived in damp cellars without light or heat. Few workers' homes had running water. Water had to be carried in from pumps in the street. Some streets did not even have working pumps. Bathrooms were totally unknown.

The industrial cities were bleak and crowded. There was little room for children to play except in the streets.

People threw their garbage and other wastes into the streets. There were few sewers and no regular garbage collection. Poor sanitation and impure water often led to outbreaks of disease. Because people lived so crowded together, diseases spread quickly. Fires also easily raged through crowded living areas.

Working people lived short lives. One out of every two children died before reaching the age of five. In Manchester in 1842, the average age at death was seventeen! In spite of all the problems, however, people flocked to the cities to find work.

The Lives of Workers

Workers led miserable lives. The hours were long, the work was hard, and the pay was low. It was difficult for most families to earn enough to meet their needs.

Factory workers got up at four or five in the morning. Even children worked. Work started at five or six in the morning. The workers stayed in the factories or mines until nine or ten at night. There were just a few breaks for meals.

The mines were damp and dangerous. Workers spent all day crawling through dark tunnels deep in the earth. Digging out coal or other minerals was back-breaking work. Dust filled the air, and many miners died of lung disease. Others were killed or injured when mine tunnels collapsed.

Factories were dirty, noisy, and poorly lit. The buildings were hot in the summer and cold in the winter. The machines were often dangerous. There were

Women shared the backbreaking and dangerous work of hauling coal from the mines.

few, if any, safety rules that owners had to follow.

Working conditions were poor for all workers. They were especially bad for women and children. About 13 out of every 100 textile workers were fourteen years old or younger. Children as young as seven often worked in factories. They either came from poor families or were orphans. Both women and children received lower wages than men, and men did not make much money.

Most workers were **illiterate**. They could not read or write. There were few schools for children to attend. Besides, most children in poor families had to help earn money. They would not have had time for school.

Workers did not look forward to much. The only day they had off was Sunday. When workers were injured on their jobs or became ill, they received no payment for the time they could not work. People too old to work had to be supported by their families.

Workers also suffered because of changes in **business cycles**. Business did not grow at an even rate. Sometimes the demand for products fell. Then workers lost their jobs. Sometimes there were more workers than there were jobs. Owners could then hire workers at lower wages. Workers desperate for jobs would take whatever pay was offered.

Checking Up
1. What new farming methods did Jethro Tull and Charles Townshend recommend?
2. What happened as a result of the practice of enclosure?
3. Why was housing so poor in industrial cities?
4. What answers would you give to the key questions at the beginning of this chapter?
5. *How was the life of a child worker different from yours?*

Benefits of the Industrial Revolution

As You Read

1. Think about these words.
   social security   pension   union   strike   standard of living
2. Look for answers to these key questions.
   a. How did reformers help improve conditions for poor people?
   b. What part did unions play in bringing about improvements for workers?
   c. What benefits for people came from industry?

Workers endured many hardships during the early years of the industrial revolution. It was at this time that the economic thinker Karl Marx developed his ideas. Marx claimed that the capitalists were taking profits that ought to go to the workers. He saw that capitalists were becoming richer and richer while the workers were becoming poorer and poorer. Marx predicted that the capitalist system would finally break down. The workers would revolt and overthrow the capitalists.

According to Karl Marx, communism would then replace capitalism. Workers would take over the ownership of factories, land, and any other property that produced wealth. Marx failed to understand that the hardships people endured in the early years of the industrial revolution were not permanent. Rather than becoming worse, the lot of the workers improved. Over time, workers as well as factory owners began to share the benefits of industrialization.

Reformers improved conditions in the textile factories of New England.

Charles Dickens

No other writer has left us a clearer picture of what life was like during the Industrial Revolution than Charles Dickens. After his birth in 1812, his family went through hard times. Because of his father's debts, Charles had to work in a factory. Later, however, he was able to attend school.

Dickens realized that writers could help bring about reforms by showing how hard life was for the poor in the industrial cities. In one book Dickens followed the adventures of an orphan, Oliver Twist. During the Industrial Revolution, England had special Poor Laws that provided at least some food, lodging, and pocket money for the poor in return for labor in workhouses. Oliver Twist grew up in such a workhouse.

One night at supper, Oliver rose from the table to ask the headmaster for a second bowl of broth. For this simple request, Oliver was sent away from the workhouse. On the streets Oliver met a gang of thieves. Although he never joined them in stealing, they tried again and again to get him into trouble. Oliver, however, found better people who were able to help him.

This drawing of Oliver Twist appeared in the original edition of Dickens's book.

Oliver Twist succeeded in making people aware of the plight of the urban poor. People who read the book often worked for reform. Dickens wrote many other famous works, such as *David Copperfield, A Christmas Carol,* and *Great Expectations.* All were set in 19th century England. These works show Dickens's great interest in people. He describes their habits and attitudes. Because of his great skill, there is a timelessness to his writing. The basic human nature he portrays does not change. His books have universal appeal for this reason.

Working for Improvements

Working conditions were terrible during the early years of the Industrial Revolution. Working conditions improved, however, through the efforts of two groups of people—reformers and the workers themselves.

Reformers. A few factory owners tried to improve conditions for their workers. One of these was Robert Owen, who owned a cotton mill in England. Owen tried to show that it was possible to run a profitable industry and still treat workers well. He turned his mill into a model factory. He hoped others would follow his example.

Owen built fine housing for his workers. He improved working conditions, reduced hours, and raised wages. He refused to hire young children, and he helped educate his workers' children. Owen's mill, which did make a profit,

Because of the belief in laissez faire, relief for the poor was reduced in the 1830s. Here unemployed workers line up for food tickets.

attracted visitors from all over England. However, few other factory owners followed his example.

Owen was one of many people who tried to improve conditions in the 1800s. These people wanted to bring about reforms, or changes, that would improve life for workers and for others who were needy. Reformers gave money to organizations that helped the poor. They started free schools for children of poor families. They helped take care of the sick, the old, and the jobless.

Reformers also tried to get governments to pass laws that would improve conditions for workers. Their goals were not easy to accomplish. The English government, for example, believed in laissez faire. It did not want to interfere with business. Nevertheless, little by little, reforms came.

One important law passed by Parliament was the Factory Act of 1833. This law stopped the hiring of children under the age of nine. Children under the age of thirteen could work only eight hours a day. Workers thirteen to eighteen years old had a twelve-hour day. The law said that children also had to be given two hours of schooling each day.

In the 1880s Germany started a system of **social security**, or a government-supported insurance plan for workers. It paid money to workers who were unemployed or too sick to work. Retired workers received **pensions**, or payments that supported them in their old age. Social security spread to other countries.

Workers unite. The greatest improvements for workers came because of their own efforts. Workers began to organize **unions**. These organizations brought the workers in a factory or other industry together to try to get better working conditions, wages, and social security.

In many countries unions were illegal. Workers united anyway, using such names as "friendship societies" to hide their real purpose. Gradually, workers gained the right to form unions.

447

Workers in the United States made their demands heard through strikes. These women factory workers went on strike in 1860.

Unions used a strong weapon against owners. They used the **strike**. All the workers in a factory would refuse to work, forcing the factory to shut down. Union members stayed on strike until their demands were met. In this way, they gradually got better pay, shorter hours, and improved working conditions.

Strikes, too, were against the law. Workers often decided to strike anyway. Many went to jail rather than give up their struggle.

People of the 19th century thought of their age as one of progress. A mid-century exhibition in London displayed the most recent inventions.

Nationwide unions took form in the United States in the 1880s.

In time industrialists met the demands of workers. By the late 1800s, workers were also beginning to get their share of the good life made possible by the Industrial Revolution.

The Benefits of Industry

Almost everywhere, industrialization began by bringing a good deal of misery to workers. However, as workers began to share more of the benefits of industrialization, life began to improve. Workers enjoyed a better **standard of living**. They lived better, ate better, and lived longer and healthier lives. As working hours were shortened, people had more time to enjoy their lives. As wages increased, people could afford better housing and more things to bring comfort to their lives.

The gap between rich and poor became narrower in industrialized countries. There were still very rich people and very poor people, but more and more people belonged to the middle class. More workers earned enough money to live comfortable lives.

Checking Up
1. What did Robert Owen do to improve the conditions of his workers?
2. Why was the Factory Act of 1833 important? How did it help improve the lot of working children?
3. What is social security? Where did it begin?
4. What answers would you give to the key questions at the beginning of this chapter?
5. *Why do you think unions and strikes were at first illegal?*

Unit 17 Summary
- New inventions helped the factory system replace cottage industry.
- The use of steam power and improvements in transportation and communication were especially important developments during the Industrial Revolution.
- New farming methods and the practice of enclosure led to a second agricultural revolution.
- Businesses grew and expanded within the capitalist system.
- Working conditions gradually improved as reformers worked for changes and workers formed unions and organized strikes.
- As the Industrial Revolution spread beyond England, more and more people began to share in the benefits of industrialization.

Unit 17 Review Workshop

What Have You Learned?

A. Choose the ending that best completes each sentence.
  1. Cottage workers were especially important in (a) the textile industry (b) English cities (c) the iron and steel industries.
  2. Cottage workers used (a) spinning wheels and handlooms (b) water-power (c) steam power.
  3. The earliest steamships were built in (a) England (b) western Europe (c) the United States.
  4. Enclosure meant (a) fencing in farmland (b) planting different kinds of crops (c) using better farm methods.
  5. The agricultural revolution led to (a) larger farms (b) smaller farms (c) more farmers.
  6. Capital includes (a) land and machines (b) money (c) all of the above.
  7. People who believed in laissez faire included (a) government reformers (b) Karl Marx (c) Adam Smith
  8. The idea of social security began in (a) England (b) Germany (c) the United States.

B. The following statements are important ideas from the unit. Explain each in two or three sentences.
  1. The invention of the flying shuttle helped spinners keep up with weavers.

  2. England used its colonies as sources of raw materials for factories.
  3. Steam power allowed people to build factories in locations away from sources of water.
  4. English exports rose rapidly during the Industrial Revolution.
  5. Steam-powered machines were used in most textile factories by the early 1800s.
  6. The Factory Act limited the number of hours children were allowed to work.
  7. In the early stage of the Industrial Revolution, people in the country were likely to live longer than those in cities.
  8. Robert Owen was both a factory owner and a reformer.
  9. Karl Marx thought that the workers would take over possession of the factories.
  10. Except for the United States and Japan, no non-European nation industrialized in the late 1800s.

Use Your Reading Skills

1. Review the chart of inventions on page 428 and the material on developments in transportation and communication. Using information in the first chapter of this unit, make a chart of your own with the title "Inventions Change Transportation and Communication."

2. Use the Index to find the page or pages that tell about the population in Manchester during the Industrial Revolution. Make a graph that shows the city's changing population. Model your graph after those in this unit.

Use Your Thinking Skills

A. The picture on this page shows one artist's ideas about the Industrial Revolution. Study it, then answer the following questions.
   1. List at least three things in the picture that have something to do with the Industrial Revolution.
   2. How do you think the artist felt about the Industrial Revolution? How can you tell?
   3. Does the artist present a fair view of the period? Why or why not?

B. Each of the persons listed below had an effect on events during or after the Industrial Revolution. Write a sentence telling why each person was important.
   1. Richard Arkwright
   2. Samuel Morse
   3. George Stephenson
   4. Jethro Tull
   5. James Watt
   6. Eli Whitney

Learn by Doing

A. Many products sold in the United States come from other industrialized countries. Make a list of as many imports as you can think of from each of the following countries.
   Great Britain   Japan
   West Germany   France

B. Do further library research on one of the inventions you read about in this unit. Then prepare a report or a poster about the inventor and the invention, how the invention came about, how it worked and what effect it had.

Read to Learn More

Find the topics listed below in the card catalog of your library. Read all or part of a book listed under one of the topics. Share what you learn with your classmates.

INDUSTRIAL REVOLUTION

AGRICULTURAL REVOLUTION (MODERN)

CAPITALISM

LABOR UNIONS

Unit 18

The Twentieth Century and Beyond

Twentieth-century cities in many parts of the world rise from what until recently was farmland.

Forces of Change

As You Read

1. Think about these words.
   colonialism   imperialism
2. Look for answers to these key questions.
   a. How did the industrial revolution lead to the spread of colonialism and imperialism?
   b. Which countries were important imperialist powers in the 1900s?
   c. How did nationalism conflict with imperialism?
3. Use this reading skill.
   One important reading skill is the ability to figure out what long, unfamiliar words mean. Many words are long because they have suffixes, endings which give a clue to the word's meaning. You will see words like *nationalism* in this chapter. The suffix *ism* can mean "loyalty to" something. So *nationalism* refers to a person's loyalty toward a nation.

As the industrial revolution spread, industrial nations needed more raw materials and more markets. They got both by establishing colonies around the world. Great Britain, France, and other European nations followed a policy of **colonialism.** That is, they established colonies. In the 1600s and 1700s mercantilism supported this policy.

These colonies became parts of the empires built by European nations in the 1800s. The practice of **imperialism,** or empire building, led some countries to expand their territories in Europe too. Weak countries fell under the control of more powerful ones.

Many of the places you have already read about were parts of empires. For example, the lands of the Incas and Mayas made up a part of Spain's empire in the Western Hemisphere. In the 1800s Egypt and parts of Africa came under the control of European nations. India, China, and other parts of Asia also felt the expansion of European power. Truly, the imperialists changed the map of the world in the 19th and 20th centuries.

Growth of Empires

From the middle 1800s until 1914, many industrial powers acquired colonies and territories in Africa and Asia. They used treaties, armies, or the threat of conquest to get these colonies. Missionaries also helped in the scramble for colonies. Thousands of Christian mis-

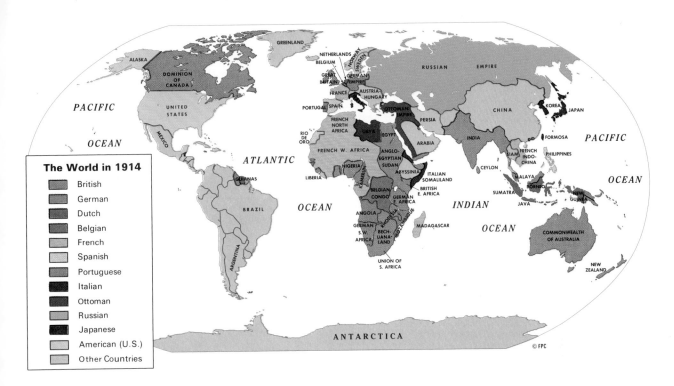

The World in 1914

- British
- German
- Dutch
- Belgian
- French
- Spanish
- Portuguese
- Italian
- Ottoman
- Russian
- Japanese
- American (U.S.)
- Other Countries

sionaries from Europe and the United States went to distant lands to teach and to convert people. They set up churches, schools, and hospitals. Traders and armies often followed the missionaries.

Africa. Great Britain, France, Germany, Portugal, and Belgium carved out large areas of Africa as their own. These colonies provided the countries with rich sources of raw materials, as well as markets for manufactured goods. For example, Zaire, which used to be called the Belgian Congo, supplied copper. Egypt, under British control, became an important source of raw cotton.

Asia. Asia and Pacific islands also became important to industrial countries. As you know from Unit 16, trade between European and Asian countries was growing. By the 1600s European trading ships were visiting the port of Canton, China. Although the Chinese

fought to keep Europeans out of China in the early 1800s, they were not successful. Other Chinese ports opened to European merchants. The United States, too, gained trading rights in China. In 1900 the United States persuaded other countries to follow an "open-door" policy in

Explorers penetrated many areas of Africa and aroused European interest.

455

China. The open door gave all nations equal trading rights in China.

The large and heavily populated country of India came under British rule. In the 1700s a British trading company was the ruler of most of India. Then, in 1858, the British Parliament brought India under government control. India became part of the vast British Empire, on which "the sun never set."

Japan did not become a part of another country's empire. Instead, it began a policy of imperialism itself. In 1863 Commodore Matthew Perry of the United States visited Japan. As you know from Unit 12, in the 1600s Japan had closed itself off to the outside world. Perry convinced the Japanese they needed to establish contact with other countries. Japan began to modernize. Some Japanese people were sent to Europe and the United States to study industrial methods. Japan underwent its own industrial revolution and sought raw materials and markets. Japan gained the island of Formosa after a war with China

Perry's modern fleet made Japan aware of the industrial powers.

Bolívar and San Martín led the South American armies against Spain.

in 1894–1895. It also got Korea after a war with Russia in 1904–1905.

The Americas. Spain, which had been the leading colonial power, lost control over its colonies when Napoleon's forces occupied Spain. When Spain tried to regain control, the colonies rebelled.

By this time the most powerful country in the Western Hemisphere was the United States. In 1823 a United States President, James Monroe, began a policy that was to keep Spain and other European powers out of Central and South America and the islands of the Caribbean. This policy, the Monroe Doctrine, helped prevent European expansion in the Americas. Only a few European colonies and territories remained in the Western Hemisphere.

Spain lost more of its colonies after a war with the United States in 1898. This war broke out when Spain tried to put down a rebellion in Cuba. The United States defeated Spanish forces in the Caribbean and the Pacific. Spain gave up Cuba, Puerto Rico, Guam, and the Philippine Islands. Cuba and the Philippines eventually gained independence.

Nationalism and Imperialism

In Unit 15 you learned that nationalism is the strong feeling that people have for their own country. The force of nationalism conflicted with the force of imperialism in many countries, especially in the late 19th and early 20th centuries. Feelings of nationalism helped break up the old Spanish and Portuguese empires in the Western Hemisphere. One by one, various parts of Latin America fought for and won independence from European rule. Colonial people in other places also rebelled against the foreign governments and companies that controlled them. There were uprisings in India in the 1850s and in China in the early 1900s. People in these places wanted freedom from European influence. Imperialist rule over these places lasted for many years. The struggle for independence from foreign rule also continued.

National unification. The 1870s saw the rise of two European nations: Italy and Germany. Italy had been divided into seven separate states. By 1871 it had been unified into a nation.

Since 1815 Germany had been a fairly weak confederation of thirty-eight states. A spirit of nationalism for a strong, united Germany grew among Germans. Many looked to Prussia, the strongest German state, for leadership. Bismarck (biz'märk), the chief minister of the king of Prussia, helped unite German states into the German Empire.

Discontent within empires. Not all the nations of Europe were independent. Many were parts of the three large empires of central and eastern Europe. The populations of the three empires included many different nationalities. Their desire for independence often led to discontent and unrest.

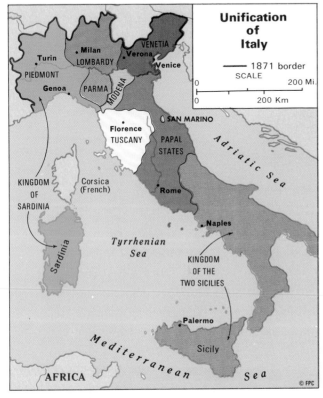

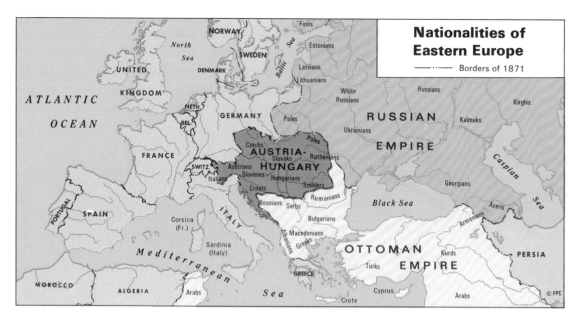

Nationalities of Eastern Europe
——···—— Borders of 1871

In Eastern Europe Russia had extended its control over many other places. By the early 1800s, the Russian Empire included much of Poland, Finland, and part of Armenia. The people in each of these places did not want to be under Russian rule. Instead, they wanted to become independent nations.

The Austro-Hungarian Empire, a large empire in central Europe, had two main parts—Austria and Hungary. There were many nationalities within the empire. Each had its own language, customs, and history. Various nationalist groups in the Austro-Hungarian Empire rebelled, but they were unable to gain independence. World War I caused the breakup of the Austro-Hungarian Empire.

The Ottoman Empire, which you read about in Units 9 and 10, also included many different nationalities. As these groups rose up against their Ottoman rulers, the Ottoman Empire lost most of its European territory. By 1913 the Turks who controlled the empire held only what is now the country of Turkey and other parts of the Middle East. The weakening of the Ottoman Empire in southeastern Europe led to the rivalry between Austria-Hungary and Russia for influence there. This rivalry was one of the causes of the First World War.

Checking Up

1. What was the open-door policy in China?

2. What was the Monroe Doctrine?

3. What two European countries became nations in 1870–1871? What three empires in Europe had many nationalities among their populations?

4. What answers would you give to the key questions at the beginning of this chapter?

5. *Why do you think various groups in empires wanted independence?*

458

Changes in Europe

As You Read

1. Think about these words.

   alliance   depression   abdicate   fascist   racist

2. Look for answers to these key questions.

   a. What were the causes of World War I?

   b. How did the Russian Revolution affect the people in Russia? in the rest of Europe?

   c. What were the policies and goals of fascist leaders such as Mussolini and Hitler?

3. Use this reading skill.

   An important reading skill is the ability to note how persons or events are both alike and different. Use this skill to compare the rise to power of both the communists and the fascists.

People made great progress during the 19th century. Several democratic governments came into being. The industrial revolution improved people's lives. Europe was the center of power in the world. Yet by 1900, Europe itself was divided into opposing countries. Competition among European countries led to large-scale wars in the first half of the 20th century.

Europe in Conflict

In the early 1900s, rivalry among many European countries was becoming more intense. Competition for overseas colonies and for greater influence in the world increased. Countries began to build up their armed forces. They were preparing to fight to win territory and increase their power.

Great Britain grew uneasy when Germany built a strong navy. France wanted to win back territory it had lost to Germany in a war in 1871. Russia was angry over the expansion of Austria-Hungary into southeastern Europe.

Balance of power. During much of modern European history, a balance of power existed among the different European countries. Whenever one country seemed to become too powerful, others joined in an **alliance** to match its strength. An alliance is an agreement among different countries to help one another in case of attack.

Two great alliances dominated Europe in the early 20th century. One was the Triple Alliance, made up of Germany, Austria-Hungary, and Italy. The other was the Triple Entente, made up of

Great Britain, France, and Russia. Countries began a race to build up strong armies and navies. Each member of the two alliances had some dispute with a member of the other alliance. If a quarrel broke out between two countries belonging to different alliances, almost all the other European countries would be brought into war.

World War I. Such a quarrel did occur. The incident that set off the first great war of the 20th century was the assassination of Francis Ferdinand, heir to the throne of Austria-Hungary, in June of 1914. Soon, most countries in Europe entered the war. The Central Powers were Austria-Hungary, Germany, and the Ottoman Empire. They fought against the Allies—Russia, France, Great Britain, and, after 1915, Italy. The United States remained neutral until 1917, when it joined the Allies. Most of the fighting took place in Eu-

rope, but there was fighting in other places too. Millions were killed in battle. Many more were wounded. Civilians as well as soldiers lost their lives, either in the fierce fighting or from hunger and disease caused by the war.

The arrival of 2 million U.S. troops in Europe helped the Allies turn back the Central Powers. Germany and its partners finally realized they could not continue the war. On November 11, 1918, Germany surrendered.

Results of the war. World War I greatly changed the national boundaries of Europe. A revolution broke out in Russia, and the people overthrew the government. Poland again became independent. Germany lost some of its territory and was forced to give up all its colonies. Austria-Hungary broke up into a number of new countries. The Ottoman Empire was broken apart by the Allies, losing its Syrian, Mesopotamian, and

460

German sinking of U.S. ships led the United States to war.

During the depression the U.S. government set up work programs.

Arabian territories. The Ottoman sultan fled, and the new Republic of Turkey was born.

During the war the United States President, Woodrow Wilson, urged that a League of Nations be formed afterward. Its main purpose was to settle problems among nations peacefully rather than by war. Several important countries, however, failed to become members of the league, including the United States itself. The league did not have much power. Countries did not have to accept the league's decisions. The league could not stop conflicts among countries.

Twentieth-Century Dictators

Much of Europe suffered great damage in World War I. It was difficult for

President Wilson hoped every nation in Europe could be independent.

many nations to recover. Business declined, prices fell, and many people were unemployed. The years after 1929 were called the Great Depression. A **depression** is a time when there is little business activity. Many people lose their jobs. During the Great Depression, people all around the world suffered. New fears arose, and new conflicts began to threaten the peace. Many Europeans were especially frightened by what had happened in Russia.

The Russian Revolution. Russia had been a troubled nation for a long time. It was ruled by a czar, or emperor, who was an absolute monarch. Russia was still basically an agricultural nation with millions of peasants working the land. It was a land of rich landowners and nobles and many poor peasants.

Although Russia was slow to industrialize, there were some factories. Like the workers in England at the beginning of the industrial revolution, the workers in Russia suffered greatly. In January 1905, a large crowd of workers marched toward the czar's palace in St. Petersburg. They wanted to ask for better working conditions. They were met not

461

by the czar but by soldiers, who fired into the crowd killing hundreds of people. Bloody Sunday, as this event was called, led to strikes by workers all over Russia.

Finally Czar Nicholas II gave in and promised to bring about some reforms. He gave the country a kind of parliament, called the Duma. The czar, however, was not pleased by having to give in to his people. He gave the Duma little power.

Russia's entry into World War I led to greater problems. Most of the Russian generals were incompetent. Russian soldiers were killed by the hundreds of thousands as they fought against better-armed and better-led Germans and Austrians. At the same time, many people in Russia were going hungry because there was not enough food. The czar did not seem able to handle Russia's problems, yet he refused to give any more power to the Duma.

More workers' strikes broke out in 1917. Soon the strikes turned into a revolution against the czar's government. Czar Nicholas II **abdicated,** or gave up his power, and a temporary government was formed. It called for the election of a national assembly. All citizens were to vote for representatives. However, this temporary government failed to take Russia out of the war. Nor did it introduce much-needed land reform.

People were not pleased. V.I. Lenin led a political group known as the Bolsheviks. The Bolsheviks believed in the doctrine of communism. They worked

Lenin returned to Russia after the czar's government was overthrown.

against the new government. Lenin adopted the slogan "Peace for the soldiers, land for the peasants, and bread for the workers."

In November of 1917, the Bolsheviks overthrew the government and seized power. The czar and his family were imprisoned and later killed. One of the first things the Bolsheviks did was to make peace with the Central Powers in 1918.

Russian communism. After the revolution Russia became the Union of Soviet Socialist Republics (USSR), or simply the Soviet Union. The Bolsheviks, who said they were leading the workers, kept all power to themselves. They followed the ideas of Karl Marx. Marx had been against private ownership of lands and property. Farms, factories, and businesses, Marx said, should belong to the people, not to private owners. The Bolsheviks communized, or in the name of the people took over the ownership of, factories and businesses.

When the Bolsheviks came to power, Russia faced many problems. Russia suffered greatly because of the war. There was a shortage of food, and many people were out of work. There was much suffering, famine, and disease. Many thousands died between 1918 and 1923. In spite of setbacks, the Soviet Union slowly began to build up its industries.

Lenin ruled the USSR like a dictator. Only members of the Communist Party, a small minority of the population, could hold high office in the government. After Lenin's death in 1924, Joseph Stalin took over the government. He strengthened his control by getting rid of anyone who opposed him. Many were killed. Thousands were thrown into prisons. A secret police force helped Stalin maintain his power and control nearly every aspect of life in the country.

Mussolini sought to restore to Italy the power of ancient Rome.

Europe reacts. Many Europeans were frightened by the Russian Revolution. They were afraid that communism might spread. In the 1920s and 1930s, leaders of new political parties in Europe used this fear to their own advantage. The most important of these groups were the **fascists** in Italy and Germany. The fascists believed in the need for a strong central government headed by a dictator. They wanted to restrict people's freedom.

The Fascists. Benito Mussolini became dictator of Italy in 1922. He was the leader of a nationalistic group called the Fascists (fash'ists). Fascist policy required every Italian to obey Mussolini. Those who opposed his rule were punished. The Fascists hoped to achieve Italian control of the area around the Mediterranean.

The Nazis. Adolf Hitler took control of the German government in 1933. He was the leader of the National Socialist, or Nazi, party. This party had goals similar to those of the Fascists in Italy. The Nazis were intense nationalists who wanted to erase the shame of German defeat in World War I. Hitler was also a **racist.** He claimed that the Germans were a master race. Thus, he believed they were superior to all other people.

Hitler directed his racist policies particularly against the Jews. He blamed them for all of Germany's problems. Nazis beat Jews and damaged their businesses while the police pretended not to notice. After World War II began, the Nazis rounded up millions of Jews from

463

Hitler claimed he would establish a thousand-year German empire.

all the countries that fell under German rule and sent them to concentration camps. About 6 million Jews died or were put to death in these camps. This is known as the Holocaust.

Others suffered as well. Anyone who disagreed with the Nazis was thrown into prison or executed. Many people fled the country to escape imprisonment. Secret police spied on people. Germans were encouraged to report members of their own family if they were suspected of being against Hitler.

Even though Hitler used terror and hatred to maintain his control, many Germans approved of his government. Industry, especially in arms production, prospered. People were working once again. The hard years of the depression were over. Germany was becoming a

proud and strong nation again. Hitler began to rebuild the nation's military forces.

One of Hitler's first goals was to unite all German people, including those who lived outside Germany's borders. There were millions of German-speaking people in Austria, Czechoslovakia, and Poland. German troops marched into Austria and took it over in 1938. The following year, Germany took over much of Czechoslovakia. Other European nations looked on in anger, but they did nothing to stop Hitler. The fear of another war was too great.

On September 1, 1939, German and Soviet troops invaded Poland. France and Great Britain, both allies of Poland, declared war on Germany. World War II began.

Checking Up

1. What were the two important alliances in Europe just before World War I?

2. How did each of the following change as a result of World War I: Russia, Austria-Hungary, Germany, the Ottoman Empire?

3. In which three important countries did dictators come to power? How did they do so?

4. What answers would you give to the key questions at the beginning of this chapter?

5. *How are the causes of World War II linked to the results of World War I?*

The Recent Past

As You Read

1. Think about these words.
   superpower   Third World
2. Look for answers to these key questions.
   a. What significant changes came about in Europe as a result of World War II?
   b. How did Asia and Africa change after the war? What are the three worlds?
   c. How are the developing countries still tied to the more industrialized world?

In the last forty years, sweeping changes have occurred in the world. A second great war fought in Europe, North Africa, and the Far East marked the beginning of a new world balance. After the war the United States and the Soviet Union became the most powerful countries in the world. Countries in Europe and Asia became their allies. New countries in Asia and Africa gained their independence. All these developments resulted from World War II.

The United States entered World War II after a surprise Japanese attack.

World War II

In the 1930s the attacks of Italy upon Ethiopia and of Japan upon China alarmed the world. Then in 1939, Germany and the Soviet Union invaded Poland. As allies of Poland, Great Britain and France declared war on Germany. World War II began. Find this event on the time line on page 367.

The Axis and the Allies. Italy, Germany, and Japan formed an alliance called the Axis. Opposing them were the Allies—Great Britain and France. At the beginning of the war, Germany had a treaty with the Soviet Union. In June 1941, however, Germany broke the treaty and attacked the Soviet Union, which then joined the Allies.

The United States at first remained neutral. Yet it sent the Allies ships, arms, and food. Then on December 7, 1941, Japan attacked a U.S. naval fleet at Pearl Harbor in Hawaii. The United States declared war on the Axis powers.

465

Fighting in the air during World War II caused destruction in European cities.

The Axis powers occupied vast territories in Europe, North Africa, and the Far East. It took nearly another four years for the Allies to defeat the Axis. Germany was finally crushed between Russian forces attacking from the east and the Allied forces from the west. German surrender came in May 1945. Japan surrendered four months later, after the United States dropped atom bombs on the cities of Hiroshima and Nagasaki.

Results of the War

Once again Europe came out of a world war with many millions dead or wounded. Bombing raids by both sides had brought terrible destruction to cities. It took years of hard work, and a great deal of aid from the United States before Europe was able to recover.

The world divided. As had happened after World War I, many borders in Europe changed after the fighting ended. The most significant change, however, was the division of Europe into two opposing parts. One part, Western Europe, saw the reestablishment of democratic governments under United States protection. The Soviet Union dominated the other part, Eastern Europe.

When World War II ended, Soviet troops occupied most of Eastern Europe. The Soviet Union established new communist governments in the nations it controlled. Attempts to stop the growth of Soviet influence led to a "cold war." The cold war was the rivalry between Western powers (the United States and its allies) and the Soviet Union for influence. There was no fighting.

Germany itself was split into two parts. The eastern part, occupied by the USSR, became the communist state of East Germany. The western part became the West German Republic. Berlin, the former capital which lay within the zone controlled by the USSR, was also di-

Stalin, Roosevelt, and Churchill, the Allied leaders, met during the war.

Soviet leaders govern the Soviet Union from the Kremlin in Moscow.

vided. It remains a divided city today, with a wall built by the communists to prevent East Germans from escaping.

The three worlds. The United States came out of World War II the most powerful country in the world. It became the leader of what is called the free world, those countries that opposed the power of communism and the Soviet Union.

After the war the Soviet Union continued to grow in strength and to influence other communist countries in Europe and Asia. By 1949 the Soviets, too, had atomic weapons. It was clear that the USSR had become the second **superpower,** one of the several very powerful countries in the world. Together, the Soviet Union and other communist countries make up the Second World.

Many of the countries of Asia and Africa that had been colonies before World War II became independent after the war. They did not want to become allied with either the Western or the communist superpowers. They are called the **Third World** countries.

Japan and China. Japan was occupied by U.S. troops for several years after its surrender. With help from the United States, the Japanese set up a democratic government. Japan has become a part of the free world and is now one of the world's leading industrial nations.

In the early 1900s, China became a republic. The most important political group in China was the Nationalist

467

Mao Tse-tung recruited peasants into the revolutionary communist armies.

party. The Communist party also organized. During World War II, Chinese forces from Nationalist and Communist groups fought separately against Japan. After the war they fought against each other for control of China. The Communists led by Mao Tse-tung (mou'zɔ dŏong') gradually drove the Nationalist forces off the mainland of China to the island of Taiwan. In 1949 China became a communist country known as the People's Republic of China.

For several years the Chinese Communists were closely allied with the Soviet Union. In the 1960s, however, China began to follow a more independent path. Since the early 1970s, the People's Republic has had friendlier relations with the United States and other noncommunist countries. The Chinese are still behind other industrial countries of the world. However, the huge number of people in the People's Republic—about one billion people—gives it the potential to become a future superpower.

468

The End of Imperialism

One of the most important changes since World War II has been the decline of colonialism and imperialism. Many of the people in colonies fought against the Axis powers. Many Asians suffered greatly during the war. After the war they wanted to be free of foreign control. Since the war almost fifty new countries have gained independence in areas that had once been colonies.

Struggles for independence. Before World War I, Palestine, the ancient homeland of the Jews, was part of the Ottoman Empire. After World War I Great Britain governed Palestine. During the early part of the 20th century, many Jews from Europe began to settle there. There were conflicts between the Jews and the Arabs who lived in Palestine. In 1948 the Jewish state of Israel was founded. Many Palestinian Arabs left. Disagreement between the Israelis and Palestinians continues.

The British granted independence to its colony, Ghana, gradually. India struggled considerably to gain its inde-

Asian and African colonies gained independence after World War II.

pendence. In other places people had to fight to gain independence. The French, for example, tried to put down rebellions in Algeria and Indochina for a number of years before pulling out.

Problems continued in Vietnam, one of the new nations of Indochina. In 1954 Vietnam was divided into two parts: communist North Vietnam (the Democratic Republic of Vietnam), and noncommunist South Vietnam (the Republic of Vietnam). Communists and noncommunists fought for twenty years.

Not until 1975, after more than ten years of United States involvement, did the civil war end. Many Vietnamese have chosen to leave their homeland, which the communists now rule.

An interdependent world. Many of the new countries are part of what is called the Third World. They have tried to stay out of the conflict between the communist and the noncommunist nations of the world. These Third World countries fiercely oppose any form of imperialist control. They hope to avoid being tied to either Western or Soviet powers. Included in this group are nations in Africa, Asia, and Latin America.

In one way, however, much of the Third World cannot escape involvement with the world's leading industrial powers. Most Third World countries have not yet become highly industrialized. Their economies are still closely linked with the industrial countries. The Third World still supplies raw materials to these countries and buys manufactured products from them. It often depends on technology from the industrial countries. Countries, not yet industrialized, are known as developing countries.

Vast supplies of oil have been discovered in developing countries like Saudi Arabia, Kuwait, Iran, Libya, and Iraq. Oil exports have brought wealth, industry, and rapid progress to them. To protect their resources, they have formed OPEC (the Organization of Petroleum Exporting Countries). OPEC has become a very powerful organization. It can control both the price and the supply of oil in the world.

One way of looking at today's world is to divide it into free world, communist world, and Third World countries. Another way is to look at the extent to which countries have become industrialized. On the one hand are the older, more highly industrialized countries. On the other are the newer, developing countries struggling to industrialize.

Checking Up

1. What countries made up the Axis powers? What were the countries that fought against them?
2. What happened to Germany and Japan after World War II? to China?
3. What is OPEC? Why is it important?
4. What answers would you give to the key questions at the beginning of this chapter?
5. *Why do you think the Third World has not become allied with either Western or communist superpowers?*

469

Maps Tell a Story of Boundaries

Look at the political map of the world in your Atlas on pages 10–11. Notice the boundary lines, or borders, between countries. What symbol marks the boundary between the United States and Canada? Where is the boundary between the United States and Mexico? Boundaries between the United States and its neighbors to the north and south are clear and easily defined. They follow either natural boundaries made by major rivers and lakes, or lines of latitude.

Look now at the boundaries between countries in the rest of the world. These boundaries seem to follow strange zigzag lines. Why such confusion? There are many reasons. Countries have fought over territory for centuries. Boundaries have been defined, redefined, wiped out, and reestablished. Boundaries may have been drawn after some victory or defeat in the past. They may go back to where different groups of people settled long ago. They may also depend on what areas remained united for long periods of time.

A Changing Map

World War I created a new set of boundaries in Europe. It even created a

470

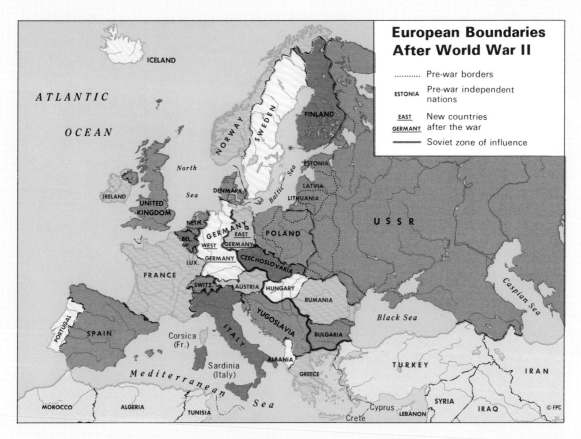

European Boundaries After World War II

.... Pre-war borders

ESTONIA Pre-war independent nations

EAST GERMANY New countries after the war

Soviet zone of influence

new group of countries. The map on page 470 tells a story of changing boundaries. By using colors, it shows boundaries before World War I. New countries formed after the war are underlined on the map. What three whole countries were once included in Austria-Hungary? What four other countries had some of their territory in the empire? What new country absorbed the former countries of Serbia and Montenegro? What three countries gave Poland its territory? From what country did France receive territory?

More Changes

Look at the second map. It shows you Europe after World War II. What territory did Germany lose? Into what two states was Germany divided? What happened to Poland's borders? What three countries did the USSR absorb?

These two great wars also changed boundaries all over the world. Germany lost its colonies after World War I. Italy gave up its colonies after World War II, and Japan lost its Far East empire. The African and Asian colonies of Britain, France, and other European countries gained their independence.

Maps continue to change today. Boundaries shift and new nations emerge. Earth's political geography, the boundaries of its countries, is a constant reminder that people control the patterns of our world.

The World of the Future

As You Read

1. Think about these words.
   prediction   trend
2. Look for answers to these key questions.
   a. What changes do scientists foresee in where people live, what they eat, and the kind of work they do?
   b. How can science help us meet our energy needs? How can technology open up a new frontier?
   c. Why is an understanding that people around the world are very much alike important?

From studying this book, you have learned many things about the past. You have read about many cultures and countries and their contributions to our world. Information about the past is important to people today, especially if they can use it to help plan for the future. Understanding the changes that have occurred can help us prepare for the changes in the 21st century.

No one is sure what the 21st century will be like. We can say that, as in the past, there will certainly be many changes. We can even make some **predictions**, or forecasts, about the kinds of changes that will take place. In fact, many scientists study the past and the present to get information they can use to predict the future. They study **trends**, or patterns, of living to try to answer questions about life in the years to come. What changes will occur in industry and agriculture? Where will people be living? How will people earn a living? What resources will be available? What new discoveries will be made?

There are predictions that try to answer these questions. Predictions are only what we *think* might happen. They can be wrong. Yet looking at some predictions about your future world can help you think about the future.

People and Settlements

Since the time of the Ice Age, the world's population has increased. In 1850, during the industrial revolution, the world's population was 1.25 billion. This number increased to 3.7 billion by 1950. It has been predicted that by 2050 the population of the world will be about 7 billion!

Where will all these people live? Already many of the world's large cities are crowded with people. Yet we think that people will continue to migrate to cities. Perhaps *you* will live in a planned city, or even in an underwater or space city.

The inside of the hub of a space city may not appear very different from what cities look like on earth.

Agricultural Revolutions

Until recently there have been new lands to settle and new lands to farm.

Future cities in space may look like huge wheels.

Now almost all the land that can be farmed is already being used to produce food. The use of fertilizers and better seeds has increased food production. Yet today there is still not enough food in many places in the world. How will people in the future have enough to eat?

Some predict that the future will bring new agricultural revolutions. More food will be grown in giant greenhouses. There controlled conditions can produce more and better crops. It is also likely that more food will come from the sea. Already people are fish farming, and harvesting seaweed. There may also be a revolution in *what* we eat. We know that soybeans are a rich source of protein and a good substitute for meat. The menus of the future may include soybean steaks and seaweed salads.

The World's People—Past, Present, Future

The history you have read in this book has been the history of the people of the world. You have read about the first farmers, the builders of cities and empires, the creators of art and architecture. Our story includes people who explored and discovered new lands, new planets, and new ideas. All the people of the past, even those we may not know, have influenced us today. They have influenced where and how we live, and the governments we have.

Although you are at the end of this book, the story of the world's people continues. Even as you are reading, people everywhere are doing things that will influence you and the way you live. Perhaps someone is discovering a new medicine. Someone else may be beginning a new space journey. Yet what people do today is truly just a continuation of what people did in the past.

What will your world of tomorrow be like? Where will you be living? What kind of work will you be doing? Some of the answers depend on you. As the future unfolds, you will have an important part in it, just as people in the past and in the present have had. In the future, you will be a person who makes a difference. What difference will you make?

Economic Changes

The agricultural revolution and the industrial revolution greatly changed the ways people earned a living. Economic systems changed also. Now another change is taking place. Some people call it a computer revolution. Others call it an information revolution. Computers are greatly increasing the amount of available information. The trend will surely continue into the 21st century. It may influence your career.

Many people fear that, in time, people will be replaced by computers. This was the same kind of fear people had during the industrial revolution. Workers were afraid machines would replace them. However, people were not truly replaced then, and they probably will not be now. Rather, new technology frees people to do other kinds of work. In the future, fewer people will be needed to produce goods, but more will be needed to provide services for others. More people will enter service careers in law, medicine, nursing, education, and government in the 21st century.

Preparation for these careers is changing too. Many aspects of education are becoming more practical. More and more students prepare themselves for technological and service careers.

Resources in the Future

You learned in Units 17 and 18 of this book that industrialized countries need many resources. An important resource today and for the future is energy. Huge reserves of oil are found in Third World nations. Yet they will not likely be enough to meet all the world's needs tomorrow. So scientists are working to find how to use new forms of energy. Two new possible sources are very old ones— the sun and the wind. Perhaps sun and wind power will run factories and automobiles.

Scientists are working at ways to harness the vast energy of the sun.

A New Age of Exploration and Discovery

Copernicus and Galileo studied the universe to learn about our solar system. Columbus, Magellan, Cartier, and others looked for new routes to Asia and found new lands instead. The curiosity that guided the early discoverers and explorers guides people today. The new frontier for exploration is space. Technology has enabled us to explore space. Spacecraft may one day carry space-age immigrants to settle new cities in space.

Connections Among the World's People

For centuries it was possible to live on our planet without knowing much about people who lived far away. Migrations of people, movements of armies, and journeys of traders helped change all that. Ideas also began to spread faster after the invention of the printing press. Changes in transportation and communication have helped us learn more and more about our world neighbors. Understanding that people around the world are very much alike increases the chances for a peaceful 21st century. Planning for this future is the responsibility of all the world's people.

Checking Up

1. How much of an increase has there been in the world's population since the industrial revolution?
2. What is the computer or information revolution?
3. How have people around the world learned more about their neighbors?
4. What answers would you give to the key questions at the beginning of this chapter?
5. *Which predictions that you read about in this chapter do you think may come true? Which may not?*

Unit 18 Summary

- By 1900 a small number of industrial nations controlled colonies and territories all over the world.
- Imperialism was often in conflict with nationalism.
- World War I led to the breakup of empires within Europe and the emergence of many new countries.
- The Russian Revolution led to a fear of communism in much of the world.
- Nazi and Fascist policies brought about World War II.
- Many new countries were born in areas once under imperialist control following World War II.
- Technology has brought important changes to the people of the world.
- Life in the 21st century may be very different from life today.

Unit 18 Review Workshop

What Have You Learned?

A. Complete each of the following sentences with the correct word from the list below.

Bismarck	Lenin
Mussolini	Russia
Francis Ferdinand	Hitler
Great Britain	Japan

1. In 1914 it was said that the sun never set on the empire of

   _____.
2. _____ won Formosa in 1895.
3. _____ helped create the German Empire.
4. The assassination of _____ set off World War I.
5. _____ led the Bolsheviks.
6. _____ was the leader of the Fascists in Italy.
7. The Nazi leader was _____.
8. A communist revolution took place in _____ in 1917.

B. Choose the answer that correctly completes each statement.

1. An empire in Europe before World War I which did not contain many different nationalities was the (a) Austro-Hungarian (b) Russian (c) German.
2. The strong feeling people have for their country is called (a) imperialism (b) colonialism (c) nationalism.
3. The Allies in World War I did not include (a) France (b) Russia (c) the Ottoman Empire.
4. The idea of the League of Nations originated with (a) Lenin (b) Wilson (c) Mussolini.
5. World War II really began when (a) Japan invaded China (b) Italy invaded Ethiopia (c) Germany and the USSR invaded Poland.
6. The Axis in World War II did not include (a) Germany (b) Turkey (c) Japan.
7. Mao Tse-tung was leader of the Chinese (a) Nationalists (b) Communists (c) on Taiwan.
8. The first woman to become prime minister of England was (a) Golda Meir (b) Indira Gandhi (c) Margaret Thatcher.

Use Your Thinking Skills

In each of the following lists, choose the word that does not belong with the others.

1. *Imperialist nations in 1900:* Great Britain, Russia, Japan, India
2. *Central Powers in World War I:* Spain, Ottoman Empire, Germany, Austria-Hungary
3. *Twentieth century dictators:* Mussolini, Hitler, Wilson, Stalin
4. *Allies in World War II:* United States, Italy, Great Britain, France
5. *Communist-controlled nations today:* USSR, China, Poland, Japan
6. *Superpowers of 1980s:* United States, USSR, China, OPEC
7. *Third World areas:* Asia, Africa, Australia, Latin America

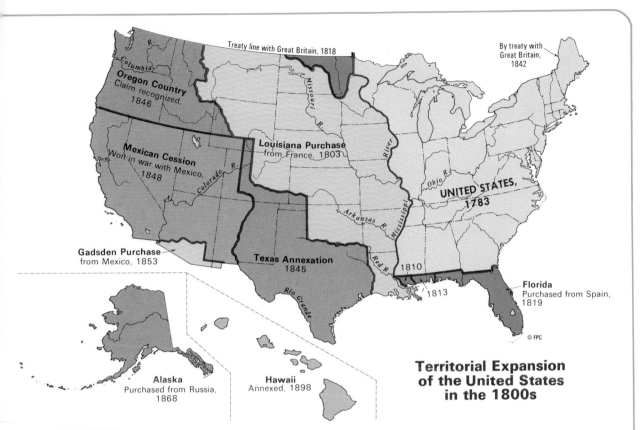

Territorial Expansion
of the United States
in the 1800s

(Map labels:)
Treaty line with Great Britain, 1818
By treaty with Great Britain, 1842
Columbia R.
Oregon Country Claim recognized, 1846
Missouri R.
Mexican Cession Won in war with Mexico, 1848
Louisiana Purchase from France, 1803
River
Colorado R.
Ohio R.
UNITED STATES, 1783
Arkansas R.
Mississippi R.
Gadsden Purchase from Mexico, 1853
Texas Annexation 1845
Red R.
1810
1813
Florida Purchased from Spain, 1819
Rio Grande
© FPC
Alaska Purchased from Russia, 1868
Hawaii Annexed, 1898

8. *Countries that were until World War II a part of empires:* Ghana, Vietnam, India, Mexico

Use Your Reading Skills

During the 1800s the United States more than doubled its size through the purchase, annexation, or conquest of land. Using the above map, find four areas that the United States purchased. When did the purchases take place? What two areas were annexed? When? What area was won in a war? What area did the United States gain by simply laying claim to it?

Learn by Doing

Certain areas in the world have been called trouble spots. These are the places where conflicts might easily occur. Some of these places are listed below. Working with several of your classmates, pick one of these areas and find out more about it. What are the problems there? Who is involved? What future does it have?

Latin America   South Africa
Eastern Europe   Southeast Asia
Middle East

Read to Learn More

Find the topics listed below in the card catalog of your library. Read all or part of a book listed under one of the topics. Share what you learn with your classmates.

IMPERIALISM   COMMUNISM
WORLD WAR I   COMPUTERS
WORLD WAR II   ENERGY

Appendix

Areas of the Oceans and Continents*

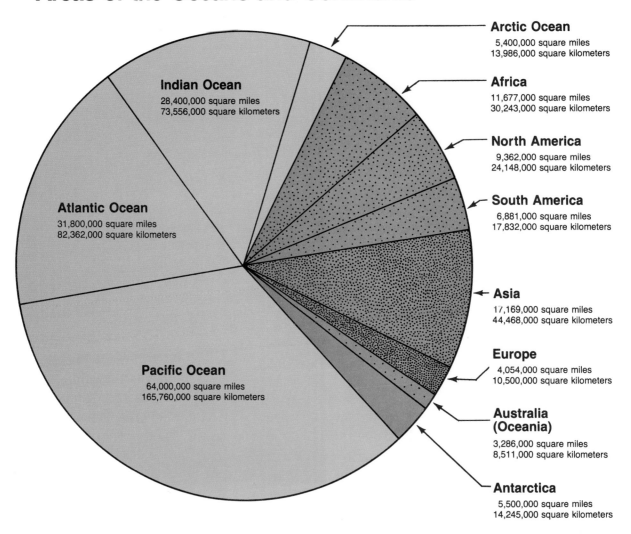

Arctic Ocean
5,400,000 square miles
13,986,000 square kilometers

Africa
11,677,000 square miles
30,243,000 square kilometers

North America
9,362,000 square miles
24,148,000 square kilometers

South America
6,881,000 square miles
17,832,000 square kilometers

Asia
17,169,000 square miles
44,468,000 square kilometers

Europe
4,054,000 square miles
10,500,000 square kilometers

Australia (Oceania)
3,286,000 square miles
8,511,000 square kilometers

Antarctica
5,500,000 square miles
14,245,000 square kilometers

Indian Ocean
28,400,000 square miles
73,556,000 square kilometers

Atlantic Ocean
31,800,000 square miles
82,362,000 square kilometers

Pacific Ocean
64,000,000 square miles
165,760,000 square kilometers

The Earth**

Total area of the earth (land and water) . . . . .197,000,000 sq. mi.; 510,000,000 sq. km.

Total land area of the earth (including inland waters and Antarctica) . . . . . . .58,000,000 sq. mi.; 150,000,000 sq. km.

Diameter of the earth (at the equator or through the poles) . . . . .8,000 mi.; 12,700 km.

Circumference of the earth (at the equator). . . . . .25,000 mi.; 40,000 km.

*All area figures are approximate.

**All figures are approximate, based on the best available sources.

478

Populations of the World's Largest Metropolitan Areas

15,589,000	New York, U.S.A.	7,000,000	Tientsin, China
13,994,000	Mexico City, Mexico	6,711,000	Chicago, U.S.A.
11,695,000	Tokyo, Japan	6,133,000	Cairo, Egypt
10,820,000	Shanghai, China	6,000,000	Chongqing, China
10,041,000	São Paulo, Brazil	5,971,000	Bombay, India
9,863,000	Paris, France	5,490,000	Jakarta, Indonesia
9,749,000	Buenos Aires, Argentina	5,000,000	Canton, China
9,478,000	Los Angeles, U.S.A.	4,904,000	Manila, Philippines
8,569,000	Osaka, Japan	4,867,000	Hong Kong (Victoria)
8,329,000	Rio de Janeiro, Brazil	4,835,000	Bangkok, Thailand
8,011,000	Moscow, USSR	4,716,000	Tehran, Iran
7,570,000	Peking, China	4,588,000	Leningrad, USSR
7,500,000	Seoul, South Korea	4,400,000	Shenyang, China
7,031,000	Calcutta, India	4,340,000	Detroit, U.S.A.
7,028,000	London, England	4,114,000	Philadelphia, U.S.A.

World's Major Seas
Area in square miles (sq. km)

1,148,500	(2,975,000)	South China Sea
1,049,000	(2,717,000)	Caribbean Sea
969,000	(2,510,000)	Mediterranean Sea
873,000	(2,261,000)	Bering Sea
613,800	(1,590,000)	Sea of Okhotsk
582,100	(1,507,000)	Gulf of Mexico
475,800	(1,232,000)	Hudson Bay

World's Largest Lakes
Area in square miles (sq. km)

143,550	(371,794)	Caspian Sea, Europe-Asia
31,820	(82,414)	Superior, North America
26,828	(69,485)	Victoria, Africa
25,300	(65,527)	Aral Sea, Asia
23,100	(59,829)	Huron, North America
22,400	(58,016)	Michigan, North America
12,700	(32,893)	Tanganyika, Africa

World's Longest Rivers
Length in miles (km)

4,132	(6,648)	Nile, Africa
3,915	(6,299)	Amazon, South America
3,892	(6,262)	Mississippi-Missouri, North America
3,461	(5,569)	Ob-Irtysh, Asia
3,434	(5,526)	Yangtze, Asia
2,903	(4,671)	Hwang Ho, Asia

Ocean Depths

Depth in feet (m)	Location	Ocean
36,198 (11,033)	Mariana Trench	Pacific
28,374 (8,648)	Puerto Rico Trench	Atlantic
25,344 (7,725)	Java Trench	Indian
17,880 (5,450)	Eurasian Basin	Arctic

Highest and Lowest Continent Points

Continent	Highest point	Elevation in feet (m)	Lowest point	Depth below sea level in feet (m)
North America	Mt. McKinley, U.S.A.	20,320 (6,194)	Death Valley, U.S.A.	282 (86)
South America	Mt. Aconcagua, Argentina	22,834 (6,960)	Valdez Peninsula, Argentina	131 (40)
Europe	Mont Blanc, France	15,771 (4,807)	Prins Alexander Polder, The Netherlands	22 (7)
Asia	Mt. Everest, Nepal-China	29,028 (8,848)	Dead Sea, Israel-Jordan	1,312 (399)
Africa	Mt. Kilimanjaro, Tanzania	19,340 (5,895)	Lake Assal, Djibouti	512 (156)
Australia	Mt. Kosciusko	7,310 (2,228)	Lake Eyre	52 (16)
Antarctica	Vinson Massif Group, Ellsworth Mountains	16,860 (5,139)	Sea Level	

NATIONS OF THE WORLD

Listed alphabetically by continent

Independent Nation	Area and Population	Population Density and Growth Rate	Capital and Population	*GNP (in millions of U.S. dollars) and Per Capita GNP	Major Exports (or chief sources of foreign income)	Major Imports
Africa						
Algeria	950,000 sq. mi. 19,026,000	20 per sq. mi. 3.2%	Algiers 1,800,000	$31,300 $1,720	petroleum, petroleum products	capital goods, food, semifinished goods
Angola	481,000 sq. mi. 6,781,000	14 per sq. mi. 2.4%	Luanda 480,600	$2,600 $440	oil, coffee, diamonds, sisal, fish, corn	machinery, iron, steel, metals
Benin	45,000 sq. mi. 3,522,000	78 per sq. mi. 2.8%	Porto-Novo 132,000	$660 $340	palm products, agricultural products	clothes, consumer goods, cement
Botswana	222,000 sq. mi. 795,000	4 per sq. mi. 2.6%	Gaborone 49,600	$230 $480	cattle, animal products, copper	food, vehicles, textiles
Burundi	11,000 sq. mi. 4,353,000	396 per sq. mi. 2.5%	Bujumbura 151,000	$610 $140	coffee, tea, hides, skins	textiles, food
Cameroon	184,000 sq. mi. 8,660,000	471 per sq. mi. 2.6%	Yaoundé 313,700	$4,900 $600	cocoa, coffee, timber, cotton	consumer goods, food, beverages
Cape Verde	1,200 sq. mi. 338,000	282 per sq. mi. 2.1%	Praia 21,500	$40 $136	fish, bananas, salt, flour	petroleum products, corn, rice
Central African Republic	242,000 sq. mi. 2,376,000	10 per sq. mi. 2.6%	Bangui 362,700	$530 $280	cotton, coffee, diamonds, timber	textiles, petroleum products, vehicles
Chad	496,000 sq. mi. 4,687,000	9 per sq. mi. 2.3%	N'Djamena 303,000	$930 $220	cotton, livestock, animal products	cement, petroleum, food, machinery
Comoros	840 sq. mi. 375,000	446 per sq. mi. 2.8%	Moroni 16,000	$69 $240	perfume oils, vanilla, copra	food, cement, fuel, chemicals
Congo	135,000 sq. mi. 1,573,000	12 per sq. mi. 2.8%	Brazzaville 310,000	$805 $540	lumber, tobacco, veneer, plywood	machinery, iron, steel, food
Djibouti	9,000 sq. mi. 286,000	32 per sq. mi. 5.1%	Djibouti 160,000	$336 $1,174	hides, skins, coffee	food, machinery
Egypt	386,000 sq. mi. 42,636,000	105 per sq. mi. 2.6%	Cairo 5,423,000	$17,800 $430	cotton, cotton products, petroleum	food, machinery, fertilizers, wood
Equatorial Guinea	11,000 sq. mi. 252,000	23 per sq. mi. 2.1%	Malabo 25,000	$70 $240	cocoa, coffee, wood	food, chemicals, chemical products
Ethiopia	455,000 sq. mi. 29,892,000	66 per sq. mi. 0.7%	Addis Ababa 1,277,200	$2,890 $100	coffee, hides, skins, oilseeds	petroleum
Gabon	102,000 sq. mi. 649,000	6 per sq. mi. 1.3%	Libreville 225,200	$3,000 $5,250	petroleum, wood, minerals, coffee	machinery, vehicles, food
Gambia	4,000 sq. mi. 609,000	152 per sq. mi. 2.8%	Banjul 47,700	$161 $280	peanuts, peanut products	textiles, food, tobacco, machinery
Ghana	92,000 sq. mi. 12,331,000	134 per sq. mi. 3.3%	Accra 716,600	$10,100 $849	cocoa, wood, gold, diamonds, manganese	textiles, food, manufactured goods
Guinea	95,000 sq. mi. 5,501,000	58 per sq. mi. 2.8%	Conakry 763,000	$1,200 $230	bauxite, alumina, coffee, pineapples	petroleum products, metals, machinery
Guinea-Bissau	14,000 sq. mi. 801,000	57 per sq. mi. 1.9%	Bissau 109,500	$170 $280	peanuts, coconuts, shrimp, fish, wool	food, manufactured goods, fuel
Ivory Coast	125,000 sq. mi. 8,156,000	65 per sq. mi. 3.3%	Abidjan 1,011,000	$9,100 $1,220	cocoa, coffee, wood, cotton, bananas	manufactured goods, consumer goods
Kenya	225,000 sq. mi. 16,759,000	74 per sq. mi. 4.0%	Nairobi 835,000	$5,300 $340	coffee, tea, livestock products	machinery, iron, petroleum, paper

*GNP: Gross National Product, or the total value of all the goods and services produced by the people of a country within one year
N/A: Not available

480

NATIONS OF THE WORLD

Listed alphabetically by continent

Independent Nation	Area and Population	Population Density and Growth Rate	Capital and Population	*GNP (in millions of U.S. dollars) and Per Capita GNP		Major Exports (or chief sources of foreign income)	Major Imports
Lesotho	12,000 sq. mi. 1,350,000	113 per sq. mi. 2.2%	Maseru 14,700	$210	$160	wool, mohair, wheat, cattle, diamonds	corn, building materials, clothes
Liberia	43,000 sq. mi. 1,872,000	43 per sq. mi. 3.1%	Monrovia 229,300	$810	$480	iron ore, rubber, diamonds, lumber	machinery, food, petroleum products
Libya	679,000 sq. mi. 3,075,000	5 per sq. mi. 3.4%	Tripoli 994,000	$20,000	$6,960	petroleum	manufactured goods, food
Madagascar	230,000 sq. mi. 8,665,000	37 per sq. mi. 2.5%	Antananarivo 468,000	$2,800	$340	coffee, vanilla, sugar, cloves	consumer goods, food, machinery
Malawi	37,000 sq. mi. 6,130,000	166 per sq. mi. 3.0%	Lilongwe 102,000	$870	$150	tobacco, tea, sugar, peanuts, cotton	manufactured goods, machinery, fuel
Mali	465,000 sq. mi. 6,735,000	13 per sq. mi. 2.7%	Bamako 440,000	$840	$130	livestock, peanuts, fish, cotton	textiles, vehicles, machinery, sugar
Mauritania	419,000 sq. mi. 1,517,000	4 per sq. mi. 1.9%	Nouakchott 135,000	$620	$400	iron ore, fish	food, petroleum, machinery
Mauritius	720 sq. mi. 961,000	1,335 per sq. mi. 1.4%	Port Louis 155,000	$870	$970	sugar, tea, molasses	food, manufactured goods
Morocco	190,000 sq. mi. 21,274,000	112 per sq. mi. 2.9%	Rabat 768,000	$14,700	$740	phosphates	manufactured goods, food
Mozambique	304,000 sq. mi. 10,461,000	34 per sq. mi. 2.8%	Maputo 750,000	$1,700	$170	cashew nuts, sugar, textiles, cotton	wheat
Namibia	318,000 sq. mi. 1,039,000	3 per sq. mi. 3.0%	Windhoek 77,400	N/A	N/A	livestock, diamonds	food
Niger	489,000 sq. mi. 5,585,000	11 per sq. mi. 2.9%	Niamey 225,300	$2,100	$410	uranium, peanuts, livestock, hides	fuel, machinery, food
Nigeria	375,000 sq. mi. 78,382,000	209 per sq. mi. 3.3%	Lagos 1,060,000	$46,500	$620	cocoa, palm products, rubber, timber, tin	machinery, chemicals
Rwanda	10,000 sq. mi. 5,198,000	520 per sq. mi. 3.2%	Kigali 117,750	$958	$210	coffee, tea	textiles, food, machinery
São Tomé and Principe	370 sq. mi. 83,000	224 per sq. mi. 1.1%	São Tomé 20,000	$20	$160	cocoa, copra, palm oil, coffee	communications equipment, food
Senegal	76,000 sq. mi. 5,757,000	76 per sq. mi. 2.7%	Dakar 914,500	$2,500	$450	peanuts, peanut products, phosphate	food, consumer goods
Seychelles	160 sq. mi. 64,000	400 per sq. mi. 1.5%	Victoria 23,000	$40	$710	cinnamon, vanilla, copra, fish	food, tobacco, machinery
Sierra Leone	28,000 sq. mi. 3,420,000	122 per sq. mi. 2.2%	Freetown 314,300	$540	$180	diamonds, iron ore, palm kernels	machinery, food
Somalia	246,000 sq. mi. 5,643,000	23 per sq. mi. 9.5%	Mogadishu 377,000	$340	$110	livestock, hides, skins, bananas	textiles, cereals, machinery
South Africa	472,000 sq. mi. 28,697,000	61 per sq. mi. 2.1%	Pretoria/ Capetown 528,000/ 892,000	$57,200	$2,040	wool, diamonds, corn, uranium, sugar, ores	vehicles, machinery, petroleum products
Sudan	967,000 sq. mi. 19,028,000	20 per sq. mi. 3.0%	Khartoum 1,621,000	$5,600	$270	cotton, peanuts, sesame	textiles, petroleum products, vehicles
Swaziland	7,000 sq. mi. 564,000	81 per sq. mi. 2.8%	Mbabane 23,000	$310	$630	sugar, iron ore, asbestos, wood, meat	vehicles, petroleum products, food

*GNP: Gross National Product, or the total value of all the goods and services produced by the people of a country within one year
N/A: Not available

481

NATIONS OF THE WORLD

Listed alphabetically by continent

Independent Nation	Area and Population	Population Density and Growth Rate	Capital and Population	*GNP (in millions of U.S. dollars) and Per Capita GNP	Major Exports (or chief sources of foreign income)	Major Imports
Tanzania	363,000 sq. mi. 18,829,000	52 per sq. mi. 3.1%	Dar es Salaam 860,000	$4,000 $220	coffee, cotton, tea, sisal, cashew nuts	manufactured goods, machinery, food
Togo	22,000 sq. mi. 2,661,000	121 per sq. mi. 3.0%	Lomé 283,000	$960 $380	phosphates, cocoa, palm kernels	consumer goods, fuel, food
Tunisia	64,000 sq. mi. 6,554,000	102 per sq. mi. 2.5%	Tunis 550,400	$6,100 $980	petroleum, olive oil, phosphates	raw materials, machinery, food
Uganda	91,000 sq. mi. 13,012,000	143 per sq. mi. 3.1%	Kampala 458,000	$930 $70	coffee, cotton, tea, copper	petroleum products, machinery, metals
Upper Volta	106,000 sq. mi. 6,895,000	65 per sq. mi. 2.3%	Ouagadougou 235,000	$870 $130	livestock, peanuts, cotton, sesame	textiles, food, consumer goods
Zaire	905,000 sq. mi. 29,344,000	32 per sq. mi. 2.9%	Kinshasa 2,242,300	$5,400 $200	copper, cobalt, diamonds, coffee	consumer goods, food, fuel
Zambia	288,000 sq. mi. 5,926,000	21 per sq. mi. 2.9%	Lusaka 684,000	$2,800 $500	copper, zinc, lead, cobalt, tobacco	machinery, food, fuel
Zimbabwe	151,000 sq. mi. 7,532,000	50 per sq. mi. 2.5%	Salisbury 627,000	$3,300 $470	tobacco, asbestos, copper, tin, chrome	machinery, wheat, petroleum products
Asia						
Afghanistan	250,000 sq. mi. 15,193,000	61 per sq. mi. 2.2%	Kabul 891,800	$3,400 $230	karakul skins, fruits, nuts, cotton	petroleum products, textiles
Bahrain	230 sq. mi. 392,000	1,704 per sq. mi. 4.0%	Manama 150,000	$1,700 $4,660	petroleum products, aluminum	manufactured goods, machinery, food
Bangladesh	55,019 sq. mi. 91,700,000	1,540 per sq. mi. 2.7%	Dacca 2,500,000	$9,100 $100	jute, hides, skins, leather, tea	machinery, food, grains, fuel
Bhutan	17,992 sq. mi. 1,318,000	73 per sq. mi. 2.3%	Thimbu 10,000	$90 $70	timber, fruits, vegetables	manufactured goods, machinery
Brunei	2,230 sq. mi. 232,000	104 per sq. mi. 5.8%	Bendar Seri Begawan 70,000	$460 $2,970	petroleum, natural gas	machinery, food, manufactured goods
Burma	262,007 sq. mi. 34,842,000	133 per sq. mi. 2.4%	Rangoon 2,186,000	$5,000 $150	rice, teak, machinery	textiles, manufactured goods
China	3,706,560 sq. mi. 1,034,364,000	260 per sq. mi. 1.4%	Peking 9,029,000	$517,000 $510	oil, minerals, metals	grain, chemical fertilizer
Cyprus	3,572 sq. mi. 629,000	176 per sq. mi. 0.8%	Nicosia 160,000	$1,970 $3,210	citrus fruits, wine, raisins, potatoes	manufactured goods, machinery
India	1,211,004 sq. mi. 686,131,000	519 per sq. mi. 1.8%	New Delhi 301,000	$116,000 $170	engineering goods, textiles, clothing	machinery, petroleum
Indonesia	736,000 sq. mi. 152,754,000	21 per sq. mi. 2.9%	Jakarta 6,397,000	$51,200 $350	petroleum, timber, rubber, coffee, tin	rice, wheat, textiles, chemicals
Iran	636,000 sq. mi. 39,097,000	61 per sq. mi. 2.9%	Tehran 4,530,200	$81,700 $2,170	petroleum, carpets, cotton, fruits, nuts	machinery, iron and steel products
Iraq	172,000 sq. mi. 13,596,000	79 per sq. mi. 3.5%	Baghdad 3,205,600	$35,200 $2,730	petroleum products	manufactured goods
Israel	8,000 sq. mi. 3,814,000	477 per sq. mi. 2.3%	Jerusalem 398,200	$17,000 $4,640	diamonds, fruits, textiles, food	military equipment, chemicals, cereals
Japan	143,000 sq. mi. 117,266,000	82 per sq. mi. 0.8%	Tokyo 8,179,000	$1,011,000 $8,700	machinery, iron and steel, chemicals	fossil fuels, food, machinery

*GNP: Gross National Product, or the total value of all the goods and services produced by the people of a country within one year
N/A: Not available

NATIONS OF THE WORLD

Listed alphabetically by continent

Independent Nation	Area and Population	Population Density and Growth Rate	Capital and Population	*GNP (in millions of U.S. dollars) and Per Capita GNP	Major Exports (or chief sources of foreign income)	Major Imports
Jordan	37,100 sq. mi. 3,150,000	85 per sq. mi. 3.4%	Amman 684,000	$2,800 $1,250	fruits, vegetables, phosphates	petroleum products, textiles, food
Kampuchea	70,000 sq. mi. 5,565,000	80 per sq. mi. N/A	Phnom Penh 270,000	$500 $50	rubber, rice, wood, pepper	food, fuel, machinery
Korea, North	47,000 sq. mi. 19,627,000	418 per sq. mi. 3.2%	Pyongyang 1,500,000	$14,100 $750	minerals, chemicals, metal products	machinery, food, petroleum, coal
Korea, South	38,190 sq. mi. 40,098,000	1,050 per sq. mi. 1.6%	Seoul 8,114,000	$60,100 $1,600	textiles, clothing, machinery, plywood	machinery, steel, petroleum, textiles
Kuwait	6,200 sq. mi. 1,418,000	229 per sq. mi. 6.3%	Kuwait 78,100	$23,500 $18,390	petroleum products	machinery, food, manufactured goods
Laos	91,430 sq. mi. 3,499,000	38 per sq. mi. 1.1%	Vientiane 176,637	$290 $90	forest products, tin, coffee, tobacco	rice, petroleum products
Lebanon	4,000 sq. mi. 3,059,000	765 per sq. mi. 2.6%	Beirut 475,000	$3,600 $730	fruits, nuts, grain, vegetables	machinery, flour, petroleum
Malaysia	128,000 sq. mi. 14,179,000	111 per sq. mi. 2.4%	Kuala Lumpur 1,081,000	$19,600 $1,480	rubber, palm oil, tin, timber	machinery, manufactured goods
Maldives	110 sq. mi. 157,000	1,427 per sq. mi. 3.0%	Male 29,600	$30 $190	fish	rice, sugar
Mongolia	604,100 sq. mi. 1,681,000	3 per sq. mi. 2.6%	Ulan Bator 403,000	$750 $500	meat products, wool, minerals	machinery, sugar, petroleum, tea
Nepal	54,590 sq. mi. 15,153,000	278 per sq. mi. 2.4%	Katmandu 171,400	N/A $130	rice, jute, timber	manufactured goods, fuel
Oman	82,000 sq. mi. 591,000	7 per sq. mi. 3.0%	Muscat 15,000	$2,600 $4,600	petroleum products	manufactured goods, machinery
Pakistan	310,000 sq. mi. 87,720,000	283 per sq. mi. 2.8%	Islamabad 77,300	$23,000 $290	rice, cotton, carpets, leather	petroleum products, sugar, machinery
Philippines	116,000 sq. mi. 49,481,000	427 per sq. mi. 2.5%	Manila 5,900,600	$29,200 $620	coconut, sugar, rice, timber, copper	petroleum products, wheat
Qatar	4,000 sq. mi. 225,000	56 per sq. mi. 4.4%	Doha 180,000	$5,000 $29,900	petroleum products	manufactured goods, machinery, food
Saudi Arabia	900,000 sq. mi. 10,112,000	11 per sq. mi. 5.6%	Riyadh 1,044,000	$77,000 $9,500	petroleum, petroleum products	manufactured goods, food
Singapore	225 sq. mi. 2,406,000	10,693 per sq. mi. 1.2%	Singapore 2,390,000	$9,000 $3,810	petroleum products, rubber	manufactured goods, petroleum
Sri Lanka	25,300 sq. mi. 14,973,000	592 per sq. mi. 1.7%	Colombo 624,000	$3,200 $220	tea, rubber, coconuts	rice, flour, petroleum
Syria	72,000 sq. mi. 8,955,000	124 per sq. mi. 3.4%	Damascus 1,156,000	$7,800 $960	petroleum, textiles, tobacco, fruits	machinery, metal products, fuel
Thailand	198,000 sq. mi. 48,328,000	244 per sq. mi. 2.3%	Bangkok 4,178,000	$27,300 $590	rice, sugar, corn, rubber, tin	machinery, fuel, metals, chemicals
Turkey	296,000 sq. mi. 46,139,000	156 per sq. mi. 2.3%	Ankara 2,106,000	$67,700 $1,530	cotton, tobacco, fruits, nuts	petroleum, metals, machinery
United Arab Emirates	32,000 sq. mi. 934,000	29 per sq. mi. 4.0%	Abu Dhabi 95,000	$21,000 $24,360	petroleum, pearls, fish	food, manufactured goods

*GNP: Gross National Product, or the total value of all the goods and services produced by the people of a country within one year
N/A: Not available

NATIONS OF THE WORLD

Listed alphabetically by continent

Independent Nation	Area and Population	Population Density and Growth Rate	Capital and Population	*GNP (in millions of U.S. dollars) and Per Capita GNP	Major Exports (or chief sources of foreign income)	Major Imports
Vietnam	111,000 sq. mi. 54,382,000	490 per sq. mi. 2.5%	Hanoi 1,443,500	$7,600 $150	agricultural and handicraft products	petroleum, steel, chemicals
Yemen, North	75,000 sq. mi. 5,305,000	71 per sq. mi. 2.3%	San'a 210,000	$3,800 $740	cotton, coffee, hides, vegetables	textiles, sugar, manufactured goods
Yemen, South	111,000 sq. mi. 1,930,000	17 per sq. mi. 2.4%	Aden 343,000	$790 $430	petroleum, petroleum products	manufactured goods, machinery
Australia and Oceania						
Australia	2,832,000 sq. mi. 14,676,000	5 per sq. mi. 1.2%	Canberra 241,300	$120,400 $8,360	agricultural products, metals	manufactured goods, raw materials
Fiji	7,055 sq. mi. 636,000	90 per sq. mi. 1.8%	Suva 63,600	$810 $1,300	sugar, coconut oil	machinery, fuel, chemicals
Kiribati	264 sq. mi. 58,000	220 per sq. mi. 1.6%	Tarawa 1,800	$40 $630	phosphate, copra	food, fuel
Nauru	8 sq. mi. 7,000	875 per sq. mi. N/A	Yaren N/A	$150 $21,400	phosphate	food, fuel
New Zealand	103,581 sq. mi. 3,152,000	30 per sq. mi. 0.0%	Wellington 137,600	$13,000 $4,350	meat, dairy products, wool	machinery, manufactured goods
Papua New Guinea	183,540 sq. mi. 3,204,000	17 per sq. mi. 2.7%	Port Moresby 121,600	$2,000 $650	copper, coconut, coffee, copra	machinery, manufactured goods
Solomon Islands	11,500 sq. mi. 233,000	20 per sq. mi. 3.4%	Honiara 18,500	$70 $320	copra, timber, fish	fuel
Tonga	377 sq. mi. 99,000	263 per sq. mi. 2.1%	Nukualofa 18,300	$30 $370	copra, coconut, bananas	food, machinery, petroleum
Tuvalu	10 sq. mi. 7,000	700 per sq. mi. 2.1%	Funafuti 2,200	$1.2 $180	copra	food, mineral fuel
Vanuatu	5,700 sq. mi. 119,000	21 per sq. mi. 2.7%	Port-Vila 14,590	N/A N/A	copra, fish, meat	food
Western Samoa	1,100 sq. mi. 157,000	143 per sq. mi. 1.0%	Apia 33,400	$70 $450	copra, cocoa, timber, bananas	food, manufactured goods, machinery
Europe and the Soviet Union						
Albania	11,000 sq. mi. 2,705,000	246 per sq. mi. 2.1%	Tirana 192,300	$1,200 $520	minerals, metals, fuel, food	machinery, metals, minerals, fuel
Andorra	180 sq. mi. 31,000	172 per sq. mi. 6.5%	Andorra 10,900	N/A N/A	livestock, wheat, vegetables	tourism, machinery, consumer goods
Austria	32,000 sq. mi. 7,506,000	235 per sq. mi. 0.0%	Vienna 1,580,600	$68,600 $9,150	iron and steel products, lumber	machinery, food, textiles
Belgium	12,000 sq. mi. 9,861,000	822 per sq. mi. 0.1%	Brussels 144,000	$112,300 $11,370	iron and steel products, textiles	machinery, fuel, vehicles, textiles
Bulgaria	43,000 sq. mi. 8,885,000	207 per sq. mi. 0.4%	Sofia 1,031,000	$26,800 $3,020	machinery, fuel, raw materials, food	machinery, fuel, minerals, food
Czechoslovakia	49,000 sq. mi. 15,375,000	314 per sq. mi. 0.6%	Prague 1,188,600	$76,500 $5,020	machinery, fuel, raw materials, food	machinery, fuel, raw materials
Denmark	17,000 sq. mi. 5,133,000	302 per sq. mi. 0.2%	Copenhagen 658,000	$70,300 $13,700	meat, dairy products, textiles	industrial machinery

*GNP: Gross National Product, or the total value of all the goods and services produced by the people of a country within one year
N/A: Not available

NATIONS OF THE WORLD

Listed alphabetically by continent

Independent Nation	Area and Population	Population Density and Growth Rate	Capital and Population	*GNP (in millions of U.S. dollars) and Per Capita GNP	Major Exports (or chief sources of foreign income)	Major Imports
Finland	130,000 sq. mi. 4,784,000	37 per sq. mi. 0.3%	Helsinki 483,700	$31,000 $6,530	timber, paper, ships, machinery	food, petroleum, chemicals, iron
France	213,000 sq. mi. 53,853,000	253 per sq. mi. 0.4%	Paris 2,102,900	$535,000 $10,010	machinery, iron and steel products	petroleum, iron and steel products
Germany, East	42,000 sq. mi. 16,759,000	399 per sq. mi. −0.1%	East Berlin 1,333,900	$89,000 $5,310	chemicals, coal, ships	petroleum, steel products, metals
Germany, West	96,000 sq. mi. 61,388,000	639 per sq. mi. −0.1%	Bonn 286,000	$766,100 $12,500	machines, tools, chemicals	manufactured goods, fuel
Greece	51,000 sq. mi. 9,556,000	187 per sq. mi. 0.7%	Athens 867,000	$39,500 $4,210	tobacco, minerals, fruits, textiles	machinery, petroleum
Hungary	36,000 sq. mi. 10,730,000	298 per sq. mi. 0.2%	Budapest 2,060,000	$35,800 $3,340	machinery, consumer goods, raw materials	machinery, food, energy sources
Iceland	40,000 sq. mi. 229,000	6 per sq. mi. 1.1%	Reykjavik 83,500	$2,380 $10,600	fish and fish products, aluminum	machinery, food, petroleum
Ireland	27,000 sq. mi. 3,431,000	127 per sq. mi. 1.2%	Dublin 544,600	$14,700 $4,500	dairy products, animals, textiles	petroleum, petroleum products
Italy	116,000 sq. mi. 57,089,000	492 per sq. mi. 0.3%	Rome 2,911,700	$320,000 $5,700	machinery, food, textiles, chemicals	machinery, food, iron, metals, wool
Liechtenstein	65 sq. mi. 27,000	415 per sq. mi. 1.9%	Vaduz 4,900	$378 $14,000	postage stamps, leather goods	machinery, petroleum products
Luxembourg	1,000 sq. mi. 365,000	365 per sq. mi. 0.2%	Luxembourg 79,600	$4,400 $12,300	iron and steel products	coal, consumer goods
Malta	121 sq. mi. 348,000	2,876 per sq. mi. 1.2%	Valletta 14,000	$760 $2,290	clothing, textiles, ships	consumer goods, fuel
Monaco	1 sq. mi. 25,000	25,000 per sq. mi. N/A	Monaco 25,000	N/A N/A	tourism, postage stamps, chemicals	machinery, consumer goods
Netherlands	13,000 sq. mi. 14,182,000	1,091 per sq. mi. 0.6%	Amsterdam 716,000	$165,100 $11,710	food, machinery, chemicals	machinery, food, chemicals, ores
Norway	125,000 sq. mi. 4,092,000	33 per sq. mi. 0.3%	Oslo 457,200	$46,300 $11,360	petroleum, natural gas, metals, pulp	food, ships, fuel, vehicles, iron
Poland	121,000 sq. mi. 35,746,000	295 per sq. mi. 1.0%	Warsaw 1,552,300	$119,200 $3,370	machinery, fuel, agricultural products	machinery, fuel
Portugal	36,000 sq. mi. 9,915,000	275 per sq. mi. 0.5%	Lisbon 861,500	$95,200 $2,740	cotton, cork, resin, canned fish, timber	petroleum, cotton, machinery, iron
Rumania	92,000 sq. mi. 22,302,000	242 per sq. mi. 0.7%	Bucharest 1,858,000	$79,000 $3,580	machinery, food, consumer goods	machinery, fuel, minerals, metals
San Marino	24 sq. mi. 21,000	875 per sq. mi. N/A	San Marino 8,500	N/A N/A	tourism, stone, lumber, wheat, nuts	consumer goods, machinery
Spain	195,000 sq. mi. 37,610,000	193 per sq. mi. 0.9%	Madrid 3,232,300	$197,000 $5,250	cars, iron and steel products, machinery	fuel, machinery, chemicals, iron
Sweden	173,000 sq. mi. 8,322,000	48 per sq. mi. 0.2%	Stockholm 649,400	$102,800 $12,390	machinery, vehicles, wood pulp	machinery, vehicles, petroleum products
Switzerland	16,000 sq. mi. 6,328,000	396 per sq. mi. −0.2%	Bern 142,900	$99,000 $15,750	machinery, chemicals, precision instruments	machinery, metals, chemicals, textiles
United Kingdom	94,000 sq. mi. 55,966,000	595 per sq. mi. 0.0%	London 6,877,100	$488,700 $8,760	machinery, chemicals, metals, food	food, petroleum, machinery

*GNP: Gross National Product, or the total value of all the goods and services produced by the people of a country within one year
N/A: Not available

NATIONS OF THE WORLD
Listed alphabetically by continent

Independent Nation	Area and Population	Population Density and Growth Rate	Capital and Population	*GNP (in millions of U.S. dollars) and Per Capita GNP	Major Exports (or chief sources of foreign income)	Major Imports
USSR (Soviet Union)	8,600,000 sq. mi. 266,754,000	31 per sq. mi. 0.8%	Moscow 8,100,000	$1,374,800 $5,210	petroleum, metals, agricultural products	complex machinery, steel products
Vatican City	0.2 sq. mi. 1,000	5,000 per sq. mi. N/A	Vatican City 729	N/A N/A	tourism, postage stamps	N/A
Yugoslavia	99,000 sq. mi. 22,451,000	227 per sq. mi. 0.8%	Belgrade 967,000	$64,400 $2,900	raw materials, consumer goods	raw materials, consumer goods
North America						
Antigua and Barbuda	170 sq. mi. 76,000	447 per sq. mi. 1.3%	St. Johns 19,000	$76 $1,000	clothing, lobsters	fuel, food, machinery
Bahamas	4,400 sq. mi. 249,000	57 per sq. mi. 3.4%	Nassau 133,300	$1,080 $4,650	medicines, cement	food, manufactured goods
Barbados	166 sq. mi. 256,000	1,542 per sq. mi. 0.4%	Bridgetown 7,600	$640 $2,360	sugar, sugarcane, electrical parts	food, consumer goods, machinery
Belize	8,970 sq. mi. 146,000	16 per sq. mi. 1.9%	Belmopan 4,500	$120 $790	sugar, clothing, fish, molasses	machinery, food, manufactured goods
Canada	3,849,000 sq. mi. 24,033,000	6 per sq. mi. 0.9%	Ottawa 738,600	$222,200 $9,350	transportation equipment, wheat	transportation equipment, steel
Costa Rica	20,000 sq. mi. 2,269,000	113 per sq. mi. 2.6%	San José 637,000	$4,000 $1,850	coffee, bananas, beef, sugar, cocoa	manufactured goods, machinery, fuel
Cuba	44,000 sq. mi. 9,796,000	223 per sq. mi. 1.1%	Havana 1,998,100	$13,300 $1,360	sugar, nickel, shellfish, tobacco	machinery, food, petroleum
Dominica	300 sq. mi. 79,000	263 per sq. mi. 0.6%	Roseau 16,800	$30 $430	bananas, lime juice, oil, cocoa	machinery, food, manufactured goods
Dominican Republic	19,000 sq. mi. 5,762,000	303 per sq. mi. 2.5%	Santo Domingo 1,103,400	$5,500 $990	sugar, nickel, coffee, tobacco, cocoa	food, petroleum, machinery
El Salvador	8,000 sq. mi. 4,879,000	610 per sq. mi. 3.0%	San Salvador 443,000	$3,500 $750	coffee, cotton, sugar	machinery, cars, petroleum, food
Grenada	130 sq. mi. 107,000	823 per sq. mi. 1.0%	St. Georges 30,813	$71 $660	cocoa, nutmeg, mace, bananas	food, machinery, building materials
Guatemala	42,000 sq. mi. 7,166,000	171 per sq. mi. 3.0%	Guatemala City 1,004,000	$6,900 $1,010	coffee, bananas, sugar, meat	manufactured goods, machinery, fuel
Haiti	11,000 sq. mi. 5,878,000	534 per sq. mi. 2.4%	Port-au-Prince 745,000	$1,500 $260	coffee, industrial products, sugar	consumer goods, food, petroleum
Honduras	43,000 sq. mi. 3,838,000	89 per sq. mi. 3.4%	Tegucigalpa 316,800	$2,164 $590	bananas, coffee, lumber, meat	manufactured goods, machinery
Jamaica	4,000 sq. mi. 2,255,000	564 per sq. mi. 1.2%	Kingston 643,000	$2,900 $1,300	alumina, bauxite, sugar, bananas	fuel, machinery, food, fertilizer
Mexico	764,000 sq. mi. 68,236,000	89 per sq. mi. 2.4%	Mexico City 9,191,300	$119,900 $1,810	cotton, coffee, sugar, shrimp	machinery, consumer goods
Nicaragua	57,000 sq. mi. 2,465,000	43 per sq. mi. 2.8%	Managua 517,000	$1,340 $540	cotton, coffee, chemical products	agricultural products
Panama	29,000 sq. mi. 1,939,000	67 per sq. mi. 2.2%	Panama City 388,600	$2,850 $1,530	bananas, petroleum products, sugar	manufactured goods, petroleum
St. Lucia	240 sq. mi. 124,000	517 per sq. mi. 1.7%	Castries 45,000	$80 $690	bananas, cocoa	food, machinery, fertilizers

*GNP: Gross National Product, or the total value of all the goods and services produced by the people of a country within one year
N/A: Not available

NATIONS OF THE WORLD

Listed alphabetically by continent

Independent Nation	Area and Population	Population Density and Growth Rate	Capital and Population	*GNP (in millions of U.S. dollars) and Per Capita GNP	Major Exports (or chief sources of foreign income)	Major Imports
St. Vincent and the Grenadines	150 sq. mi. 116,000	773 per sq. mi. 2.9%	Kingstown 22,800	$40 $380	bananas, arrowroot, copra	food, machinery, chemicals
Trinidad and Tobago	2,000 sq. mi. 1,176,000	588 per sq. mi. 1.5%	Port-of-Spain 47,300	$4,500 $3,960	petroleum, petroleum products	petroleum, metals, machinery, food
United States	3,619,000 sq. mi. 226,505,000	63 per sq. mi. 0.9%	Washington, D.C. 674,000	$2,626,000 $11,590	machinery, chemicals, grain	mineral fuels, machinery, metals
South America						
Argentina	1,047,000 sq. mi. 27,874,000	27 per sq. mi. 1.6%	Buenos Aires 2,985,000	$62,000 $2,300	meat, corn, wheat, wool, hides, oilseeds	machinery, fuel, iron, steel
Bolivia	424,000 sq. mi. 5,420,000	13 per sq. mi. 2.6%	La Paz/Sucre 696,800/66,300	$4,100 $800	tin, petroleum, lead, zinc, silver, gold	food, chemicals, medicines
Brazil	3,290,000 sq. mi. 123,388,000	38 per sq. mi. 2.3%	Brasília 978,600	$215,000 $1,800	coffee, iron ore, cotton, soybeans	machinery, wheat, chemicals, copper
Chile	292,000 sq. mi. 11,091,000	38 per sq. mi. 1.5%	Santiago 3,853,000	$19,000 $1,740	copper, iron ore, paper products	petroleum, wheat, sugar, cotton
Colombia	440,000 sq. mi. 27,025,000	61 per sq. mi. 2.1%	Bogotá 4,293,900	$26,200 $1,000	coffee, fuel, cotton, tobacco, sugar	machinery, paper, fertilizers
Ecuador	106,000 sq. mi. 8,124,000	77 per sq. mi. 3.0%	Quito 807,000	$8,600 $1,100	petroleum, bananas, coffee, cocoa, sugar	agricultural machinery
Guyana	83,000 sq. mi. 850,000	10 per sq. mi. 1.4%	Georgetown 63,200	$520 $630	bauxite, sugar, rice, alumina, shrimp	manufactured goods, machinery, food
Paraguay	157,000 sq. mi. 3,230,000	21 per sq. mi. 2.4%	Asunción 529,000	$2,000 $840	cotton, oilseeds, meat products	fuel, machinery, motors, beverages
Peru	496,000 sq. mi. 17,843,000	36 per sq. mi. 2.6%	Lima 4,376,100	$11,100 $640	copper, fish, silver, iron, cotton, sugar	food, machinery, iron, steel
Surinam	55,000 sq. mi. 388,000	7 per sq. mi. −0.6%	Paramaribo 102,300	$820 $2,130	alumina, bauxite, aluminum, rice, wood	petroleum, iron, steel, cotton
Uruguay	72,000 sq. mi. 2,934,000	41 per sq. mi. 0.6%	Montevideo 1,238,100	$7,000 $2,400	wool, hides, meat, textiles	petroleum, metals, machinery
Venezuela	352,000 sq. mi. 15,284,000	43 per sq. mi. 3.3%	Caracas 2,944,400	$49,000 $3,970	petroleum, iron ore, coffee	industrial machines, machinery, wheat

*GNP: Gross National Product, or the total value of all the goods and services produced by the people of a country within one year
N/A: Not available

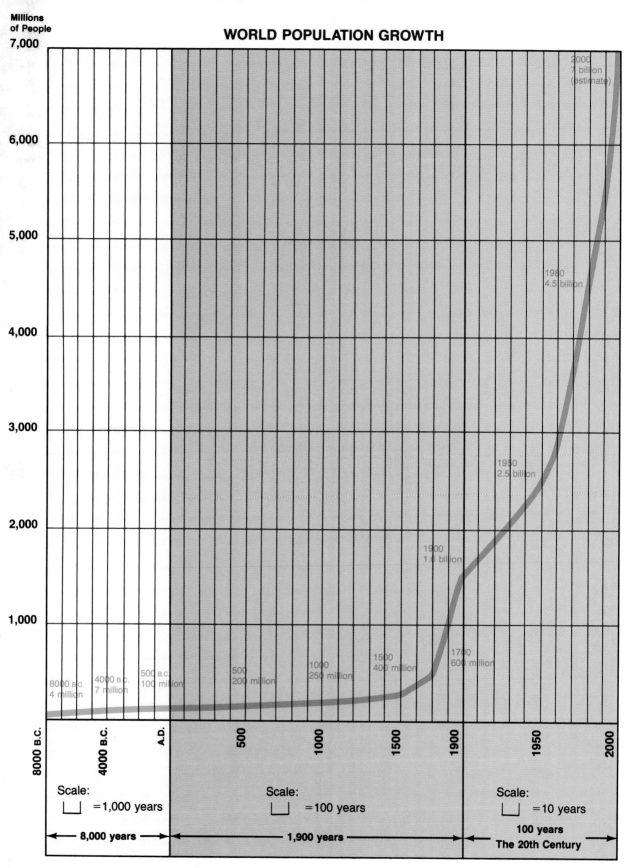

WORLD POPULATION GROWTH

Millions
of People

7,000 — 2000
7 billion
(estimate)

6,000

5,000 — 1980
4.5 billion

4,000

3,000 — 1950
2.5 billion

2,000 — 1900
1.6 billion

1,000 — 1700
600 million

1500
400 million

1000
250 million

500
200 million

500 B.C.
100 million

4000 B.C.
7 million

8000 B.C.
4 million

8000 B.C.   4000 B.C.   A.D.   500   1000   1500   1900   1950   2000

Scale:
⌐⌐ =1,000 years

Scale:
⌐⌐ =100 years

Scale:
⌐⌐ =10 years

◄— 8,000 years —►

◄————— 1,900 years —————►

100 years
The 20th Century

488

The graph above is actually three graphs combined. Each colored panel is a graph drawn on a scale that differs from the scales of the other two. Placing the graphs side by side makes it possible to show population growth since the end of the Ice Age on a single graph curve. If only one graph were drawn using the scale of the orange panel, the yellow panel would be 13¼ inches wide and the red panel would be only 5⁄32 of an inch wide.

THE WORLD ENERGY PICTURE

World Energy Sources

- ▨ Coal
- ▨ Oil
- ▨ Natural gas
- ☐ Hydroelectric and geothermal power
- ▨ Nuclear power

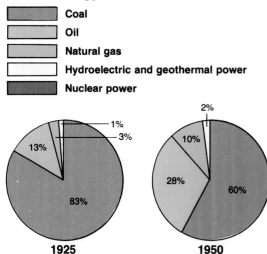

1925 — 83%, 13%, 3%, 1%

1950 — 60%, 28%, 10%, 2%

1975 — 48%, 31%, 18.5%, 2%, 0.5%

1980 — 45%, 27%, 19%, 5%, 4%

Major Nuclear Power Producers

Country	Working plants	Plants planned or under construction	Capacity of working plants*
United States	71	130	54,180
Japan	20	10	12,840
Great Britain	30	6	9,040
USSR	22	14	8,475
France	15	36	7,800
West Germany	14	13	7,050
Canada	8	15	5,590
Sweden	6	6	3,850
Belgium	3	4	1,740
Italy	4	5	1,490
East Germany	4	3	1,390
Spain	3	15	1,120
Switzerland	3	4	1,060

*In thousands of kilowatt–hours (as of 1982)

Population and Energy

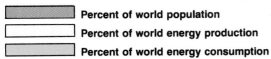

- ▨ Percent of world population
- ☐ Percent of world energy production
- ▨ Percent of world energy consumption

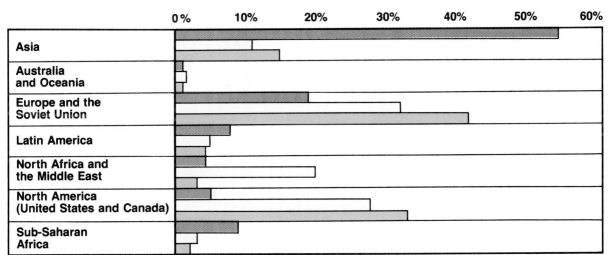

0% 10% 20% 30% 40% 50% 60%

- Asia
- Australia and Oceania
- Europe and the Soviet Union
- Latin America
- North Africa and the Middle East
- North America (United States and Canada)
- Sub-Saharan Africa

489

Glossary

In this Glossary you will find many words and phrases used in this book, including all those listed at the beginning of each chapter. You may use the Glossary as you would a dictionary. But only the word meaning that will be most helpful to you in the study of this book is given in the Glossary. You can find more meanings if you look up the words and phrases in a dictionary. Every word has been spelled phonetically, or by sounds, within parentheses following the word, and those sounds are marked to help you pronounce the word correctly. The Pronunciation Key below shows what the marks mean and gives examples of how to pronounce the sounds.

Pronunciation Key

a at	e met	ī hike	o͞o good
ā fade	ē me	ō open	o͞o soon
ã air	ə about; after; up	ô for; awful	ou loud
ä far; father; hot	i it	oi oil	zh garage

abdicate (ab'də·kāt) To give up a high office or title.

absolute monarch (ab'sə·lo͞ot' män'ərk) A king or queen who holds complete and unlimited power.

acupuncture (ak'yo͞o·pəngk'chər) Chinese medical practice involving the piercing of certain parts of the body with special needles.

adapt (ə·dapt') To change, often to meet some special need.

agora (ag'ə·rə) The marketplace in an ancient Greek city, a central gathering place.

agricultural revolution (ag'ri·kəl'chər·əl rev'ə·lo͞o'shən) The change from food gathering to food producing and the other changes in people's lives brought about by the development of farming.

agriculture (ag'ri·kəl'chər) The practice of farming; growing crops and raising livestock.

alliance (ə·lī'əns) An agreement among nations to band together for some special purpose, as to help one another in case of attack by an enemy.

ally (al'ī) A country that joins with another country for common support and protection.

ambassador (am·bas'ə·dər) A person who represents his or her government in a foreign country.

amendment (ə·mend'mənt) A change or addition to something.

ancestor (an'ses'tər) One from whom a person is descended.

annexation (an'ek·sā'shən) The act of joining a new territory to a state or nation.

anthropologist (an'thrə·päl'ə·jəst) A scientist who studies people and their way of living.

apprentice (ə·pren'tis) A person who works for and learns a trade from a skilled worker; in the Middle Ages, a young person who trained under a master.

aqueduct (ak'wi·dəkt') A structure used to carry water over long distances.

archaeologist (är'kē·äl'ə·jəst) A scientist who studies very old remains in order to learn about the past.

architecture (är'kə·tek'chər) The art and science of designing buildings.

aristocracy (är'ə·stäk'rə·sē) A form of government in which an upper class of wealthy or noble-born people hold power.

armada (är·mä'də) A fleet of warships.

assembly (ə·sem'blē) A group of persons gathered together for a special purpose, such as making laws; a legislature.

astrolabe (as'trə·lāb') An instrument used to help sailors find their way by measuring the height of the sun or stars above the horizon.

astronomy (ə·strän'ə·mē) The study of stars, planets, and other heavenly bodies and their movements.

atrium (ā'trē·əm) A central courtyard in a Roman house.

axis (ak'sis) An imaginary line through the center of the earth from the North to the South Pole.

balance of power (bal'əns əv pou'ər) The distribution of power among nations so that no one nation is strong enough to conquer the others.

490

balance of trade (bal'əns əv trād) The difference in value between a nation's imports and exports.

bamboo (bam·boo') A high, treelike grass; the hard stalk of such a plant, used to make houses, furniture, baskets, and other items.

barbarian (bär·bâr'ē·ən) 1 To the Greeks, anyone who was not a Greek. 2 A person belonging to a group regarded as uncivilized.

barter (bär'tər) To trade goods or services without the use of money.

basin (bā'sən) An area of land largely enclosed by higher land.

Bedouin (bed'ə·wən) A nomadic Arab.

boundary (boun'də·rē) A border; a line between separate political units.

bushido (boosh'i·dō') "The way of the warrior"; code of behavior of the samurai class in feudal Japan.

business cycle (biz'nis sī'kəl) A repeating pattern of growth and decline in industry.

Byzantine (biz'ən·tēn') Relating to the art or culture of the Byzantine Empire, the eastern part of the later Roman Empire.

cacao (kə·kou') A tropical tree producing seeds, or beans, from which chocolate is made.

caliph (kā'lif) A successor to Muhammad.

canal (kə·nal') A channel dug for irrigation or transportation.

cape (kāp) A point of land stretching out into a body of water.

capital (kap'ə·təl) Wealth that can be used to create more wealth.

capitalism (kap'ət·əl·iz'əm) An economic system based on private ownership of business and industry.

capitol (kap'ə·təl) The building where a legislature meets.

caravan (kär'ə·van') A train of pack animals that carries traders and their goods overland.

caste (kast) The Hindu system of dividing people into groups according to the kind of work they do or by the class into which they were born.

cataract (kat'ə·rakt') A high waterfall.

cathedral (kə·thē'drəl) A great church; the seat of a bishop.

Caucasian (kô·kā'zhən) The race, or division of humans, to which most Europeans and Middle Easterners belong.

causeway (kôz'wā') A raised road; highway.

cavalry (kav'əl·rē) Soldiers who fight on horseback; a unit of such mounted soldiers.

cenote (si·nōt'ē) A natural underground water source found in limestone areas such as the Yucatán Peninsula.

central government (sen'trəl gəv'ərn·mənt) A government that brings all parts of a country together under a single authority.

city-state (sit'ē·stāt') A self-governing city that controls the villages and farmlands surrounding it.

civilization (siv'ə·lə·zā'shən) A high degree of development attained by people in such areas as government, arts, technology, and education.

civil law (siv'əl lô) The branch of law that deals with the affairs of private citizens.

civil service (siv'əl sər'vis) People in government service, often chosen and promoted through examinations.

civil war (siv'əl wôr) A war fought between groups or sections of a single country.

clan (klan) A group made up of several, sometimes related, families.

clergy (klər'jē) Priests and others involved in the religious life.

climate (klī'mit) The average weather conditions in a place over a period of time.

climatograph (klī·mad'ə·graf) A graph showing average monthly temperature and precipitation for a particular place.

cold war (kōld wôr) A conflict between nations that does not involve actual fighting.

colonialism (kə·lō'nē·əl·iz'əm) The system of setting up colonies for the benefit of the home country.

colony (käl'ə·nē) A territory belonging to and ruled by a foreign power.

coming of age (kəm'ing əv āj') The time at which a young person is considered an adult, marked by special ceremonies in many cultures.

commercial (kə·mər'shəl) Done mainly for sale or profit, as *commercial agriculture.*

communication (kə·myoo'nə·kā'shən) The sending and receiving of messages.

communism (käm'yə·niz'əm) An economic system under which most property is held by the state.

Congress (käng'grəs) The legislative, or lawmaking, assembly of the United States.

constitution (kän'stə·too'shən) A document setting down the basic laws and principles of a government.

consul (kän'səl) The highest ranking official in the Roman government.

491

continental drift (känt′ən·ent′əl drift) The theory that continents have long been moving over the earth, and that these movements helped change the earth's surface.

contract (kän′trakt) A formal agreement between two or more people to do something.

crop rotation (kräp rō·tā′shən) A system of planting a different kind of crop in a field each year in order to keep the soil fertile.

Crusade (krōō·sād′) One of a series of Christian invasions of the Holy Land in the later Middle Ages.

culture (kəl′chər) The skills, customs, arts, and ways of life of a given people at a given time.

cuneiform (kyŏo·nē′ə·fôrm′) The Sumerian form of writing using wedge-shaped characters that stand for words or syllables.

cursive (kər′siv) Written with the letters joined together.

delta (del′tə) Land built up by deposits at a river's mouth.

democracy (də·mäk′rə·sē) Government by the people; a form of government in which all citizens share power.

depression (di·presh′ən) A period of lowered business activity and high unemployment.

desert (dez′ərt) A dry, barren area of land where few plants can grow.

despot (des′pət) A person with unlimited power; a tyrant.

dialect (dī′ə·lekt′) A form or variety of a language.

dictator (dik′tā·tər) A person who holds total power and authority in a government.

dike (dīk) A wall of earth or stone built by people to hold back flooding.

diplomat (dip′lə·mat′) A person who represents his or her country in another country.

division of labor (də·vizh′ən əv lā′bər) The assigning of specialized jobs to different people.

domesticate (də·mes′ti·kāt′) To tame or adapt in ways that are helpful to people.

draft animal (draft an′ə·məl) A domesticated animal used to pull a plow or wagon.

drama (dräm′ə) A play; a story acted out by actors.

dynasty (dī′nəs·tē) A line of rulers belonging to the same family; the period in which a certain family ruled.

ebony (eb′ə·nē) A hard, dark wood from tropical trees.

eclipse (i·klips′) A darkening of the sun when the moon comes between it and the earth, or of the moon when the earth's shadow falls over it.

economy (i·kän′ə·mē) The development and management of the resources of a country; a system for such management.

elevation (el′ə·vā′shən) The height of land above sea level.

embalm (im·bäm′) To treat a dead body in order to protect it from decaying.

emir (i·mir′) A Muslim commander in North Africa, the Middle East, and central Asia.

emperor (em′pər·ər) The ruler of an empire.

empire (em′pīr) A group of territories under the control of a single power.

enclosure (in·klō′zhər) The practice of fencing in farmland.

Enlightenment (in·līt′ən·mənt) The European philosophic trend of the 1600s and 1700s marked by great trust in human intelligence, reason, and education; the Age of Reason.

equator (i·kwāt′ər) An imaginary line around the earth that is halfway between the North and South poles.

erode (i·rōd′) To wear away. For example, wind and rain can erode soil.

estate (ə·stāt) **1** The land owned by an individual, including the buildings on it. **2** One of the three classes of society in France before the French Revolution.

experiment (ik·sper′ə·mənt) To try something out in hopes of making a discovery; to test something to see how it works.

export (ek·spôrt′) v. To send something outside a country for sale. (ek′spôrt) n. Something sent outside a country for sale.

extended family (ik·sten′dəd fam′ə·lē) A group of related people.

extinct (ek·stingkt′) No longer existing or active.

factory (fak′tə·rē) A building or buildings where goods are made.

fallow (fal′ō) Unused or unplanted land.

fascist (fash′əst) A person who believes in the need for a strong central government in which there is only one unopposed political party.

festival (fes′tə·vəl) A celebration; a time of feasting and ceremonies.

feudalism (fyōō′dəl·iz′əm) A political and social system based on a relationship between lords, who provided land and protection, and their vassals, who pledged loyalty and service to their lord.

fief (fēf) The land given to a vassal by a lord under the feudal system; a feudal estate.

fjord (fē·ôrd′) A narrow inlet of the sea between steep banks or cliffs, usually formed by a glacier.

flake tool (flāk tōol) A late Stone Age tool made from the sharp flakes chipped off a larger stone and used for cutting, scraping, and chopping.

floodplain (fləd′plān′) Level land built up by deposits from a river that overruns its banks.

fortress (fôr′trəs) A stronghold; a fort.

forum (fôr′əm) A marketplace or public square in an ancient Roman city.

freeholder (frē′hōl′dər) A person who owns a piece of land.

fresco (fres′kō) A painting made on wet plaster; wall painting.

gatherer (gath′ər·ər) A member of a group that lives on food that can be found growing wild.

geologist (jē·äl′ə·jəst) A scientist who studies the earth's crust, rocks, and rock formations.

glacier (glā′shər) A large body of slowly moving ice.

gladiator (glad′ē·āt′ər) A professional armed fighter in Roman times who performed to entertain audiences.

Gothic (gäth′ik) A style of architecture of the late Middle Ages, used for many cathedrals.

granary (gran′ər·ē) A building used for storing grain.

grid (grid) Two sets of lines that cross each other, as on a map.

guano (gwän′ō′) The droppings of sea birds, used as a fertilizer.

guild (gild) An association of workers in the same craft or trade.

gymnasium (jim·nā′zē·əm) A place equipped for games, sports, and physical training; in ancient Greece, an open field devoted to such activities.

hand ax (hand aks) A sharp, pointed stone tool made by chipping away the sides of a rock and used as a hand-held ax by Stone Age people.

heir (ār) A person who inherits or is entitled to inherit something, such as a title or property.

Hellenistic (hel′ə·nis′tik) Relating to Greek civilization after the time of Alexander the Great.

hieroglyphics (hī′rə·glif′iks) 1 The Egyptian system of writing. 2 Picture writing used by Egyptians, Mayas, and other early peoples.

highland (hī′lənd) An area of hills, mountains, or plateaus.

history (his′tə·rē) The period of time following the development of writing; the study of the events since the development of writing.

Ice Age (īs āj) The most recent of several long, cold periods when glaciers covered much of the earth, ending about 10,000 years ago.

idol (īd′əl) An image of a god, usually an object of worship.

illiterate (il·it′ə·rət) Unable to read or write.

imperialism (im·pir′ē·ə·liz′əm) The policy of empire building; the control of weaker nations, colonies, or territories by a strong nation.

import (im·pôrt′) v. To bring something into a country from a foreign country or place. (im′pôrt) n. Something brought from a foreign country.

Indo-European (in′dō·yŏor′ə·pe′ən) 1 A family of languages that includes most European and many southwestern Asian languages; the ancient language that was the source of these modern languages. 2 The people who spoke that ancient language.

industrialist (in·dəs′trē·ə·ləst) A person who owns or controls a large industry.

industrial revolution (in·dəs′trē·əl rev′ə·lōo′shən) The changes that resulted when new inventions and better machines shifted manufacturing from homes to factories.

industry (in′dəs·trē) Manufacturing; a special type of production and sale of goods, such as the textile industry.

infantry (in′fən·trē) Foot soldiers; the branch of an army made up of foot soldiers.

inflation (in·flā′shən) Rising prices, often caused by an increase in the amount of money or gold in circulation.

International Date Line (in′tər·nash′ən·əl dāt līn) The imaginary line on the earth, at or near 180° longitude, where each new day begins.

invention (in·ven′shən) The making of something new and different.

irrigation (ir′ə·gā′shən) The bringing of water to dry land in order to water crops.

Islam (is′läm) The Muslim religion, founded by Muhammad and based on belief in one God called Allah.

isolation (ī′sə·lā′shən) The state of being set apart from others; separation.

isthmus (is′məs) A narrow strip of land that connects two larger areas of land.

493

joint-stock company (joint'stäk' kəm'pə·nē) A business that is owned by many shareholders, each of whom buys stock in the company and shares its profits or losses.

journeyman (jər'nē·mən) A skilled craftworker at a stage between apprentice and master.

joust (joust) A contest between two mounted knights armed with lances.

khan (kän) A title given to the leader of a nomadic tribe on the Eurasian steppe.

knight (nīt) A trained soldier of feudal society.

Koran (kə·rän') The sacred book of Islam.

laissez faire (le'sā fãr') A policy of no government interference in economic matters; letting business owners operate as they please.

landform (land'fôrm') A feature of the earth's surface. Mountains, hills, plains, and plateaus are the four major landforms.

latitude (lat'ə·tōōd') The distance in degrees north or south of the equator.

league (lēg) A union of people, groups, or countries formed to help one another.

legend (lej'ənd) A story that may or may not be based on fact, often about the adventures of some great hero of the past.

legion (lē'jən) A Roman army group of about 4,000 fighting men.

levee (lev'ē) A wall of earth built up along a riverbank to hold back floodwaters.

literature (lit'ə·rə·chŏŏr) Creative writing, such as poems, plays, and novels.

local relief (lō'kəl ri·lēf') The difference, or change, in elevation from one place to another in the same area.

loess (les) A fine and very fertile yellowish-brown soil created by the crumbling action of glaciers and later deposited by winds.

longitude (län'jə·tōōd') The distance in degrees east or west of the prime meridian.

maize (māz) Corn.

mandate (man'dāt) A command; order.

manor (man'ər) The estate of a feudal lord.

manufacture (man'yə·fak'chər) To make goods.

map scale (map skāl) The measuring device found on maps that compares distances on the map with distances on the earth's surface.

marathon (mãr'ə·thän') A footrace of 26 miles, 385 yards, named after the story of a Greek who ran from Marathon to Athens in 490 B.C. to bring the news of a Greek victory.

market (mär'kət) A place where goods can be bought and sold.

master (mas'tər) A skilled craftworker; in the Middle Ages, a person who owned and operated a business and belonged to a guild.

meditation (med'ə·tā'shən) The act of thinking deeply.

mercantilism (mər'kən·ti·liz'əm) An economic policy designed to enrich a nation by controlling imports and exports, using tariffs to secure a favorable balance of trade, and using other methods to increase the supply of precious metals.

meridian (mə·rid'ē·ən) A north-south line of the global grid; also called a line of longitude.

Middle Ages (mid'əl āj'əz) The thousand-year period (A.D. 500–1500) of European history coming after the ancient civilizations of the Greeks and Romans and before modern times.

middle class (mid'əl klas') The social class between the landholding nobles and the land-working peasants in the Middle Ages, and between the propertied class and factory workers during the industrial revolution.

migrate (mī'grāt) To move from one place to another.

minaret (min'ə·ret') A tall, slender tower attached to a mosque from which Muslims are called to prayer.

monarchy (män'ər·kē) A government headed by a royal ruler, usually a king, a queen, or an emperor.

monastery (män'ə·ster'ē) A community of religious people, usually monks.

Mongoloid (mäng'gə·loid') The race, or division of humans, to which most East Asians belong.

monopoly (mə·näp'ə·lē) An exclusive right to produce or sell a product or service.

monotheism (män'ə·thē·iz'əm) The belief in a single God.

monsoon (män·sōōn') A seasonal wind in southern Asia.

Moor (mŏŏr) A North African Muslim.

moraine (mə·rān') A ridge of rocks and soil carried by a glacier and left behind as the glacier melted.

mosaic (mō·zā'ik) A picture or design made of many small pieces of colored stone or glass covering a wall or floor.

mosque (mäsk) A Muslim place of worship.

mountain (moun'tən) High, rocky land, usually with steep sides and a pointed or rounded top, higher than a hill.

movable type (mōo′və·bəl tīp) Carved or molded letters that can be used and reused to spell words, used in printing.

muezzin (mōo·ez′ən) A crier who calls people to prayer in Muslim countries.

mummy (məm′ē) A body preserved by embalming, as by the ancient Egyptians.

Muslim (məz′ləm) A person who accepts Islam; a follower of Muhammad and his teachings.

myth (mith) A traditional story about gods or heroes, often explaining something in nature or in the distant history of a group of people.

nation (nā′shən) The people of a territory united under a single government; a country.

nationalism (nash′nəl·iz′əm) Strong feelings of unity within and loyalty to a nation.

navigation (nav′ə·gā′shən) The art or science of guiding ships at sea.

noble (nō′bəl) A person belonging to a family of high social rank, often related to a ruler.

nomad (nō′mad) A person with no permanent home; member of a group of wandering herders.

Northwest Passage (nôrth′west′ pas′ij) A water route from the Atlantic to the Pacific Ocean around or through the northern part of North America.

oasis (ō·ā′səs) A place in a desert where water is found in a spring or well, making the growing of crops possible.

obelisk (äb′ə·lisk′) A tall, tapering pillar with carvings on it telling about a pharaoh, usually set near a temple by the ancient Egyptians.

odyssey (äd′ə·sē) A long, wandering trip.

ore (ôr) Rock containing metal.

outcaste (out′kast′) A person who is born outside a caste in India

overseer (ō′vər·sir′) A person who supervises others.

paddy (pad′ē) A rice field; flooded field.

papyrus (pə·pī′rəs) A reedy plant found along the Nile; paper made from the plant.

parallel (pär′ə·lel) An east-west line of the global grid; also called a line of latitude.

Parliament (pär′lə·mənt) The lawmaking body in Great Britain.

patrician (pə·trish′ən) A member of one of the old and powerful families in ancient Rome.

patron (pā′trən) Someone who helps support another person, usually an artist.

peasant (pez′ənt) A poor farm worker.

pebble tool (peb′əl tōol) The earliest type of Stone Age tool that has been found; a small chipped stone with a sharp point used for chopping, cutting, and digging.

peninsula (pə·nin′sə·lə) A body of land almost surrounded by water.

pension (pen′shən) A regular payment made to someone who has retired or is unable to work.

permanent (pər′mə·nənt) Long-lasting; meant to last without change.

pharaoh (fer′ō) A title for ancient Egyptian kings.

philosopher (fi·läs′ə·fər) A thinker who seeks the truth.

philosophy (fi·läs′ə·fē) The love of wisdom.

physical map (fiz′i·kəl map) A map that shows the natural features of the land, such as elevation and rivers.

pilgrimage (pil′grə·mij) A special trip made to some holy place.

plain (plān) An area of broad, level land.

plateau (pla·tō′) An area of high, flat land.

plebeian (pli·bē′ən) A member of the Roman lower class; any Roman not a member of the patrician class.

population (päp′yə·lā′shən) The number of people in a certain area.

precipitation (pri·sip′ə·tā′shən) Moisture that falls to the earth, such as rain, snow, and sleet.

prediction (pri·dik′shən) A forecast of what will happen.

prehistory (prē·his′tə·rē) The entire period of time before the development of writing.

prime meridian (prīm mə·rid′ē·ən) An imaginary line on the earth's surface running through Greenwich, England, from the North Pole to the South Pole and used as the starting point from which degrees of longitude are measured.

profit (präf′ət) Gain; the difference between the expenses of producing a product and the price received for selling it.

projection (prə·jek′shən) A grid picked up off the globe and placed on a flat surface.

property (präp′ər·tē) Something owned.

protectorate (prə·tek′tə·rət) A weaker nation under the control of a stronger one.

province (präv′əns) An administrative district.

pyramid (pir′ə·mid′) **1** A huge tomb built by the ancient Egyptians as a burying place for a pharaoh. **2** A Mayan temple with a similar shape.

racist (rā′səst) One who practices policies of discrimination or persecution based on the idea that one race of people is better than another.

radiocarbon dating (rā′dē·ō·kär′bən dā′ting) A method used to tell the age of ancient remains by measuring the amount of radioactivity left.

ransom (ran′səm) Money or goods paid for the release of a captured person or property.

raw material (rô mə·tir′ē·əl) A resource used to make a finished product.

rebellion (ri·bel′yən) An uprising against a government.

Reformation (ref′ər·mā′shən) The religious movement in the 1500s that protested practices of the Roman church and resulted in the establishment of Protestant churches.

reformer (ri·fôr′mər) A person who tries to improve conditions.

refugee (ref′yōō·jē′) A person who flees from a country because of danger or other problems.

regent (rē′jənt) A person who rules in place of a king, an emperor, or some other ruler.

Renaissance (ren′ə·säns′) The European revival of classical ideals in art, from the late 1300s to about 1600.

representative (rep′ri·zent′ət·iv) A person who acts or speaks for others; an elected official.

republic (ri·pəb′lik) A form of government in which citizens elect officials to represent them.

reservoir (rez′əv·wär′) An artificial lake or pond where water is stored for future use, often formed by a dam.

Restoration (res′tə·rā′shən) The reestablishment of the English monarchy in 1660; the period in England (1660–1688) between that event and the Glorious Revolution.

revolution (rev′ə·lōō′shən) 1 A remarkable or complete change of any kind; the throwing over of a government. 2 One complete orbit of a planet around the sun, or of a moon around its planet.

rift valley (rift val′ē) A valley formed by the sinking of land into a long, deep trench.

Romance language (rō·mans′ lang′gwij) A language based on Latin, the Romans' language.

royal (roi′əl) Relating to kings or queens.

rural (rŏŏr′əl) Relating to the country or farming areas rather than urban areas.

sakia (säk′ē·yə) A type of waterwheel developed late in Egyptian history and used throughout the Middle East and North Africa.

samurai (sam′ə·rī′) A member of the military class in feudal Japan.

scribe (skrīb) A person employed to write letters, legal contracts, and other documents; a monk who copied manuscripts.

scroll (skrōl) A roll of paper or parchment, usually with writing or artwork on it.

sea level (sē lev′əl) The level at which the ocean meets the land.

sect (sekt) A group that has broken away from an established religion or church.

senator (sen′ə·tər) A member of the Roman Senate, the group that advised the consuls.

serf (sərf) A member of the lowest feudal class; a farm worker bound to the land owned by someone of a higher class.

shadoof (shä·dōōf′) A pivoted pole with a weight at one end and a bucket at the other, used for raising water in irrigating land.

shaman (shäm′ən) A person said to be able to talk to and influence spirits.

Shinto (shin′tō) The main religion of Japan.

shogun (shō′gən) A military and political leader in Japan from the late 1100s until 1868.

shrine (shrīn) A place of worship, often one containing some sacred object.

slag (slag) Waste matter left over after metal has been taken out of ore by smelting.

slash and burn (slash ənd bərn) A method of farming in which a forest is cleared by cutting down and burning trees and brush.

smelt (smelt) To melt ore to separate the pure metal from impurities.

snow line (snō līn) The level of a mountain above which there is always snow.

social class (sō′shəl klas) A group of people with the same rank or social standing, often determined by wealth or power.

social security (sō′shəl si·kyŏŏr′ə·tē) A government-supported system of insurance for workers that pays money to the unemployed, the sick, and the aged.

society (sə·sī′ə·tē) All the people of a community regarded as a whole.

solar system (sō′lər sis′təm) Our sun, the nine planets, and their revolving moons.

source (sôrs) The place where a river begins, usually in highlands.

specialize (spesh′ə·līz′) To adapt something to a particular use.

sphinx (sfingks) A mythical creature with the body of a lion and the head of a person, ram, or hawk; the famous Egyptian statue.

standard of living (stan'dərd əv liv'ing) The level of comfort enjoyed by a person or group.

steppe (step) A vast area of dry, level grassland, found in Asia and eastern Europe.

Stone Age (stōn āj) The long prehistoric period when people used tools made of stone.

strait (strāt) A narrow stretch of water that connects two larger bodies of water.

strike (strīk) A work stoppage; organized refusal to work until certain conditions are met.

succession (sək·sesh'ən) The order in which one person follows another to power.

sultan (səl'tən) The title of a powerful Muslim ruler.

superpower (soō'pər·pou'ər) An extremely powerful nation, usually one having power over other powerful nations.

surplus (sər'pləs) Something more than what is needed; something left over.

taboo (tə·boō') Restricted or forbidden.

tariff (tār'əf) A tax on imports.

technology (tek·näl'ə·jē) All the tools and methods people invent and use to do work and provide for their needs.

terrace (ter'əs) A flat platform of earth built into a hillside, used for planting crops.

textile (tek'stīl) A woven fabric; cloth.

theory (thē'ə·rē) An idea, or explanation, as to why or how something works.

Third World (thərd wərld) Those nations that refuse to ally themselves with either the communist nations or the free world; mostly the developing nations of the world.

tithe (tīth) A tenth of something, such as income, paid as a tax to a church by its members.

tortilla (tôr·tē'yə) A thin, flat pancake made from corn dough.

tradition (trə·dish'ən) A long-established custom, belief, or way of doing something.

treaty (trē'tē) A formal agreement, as between nations.

trend (trend) A pattern of events that may indicate the direction of future changes.

tribune (trib'yoōn) A Roman official elected to protect the interests of the plebeians.

tribute (trib'yoōt) A yearly tax paid by one state or nation to another for protection against invasion.

tyrant (tī'rənt) Any ruler who seized and held power illegally in ancient Greece; a cruel and evil ruler.

union (yoō'nyən) An organization of workers banded together to improve their working conditions and wages.

urban (ər'bən) Relating to cities or towns.

urban hearth (ər'bən härth) One of the areas where the world's first cities developed.

utopia (yoō·tō'pē·ə) A perfect place; a political and social system with no problems.

vassal (vas'əl) A person who held land under the feudal system and who promised to pay taxes to the lord and to fight for the lord who provided the land.

veto (vē'tō) An order setting aside some law or action.

Viking (vī'king) A member of any group of Scandinavian seagoing raiders who attacked many coastal parts of Europe between the 700s and the 900s.

volcanic ash (väl·kan'ik ash) A layer of rock particles and dust that is thrown out of an erupting volcano.

wadi (wäd'ē) A desert streambed that is usually dry but fills with water during a rainstorm.

yurt (yərt) A circular tent used by some nomadic tribes of the Eurasian steppe.

ziggurat (zig'ə·rat') A pyramid-shaped temple built by the Sumerians.

Index

This Index will help you find the topics, pictures, maps, charts, graphs, and diagrams you need in your work. It is arranged in alphabetical order. It has guide words like those in your dictionary. It will show you what you can find in the book about persons, places, or things.

Italic letters before page references refer to the following: *c.* stands for chart; *d.* stands for diagram; *g.* stands for graph, *m.* stands for map; and *p.* stands for photo or illustration.

Japan *(continued)*
post-World War II, 467, 471
samurai, 320–321; *p.* 320
size and latitude comparison
of, with U.S., *m.* 307
in World War II, 465–466
See also **Shinto; shoganate**
Japan Current, 308; *m.* 308
Java, 361, 362
Jefferson, Thomas, 417, 418
Jenne, 358
Jerusalem, 77, 265, 268, 293,
294; *p.* 77
Jesuits, 388
Jesus, 152, 258, 259
Jews
in Islam, 259, 262
Nazi treatment of, 463–464
in Palestine, 468
in Spain, 392
See also **Hebrews**
Jimmu, 316
Joan of Arc, *p.* 390
John, king of England, 391
joint-stock companies, 410, 434
journeyman workers, 297
jousts, 289; *p.* 288
Jupiter, 142

K
Kaaba, 258, 260
Kamakura, 319, 321, 322
kamikaze, 322
Kammu, 317
Kant, Immanuel, 400
Karakorum, 247, 251
Karanga, 348, 349
Karnak, temple at, 96
Kay, John, *c.* 428
Kepler, Johannes, 401–402
Kerma, 168–169, 173, 174
Khafre, 97
Khanbaligh, 251
Khartoum, Sudan,
climatograph 85
Khingan Mountains, 244
Khufu, King, 93
knights, 286–287; *p.* 287
Knossos, 104
Kon-Tiki, 334; *m.* 334; *p.* 334
Koran, 258, 259, 266, 273, 357
Korea, 104, 313, 314, 456
Kremlin, *p.* 467
Kublai Khan, 248, 251, 322

Kumbi Saleh, 354, 355
Kung-Fu-tzu, 198
Kush, *m.* 169
agriculture in, 170–171
contributions of, 180–181,
352
final days of, 178–180
flourishing of, 176–177
geography of, 168–170
influence of Egypt, 174–176
life in, 170–171
Kuwait, 469
Kyoto, Japan, 317
Kyushu, 313

L
labor, 442–444, 447–449
Lafayette, General, 418
laissez faire, 438, 447
Lancaster, House of, 391
land bridges, Ice Age, 41–42
landforms
of Africa, 183; *m.* 183
of Europe, 398–399; *m.* 398
land use
in China, 190–191; *m.* 190
in Greece, 115
language(s)
Arabic, 257, 264–265
Chinese, 201
development of, 47
Indo-European, 103
Japanese, 318
Latin, 160–161, 333, 377
Quechua, 333
Romance, 160
Tagalog, 409
Lao-tzu, 199
La Salle, Sieur de, *c.* 383
latitude, 30
laws
Code Napoleon, 420
Code of Hammurabi, 70; *p.*
70
common, 413; *p.* 413
Islamic, 359
Mongol, 247
Roman, 158, 413
League of Nations, 461
Lenin, V. I., 462, 463; *p.* 462
Libya, 469
literature
ancient Greek, 118
Japanese, 318

Muslim, 268; *p.* 269
Renaissance, 377
Roman, 160–161
Liu Pang, 203
Livy, 161
llamas, 331, 337; *p.* 331
local relief, 182
Locke, John, 403–404, 417
loess, 45
longitude, 30
lines of, 31
and time, 33, 35
Louis XIV, king of France, 390
Louis XVI, king of France, 419
Lowell, Massachusetts, *p.* 445
Loyola, Ignatius, 388
Luther, Martin, 386–387; *p.*
387

M
Macedonia, 132, 148, 149
Machu Picchu, *p.* 327
Magellan, Ferdinand, 380–381,
407, 475; *c.* 383
Magellan, Strait of, 380
Magna Charta, 391, 412; *p.* 390
Magyars, 283
Malay Peninsula, 362
Mali, 265, 354, 355, 358, 359
agriculture in, 356
empire of, 355–357
mosque in, *p.* 265
Mama Ocllo, 331–332
Manchester, England, 430,
442, 443
Manco Capac, 331–332
Manco Inca, 343
Mandate of Heaven, 197
Mandingoes, 355
manor system, 290–292, 296;
p. 290, 291
Mansa Musa, 356–357; *p.* 347
Mao Tse-tung, 468
map making, *p.* 162, 267, 370,
371
maps
distortion on, 29; *d.* 29
Mercator's, 32
projections of, 32–33
scales on, 250–251
maps, historical
Akkadian Empire, 75
Alexander the Great's
empire, 133

Acknowledgments

Artwork

Colrus, Bill, 43, 57, 61, 88, 90, 91, 93, 94, 95, 100, 119, 269, 407
Cymerman, John, 148, 176, 181, 202
Dunnington, Tom, 78
Gray, Stuart, 219, 220, 222
Killgrew, John, 73, 77
Newman, Deirdre, 113, 224, 231
Powers, Tom, 45, 156, 163, 170
Shaw, Charles, 287, 289, 291, 332, 336, 341, 345, 353, 354, 359, 360
Tsugami, Kyuzo, 325

Photographs

Cover: Adam Woolfitt/Woodfin Camp
Page 28: National Aeronautics and Space Administration
29: Michal Heron
31: Eric Carle/Shostal Associates
35: Dave Forbert/Shostal Associates
37: Klaus D. Francke/Peter Arnold, Inc.
39: Shelly Grossman/Woodfin Camp
41: Bill N. Kleeman/Tom Stack & Associates
47: E. R. Degginger
48: John Launois/Black Star
49: top, Ward Wells/Shostal Associates; bottom, John Launois/Black Star
50: Ward Wells/Shostal Associates
52: E.R. Degginger
53: left, Freelance Photographers Guild; right, The Granger Collection
54: Historical Pictures Service
55: The Granger Collection
59: The Metropolitan Museum of Art, Gift of John D. Rockefeller, Jr., 1932
62: Historical Pictures Service
63: Charles Harbut/Archive
64: Liason Agency, Inc.
65: top left, Lee Boltin; top right, Shostal Associates; bottom, Museum of Science and Industry
66: top, The Granger Collection; bottom, Dr. George Gerster/Photo Researchers
68: Igor Eigeland/Black Star
70: Historical Pictures Service
71: The Granger Collection
72: top, Ken Proctor/Shostal Associates; bottom, Harold Simon, Tom Stack & Associates
74: top, Courtesy of The British Museum; bottom, The Granger Collection
77: Richard Steedman/The Image Bank
83: Robert Harding Associates
89: The Metropolitan Museum of Art
96: top left, Robert Harding Associates; top right, The Metropolitan Museum of Art; bottom, Kurt Scholz/Shostal Associates
97: Farrell Grehan/Photo Researchers
99: Egyptian Expedition/The Metropolitan Museum of Art

101: top, The Granger Collection; bottom, Historical Pictures Service
102: left, The Granger Collection; right, Dr. George F. Dales, University of California
104: Historical Pictures Service
107: top left and right, Historical Pictures Service; bottom, The Granger Collection
109: E.R. Degginger
111: The Granger Collection
118: left, Professor Saul Weinberg/Archaeological Institute of America; right, The Granger Collection
121: William Hubbell/Woodfin Camp
122: top, Joseph Szaszfai/Courtesy of Wadsworth Atheneum, Hartford; bottom, National Archives
126: The Bettmann Inc. Archive
127: Historical Pictures Service
130: E. Streichan/Shostal Associates
131: left, Freelance Photographers Guild; right, William Hubbell/Woodfin Camp
133: The Granger Collection
134: from *A History of Technology, Vol. II,* Oxford University Press, 1956
139: Ray Manley/Shostal Associates
141: The Granger Collection
142: from *Citizens of Rome,* The Hamlyn Group
145: Historical Pictures Service
149: Adam Woolfitt/Woodfin Camp
151: top, The Granger Collection; bottom, Historical Pictures Service
152: The Louvre
154: Editorial Photocolor Archives, Inc.
155: top, Albert P. Brown/Tom Stack & Associates; bottom, The Granger Collection
156: Eric Carle/Shostal Associates
157: The Granger Collection
158: National Park Service
159: top, Vance Henry/Taurus; bottom, Courtesy of The National Museum of Wales
160: E. Streichan/Shostal Associates
162: Courtesy of The British Library
167: Douglas Waugh/Peter Arnold, Inc.
171: Klaus D. Francke/Peter Arnold, Inc.
172: top, C. Miller/Shostal Associates; bottom, Ken Proctor/Shostal Associates
174: The Granger Collection
175: top left, Werner Forman Archive; bottom right, Sudan Antiquities Service
177: Werner Forman Archive
178: Shostal Associates
179: Seymour Green, Ltd./Shostal Associates
180: Courtesy of Inland Steel
187: Fred Ihrt/The Image Bank
193: Courtesy of Fine Arts Museum, Boston, Bequest of Charles B. Hoyt
194: from *Science and Civilization in China,* Cambridge University Press

195: Suzanne Engelmann/Shostal Associates
197: Courtesy of Museum of Fine Arts, Boston
198: The Granger Collection
201: left, Freer Gallery of Art, Smithsonian Institution, Washington, D.C.; right, The Granger Collection
203: The Granger Collection
204: Courtesy of the Cultural Relics Bureau, Beijing and The Metropolitan Museum of Art, New York
205: Courtesy of the Freer Gallery of Art, Smithsonian Institution, Washington, D.C.
206: left, Paolo Koch/Photo Researchers; right, The British Library
207: from *Science and Civilization in China,* Cambridge University Press
208, 209: The Granger Collection
213: Robert Frerck/Odyssey Productions
219: Courtesy of the Peabody Museum, Harvard University
222: P. Cheesman/Shostal Associates
223: Robert Frerck/Odyssey Productions
224: Courtesy of the Peabody Museum, Harvard University
225: Courtesy of the Peabody Museum, Harvard University, photograph by Hillel Burger
228: top left and right, Rhoda Sidney/Monkmeyer; bottom, Robert Frerck/Odyssey Productions
229: Culver Pictures
231: Courtesy of the Peabody Museum, Harvard University, photograph by Hillel Burger
233: Eric Carle/Shostal Associates
235: Courtesy of the Freer Gallery of Art, Smithsonian Institution, Washington, D.C.
236: left, Sovfoto; right, Roland Michaud/Woodfin Camp
237: Sovfoto
239: top, Roland Michaud/Woodfin Camp; bottom, Kenneth W. Fink/Bruce Coleman, Inc.
240: Marc F. Bernheim/Woodfin Camp
241: left, Roland & Sabrina Michaud/Woodfin Camp; right, Bruno J. Zehnder/Peter Arnold, Inc.
242: The Granger Collection
244: Courtesy of The Metropolitan Museum of Art; Gift of the Dillon Fund
245: Courtesy of the Freer Gallery of Art, Smithsonian Institution, Washington, D.C.
246, 247, 248: The Granger Collection
255: Robert Azzi/Woodfin Camp
258: Abu Hander/Woodfin Camp
259: Jonathan T. Wright/Bruce Coleman, Inc.
261: Spencer Collection, The New York Public Library, Astor, Lenox and Tilden Foundations
263: Jonathan Elk, III/Bruce Coleman, Inc.

264: Robert Weinreb/Bruce Coleman, Inc.

265: E. Streichan/Shostal Associates

267: top, The Metropolitan Museum of Art, Bequest of Edward C. Moore, 1891. The Edward C. Moore Collection; bottom, The Granger Collection

268: Courtesy of the Freer Gallery of Art, Smithsonian Institution, Washington, D.C.

269: left, Jessica Ehlers/Bruce Coleman, Inc.; right, Roland & Sabrina Michaud/Woodfin Camp

270: top, Robert Azzi/Woodfin Camp; bottom, John Elk, III/Bruce Coleman, Inc.

271: The Granger Collection

277: The Granger Collection

279: Photo Researchers © Belzeaux

280, 281: The Granger Collection

282: top, M. Timothy O'Keefe/Bruce Coleman, Inc.; bottom, The Granger Collection

283: top, The Granger Collection; bottom, Courtesy of the Viking Ship Museum

286: Ray Manley/Shostal Associates

288, 290, 292: The Granger Collection

294: Historical Pictures Service

295, 296, 297, 298, 299, 300, 303: The Granger Collection

305: Mike Yamashita/Woodfin Camp

309: Frederick Raucher/Shostal Associates

311: left, Mike Yamashita/Woodfin Camp; right, The Metropolitan Museum of Art, The Michael C. Rockefeller Memorial Collection, Gift of Mrs. John D. Rockefeller III, 1958

312: Courtesy of The Freer Gallery of Art, Smithsonian Institution, Washington, D.C.

313: Mike Yamashita/Woodfin Camp

314: Joseph D. Barnell/Shostal Associates

315: top, Sekai Bunka Photo; bottom, The Metropolitan Museum of Art, The Henry G.C. Packard Collection of Asian Art, Gift of Harry G.C. Packard and Purchase, Fletcher, Rogers, Harris Brisbane, Dick and Louis V. Bell Funds, Joseph Pulitzer Bequest and The Annenberg Fund, Inc. Gift, 1975

317: Courtesy of the Freer Gallery of Art, Smithsonian Institution, Washington, D.C.

318: Isabella Stewart Gardner Museum, Boston

320: The Granger Collection

321: Burt Glinn/Magnum Photos

322: left, Courtesy of Japan Air Lines; right, Courtesy of the Museum of Fine Arts, Boston

327: Loren McIntyre

331: P. De Orlandini/Shostal Associates

333: Loren McIntyre

334: Courtesy of Mrs. Thor Heyerdahl

338: top, Eric Carle/Shostal Associates; bottom, Loren McIntyre

339: Loren McIntyre

340: Courtesy of the American Museum of Natural History

342: The Granger Collection

347: Bibliothequé Nationale

348: Tom Nebbia/Woodfin Camp

349: Courtesy of the World Bank

352: Nicholas Devore III/Bruce Coleman, Inc.

353: J.M. Bertrand/Shostal Associates

356: John Elk, III/Bruce Coleman, Inc.

362: left, Ernst Haas; right, Norman Myers/Bruce Coleman, Inc.

363: Craig Varden/Shostal Associates

367: Dave Forbert/Shostal Associates

369: John Elk, III/Bruce Coleman, Inc.

370: The Bettmann Inc. Archive

371: top, The Granger Collection; bottom, The British Library

373: Historical Pictures Service

374: The Granger Collection

375: top left, Editorial Photocolor Archives, Inc.; top right, Robert Gamm/Shostal Associates; bottom left, Shostal Associates; bottom right, European Color Slides

376: top left, Editorial Photocolor Archives, Inc.; top right, The Granger Collection; bottom left, Editorial Photocolor Archives, Inc.; bottom right, Eric Carle/Shostal Associates

377: The Granger Collection

379: Rare Book Division, The New York Public Library, Astor, Lenox & Tilden Foundations

382: Historical Pictures Service

384: National Aeronautics and Space Administration

385, 387, 388: Historical Pictures Service

391: top, The Granger Collection; bottom, Historical Pictures Service

393: Historical Pictures Service

397: The Granger Collection

401: top left, The Granger Collection; top right and bottom right, Historical Pictures Service

402, 403: Historical Pictures Service

408: The Granger Collection

409: Freelance Photographers Guild

410: New York Public Library, Rare Book Division; Astor, Lenox, and Tilden Foundations

411: The Granger Collection

412: Historical Pictures Service

413: Eldred Wade/Shostal Associates

414: bottom, The Granger Collection

415: Historical Pictures Service

416: The Granger Collection

417: Roloc

418: The Granger Collection

419: top, Historical Pictures Service; bottom, The Granger Collection

420: The Granger Collection

425: Science Museum, London

426, 429: The Granger Collection

430: top, The Granger Collection; bottom, Prints Division, The New York Public Library, Astor, Lenox and Tilden Foundations

435: Culver Pictures

438: left, The Granger Collection; right, Courtesy of the American Petroleum Institute

440: The Granger Collection

441: Eric Carle/Shostal Associates

442: top, Culver Pictures; bottom, The Granger Collection

443, 444, 446, 447: The Granger Collection

448: top, The Granger Collection; bottom, The Bettmann Inc. Archive

449: The Granger Collection

451: Historical Pictures Service

453: Jim McNee/Tom Stack & Associates

455: Historical Pictures Service

456: Historical Pictures Service

461: top left, Courtesy of National Archives; top right, Library of Congress; bottom, Wide World

462, 463, 464, 465, 466: Wide World

467: J. Messerschmidt/Bruce Coleman, Inc.

468: top, Wide World; bottom, Mark Kauffman, Life Magazine © Time, Inc.

473: National Aeronautics and Space Administration

475: Michal Heron/Woodfin Camp